ROSALYN RABARA
SO-AWU-133

# EXPERIENCES
# THE READER FOR
# DEVELOPING WRITERS

### JOHN C. LOVAS

DE ANZA COLLEGE

 HarperCollins*CollegePublishers*

Acquisitions Editor: Ellen Schatz
Developmental Editor: Thomas Maeglin
Cover Illustration/Photograph: Diana Org/Superstock
Electronic Production Manager: Angel Gonzalez Jr.
Project Coordination/Text Design: Ruttle Graphics, Inc.
Electronic Page Makeup: Ruttle Graphics, Inc.
Manufacturing Manager: Willie Lane
Printer and Binder: R. R. Donnelley & Sons Company
Cover Printer: The Lehigh Press

For permission to use copyrighted material, grateful acknowledgment is made to the copyright holders on pp. 338–339, which are hereby made part of this copyright page.

EXPERIENCES: THE READER FOR DEVELOPING WRITERS

Copyright © 1996 by HarperCollins Publishers, Inc.

All rights reserved. Printed in the United States of America. No part of this book may be used or reproduced in any manner whatsoever without written permission, except in the case of brief quotations embodied in critical articles and reviews. For information address HarperCollins College Publishers, 10 East 53rd Street, New York, NY 10022. *For information about any HarperCollins title, product, or resource, please visit our World Wide Web site at **http://www.harpercollins.com/college** .*

Library of Congress Cataloging-in-Publication Data
Lovas, John C., 1939–
      Experiences : the reader for developing writers / John C. Lovas.
            p.      cm.
      Includes index.
      ISBN 0-673-46878-X (Student Edition)
      ISBN 0-673-468798 (Instructor's Edition)
      1. College readers.  2. English language—Rhetoric.   3. English
language—Grammar.    I. Title.
PE1408.L7  1995
808 .0427—dc20                                                    95-17059
                                                                          CIP

95 96 97 98 9 8 7 6 5 4 3 2 1

## Dedication

To Brenda, Timothy, Gregory, and Desmond,
in all our agonies and ecstasies.

# Contents

# To The Instructor

## The Purpose

For more than ten years, my colleagues and I at De Anza College, a large community college in the heart of Silicon Valley, California, have been dissatisfied with the readers available for the pre-college composition course (the developmental course that prepares students for Freshman English and college reading and writing). In my experience, most of those readers are really variations on Freshman English texts, but in some way "simplified": either the selections are fewer and shorter, or include more journalistic essays and fewer literary ones, or the tone is too friendly and informal. But they always seem to take the assumptions of the Freshman English reader as the basic framework. This tradition assumes that closely examining essays on subjects of academic and intellectual interest will activate students' background knowledge based on previous schooling and reading in newspapers and magazines, helping them formulate ideas for writing.

The problem with this approach is that most of the students who need developmental reading and writing in community colleges and in many universities need a preparatory experience that directly addresses what they don't know. This text attempts to address that different need. Here are my most important assumptions about:

### STUDENTS

- Most students who do not qualify for Freshman English did not read extensively in high school and do not read newspapers and magazines regularly. Thus, they do not have a background of reading-based knowledge to activate by close scrutiny of model essays.
- Students can best be introduced to critical reading and writing through topics they know chiefly from their experience rather than their schooling. Some topics are nearly universal, regardless of the individual's age, gender, cultural background or economic status (e.g., family, work, music, food, television).

### ADULT LEARNERS

- Adult learners do have considerable knowledge based on experience and observation, though they often do not recognize how much they do know and how to make use of what they know.
- Controversial material, reflecting several viewpoints, has the best chance of engaging the interest and commitment of adult learners.

Both the reading and writing should focus on the discovery of meaning, not the mastery of form through exercises.

### READING

- Developing a reading-based knowledge for writing involves both breadth and depth. Reading material should be high interest, of varying levels of difficulty, reflecting divergent viewpoints. The reading should be sufficient in number and variety to create in the student a developing sense of confidence about the subject area.
- An effective reader has a clear but flexible organization, allowing teachers of varying experience and philosophy to use the materials in ways most suited to their individual skills and interests. No single theoretical orientation should dominate such a reader.

### WRITING

- All writers write best about what they know. The college composition course needs to show developing writers how to link the knowledge they already have with reading that provides new ideas and critical perspectives.
- Developing writers do best when they are asked to build on existing knowledge and experience through the required reading rather than when they are made to feel how much they don't know by reading on completely unfamiliar subjects. The latter effect is produced by many existing readers.

This text attempts to incorporate all of these assumptions both through the principle of selection of materials and through the organization and presentation of those materials. *Experiences* assumes the students' life experiences provide a solid basis for developing critical reading and writing skills.

## THE AUDIENCE

The primary audience for this book is students in both community colleges and those universities that provide a composition course preparatory to Freshman English. The text has sufficient material for a semester-long course, but is well-suited to a one quarter course as well. Though the majority of these students are under age 25 (thus not too distant from high school), many of the students in such courses are returning after many years engaged in work and family. These students are from diverse ethnic backgrounds and for many English is not their first language (though they have had considerable experience with English to get into this course). A special challenge in these courses is to find subjects that virtually every student has access to and potential interest in.

# The Content

This text consists predominantly of opinion pieces that commonly appear on the op-ed and feature pages of major daily newspapers. However, each section also includes one or two essays of greater complexity and sophistication, to provide students with a stretch and to help them anticipate the kind of reading they can expect in Freshman English. Each section will also include one or two pieces that emphasize information more than opinion as a way of providing more background knowledge on the given topic. My experience has been that many students read material that has not been assigned for class discussion because their interest in the topic has been piqued.

# The Pedagogy

Perhaps one of the most distinctive features of this book is the nature of its topics. Each has been selected for its concreteness, accessibility, and the likelihood that most adults have had more than casual experience with that topic, even if they have not read or reflected much about the topic. Several theoretical concerns converge here. One is the recent concern about students' background knowledge, an issue given prominence by E. D. Hirsch, Jr.'s *Cultural Literacy*. But rather than promote learning some list of culturally salient facts, this approach will introduce critical perspectives on familiar topics. Some research suggests that a very high percentage of students who are placed in developmental courses still fit what Piaget characterized as "concrete operational" learners. Abstracting and theorizing are particularly challenging for such learners. Thus, the material in this reader is intended to provide grounding in the familiar at the same time the student writer is being pushed to develop defensible generalizations, abstract ideas, and critical perspectives on those ideas.

Cultural diversity should be part of the fabric of any set of good teaching materials. My selection of pieces within topics seeks material that is controversial, sometimes offering unusual perspectives. Thus, material reflecting both ethnic and gender difference serves nicely the teaching goals of the text. But my experience suggests this material works best when it is presented as part of the consideration of some inclusive topic that provides common ground for all.

The reading level varies within each topic area. Most pieces are short and accessible to readers with high school reading ability. A few are below that level. Each topic has at least one more demanding piece, the sort that might well be used in the Freshman English course. Stephen Krashen of the University of Southern California makes a compelling argument that most readers, in order to develop in skill, need to encounter material that is one increment above their current level. By insuring that the material here is demanding, but not well beyond most students' current reading level, students are presented challenges at which they can succeed. Further, this variation in level of difficulty allows instructors to use the material in at least two ways. One approach would focus on the shorter, more accessible pieces that begin each chapter, only occasionally taking up the longer, more demanding pieces, perhaps later in the term. Another approach would be to focus class discussion and instruction on the more difficult pieces, using the shorter pieces primarily as background material.

The more writers feel they know a subject, the more confidently and critically they can write about that subject. By providing a number of opinion pieces that explore different aspects and different perspectives of a familiar topic, this book should help student writers develop both confidence and critical thinking skills.

## The Format

Each chapter is introduced by a short headnote, suggesting the various dimensions of the topic and some of the perspectives to be encountered in that chapter. Each reading is introduced by an even shorter headnote that will emphasize questions intended to arouse interest and motivate reading. Each reading is followed by suggestions for reflection, which may be written or oral (in class). Each chapter concludes with a series of suggestions for writing, ranging from short responses and journal entries to full-length papers.

The sequence of topics is vaguely developmental. I don't want to make strong claims about this feature, but the sequence (Family, Parent/Child, Food, Television, Music, Consuming, Driving and Riding, Work, Male/Female) approximates the sequence in which most Americans encounter those experiences in their lives. Presumably, that order represents a pattern moving from greatest amount of experience to least, though this breaks down in some categories. Within chapters, I have established a pattern of short and more general pieces to begin, followed by longer, more complex pieces. The primary type is the argument, but expository and narrative pieces can be found throughout.

# So What Good Is Reading Anyway?

## A Note to the Student Who Bought This Book

When you are a child, "so what?" can be a rude question. But, when you are a college student, it is a very good question. When you are advised to study certain subjects or required to meet certain requirements, asking "so what good is it?" can help you understand why you are trying to learn what has been asked of you or recommended to you.

So why read? Part of the answer may seem so obvious that it doesn't need saying. But here goes anyway.

- Reading provides basic information so you can get through the day. You need to know how to read to use the telephone book, the TV schedules, ATM instructions, directions on a food package, traffic signs, bus and train schedules, and the instructions for power tools, electronic equipment, or a computer program.
- Reading provides useful information about the world around you. You need to know how to read to get the weather forecast, the box scores and teams statistics on your favorite sports team, the specials at the grocery store, sale items at a clothing store, and reports about crimes in your neighborhood.
- Reading provides inspiration. Reading is the chief means of learning the stories of great deeds and great adventures of the men and women of the past. Stories can inspire us by telling of great acts of heroism and generosity, and stories can caution us by telling of acts of greed, violence, and terror.
- Reading provides us with concepts, the tools of thinking. Reading is the chief vehicle we have for gaining new knowledge, knowledge that can lead to a better job, healthier life, or more satisfying relationships.
- Reading provides us with new ideas and new understandings about ourselves and the world. Reading can take us to places we've never been and to times we can never live in. Reading can challenge us to examine what we believe and value, to clarify what is good and bad, and to help us form our judgment about how to spend our time, money, energy, and even our vote.

This book cannot accomplish all of that, but you can. Decide how reading can help you improve your life. Then use the information, concepts, ideas, and inspiration from the writers collected here to help you make the improvement you want.

# Acknowledgments

This book had its genesis in conversations with my colleagues at De Anza College, James Goldsberry and Gary Cummings. My debt to Cummings is especially deep, for his early encouragement on this project and his very useful comments on an early version of the text. Jerome Garger of Lane Community College and Sally Wood and James Luotto of De Anza provided invaluable close readings of draft chapters. I am also indebted to those colleagues at De Anza who used various chapters with their students: Judy Hubbard, Kate Hunter, Carolyn Keen, Jean Miller, Alan Simes, William Spencer, Nell Sullivan, and Sally Wood. Donald McQuade of the University of California, Berkeley, provided wise counsel on the publishing process. Joel McLemone and Garrick Wohlstrand contributed invaluable assistance in preparing the text for publication. The final shape of the book owes a great deal to the perceptive and tactful suggestions of Don Barshis, Wilbur Wright College; Kate Mangelsdorf, University of Texas at El Paso; Teddie McFerrin, Collin County Community College; Christine Perri, Harold Washington College; Diane Scott, San Diego Mesa College. Finally, Mark Paluch, Laurie Likoff, Patricia Rossi, Ellen Schatz, and Tom Maeglin of HarperCollins and Michael Gibbons of Ruttle Graphics, Inc. provided a high degree of professionalism in keeping the project focused. My wife Brenda supported this project in every way, from suggesting readings to proofing copy. Thanks, finally, to my brother Michael for the use of his Oregon "digs," where much of this work was incubated, and to my son Gregory for his expert advice on cartoons. Though I would love to spread the blame around, any weaknesses in the final version of the book are solely my responsibility.

# THIS MODERN WORLD by TOM TOMORROW

**Find Tom Tomorrow's definition of a reader in this cartoon. Would your definition of a reader differ in any way?**

# WAYS OF READING

## APPROACHES TO READING

Since you already know how to read, why does this book begin with a section about reading? As the title suggests, there are many ways of reading. You probably started reading with something like this:

The dog.
The dog ran.

That is the entirety of Lesson I of McGuffey's *First Eclectic Reader*, first published in 1879. Most beginning school readers still involve simply recognizing words in print that a child already uses in conversation. But you are in college now, a far remove from your days of "See Spot. See Spot run." Yet you still practice those beginning lessons. You look at words on the page, recognize that they correspond to words you know, and then you make some sense of them. Of course, that first lesson doesn't give you very much to make sense of. "The dog ran." So what? In fact, many questions come to mind. What kind of dog was it? Why did the dog run? Where was it running? Was it chasing something? Was it being chased? Was it just running for the fun of it? We get no answers to any of these questions. But asking those kinds of questions is the heart of reading. And those kinds of questions often lead us to write. As a quick exercise, take two minutes to elaborate on "The dog ran." Try to answer some of the previous questions.

Look at what you have written. Does it have more meaning than "The dog ran"? What did you add that gave it more meaning? Did you add details about the dog and about the running? Did you give reasons for the running?

Did you introduce other dogs, other animals, or human beings? Did you try to convey the importance of what you had written?

This business of questioning, reading, thinking, and then writing are fundamental to college work, to professional work, and to this book. Whether the subject is simple and easy or complex and hard, you will use these basic processes of questioning, reading, thinking, and writing over and over again. When you read, you try to make sense out of another person's writing. Part of being a reader means knowing something about being a writer. You also need to know something about the writer's language, the kinds of words used and the kinds of sentences used. But most reading has elements that you don't yet know (as you quickly realized about the previous dog statements). This working from the known to the unknown is basic to reading and to learning. Writing offers one of the best ways to explore what you don't yet know, and what you are trying to learn. This book will give you many opportunities to learn new facts, gain new knowledge, and confront new ideas.

A good way to think about reading is to imagine yourself as a talk show host or an interviewer. See each piece of reading as your guest, a possible source of useful ideas, interesting information, and controversial opinions. Like some talk show guests, some pieces of reading are very open and cooperative, giving up their ideas, information, and opinions with just minimal effort on your part. But many pieces of reading require background research, probing questions, and even a sort of confrontation, where you state your own reaction and your own opinions in an effort to get a clearer understanding of what the piece of reading actually means. Just as a talk show host must prepare very thoroughly for the more challenging guests, you must prepare thoroughly for the more demanding reading you face. You can see that a reader must be a very active person, one who works hard to get the reading to make some sense.

## GETTING A SENSE OF THE WHOLE

Virginia Woolf, an important but often difficult to read writer, offered this view of "the common reader": get the idea of reading

> [He] differs from the critic and scholar. He is worse educated, and nature has not gifted him so generously. He reads for his own pleasure rather than to impart knowledge or correct the opinions of others. Above all, he is guided by an instinct to create for himself, out of whatever odds and ends he can come by, some kind of whole—a portrait of a man, a sketch of an age, a theory of the art of writing.

Woolf's phrase "some kind of whole" simply means you should find a meaning, something that makes sense to you. Woolf sees readers as active persons—people who create, people who make models in their minds that roughly correspond to the real world experience or the idea that the writer presents. This view of reading has a lot in common with the way a map guides you during a trip. A map can help you get where you are going. A good map contains the essential features of the area you are traveling. But the map is simply a tool. Your goal is to get to your destination and, perhaps, to enjoy yourself along the way. You would never confuse the lines on the map as the actual roads or the little dots as the towns and cities you travel through. The same is true with various reading methods. They can guide you and help you find your way through the reading. But getting to your destination—finding meaning in your reading and enjoying it—will be your chief concern.

## Feeling the Effort of Reading

READ and Understand

Perhaps you had some difficulty making sense out of what Virginia Woolf wrote. Good. That means you qualify as what Mortimer Adler, a law professor and educational reformer, calls "the average reader":

2) know how to get there & what it is about

> … and that means most of us who have learned our ABC's. We have been started on the road to literacy. But most of us also know that we are not expert readers. We know this in many ways, but most obviously when we find some things too difficult to read, or have great trouble in reading them; or when someone else has read the same thing we have and shown us how much we missed or misunderstood.
>
> If you have not had experiences of this sort, if you have never felt the effort of reading or known the frustration when all the effort you could summon was not equal to the task, I do not know how to interest you in the problem. Most of us however, have experienced difficulties in reading, but we do not know why we have trouble or what to do about it.
>
> I think this is because most of us do not regard reading as a complicated activity, involving many different steps in each of which we can acquire more and more skill through practice, as in the case of any other art. We may not even think there is an art of reading. We tend to think of reading almost as if it were something as simple and natural to do as looking or walking. There is no art of looking or walking.

This book assumes, as Adler does, that there is an art to reading. In other words, you can be shown a series of steps or guides, which you can practice until your skill improves noticeably. This process is not as simple as it sounds. Earlier, I suggested you may have found the Virginia Woolf quotation difficult. This experience is a natural part of reading, not a sign of your inadequacy. Let me go back to my map comparison. A common sense view says a map should keep you from getting lost during your travels. Most of us get rather upset if we get lost. When you enter new territory, you are almost certain to feel some confusion and be somewhat lost. Reading material that is unfamiliar, dealing with new ideas and information, often creates that feeling of being a little bit lost. This is not a bad thing. In fact, you get that feeling only when you recognize something new and unfamiliar, when you realize that you haven't been there before. Most learning begins with that feeling, recognizing you are in a new place. As a student, your schooling provides you with a map, a guide to your learning. Your schooling should also present you with new material—to get you a little lost—so you can be challenged to go beyond what you already know.

This book also assumes that your increased skill in reading will help you as a developing writer. Reading provides raw material for writers. Your own writing also becomes material that you read. You can improve your own writing by carefully and critically rereading what you have written. This book offers many opportunities to practice reading and to use what you learn in your writing.

## Reading the World As Well As the Word

Adler indicates that the process of reading is complicated. It may be more complicated than he suggests. He says there is no art of looking, but John Berger, a contemporary critic, would not agree with Adler on that point. Before we read words, we "read" the world we experience. We see or observe the people and objects around us. We discover patterns in what we see and we experience unique moments. All this activity counts as part of our reading of the world. As Berger explains in *Ways of Seeing*:

knowledge in experience

> Seeing comes before words. The child looks and recognizes before it
> can speak.
> But there is also another sense in which seeing comes before words. It
> is <u>seeing</u> which establishes our place in the surrounding <u>world</u>; we explain
> that world with words, but words can never undo the fact that we are sur-
> rounded by it. The relation between what we see and what we know is
> never settled. Each evening we *see* the sun set. We *know* that the earth is
> turning away from it. Yet the knowledge, the explanation, never quite fits
> the sight....
> The way we see things is affected by what we know or what we be-
> lieve. In the Middle Ages when men believed in the physical existence of
> Hell the sight of fire must have meant something different from what it
> means today. Nevertheless their idea of Hell owed a lot to the sight of fire
> consuming and the ashes remaining—as well as to their experience of the
> pain of burns. (7–8)

Berger addresses one of the great complications involved in reading: how do you connect the words to your experiences. Actually, your experiences often present you with questions that can motivate you to read more about a topic. Here again, you want to think of reading as active work, a conversation between your experience of the real world and the world created by the words on a page.

I say a lot about what you experience and its connection to what you read because this book will encourage you to make those connections as often as possible. Everyone has a great deal of practical experience. You have seen much and done much by the time you enter a college classroom. Sometimes, you may feel there is little connection between what you already know and what you are asked to learn in college classrooms. For example, you have been eating since the day you were born. You have experienced many different foods and developed strong likes and dislikes about both particular foods and particular ways of preparing food. So, you would be able to write a great deal in support of your opinions about foods you like and don't like. On the other hand, if you were asked to explain the mating habits of the tsetse fly, you'd probably have very little to say.

Notice that the readings in this book are grouped under headings that should be immediately familiar to you. Each of us has a family. We eat, and we watch television (often at the same time). We have listened to music, perhaps even made music. We have ridden in and driven automobiles. We have shopped. We have worked (though not always for pay). We are either men or women. So, in a general sense, what you read here will be familiar. Because the work in this book will prepare you for the kinds of reading and writing demanded in college courses, you will also encounter the unfamiliar and the difficult. But that's what you expected, isn't it? You don't take a course to do what you already know well, but to increase your knowledge and improve your skills.

## HANDLING DIFFICULTIES IN YOUR READING

This first chapter presents some approaches to the kind of reading a beginning college student must do. There are no simple formulas for reading, partly because we often have different reasons for reading. Consider what Michel Montaigne, a 16th century French writer who helped establish the essay as a form of writing, said about reading:

> In books I only look for the pleasure of honest entertainment; or if I study, the only learning I look for is that which tells me how to know myself, and teaches me how to die well and to live well …
>
> When I meet with difficulties in my reading, I do not bite my nails over them; after making one or two attempts I give them up. If I were to sit down to them, I should be wasting myself and my time; my mind works at the first leap. What I do not see immediately, I see even less by persisting. Without lightness I achieve nothing; application and over-serious effort confuse, depress, and weary my brain. My vision becomes blurred and confused. I must look away, and then repeatedly look back; just as in judging the brilliance of a scarlet cloth, we are told to pass the eye lightly over it, glancing at it several times in rapid succession. (160–161)

It should be reassuring to know that famous writers can find reading difficult and confusing. Montaigne even seems to say that when reading is hard he just gives up. What he means, though, is that if you are having trouble making sense of what you read, don't persist with the same approach. In fact, Montaigne's technique can be quite useful in dealing with reading that is hard to understand. Instead of getting bogged down on a sentence or paragraph, look away—then look back, rapidly scanning the entire piece. Take in several small parts to get involved with the reading. That can give you just enough understanding to ask questions that the reading might answer for you. Just as a good talk show host must develop questions that will get guests to reveal themselves, you need to develop good questions to find answers from what you read.

When you find yourself reacting to some piece of reading with "This is BOR-ing!", you might try another approach. Imagine the writer sitting down next to you on a bus or a plane or in a fast food restaurant—a complete stranger. Perhaps this person looks unimportant or eccentric or hostile. Imagine, though, that, despite the person's appearance, he or she has some story to tell, some piece of information you don't have or some opinion you haven't encountered before. Consider that every person who becomes a friend was first a stranger—and that finding a friend is always possible with a new piece of writing. Now read this "boring" piece trying to learn something about the person you imagine wrote it. Try to understand why the person said this (even if you think what was said is silly or stupid or misguided). Can you see how your own attitudes may play a role in how you read and in how well you read? Keeping an open mind, at least to start, is one important approach to reading.

Let me illustrate this aspect of reading another way. Married couples, lovers, and family members often have conflicts that grow out of communication difficulties. When you know another person well, you often interrupt when that person says things that upset you, even before he or she has finished speaking. One technique for handling such conflicts is to suggest that the two people in conflict (let's call them Hortense and Seymour) write letters to one another. That way, both Hortense and Seymour can complete their thoughts without interruption. When they read the other person's letter, they read it at least twice. First, they read it with the heart (with emotions and feelings); then, they read it with the head (with reason and logic). Though this approach will not eliminate all of Hortense and Seymour's conflicts or differences in viewpoints, it does give each of them a much better chance of understanding what the other person really thinks and really feels. Try to apply this technique when you read. Read an article or essay once with the heart, letting your own feelings express themselves. Then read it again, with the head, letting your mind make sense out of the writer's ideas and opinions.

## LEARNING TO DESCRIBE A FISH (OR ANY OBJECT OF STUDY)

Ezra Pound, one of the most influential American poets of the 20th century, offers another way of reading in a book called *The ABC of Reading*:

The proper method for studying poetry and good letters is the method of contemporary biologists, that is careful first-hand examination of the matter and continual COMPARISON of one "slide" or specimen with another.

No man is equipped for modern thinking until he has understood the anecdote of Agassiz* and the fish:

A post-graduate student equipped with honours and diplomas went to Agassiz to receive the final and finishing touches. The great man offered him a small fish and told him to describe it.

Post-Graduate Student: "That's only a sunfish."

Agassiz: "I know that. Write a description of it."

After a few minutes the student returned with the description of the *Ichthus Heliodiplodokus,* or whatever term is used to conceal the common sunfish from vulgar knowledge, family of *Heliichtherinkus,* etc., as found in textbooks of the subject.

Agassiz again told the student to describe the fish.

The student produced a four-page essay. Agassiz then told him to look at the fish. At the end of three weeks the fish was in an advanced state of decomposition, but the student knew something about it. (17–18)

*you have to know the info & live w/ it / live w/ Reading*

If you are like me, you had no trouble reading Pound's anecdote, but you had trouble understanding his point. I found I had to reread the passage a few times, but finally I saw that Pound makes two very important points about learning and reading. First, he wants us to see that close observation of real life, of our own experiences and surroundings, constitutes a powerful way of learning. Second, he suggests that when we read, we are always involved in making comparisons like these:

- How does what this writer says compare to what I already believe?
- How does it compare to what I know from observing and experiencing in the world?
- Does it add to my knowledge?
- Does it challenge my beliefs in some small or large way?

## SUMMING UP

A lot of ground has been covered in this first section, so let's sum up. When you encounter demanding reading, you should:

1. Read with questions in mind.
2. Get some sense of the author's main point.
3. Recognize how much work reading requires.
4. Compare your own experience and knowledge in the world to the ideas and opinions you are reading.

*5) GET THE MEANING of THE READING.*

*Louis Agassiz, Swiss-born natural historian and geologist, who became the most influential teacher of science in America in the nineteenth century.

5. Recognize how your attitudes, sometimes your resistance, contribute to how much you get from reading.
6. Vary the approach until you get what the writer has to offer.

Before I show how these approaches might be applied to the essays in
this book, you may find it useful to conduct a self-assessment of your past
experiences and current feelings about reading. This next section offers you
a way of looking at your own reading, past and present.

## Your Reading Autobiography: An Exercise

Everyone has had different experiences with reading and studying in childhood. Sometimes those experiences affect how we feel about reading when
we are adults. In the following, you will find several brief accounts of early
reading experiences, some by people who became successful writers as
adults and some by characters created by writers. Read each of these excerpts (or as many as your instructor suggests). As you read each passage,
ask yourself how the writer's experience is similar to or different from your
own. After you complete the reading and as a preparation for writing, use
some scratch paper to respond to some or all of these suggestions:

1. Make a list of the similarities or differences from your own reading
   experiences that you noticed as you read.
2. Recall your greatest success or greatest difficulty with reading
   when you were younger.
3. Think of the book, article, or poem that had an important effect on
   you and the one that was most difficult for you.
4. Estimate what part of your typical day is spent reading.
5. List the types of material you usually read (newspapers, magazines,
   books, reports, manuals, comics, packaging).
6. Recall a person who helped you become a reader—or a better
   reader.

Using the material you develop from the reading and from the notes you
make in response to suggestions 1 through 6, write your own "autobiography as a reader." This should be a story of important experiences you can recall as you learned to read and as you had difficulties or successes with reading. You should try to accomplish two things in this brief autobiography.
First, develop a clearer idea of your own strengths and weaknesses as a
reader. Second, convey to your instructor your feelings about reading and
what you hope to gain from a college course in reading and writing. Your
paper should be at least one page but no more than two pages.

1: Kim Chernin, a poet and novelist, recounts her mother's experience after emigrating from Russia to the United States:

> *I was happy with America. No, it was something more. I was
> enamored. In the apartment there was running water, a toilet in-
> side. My father bought us clothes. In America everything was new.
> There were pavements on the street. It was just like Zayde said:
> there were no old people in America. There was more sun in
> America. Everything was painted in America. We were in love
> with this shining world.*
>
> *Then I went to school. You remember, I could read and write
> in Russian and Yiddish. I knew a little Latvian. But here in Amer-
> ica I was put in the first grade. Before now, always, I was proud
> of my learning. I knew arithmetic, I knew history, I knew many
> things. But none of this I knew in English. There I was sitting,
> eleven years old, in a room with six-year-old children. I felt
> ashamed.* [In My Mother's House, *36*]

2: Maxine Hong Kingston presents a painful picture of being called
on to read in first grade:

> *It was when I found out I had to talk that school became a mis-
> ery, that the silence became a misery. I did not speak and felt bad
> each time that I did not speak. I read aloud in first grade, though,
> and heard the barest whisper with little squeaks come out of my
> throat? "Louder," said the teacher, who scared the voice away
> again. The other Chinese girls did not talk either, so I knew the si-
> lence had to do with being a Chinese girl.*
>
> *Reading out loud was easier than speaking because we did not
> have to make up what to say, but I stopped often, and the teacher
> would think I'd gone quiet again. I could not understand "I." The
> Chinese "I" has seven strokes, intricacies. How could the Ameri-
> can "I," assuredly wearing a hat like the Chinese, have only three
> strokes, the middle so straight? Was it out of politeness that this
> writer left off strokes the way a Chinese has to write her own name
> small and crooked? No, it was not politeness; "I" is a capital and
> "you" is lower-case. I stared at that middle line and waited so
> long for its black center to resolve into tight strokes and dots that I
> forgot to pronounce it. The other troublesome word was "here," no
> strong consonant to hang on to, and so flat, when "here" is two
> mountainous ideographs. The teacher, who had already told me
> every day how to read "I" and "here," put me in the low corner
> under the stairs again, where the noisy boys usually sat.* [The
> Woman Warrior, *193–194*]

3: Sandra Cisneros tells of Esperanza, a girl growing up in the Latino
quarter of Chicago, who reads to her dying Aunt Lupe:

> *I took my library books to her house. I read her stories. I liked
> the book* The Waterbabies. *She liked it too. I never knew how sick*

she was until that day I tried to show her one of the pictures in the book, a beautiful color picture of the water babies swimming in the sea. I held the book up to her face. I can't see it, she said, I'm blind. And then I was ashamed.

She listened to every book, every poem I read her. One day I read her one of my own. I came very close. I whispered it into the pillow:

> I want to be
> like the waves on the sea,
> like the clouds in the wind,
> but I'm me.
> One day I'll jump
> out of my skin.
> I'll shake the sky like a hundred violins.

That's nice. That's very good, she said in her tired voice. You just remember to keep writing, Esperanza. You must keep writing. It will keep you free, and I said yes, but at that time I didn't know what she meant. (The House on Mango Street, 60–61)

4: In her novel for children, *Dorp Dead,* Julia Cunningham creates a vivid character, Gilly Ground, who masks his real ability behind poor spelling and clumsiness:

I guess I was always what is called different, or way out, or a little nuts. Like me or not, that's how it is. Oh, I look like any other eleven-year-old with a thatch of roughly cut brown hair, the correct number of fingers and toes, green eyes that can open or shut with sun or sleep, and a sort of over-all foxy face, narrow at the chin. But I have a secret that nobody, not my dead grandmother or Mrs. Heister at the orphanage or my various unfortunate teachers, ever guessed. I am ferociously intelligent for my age and at ten I hide this. It is a weapon for defense as comforting as a very sharp knife worn between the skin and the shirt. When a person hasn't money in the pocket, good leather to walk around in, clothes that are his own, and a home address to back him up, I figure he has to have something else—anything. And I'm lucky. I'm not just bright, I'm brilliant, the way the sun is at noon. This is not a boast. It's the truth. It's my gold, my shelter, and my pride. It's completely my possession and I save it like an old miser to spend later. I purposely never learn to spell, which for the simple indicates stupidity. I fall all over my tongue when I am asked to read in school, and when we have a test in arithmetic I dig in the wrong answers very hard with a soft pencil and then smudge them over with my thumb to make it look as though I had tried. (Dorp Dead, 3–4)

5: In his autobiography, Malcolm X gives a dramatic account of his
   unusual approach to reading improvement:

> *Many who today hear me somewhere in person, or on televi-*
> *sion, or those who read something I've said, will think I went to*
> *school far beyond the eighth grade. This impression is due entirely*
> *to my prison studies.*
>
> *It had really begun back in the Charlestown Prison, when*
> *Bimbi first made me feel envy of his stock of knowledge. Bimbi*
> *had always taken charge of any conversation he was in, and I*
> *had tried to emulate him. But every book I picked up had few sen-*
> *tences which didn't contain anywhere from one to nearly all of*
> *the words that might as well have been in Chinese. When I just*
> *skipped those words, of course, I really ended up with little idea of*
> *what the book said. So I had come to the Norfolk Prison Colony*
> *still going through only book-reading motions. Pretty soon, I*
> *would have quit even these motions, unless I had received the mo-*
> *tivation that I did.*
>
> *I saw that the best thing I could do was get hold of a dictio-*
> *nary—to study, to learn some words. I was lucky enough to rea-*
> *son also that I should try to improve my penmanship. It was sad. I*
> *couldn't even write in a straight line. It was both ideas together*
> *that moved me to request a dictionary along with some tablets*
> *and pencils from the Norfolk Prison Colony school.*
>
> *I spent two days just riffling uncertainly through the dictio-*
> *nary's pages. I'd never realized so many words existed. I didn't*
> *know which words I needed to learn. Finally, just to start some*
> *kind of action, I began copying.*
>
> *In my slow, painstaking, ragged handwriting, I copied into my*
> *tablet everything printed on that first page, down to the punctua-*
> *tion marks.*
>
> *I believe it took me a day. Then, aloud, I read back, to myself,*
> *everything I'd written on the tablet. Over and over, aloud, to my-*
> *self, I read my own handwriting.*
>
> *I woke up the next morning, thinking about those words—im-*
> *mensely proud to realize that not only had I written so much at*
> *one time, but I'd written words that I never knew were in the*
> *world. Moreover, with a little effort, I also could remember what*
> *many of these words meant. I reviewed the words whose meanings*
> *I didn't remember. Funny thing, from the dictionary's first page*
> *right now, that "aardvark" springs to my mind. The dictionary*
> *had a picture of it, a long-tailed, long-eared, burrowing African*
> *mammal, which lives off termites caught by sticking out its tongue*
> *as an anteater does for ants.*
>
> *I was so fascinated that I went on—I copied the dictionary's*
> *next page. And the same experience came when I studied that.*
> *With every succeeding page, I also learned of people and places*
> *and events from history. Actually the dictionary is like a minia-*
> *ture encyclopedia. Finally the dictionary's A section had filled a*

*whole tablet—and I went on into the B's. That was the way I
started copying what eventually became the entire dictionary. It
went a lot faster after so much practice helped me to pick up
handwriting speed. Between what I wrote in my tablet, and writing letters, during the rest of my time in prison I would guess I
wrote a million words.*

*I suppose it was inevitable that as my word-base broadened, I
could for the first time pick up a book and read and now begin to
understand what the book was saying. Anyone who has read a
great deal can imagine the new world that opened. Let me tell you
something: from then until I left that prison, in every free moment
I had, if I was not reading in the library, I was reading on my
bunk. You couldn't have gotten me out of books with a wedge. Between Mr. Muhammad's teachings, my correspondence, my visi-
tors—usually Ella and Reginald—and my reading of books,
months passed without my even thinking about being imprisoned.
In fact, up to then, I never had been so truly free in my life.* (The
Autobiography of Malcolm X, *171–173*)

6: Robert Coles, a child psychiatrist and prolific writer, couldn't listen
to his favorite radio programs on the large Philco in the parlor because of his parents' reading habits:

*I remember one evening, when my father was saying good
night to me, we had, as was our custom, what he called a "brief
evening chat." Putting on a serious face and feeling a bit nervous
at the prospect of challenging what by then I knew to be a much-
cherished activity, I managed to voice my query: "Why do Mom
and you read out loud to each other?" He wasn't surprised by the
question, but he wanted to know how much thought I'd given to
the subject. He asked me whether I'd discussed his reading habits,
and my mother's, with anyone else. I told him that Bill [Coles'
brother] and I had indeed learned that none of our neighborhood
friends had parents who were so inclined. I also told him that I
had tried reading a book,* Robin Hood, *with a good friend who
lived next door, Benedict, and we had concluded that the exercise
was slow, cumbersome, boring. Dad, sensing more at stake, wondered whether I'd be happier if he and Mom read upstairs rather
than in our living room....*

*I can still remember my father's words as he tried to tell me,
with patient conviction, that novels contain "reservoirs of wisdom," out of which he and our mother were drinking. A visual
image suddenly crossed my mind—books floating like flotsam
and jetsam on Houghton's Pond, near Milton, Massachusetts,
where we lived. I never told my father what had appeared to me,
but he knew its essence by my glazed eyes. He made his pitch anyway: "Your mother and I feel rescued by these books. We read
them gratefully. You'll also be grateful one day to the authors."
Grateful? I was most certainly grateful, seconds later, when I felt
my father's facial stubble on my cheek. No more moral explica-*

*tion—only that last, Yorkshire-accented "Good night, Bobby,"*
*and my ever-optimistic rejoinder: "See you in the morning." (The*
Call of Stories, *xi-xii)*

# READING AN ESSAY

At the end of Section 1, "Approaches to Reading", I listed six principles that should guide your work as a reader. Let me review them:

1. Read with questions in mind.
2. Get some sense of the author's main point.
3. Recognize how difficult reading is.
4. Compare your own experience and knowledge in the world to the ideas and opinions you are reading.
5. Recognize how your attitudes, and sometimes your resistance, contribute to how much you get from reading.
6. Vary the approach until you get what the writer has to offer.

In this section, I will describe seven techniques that will help you put those principles into practice. Each of these techniques will be applied to an essay like those in this book. To begin your practice, read the essay "If We Cannot Save Our Children, We Are also Doomed" by historian Gary Wills. Read with your heart, noticing your feelings and noting which part of the essay creates those feelings.

◆

# IF WE CANNOT SAVE OUR CHILDREN, WE ARE ALSO DOOMED

GARY WILLS*

◆

In the week of the Los Angeles riots, a man drove his defective and runaway car, containing five children, into Lake Michigan, where it promptly sank. The man slipped out the door, but divers who were there by chance    1

---

*Gary Wills is a historian at Northwestern University. He wrote this article for the *Los Angeles Times*.

went down repeatedly in search of the children. The papers were full of the divers' heroism, and a general good cheer spread from the fact that three of those children, retrieved unconscious from the icy water, lived—to be returned to a poor neighborhood that may destroy them more slowly but as completely as the lake would have done.

A child in the water, a girl in a well, a boy trapped in a cave—whole countrysides will mobilize to rescue that single, imaginable human being. Some countrysides, in fact, will mobilize to guide a bewildered whale back to safety. But children go under every day in the dark rivers that are our city streets. Charles Dickens makes us picture one lost child in the filthy alleys of 19th-century London; but we do not see child after child alone and frightened, every night, in Los Angeles. We do not see, or want to see.  2

To see, and not to rescue, such children is corruptive of our most basic instincts. But rescue on such a scale is a daunting task. We might be drawn down into those dark currents ourselves. So we skirt them, avert our eyes, blame those caught in their murky coils. If we avoid them perhaps we, at least, will be saved.  3

But these are dark holes that will draw us in if we ignore them. The children are taking down our cities with them, and our moral authority as well.  4

There is something as symmetrical as doom about this. We listen, on television, to Sally Struthers begging us to "Save the Children" in some village halfway around the world—and let our own nation's children live only by hardening their hearts. We proudly lecture other countries on their human-rights records—and take away the most elemental right from these infants, the right to hope. We call our country the leader of the free world—while these children are imprisoned in inescapable misery. We feel obliged, now, to help the former Soviet Union address its most intractable problems—while deftly avoiding our own.  5

Then, to cap it all, we suffer the obscenity of our president informing us that those children are drowning in despair because we gave them too much. We passed "bleeding heart" legislation in the 1960s, gave them "liberal guilt money," that made them too soft to survive—unlike our tough white self—determining babies in the suburbs.  6

Even the attempts to help these children are turned against them. "Old failed solutions" just testify to the futility of rescue attempts, we are told. We ask other countries to solve worse problems with fewer resources, but throw up our hands at the task of saving our own cities, our own work force, our own fellow citizens.  7

It is subtly paralyzing to speak of these tragedies simply as "a problem." Rescue attempts are tried and fail when a child is down a well. We do not say the first attempts did not solve the problem and walk away. Besides, saving the cities is not a thing one can approach and "solve" once and for all.  8

We defend ourselves with continuing military plans, many of which have failed. Rockets blew up, planes crashed, tanks broke down, dollars disappeared, but we did not think defense was a problem we could walk away from if we had not solved it by the end of a year or a decade.  9

Others say that it is unrealistic to speak of work on our cities at the scale    10
of a Marshall Plan. The parallel is not apt, they argue. Well, it is certainly not
exact. In the Marshall Plan, we helped foreigners. These are citizens. The
problems then were distant. These are at our doorstep.

People tell us they are willing to help if only someone would tell just    11
what to do. People lie. Aid for Families with Dependent Children comes to
less than 2 percent of federal spending; yet politicians rise to power by attacking "welfare queens." Help to the poor is said to rob them of self-reliance; yet middle class entitlements have mushroomed.

Continual calls for help from the deprived suggests insatiability: Will    12
nothing satisfy those people? Nobody says that of retired people, whose demands have grown along with their federal support.

Things do not "work" with the poor because we do not want them to    13
work. Because of racism. Because we do not see the lonely, trapped child in
the ghetto. We see the lurking brute the jury saw in a Rodney King surrounded by dozens of armed men who could not feel safe till the 50th blow
was dealt out.

Until there is a willingness to face the hole in our culture, it will    14
grow. Given that willingness, however, crash efforts, trial efforts, overlap-
ping efforts, redundant efforts will follow, will supplement and correct
and compensate for each other. That is how we address things we really
care about—our own health, our colleges, our defense, our immediate
families.

We do not begrudge what was wasted on the Manhattan Project, the    15
Marshall Plan, the moon landing. If it was worth doing, it was worth the
messiness and uncertainties of large effort.

A combination of efforts is usually necessary—one program making up    16
for the deficiencies of another. What will not work is a hands-off, cheap and
remote plan like "enterprise zones."

Right-wingers like to think the market can solve anything if government    17
can just remove taxes and regulations. Among other things, this makes it unnecessary for the rest of us to care much or do much after "unleashing"
business forces. But making the inner cities a place for high-risk ventures at
low wages will not break down the isolation of the urban core—it will increase it.

Among other things, it will not take white workers into the poor area or    18
black workers out of it. A jobs program to restore the national infrastructure—funded from unused pension money—can do both.

When Patty Hearst was kidnapped, conservatives like William F. Buck-    19
ley urged leniency for the crimes she committed under duress. He has not
often been heard pleading for the children who were kidnapped at birth,
brought up in circumstances far more demoralizing than those of any Fagin's den in Dickens. Buckley could imagine Hearst as if she were his own
daughter. He cannot, apparently, imagine the same thing of black and Latino
children who commit crimes under far more imperious influences than
Hearst's brief period of captivity faced her with.

Until these children become our own, we continue to twist and distort   20
them into our enemies—and these are enemies we cannot afford to have. If
we cannot save them, we cannot save ourselves. That is the symmetry of it.
That is our doom.

Now that you've finished reading the essay, in order to give you some
basis for comparison, I will describe how I reacted on my first reading of
Wills' essay. My response is not a model, or the "correct" way to react. But it
illustrates how one experienced reader reacted to Wills' argument.

## Response

*First, Wills' concern about saving children attracted me very much. I am a
father and a teacher. My whole life has been involved in helping young people develop and become successful. I quickly sympathized with Wills' focus
on children—those who are endangered through accidents and those who
are endangered because they live in difficult and dangerous circumstances.
When he mentioned many cases where Americans have tried to help people
in other countries, especially children in other countries, I shared his feeling
that we should be equally concerned with the poor and the powerless in our
own country. But when he seemed to blame middle class people, retired
people, the Rodney King jury, and racism, I was a little bit uncomfortable. I
didn't really disagree with what Wills was saying, but I was also uncertain
that his blaming explained the problem. His example (in paragraph 19) of
contrasting how a conservative commentator sympathized with Patty
Hearst, a rich white woman, but not with poor black and Latino children
was powerful. This evoked my usual sympathy for the underdog. But at the
end, when he wrote, "That is our doom," I was confused. For me, "doom" is
a very powerful word. As a child, I had a lot of religious training. "Doom"
makes me think of "doomsday," or the end of the world. The riots in Los Angeles were terrible, horrifying, but they did not seem like the end of the
world to me. Perhaps my natural optimism resisted this very pessimistic
ending. But it bothered me. I knew I would have to reread the Wills essay to
see if I really disagreed with his ending or if somehow I misunderstood it.*

The previous paragraph is an example of what will be called a "reading
response" in this book. You can begin to understand what you have read by
quickly writing your response, stating what you felt, what you liked, and
what you didn't like in the essay you read. You shouldn't expect to grasp the
full meaning of an essay after just one reading. But writing a quick response
in a notebook or journal can help you see what parts of the essay present you
with difficulties—parts you don't understand, parts you don't agree with,
parts that irritate you, or parts that make you uncomfortable. These points of
difficulty and irritation offer the best place to begin your rereading.

Now that you have finished reading the essay with your heart, you are ready to begin the work of reading with your head, which is commonly called critical reading. This process can be quite useful and can be applied to most of the readings in this book.

*find questions / imagine you are the writer or / you know them or / find things that / are interesting in / the article / write down info's*

# QUESTIONS

First, go back to the title. The title actually states an argument. We face doom unless we save our children. But the title also raises many questions. Who are "we"? What must our children be saved from? How can they be saved? What doom do we face? By simply reading the title carefully we can create some initial tools for grasping the point Wills is making. Actually, this questioning technique can be used even before you read an article. You may find it helpful to turn the title into a series of questions and then predict what answers the writer will give to those questions. As you read, you can see how close you came to predicting the writer's answers.

The first question illustrates how reading involves more than just understanding words. Although he never states it in so many words, the "we" Wills refers to is all Americans, all of us in the United States of America. How can I be sure of that? Look at paragraph 5. The phrases "our own nation's children" and "our country the leader of the free world," when used by an American, makes it clear who "we" are.

The second question requires even more careful rereading. The opening paragraph talks both about the Los Angeles riots of 1992 and of a man driving a car with his children into a lake. Are we to save our children from drowning, as the heroic divers did in Michigan? Or from something else? Notice the last part of the first paragraph: "to be returned to a poor neighborhood that may destroy them more slowly but as completely as the lake would have done." As he writes at the end of his second paragraph, Wills wants us to save "child after child alone and frightened, every night in Los Angeles." Do you see how we have followed Montaigne's advice of looking away and repeatedly looking back? When you reread, you should not look at every sentence in order. Instead, you should look for the phrases and sentences that answer the questions that have formed in your mind.

# REFERENCES

Another question generated from the title—how can the children be saved—is more complex still. Most of Wills' article addresses this question. Wills also assumes that we have read some things he has read, that we know things he knows, and that we have seen television programs he has seen. But that won't be true for every one of his readers. In paragraph 2, he refers to Charles Dickens, assuming we know that Dickens wrote many novels in England in the early nineteenth century that portrayed social problems, especially those facing children. In paragraph 19, he mentions Dickens again, this time assuming we know that Fagin was the evil villain who enticed young boys to work for him as pickpockets in *Oliver Twist*. In paragraph 5, he assumes we know that Sally Struthers is an actress who became famous as the daughter of Archie Bunker on the television show *All in the Family* and who now makes appeals in commercials on behalf of hungry children who live far from the United States. He also assumes we know what the Manhattan Project and Marshall Plan were, who Patty Hearst and William F. Buckley are, and what Aid for Families with Dependent Children, "welfare queens," and "enterprise zones" are. If you don't know what he assumes you know, you need to find out. Use a dictionary, an encyclopedia, a fellow student, or your teacher to get the information you need.

## VOCABULARY

Wills is a college professor and uses many words that come easily to him because he makes his living doing intellectual work. But some of those words may not be part of your everyday vocabulary. So you need to do another piece of work: figure out the meaning of words you don't know and words you are not sure of. To compare your reading of the article with others, here is a list of words that many of my students don't know or are not sure of.

Paragraph   2: mobilize

Paragraph   3: corruptive, daunting, avert, murky

Paragraph   5: symmetrical, intractable, deftly

Paragraph   6: self-determining

Paragraph   7: futility

Paragraph   8: subtly

Paragraph 11: entitlements

Paragraph 12: insatiability

Paragraph 13: lurking

Paragraph 14: redundant

Paragraph 15: begrudge

Paragraph 16: deficiencies

Paragraph 17: right-wingers, ventures, urban core

Paragraph 18: infrastructure

Paragraph 19: leniency, duress, demoralizing, imperious

Paragraph 20: distort, symmetry

Is it necessary to check every word you are not sure of in a dictionary? Not always. For instance, in the second sentence of paragraph 3, the context of "daunting" (that is, reading the words that come before and after it) makes it possible to guess that the word means "difficult" or "challenging." Even if you cannot give a good dictionary definition of such a word, you may have a good sense of the meaning as you read. But if you don't know what "entitlements" (last sentence of paragraph 11) or "infrastructure" (last sentence of paragraph 18) are, Wills doesn't give you any clues about their meaning. You need to look up those words or ask someone for the definitions.

## NEGATIVES

Perhaps you noticed that Wills gives a great deal of attention to stating what will *not* save the children, expecting us as readers to figure out what will save them. This aspect of an essay is often the most demanding. The writer cites examples of what doesn't work, of what has gone wrong, and of what needs changing, only hinting at what will work, what is right, and what doesn't need to be changed. Here, the principle of contrast serves as an essential reading tool for getting the full meaning of an essay. Paragraph 5 is a good example of what Wills does throughout his essay. He lists what we do for others—Save the Children, lecture them on human rights, help the former Soviet Union—and argues we do not make the same efforts for American children "imprisoned in inescapable misery." Notice in paragraph 16 he describes what is needed in general terms ("a combination of efforts") and is more specific about what won't work ("a hands-off, cheap and remote plan like 'enterprise zones'"). Finally, his Patty Hearst/William F. Buckley example is also a negative, illustrating what won't save the children.

Now that I have looked at the essay more carefully, I see that Wills makes his best case for what is wrong, what doesn't work (in his view), and is very general about what should be done. So, I am still a bit uncertain about Wills' answer to how we will save the children.

## REPETITIONS

Another useful rereading technique involves looking for repetitions, words or phrases that a writer uses more than once. Often, a key idea can be found in the repetitions. Notice that in paragraph 4, Wills speaks of "dark holes" and in paragraph 14 he refers to "the hole in our culture." He not only repeats "hole," but it seems an unusual word for the topic. But a hole is a kind of negative space. It's where something isn't. That fits with Wills' generally negative picture.

Now I return to the last sentence in paragraph 2: "We do not see, or want to see." I think I am finally close to Wills' point. He is saying that we have a blind spot in our culture, a place either we do not look at or do not want to look at. This place is those parts of our cities where children live in deprived circumstances, lacking adequate food, housing, health care, and education. This fits with the first sentence of his concluding paragraph where he argues that if we do not see these children and make them our own children, then we will make them our enemies.

Then, in his final sentence, he returns to the words "symmetry" and "doom" that he first used in paragraph 5, and concludes that if we don't save these children we will meet our "doom." Now that I see his point more clearly, I can better say where we agree and disagree. Wills convinced me that we are not giving adequate attention or effort to the needs of these children. I know many people do not want to look at these problems. But I also know many people who do acknowledge these problems and are doing something about it. So, I'm not persuaded that the "we" applying to "all Americans" is really justified. And I'm still not persuaded the situation justifies a prediction of "doom." In fact, I remain vague about just what doom Wills is predicting. Does he foresee an Armageddon in America in which blacks and whites engage in a battle to the death? Or does he mean a cultural doom in which American ideals are so compromised that our culture is lost? I don't know, and his essay doesn't really tell me.

## Nutshell

At this point, you can sum up your understanding of Wills' essay. A very useful method for summing up is the nutshell. The term comes from the expression "putting it in a nutshell." To create a nutshell, write one sentence that states Wills' main point. Then write two to five sentences, each of them stating one of his supporting points or arguments. The result will be a nutshell of his essay. Here's my nutshell:

Main Point: Unless Americans recognize the plight of poor and neglected children in the United States, we are doomed as a people.

1. We try to help children all over the world, but not those in our own country.
2. We don't look at saving our children the same way we look at military needs, technology development, or foreign aid.
3. We don't make the same allowances for the poor and programs serving them that we make for the elderly and other national priorities.

4. This problem will be solved only if we establish programs that re-build the urban centers and only if we are really sensitive to the needs of the children there.

Notice this gives you a kind of "bare bones" version of Wills' essay, though it omits a great deal of detail and does not capture every point he makes. Nutshells are useful devices for testing how well you have under-stood what you have read. You can also use them to test your own writing to see if you have made the points you intended to make.

Now, do I assume you can get all this analysis out of two or three read-ings of an essay like this? Probably not at the beginning of your course. But this is the kind of reading you will practice throughout this book. This is the kind of reading that will help you prepare to write in college. Before you can fully develop your own opinion of Wills' ideas, you have to understand his argument. Once you grasp his point, you can more easily decide where you agree and disagree and why. Those points of agreement and disagree-ment can be the basis of the points you will make in your own writing on this subject.

Now I will ask you to read another essay, one that approaches this sub-ject from a different, though not necessarily contradictory, point of view. Use this essay to practice each of the techniques that were illustrated previ-ously with the Wills essay. This provides you a good chance to be an active reader. As you read and reread the Lawrence Harrison essay, keep a pencil and notepad handy. Use the pencil to mark the essay as you read. Using checks, question marks, and exclamation points in the margin can indicate passages you found interesting, confusing, or provocative. Underline unfa-miliar words, names, and references that you can look up later. If you notice repetitions or lists, note the emphasis in the margin or in a reader's note-book or journal. As questions or new ideas occur as you read, jot them down briefly. That way you won't forget them.

The Harrison essay demands even more work than the Wills essay. Har-rison refers to many people and historical situations that may be unfamiliar to you. You may want to work in groups on this essay, sharing the informa-tion you find in dictionaries, encyclopedias, and other reference tools. By applying each of the techniques listed below you should understand the Harrison essay.

- Responses
- Questions
- References
- Vocabulary
- Negatives
- Repetitions
- Nutshell

# Moving Into Middle Class

## Racism and discrimination still obstacles, but the majority of black Americans are in the mainstream

### Lawrence E. Harrison*

R ap performer Sister Souljah says middle-class blacks "do not represent the majority of black people." But the large majority of America's blacks are middle class.

Surprised? The Los Angeles riots and the recession notwithstanding, it's true, if you define the middle class as white collar and skilled blue collar; or if educational achievement is the determinant; or if everyone above the poverty line is middle class or higher. Only one out of six American blacks was in the middle class in 1950, compared to four out of six today.

The point is, if two-thirds of America's blacks are achieving such progress, racism and discrimination cannot be the sole or even chief obstacles for the one-third who remain behind, mostly in the ghetto.

A more important factor behind the tragedy of the ghetto may be the anti-progress values and attitudes inculcated by slavery perpetuated by the isolation of Jim Crow, and magnified by the toxic pathology of the ghetto, a pathology fed in part by the "me," "now," consumerist values of the broader society.

Many writers have stressed that slavery is destructive of progressive values. Harvard historian Stephan Thernstrom speaks of a black "cultural pattern—an emphasis on consumption rather than saving, an aversion to risk-taking investment" that would logically have its roots in the slavery experience. Alexis de Tocqueville wrote in 1835, "Slavery ... dishonors labor; it introduces idleness to society."

But cultures can change, a fact eloquently testified to by the two-thirds of American blacks who are now in the mainstream.

---

*This article is adapted from Lawrence E. Harrison's book, *Who Prospers: How Cultural Values Shape Economic and Political Success* (Basic Books). He wrote this for the *Washington Post.*

Why does the black success story leave so many incredulous?    7

Because, not just in the wake of Los Angeles, the ghetto has domi-    8
nated media treatment of blacks, the priorities of black leaders and the attention of the academic community, a pattern vastly reinforced by the
Los Angeles riots.

As an example, the National Research Council's lengthy 1989 study, "A    9
Common Destiny: Blacks and American Society," characterizes the status of
black Americans as "a glass that is half full … or a glass that is half empty."

Both the media and political leaders tend to choose the half-empty de-    10
scription. But the statistics make it clear that the glass is really more like two-
thirds full:

* In 1940, 93 percent of blacks and 65 percent of whites were in    11
  poverty; in 1990, the rate was 31 percent and 10 percent respectively.

* In 1940, the median number of years of education was seven for    12
  blacks, 10.7 for whites; in 1990, 12.4 and 12.7 respectively.

* In 1941, there was one black in the House of Representatives; to-    13
  day there are 26.

* In 1960, 22 percent of black adults and 64 percent of white    14
  adults had a high school diploma; in 1988, 67 percent and 87
  percent respectively.

* In 1940, 35 percent of voting-age blacks registered to vote; in    15
  1988, 65 percent.

* In 1940, 3.1 percent of Southern blacks registered; in 1988, 63.7    16
  percent.

* In 1970, there were 171 black members of legislatures and city    17
  councils in eight Southern states; in 1990, 1,876.

* In 1941 there were 10 black judges; in 1986, 841. The election    18
  of David Dinkins as mayor of New York City and Douglas Wilder
  as governor of Virginia underscores what amounts to a political
  revolution.

It's these statistics that prompted Octavio Paz, the Mexican intellectual    19
who has never been stingy in his criticism of the United States, to observe
in 1986, "It is not beyond the bounds of possibility that by the end of this
century the United States will have become the first multiracial democracy
in history."

The gains made by the majority of black Americans suggest that the pri-    20
mary solution to the problems of those left behind, while admittedly difficult and of long duration, must emphasize similar access and acculturation

to the mainstream. Still, some black leaders, and white and black intellectuals, are telling the ghetto dwellers that the opportunity isn't there, that they are impotent because of racism and discrimination.

The promotion of many black leaders of apartness, of identity with   21
Africa, of a sense of community circumscribed by color, is both contrary to Martin Luther King Jr.'s vision of an integrated society and a major obstacle to the continued working of the melting pot for blacks. This reverse apartheid propagates a we-vs.-them psychology on the part of blacks that contributed to the Los Angeles rioting.

Harvard sociologist Orlando Patterson, author of the prize-winning   22
"Freedom," makes a compelling case against reverse apartheid: "America, while still flawed in its race relations and its stubborn refusal to institute a rational, universal welfare system, is now the least racist white-majority society in the world; has a better record of legal protection of minorities than any other society, white or black; offers more opportunities to a greater number of black persons than any other society, including all of Africa; and has gone through a dramatic change in its attitude toward miscegenation."

Columnist William Raspberry of The Washington Post draws the logical   23
conclusion: "The need is not to reach back to some culture we never knew, but to lay full claim to the culture in which we exist."

Why should one believe that culture is the principal obstacle to   24
progress in the ghetto?

For one thing, other obstacles have diminished markedly. For example,   25
in 1958, 55 percent of white Americans would not move if a black family moved next door; in 1978, 85 percent. In 1958, 78 percent of Southern parents objected to desegregated schools; in 1980, 5 percent.

Fifty years ago, the white image of blacks was shaped by stereotypical   26
entertainment characters like "Amos 'n' Andy." Today, Bill Cosby, Oprah Winfrey and Magic Johnson are among our heroes, and many whites think Gen. Colin Powell would make an excellent President.

Further evidence of the overriding influence of culture is the perfor-   27
mance of black West Indian immigrants, acculturated to British values and institutions, in the United States (they now account for about 1 percent of the national black population).

They have produced a disproportionate number of leaders—for exam-   28
ple, Marcus Garvey, Stokely Carmichael, Malcolm X, Shirley Chisholm, Sidney Poitier, Harry Belafonte, Godfrey Cambridge, Franklin Thomas (president of Ford Foundation) and Powell. As economist Thomas Sowell has pointed out, after the first generation, Caribbean immigrants have achieved income and educational levels that exceed the national average for all Americans, and average family size, unemployment and crime rates below the national average.

The descendants of "free persons of color"—blacks who either were   29
never slaves or were freed before the Civil War—have performed similarly

to the Caribbean immigrants. The ancestors of many of Washington's black elite were freedmen.

Even with the larger societal erosion of the values of work, educa- ³⁰ tion, excellence, frugality and community, the broader society provides a far more progress-prone culture than does the ghetto. While it is difficult to change the value system of adults, public policy can play a helpful role. For example, welfare reform focused on work incentives and coupled with expanded job opportunities should have high priority, as should programs to encourage access of blacks to jobs and living arrangements outside the ghetto.

We surely can do better in inculcating progressive values in children ³¹ through expanded Head Start and supervised play and day care; busing to schools where the student body includes significant numbers from the cultural mainstream, black and white; courses that better prepare high school youngsters for effective child-rearing; and increased contact between blacks who are in the mainstream and those who aren't.

Racism and discrimination are still ugly facts of life in America. But they ³² should not become an excuse for ignoring the most important challenge for disadvantaged black Americans—which is whether they will permit the melting pot to work for them, as it has for so many other ethnic groups that have found their way out of the ghetto.

What is the main difference between Wills' piece and Harrison's? Though Harrison addresses racism, discrimination, and the cultural issues they create, he does so in mostly affirmative rather than negative terms. He cites evidence of how far African-Americans have come since 1940. In this way, he suggests that we can best deal with continuing problems of poverty and racism by understanding the factors that allowed such a large portion of African-Americans to enter the middle class over the past 50 some years. Now that I have read the Harrison essay, I can see more clearly what I didn't like about Wills' essay. Wills did a good job of saying what was wrong, but he didn't acknowledge that anything was right, that anything had worked. Harrison's essay makes a strong case that improvements have been made and that we might continue to improve in this area if we understand what led to the success we have had. Together, the Wills essay and the Harrison essay give me a fuller sense of the situation. I have a better sense of what I think, now that I have read both arguments.

This process of reading several essays, some easy and some difficult, will be repeated in every chapter of this book. You can develop your own ideas for writing by reading and understanding several different views on a subject. As you write responses to what you read and as you write out each writer's main point, you will be accumulating the material from which your own paragraphs and essays can be developed. At the end of every chapter, several suggestions for writing will be presented to help you develop your own ideas and opinions.

**Most people have both routines and fears associated with the act of writing. What are your common routines and greatest fears when you are faced with a writing task?**

# READING, THINKING, WRITING

Learning how to write requires many different skills. To start, you have to write—a lot. To have a subject to write about, you have to read and to think—a lot. Many books have been written about learning to write. Your instructor knows a lot about learning to write. This chapter cannot substitute for the information and insights provided in a full-length book about writing. It is intended to complement the advice your instructor will provide in class.

This chapter will provide a number of topics that most college writers find important as they do the hard work of reading, thinking, and writing. Each topic gives suggestions that might apply to the writing tasks you face in this course and in other college courses. Most topics will raise questions to discuss further with your instructor and your classmates. Some topics will also refer to other sources of information about writing.

The order of topics roughly follows the different stages in the writing process. But any topic can be studied at any time. Writing is very complex and very individual. You may have a question about spelling, a question about organizing your material, or a question about finding your material. The best time to address such questions is when they first come up. Use the material in this chapter as your instructor suggests or whenever it helps you answer a question about writing.

# READ TO WRITE

## COLLABORATING AND ACTIVE LISTENING

Talking with others can help you clarify your own ideas and broaden your perspective on those ideas. That's why working in groups with classmates can help you understand a reading or improve a piece of writing. Everyday living requires working together—collaborating. Living in a household with other people requires all the basic elements of collaboration: identifying what needs to be done, agreeing on who will do it and when, communicating changes and resolving conflicts, and agreeing on some standards so that all members of the household recognize that the task has been completed satisfactorily. However, anyone who has tried to set up a new household knows this is not easy to do.

Collaborating in a classroom on reading or writing has several advantages. You can benefit from other viewpoints, since each of your classmates will bring different values and experiences to the reading. You can benefit from the efforts of others, so that not everyone has to do all the same background work. You can get some motivation, since you'll see that you are not alone in the struggle to make sense out of a reading or produce writing that carries meaning and value. You can also develop some skills in interpersonal communication that will help you in many professional and work situations.

Effective collaborating involves a number of steps.

- Clarifying the task: The group must agree on what needs to be done. If your instructor has asked you to identify the main point of an article, then each member of the group must acknowledge that task.
- Clarifying your role: In some groups, everyone contributes in the same way. Other times, each member has a specific role to play as the group works. Examples of those roles might be facilitator, timekeeper, notetaker, summarizer, and researcher.
- Clarifying the outcome: The group needs to know what result is expected of the group's effort. Perhaps each member will report orally or in writing. Perhaps only a spokesperson will report the group's results. Or, perhaps the notetaker or summarizer will write on behalf of the group.

Often, controversial ideas will generate strong differences of opinion among group participants. In a writing course, your purpose is not to force your views on others, but to persuade them to consider the merit of your arguments. If strong, conflicting views are expressed in a group, try to understand the reasons for each view. People of good will can always agree to disagree.

- Being prepared to work: If a task was assigned prior to the group's work (such as reading some articles or completing an exercise), every group member must have done his or her work. Otherwise, some group members may freeload on others.
- Encouraging participation by all group members: Even in small groups, some members will be aggressive, perhaps even try to dominate the group's work, while others will be passive, reluctant to volunteer their thoughts and opinions.
- Using effective communication techniques: Learning these skills can be an entire course in itself. But essentially, this means making an effort to contribute, being honest about your knowledge and your opinions, sharing time by some form of turn-taking, not interrupting when another group member is speaking, and employing active listening.

This last technique may require some practicing. Active listening involves attending to another group member while they speak, sending both verbal and non-verbal clues that you are listening and understanding (head nods or saying, "Uh-huh" or "yes" are examples of clues), asking for clarification or amplification when you don't understand the speaker, and restating what a person has said to acknowledge that you "got it." Sarcastic remarks, put downs, personal attacks, and non-verbal dings such as rolling your eyes, smirking, or turning your body away from the speaker are all ways of undercutting active listening in a group.

Working in a group can be extremely satisfying or extremely frustrating. Learning how to work effectively with others will increase the quality of your work and your level of satisfaction with that work.

## EXERCISE

To practice collaborating in which each participant has a role, form groups of three. Assign each group member the role of sender or speaker, receiver or listener, and recorder or notetaker. The speaker should describe an experience in which he or she felt in danger of death. The listener should try to understand the speaker's story, giving active feedback (both verbal and nonverbal) and seeking clarification when some point is not clear. The notetaker should observe the conversation between speaker and listener, noting how the speaker clarifies points, how the listener communicates understanding, and how both speaker and listener manage difficulties in understanding. If time is available, this process should be repeated so that each member of the group takes each role.

# PREPARING TO WRITE

We write about what we know. We write best about what we know best. These statements may seem obvious, but they are worth thinking about in some depth. In order to write anything, you need a subject to write about. To write convincingly, you must know about the subject. The greater your confidence in your knowledge, the more perspective and confidence you bring to your writing. Let's explore these ideas in greater detail.

Members of Congress like to ask witnesses, "What did you know and when did you know it?" Writers, too, must ask, either deliberately or unconsciously, "What do I know and how do I know it?" Let's consider the four chief ways you have of knowing:

1. *Experience.* Just by living, you accumulate an enormous fund of information. Most of what you know about your first language you learned through experience. You learned to walk and put food in your mouth from experience. Most of what you know about getting through your day, you learned from experience. Just doing things and noticing the results develop an enormous knowledge base in every human being. If you have a hobby or a favorite sport, think about how much you learned just by doing what the hobby or sport requires.

2. *Observation.* Intertwined with experience is our observation of others' experiences. Often, when we find ourselves in difficulty, we observe others to see how they do something. Before you rode a bicycle or a skateboard, you observed others. Most of you have spent hundreds, perhaps thousands, of hours observing other drivers before you ever began to practice on your own. Most of your knowledge of the natural world (what's the difference between a cow and a horse?) comes from simple observation. If you have a pet, think of how much you know about that pet just from watching it eat, sleep, play, and move around.

3. *Instruction.* As you go through life experiencing and observing, you have been receiving instruction. At first, teaching comes from parents and other caretakers. As you grow, friends, neighbors, teachers, policemen, and other public officials provide you with instruction, usually in oral form, but sometimes in written form. Most of the rules we know have been provided to us this way. The best instruction takes account of what you already know from experience and observation.

4. *Reading.* Once you learned to read, you controlled a powerful means of self-instruction. Reading allows the voices, ideas, and insights of people far away and long ago to come to you as you choose. If you want to know how to start a campfire, you can read

a Boy Scout handbook—or you can find books that describe how Native Americans built fires hundreds of years ago. Or, closer to home, you can read the directions on a fire log wrapper. Think about the reading you do every day: traffic signs, street signs, billboards, package wrappers, instructions on forms. Even if you don't think of yourself as a reader, you probably get a lot of information everyday by reading.

By the time we are adults, these ways of knowing have become so interconnected that most of us are no longer aware of *how* we know *what* we know. Because so much of what we know seems second nature, we often focus our attention on what we don't know. When that happens, it is hard to write. If you think you know nothing—or very little—about a subject, you don't have much to write about. Preparing to write requires, first of all, that you find out what you know about a subject. Here's an exercise that will help you inventory your knowledge about a subject.

## Exercise

Across the top of a piece of paper, write the four headings "Experience," "Observation," "Instruction," and "Reading." Using one of the articles from Chapter 3 or Chapter 4, list as many areas of knowledge related to the subject of the article that you can, placing each one under the heading that seems to fit best. Use phrases or fragments as a kind of shorthand so that you can do this task as rapidly as possible. Complete your work in less than 10 minutes.

Form a group with other students who have read the same article. See how you can extend your knowledge by listening to what other students know about the subject that you didn't know—or hadn't yet thought of. Add new phrases and fragments to your lists.

When your group has completed sharing its information and ideas, describe in a few sentences your current state of knowledge on this subject. If you feel you still don't know enough to write about the subject, write two or three questions you have about areas that you still feel uninformed on.

## Predicting and Questioning

When we first learn to read, just being able to pronounce the words we find on the page seems a major accomplishment. Once we gain fluency and learn to read silently and more efficiently, we often read to simply understand what is being said. However, academic and professional reading requires more than that. You need to have a critical understanding of what you read. Developing the habit of reading critically requires awareness of the tasks involved and regular and repeated application of each element of the tasks.

Chapter 1 contains a brief discussion of the process of predicting and questioning as you read.

## Predicting

Predicting involves anticipating what a writer's subject will be and guessing about the writer's approach and attitude toward that subject. You might be asking yourself, "Why bother? I'll just read and see what happens. It's more fun that way." Actually, that reaction makes sense. Reading should have a feeling of spontaneity and the possibility of a surprise. Whether you are aware of it or not, you already predict when you read. For instance, when you've been given a reading assignment, have you ever looked to see how many pages it involves? Why did you do that? Probably, you wanted to predict how long it would take. If you look at the reading material and it is very long and in small print with no illustrations, you may predict that it will be hard and boring. In short, predicting is closely related to expectations. Your previous experience with reading leads you to have expectations of new reading. Generally, you will assume that a piece of reading that looks like one you have read before will provide a similar reading experience. Often when readers find a writer whom they enjoy, they will look for more books by the same person. They are predicting they will have a similar experience with the other books.

Some predictions—or expectations—can motivate you to read. If you believe that a book offering the ten steps to becoming a millionaire will really work, you'll read it eagerly, learning all you can so you too can get rich. Other predictions—"here's another dry textbook full of useless information that I'll forget right after the test"—can create barriers to effective reading. So you need to recognize the predictions you are actually making when you approach a reading assignment. Ask yourself whether those predictions are motivating you or turning you off. If they are turning you off, you'll need to try to change your expectations in some way. Instead of remembering a piece of reading that turned out badly, try to think of one that turned out well. Even a reading you don't like may provide you with new information. A reading that makes you angry can stimulate you to argue against it. To sum up:

- Recognize the predictions you are actually making when you approach a piece of assigned reading
- Determine whether those predictions are helpful or hurtful.
- When they are hurtful, take deliberate steps to alter your predictions to more helpful ones

## Exercise

Turn to the Table of Contents of this book. Pick out any article you have not read. Based only on the title and the author's name, write down what you think the topic of the article is, what the author's opinion on that topic will be, and what the author's attitude about the topic is. Put these notes aside while you read the section on "Questioning."

## QUESTIONING

You can focus your predictions by questioning what you read. Eventually, questioning should become a habit, but to start you may need to be more formal and systematic about questioning your reading. The most fundamental question relates to your purpose. Why are you reading this piece? Are you looking for specific information, such as an address, name, or number? Are you trying to learn a concept or process, such as the concept of surface tension or the process of photosynthesis? Are you trying to grasp an idea, such as Darwin's theory of evolution? Are you trying to understand a writer's opinion, following the argument and evidence the writer offers in support of the opinion? Each purpose will lead to a different reading strategy. Most of the reading in this book assumes a purpose related to the last question.

If your purpose in reading is to understand a writer's point, specific questions, like the ones listed here, can motivate your reading.

- What does the title tell me about the subject of the reading? What does the title tell me about the writer's approach to the subject?
- Does the first paragraph confirm what I thought the title told me? What does the first paragraph tell me about the importance of this subject? In other words, why should I care?
- What does the author say that is new to me? Are these new ideas or just old ideas in new words? Or are these old ideas in new situations?
- What experience have I had with the material in this reading? If I have had no experience like this, do I know someone who has?
- What does the writer's mood seem to be? Can I find an explanation in the reading for the writer's mood? What do I know about the writer? Does that help me understand the writer's mood and attitude?
- What words or phrases does the writer repeat? What examples does the writer use? What is the point of each example?
- Does the last paragraph confirm the approach indicated in the first paragraph and the title? If the last paragraph goes beyond the opening ideas, what has been added? Did the writer prepare me for what was added by providing information, explanations, examples, and reasons? Can I find them in the reading?

As you work with this process of predicting and questioning, you'll develop your own ways of using predictions and questions. In short, keep an open mind, be curious, and pursue a writer's argument until you understand it.

## EXERCISE

Turn to the article you chose for the previous exercise. Scan the entire article for about 30 seconds to get an impression of the whole piece. Now, write three questions you would like answered by the article based on your predictions and impression.

Finally, read the entire article carefully. When you finish, make notes on how accurate each of your predictions were and how fully each of your questions were answered.

# KNOW THE WORDS: VOCABULARY IS A KEY TO MEANING

We improve as readers from reading that challenges us. Such reading should be, in some way, better than us. For most readers, the obvious challenge lies in vocabulary—certain words and expressions used by a writer are new or unusual. Sometimes, we don't know the words at all. Other times, we know the words, but the writer uses them in some unusual way. In still other situations, writers refer to people or events that we are not familiar with. In every case, as a reader, you need some method for learning what you don't know.

The best way to learn words is to look them up in a dictionary. In fact, as a college student, you should always have a college edition of a reputable dictionary within easy reach when you are studying. You never know when a writer will surprise you with unfamiliar words or phrases. As a reader, you need to find a technique for developing your command of vocabulary. Adopt one of these procedures as you read:

1. Look up each unfamiliar word as you encounter it.
2. Underline or put a check next to unfamiliar words as you read, waiting until you have finished the entire article before you go to the dictionary. That way, your concentration on the writer's ideas is not interrupted.
3. As you read, make a guess at what new words and phrases mean from the *context* (the sentence before and the sentence after the one you are reading) and put a pencil mark in the margin next to the sentence containing the new word. When you have finished reading the whole article, go back to the words and phrases you didn't know. If you are still uncertain, use a dictionary.

## EXERCISE

Choose one of the three techniques for learning new words previously described and use that technique while reading one of the articles in this text.
Then, use a second technique while reading a different article. Write a short
paragraph explaining which procedure you preferred and the reasons you preferred it. If you have time, compare your experience with a classmate's by reading one another's paragraphs.

You will find, however, that not every unfamiliar word or phrase can be
found in a dictionary. In those cases, you need other strategies. This is most
common when writers assume knowledge that their readers do not share with
them. These differences between writer and reader can come from differences
in age, geography, or life experience. To illustrate, my 16-year old son recently
mentioned he was visiting a friend in the next town. Since he didn't have access
to a car that evening, I asked him how he planned to get there. "On the shame
train," he replied. I had no idea what a "shame train" was. As it turns out, it is a
transit system bus. You can be sure "shame train" is not in any dictionary. When
you encounter such new expressions, or even very old expressions, you may
need to ask someone who might be more familiar with the subject. For instance,
if you wanted to know what a "coax gage" is, you would ask a trained auto tech-
nician. If you didn't know who Ozzie and Harriet were, you could ask someone
who was at least 10 years old in the 1950s or 1960s.

## EXERCISE

To get some practice in checking out meanings that may not be immediately
clear to you, work in groups to identify the meanings of these words and expressions from "The Ties That Bind 'Wiseguy'" in Chapter 6 "Television."

| | |
|---|---|
| tapped out | largely voyeurs |
| demise | quaff |
| the black hats | weird empathy |
| entrepreneurs | beefy Stallone-ish looks |
| hood | heterosexual |
| pungent | homoeroticism |
| jawing | cult status |
| 30 pieces of silver | Norman Rockwell painting |
| windup | muscle shirts |
| twinge | Ricky and David Nelson |
| coquette | homophobe |
| munitions freak | mundane Canellism |
| psychotic incestuous geniuses | hallucinatory |
| decadent | |

In addition to determining the meaning as writer Joyce Millman uses the
expressions, make note of what method you used to learn the meaning.

# WHAT'S THE POINT? FINDING THE MAIN IDEA

Writers try to make a point to their readers. If they didn't, writing would be pointless. As a reader, you need to figure out what point a writer is making. Sometimes writers state and restate their point so often and in so many ways that it is easy to figure out what point they are making. Other times writers make their point in less obvious, more roundabout ways. Whatever the situation, as a reader, you still have to figure out what the writer is saying before you can decide what you think about the writer's point.

I don't know an easy or simple formula for figuring out a writer's main point. The best way to get good at this is to read pieces from lots of different writers until you get a feel for the many different ways writers make their points. Of course, you need to read with attention and focus. Just reading through an article once allows you to become aware of the writer's subject and some of her concerns, but you probably won't be certain of the point after one quick reading.

The real trick, then, is not learning how to read, but learning how to reread. The first reading of an article let's you get familiar with the territory. It lets you form some preliminary impressions. To really grasp the article's meaning, you want to do effective, efficient rereading. To do that, you must develop techniques for reentering the text to get a deeper understanding of the writer's point. Here are some techniques to practice for identifying the main point of an article.

## EXERCISE

1. Using a reading assigned by your instructor, make a quick list of what you already know about the article's topic using the headings *Experience, Observation, Instruction,* and *Reading.*
2. Write two or three questions that the article has raised for you.
3. Reread the first paragraph and the last paragraph. Has the writer linked them together in any way? State any connection you find between the two paragraphs.
4. Notice any repeated phrases or ideas in the article. Do these reflect the writer's emphasis?
5. Based on what you know now, state the writer's point in a single sentence.
6. Form a group with other students. Exchange your statements of the writer's point. Try to identify where you agree. Discuss where you disagree. Keep an open mind. Someone else may help you see the writer's point. There's no need to defend your first version if you see that there is a better way of stating that point. You don't score points

by being the first to get it right. You simply need to understand what the writer says.

7. With the whole class, discuss any problems your group encountered in trying to agree on what the writer's point was.

# MAPPING AND CLUSTERING

Most of the time we think in words. But we also think in shapes and colors and sounds and forms other than words. These more visual and aural ways of thinking help some people to understand ideas and concepts more easily. We show greater understanding when we can find more than one way to represent what we know. For these reasons, the related techniques of mapping and clustering help you get a clearer sense of what you read and of what you think.

Mapping applies to a way of visually representing the important elements of a piece you have read. Typically, you make a circle or oval in the middle of a piece of paper. Inside the circle you write a word or phrase that expresses the main topic or subject of the article or essay, perhaps a key phrase from the title of the article. Then, you make circles for each of the main points the writer uses to support the main topic, expressing each support point in a word or phrase. You can connect these circles to the central circle by lines. Finally, you can find the actual support (examples, facts, quotations from experts) the writer uses to back these support points, putting each of them in a circle connected to the circle expressing the support point. The result of this work provides you with a visual, non-linear representation of the important elements of a reading. Some students find this mapping process more helpful than outlining or summarizing, which depend entirely on words for representing the ideas of an author. Study the map shown in Figure 2.1 which represents the main elements of Norman Podhoretz' "Real Dads Do Not Play Mom" in Chapter 3.

Clustering involves the same technique as mapping, but in this case, you use the circles as a way of displaying what you know and what you think about a particular topic or subject. If you were trying to write about an ideal parent, you could begin by putting that phrase in the middle circle, then try to think of each important feature or quality the ideal parent has (putting each one in a circle connected to the middle circle), and then you could think of specific situations in which such a parent might display that quality (connecting these to the appropriate circle). Because the cluster can be developed in any sequence, just as the ideas come to you, it may help you get your ideas out more fully and more quickly. Study the cluster example shown in Figure 2.2.

Both mapping and clustering are useful techniques for your repertoire as a developing writer.

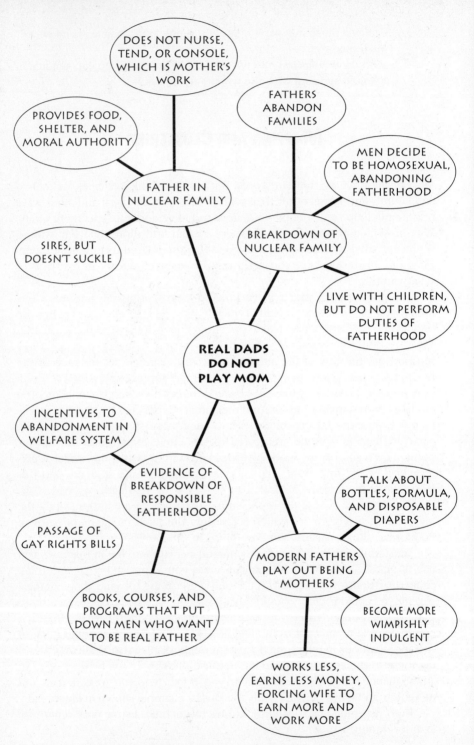

Figure 2.1   Read Dads Do not Play Mom (Map)

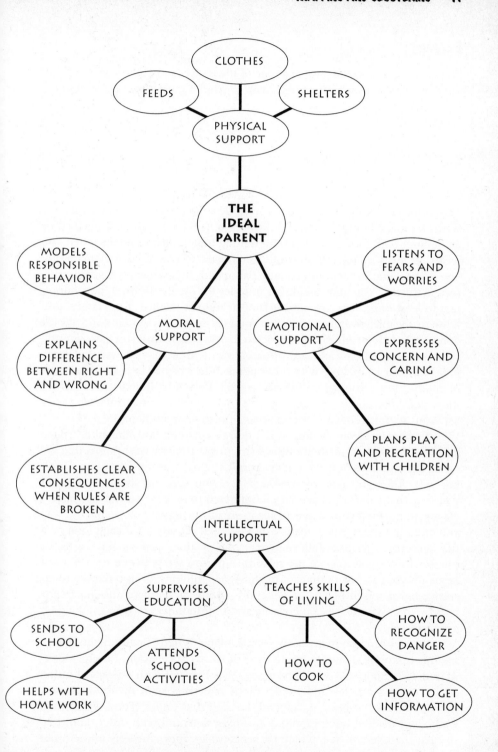

Figure 2.2   The Ideal Parent (Cluster)

## EXERCISE

To practice these techniques, map one of the articles in Chapter Seven, Music. Then, do a cluster on your favorite style or type of music (e.g., classical, rock, rap, country).

# NUTSHELLING AND OUTLINING

At several points in this chapter, I have described the list as an important writer's tool. When you give a list structure, you create either a nutshell or an outline, both of which are useful writing tools. A list develops when you write just any idea related to a topic as it occurs to you. A nutshell or an outline is the same list rearranged and elaborated. Rearrangement gives structure to the list. You may decide on an order for the items, from most important to least important, from most familiar to least familiar, from largest and costliest to smallest and least costly. You may decide some items on your list don't really belong and should be deleted. You may realize you have omitted some important items and add them. As you rearrange, you may find some items on your list belong with other items. When one item is actually a part of another item, you subordinate it, usually shown by indentation. Each of these decisions about rearranging your lists contributes to structuring your list. Your rearranged list may end up as a nutshell or an outline.

In Chapter 1, nutshelling was briefly explained and illustrated (page 22). "Putting it in a nutshell" allows you to see the essential points that another writer makes. But the nutshell can be equally useful for you as a writing tool. After you have drafted a paper, you can "nutshell" it to see if you've actually made the points you intended to make. You can also have a classmate nutshell your paper to see if a reader will get your points the way you intended them. A key feature of a nutshell requires that each item be a full sentence. Writing full sentences rather than just single words or phrases forces you to state the relationships you see between the different items on your list or outline. It pushes your thinking from tentative to assertive because sentences are generally assertions. Perhaps the nutshell is most helpful when it tests the clarity and thoroughness of your thinking on a subject.

Outlines can also help clarify your thinking. When I first thought of writing this textbook, I simply wrote a list of words (Television, Family, Music, Automobile, Sports, Work, Consuming, Male-Female) with no special order. As I collected articles and tried various exercises with my students, my thinking about the book developed. I added two topics (Food, Parent and Child) and deleted one (Sports). I also experimented with order, until I arrived at the one you see, which presents topics approximately in the order in which most human beings experience them in their lives. I used the same approach in developing the material in this chapter. Originally, I had about ten writing topics in mind. But, as I worked with my students and as other professors read my drafts, suggestions for more writing topics developed. The end result is an outline, which in this book is called "Table of Contents."

Informal topic outlines will be most useful in writing the relatively short papers (300–700 words) for courses like this one. An informal outline simply lists key points in a word or phrase, in the order you plan to take them up in your essay. You can keep such an outline handy while you write to remind you of the next point you plan to make. You can elaborate that outline by jotting down the examples you plan to use to develop each point. In that case, your outline would have more form: topic headings with subordinate points for your examples.

In longer writing projects, such as a research paper, a more formal outline will probably emerge from your efforts at planning and drafting, much as the "Table of Contents" for this book emerged as ideas developed and as users and reviewers commented on the materials. Many software programs for computers provide "outliners," or "to-do lists" that make structuring your ideas more convenient. Most handbooks will provide the details of how to present a formal outline.

## EXERCISE

To practice nutshelling, use an article from the text assigned by your instructor. Use the techniques in this chapter to identify the main point of the article, then state that point in a single sentence. Now identify the major points of support for the main point. State each support point in a single sentence. You now have a nutshell.

To practice the informal outline, list the key points made in one of the articles in this text. Under each key point, list at least two points of support found in the article. You now have a topic outline.

# SUMMARIZING

A summary demonstrates you have understood what you have read and that you can restate that understanding in your own terms. Summary writing is one of the most useful tools in both academic and professional work, but often is not explained or practiced adequately. You probably have been asked to summarize an article, lecture, story, or part of a textbook, but you may not know just what is called for in a summary.

Actually, a summary can take many forms. A very brief summary is a synopsis, such as this account of the movie *E.T.*:

E.T., which stands for extra-terrestrial, relates the adventures of a kid-sized alien, accidentally left behind when his space ship departs the earth. He is discovered by a family of American suburban kids who play with him and hide him until his loneliness gets so severe that he is dying, literally, to phone home and arrange a rescue. Government authorities and research scientists discover him and take over, but ultimately the faith and love of the kids who found him rescue E.T. from being a researcher's curiosity.

Notice that a synopsis is very brief, containing only the most important elements of the original. In this form of a summary, you don't get much of a feel of what the original was like. None of the really funny or really sad scenes are included here. None of the specific actions or words of the characters are included. Often the purpose of a synopsis is to provide just enough information about the original so that you can decide whether you want to read (or see) the full version.

## Exercise

Write a synopsis of no more than 50 words of the last movie you saw or the last episode you watched of your favorite TV program.

In many kinds of writing, a summary doesn't point you to the original, but substitutes for it. This kind of summary writing can be very important in many college courses. For instance, a professor may want you to demonstrate your grasp of a reading he has assigned and so asks you to summarize it. Usually, your professor wants more than a synopsis. In such a summary, it is important to convey not only the author's main point, but also each key support point used to establish the main point. In addition, you should include direct quotations and paraphrases of the writer's examples, evidence, and other forms of support for key points. To write an effective summary, you need to read the original carefully, several times, and then retell the original, stating the writer's main point and his chief arguments for that point, and mentioning the kind of evidence the writer offers for that main point.

Based on the discussion of Gary Wills' essay in Chapter 1, I have all the elements I need to write a summary. Here's how I would summarize Wills' article:

*When a man performs an act of heroism, saving the lives of children, people rejoice. Dramatic stories of rescues of children, or even animals like whales, catch our imagination. But the everyday dangers facing children in Los Angeles, we do not see. Wills states, "To see, and not to rescue, such children is corruptive of our most basic instincts." Should we fail to look at these dark places, the children will bring down our cities and our moral authority.*

*"There is something as symmetrical as doom about this." While we Americans donate money to "save our children" in Africa and while we lecture others on civil rights, we do not address the plight of poor children in our own country. Even when we try to help poor urban children, we give up too quickly or too easily, though we never do that in developing new military weapons.*

*Some people say they would help if they knew what to do. But we say helping the poor robs them of self-reliance and creates welfare queens. At the same time government help to the middle class increases.*

*"Things do not 'work' with the poor because we do not want them to work." This hole in our culture will not be filled until we are willing to face it. Our experience as a nation shows that when we are willing to face an issue (colleges, defense, health, our own families) we will work at it until we find a solution, even if some efforts fail.*

*The approaches of right-wingers, that market forces can solve anything, let us off the hook. But without some intervention, white workers will not enter poor areas and black workers will not be able to get out. When conservative William Buckley urges leniency for Patty Hearst, he can imagine her as his own daughter. But apparently he can't imagine black and Latino children as his own when they commit similar crimes.*

*Until the poor children of the cities become our own, they will be our enemies. If we cannot save them, we cannot save ourselves, a situation of symmetry that will spell our doom.*

Compare this summary to the original to see what parts were omitted (less important) and what parts were left in (more important).

Most of the time, in your writing, you will not write complete summaries, such as this one of Wills' piece. You will find it useful to summarize parts of what you read to use in your own writing as part of the evidence (examples and illustration) you use to develop your own ideas, your own main point or thesis. The term "paraphrase" describes this use of summary. You take the ideas and concepts of someone else and express the key elements in your own words as a way of illustrating what that writer has to say and what you are going to comment on, or as a way of buttressing your own argument as part of your essay. Sometimes in a paraphrase you will quote portions of the original (a phrase here, a sentence there). When you do this, you need to place the quoted material in quotation marks. And of course, you need to mention the writer or source by name in your paper, acknowledging that you are taking material from another writer.

A word of caution: Using the exact words of another writer without recognizing your source by using quotation marks results in plagiarism, the unacknowledged use of another's words and ideas. Even when you paraphrase material from another source, using your own words, you must name the source in your text. Failure to do so would again be plagiarism, a serious violation of scholarly ethics.

# EXERCISE

To practice paraphrasing, read the letter Gwendolyn Brooks writes to her daughter in "Mothers and Daughters" (p. 106), stating her key ideas in your own words. Limit your paraphrase to 100 words.

To practice summarizing, retell the main points of Wendy Ho Iwata's "Boy Crazy" (p. 109). Limit the summary to 300 words.

# THINK TO WRITE

## THE LIST: A TOOL OF THE MIND

We write to communicate. We want to convey information, ideas, feelings, and images to others. That seems an obvious role of writing. Yet writing does more than that. Certain kinds of writing are mental aids, tools our minds can work with. One of the most common tools—so common that it may seem obvious—is the list. Psychologists have demonstrated through various memory experiments that under normal circumstances we can hold only five to nine items in our active (or short-term) memory at any given moment. That's probably why we have trouble remembering all the names of Santa Claus' eight reindeer or Walt Disney's seven dwarfs. Both tasks approach the upper limits of our active memory. To help your memory, write down the names of the reindeer or the dwarfs as you think of them. Now your active memory no longer needs to keep those names in mind and is free to recall the ones you haven't thought of. The result, of course, is you have written a list.

Most of us write lists so often that we forget it's a form of writing. We make out grocery lists, lists of things to do, lists of what to tell the mechanic to work on, lists of the albums we own. Because lists are such a simple tool, they are a powerful tool. You can make one up almost anywhere at any time as an aid to memory. Lists can also be a tool in helping you think as you prepare for writing. One kind of list comes from brainstorming—writing down every idea that you can think of as fast as you can on a particular subject. Sometimes lists are more organized. First, you think of some categories (Homework and Housework, for example), and then you list all the items you want to remember under that category.

Let's consider how you might use this tool to read and write more effectively. First, after you have read an article, you can list all the opinions the writer has stated. That helps you understand what point the writer is making. After you have such a list, you could make a second list, one that contains opinions that the writer didn't state. You could make still another list—opinions that counter the writer's opinions. Making these lists should help you to understand better what you have read. What's more, once you have completed such lists, you have material you can begin to think about for your own writing about the article you have read.

Writers also use lists to inventory what they already know about a subject. With that aid to memory, writers can then try to list what they don't know about the subject. The second list serves as a guide to what reading, interviewing, or other research they need to do if they are to write knowledgeably on a subject.

The list can also be used by a writer to illustrate a point or provide evidence for an argument. For an example, see paragraph 8 of Barry Walters' article "Still Hot, Still Sexy, Still Dead" (p. 208) to see how his list of several songs by The Doors shows what attracted him to the music. For more extensive use of listing, see Mark Leyner's "Pass the Chips" (p. 176), where his use of letters and names in series provides the bulk of support for his ideas.

## EXERCISE

To practice these techniques, select an article in Chapter 6. After reading the article once, develop three lists: "Author's Opinions," "Other Opinions," and "Points That Counter the Author's Opinions." Now read the article a second time, listing each point you can find for each of the three headings. You may have to think up most of the points for the third list.

# MEMORY: THE WINDMILL OF YOUR MIND

Our memories serve as the storage devices for our minds. Each of us has an enormous resource in our memory, though not all of us have learned to use that resource well. Inexperienced writers and rusty writers often say "I can't think of anything to write about" or "I don't have anything to say on this subject." While sometimes those statements are accurate, many times they reflect poor memory habits. The following article written by Barbara McGarry Peters of the Health and Fitness News Service, offers both insights and memory recovery techniques.

# TRICKS OF THE MEMORY GAME

BARBARA MCGARRY PETERS

Have you ever stumbled over the name of a friend who appears unexpectedly, searched in vain for glasses or keys when in a hurry, forgotten to run an important errand or lost your train of thought?

Most adults, beginning in their 30s, noticed slight memory lapses and start to have doubts about their ability to remember. But most people, say memory experts, have a better memory than tests show. And their memories improve dramatically after they learn how short- and long-term memory work.

Some people might seem to have photographic memory abilities. They might slip up on occasion, but most of the time they capture facts, figures and faces in sharp focus on their memory "film." How do they do it?

Chances are these "human cameras" have a healthy lifestyle. Buoyant health enhances memory. Your diet, stress levels, exercise and sleep habits play important roles.

People with photographic memories also use tricks to engrave facts indelibly in their minds. Here are several that you might find helpful.

- Observe with all your senses. "Nothing is in the mind that was not first in the senses," National Institute of Mental Health (NIMH) neuropsychologist Mortimer Mishkin quotes from Thomas Aquinas. "It's all the information we take in, store in the brain and then recall when we come across something—an object, a face, a place—that reminds us of that stimulus."

  When you store facts in your sound, sight, touch, taste and smell memories, you have more cross-references to draw on the next time you want to retrieve information.

- Be a detective when you meet someone new. Take in the features of the person's face, color eyes, marks of distinction, texture and style of clothing; take in the setting—fragrant flowers on the oak table, books stacked on the desk, chilly air blowing in from an open window, thick rug beneath your feet.

  When you see that person again and can't place him or her, try to evoke details from the setting where you met. Little by little the picture your "mind camera" snapped that day will start developing, and a name or place will surface.

- Dredge up information buried deep in your memory with three tricks of the trade: relaxation, focus, and concentration. The arch enemies of a good memory are stress and distraction. Settle on one person or one paragraph at a time rather than letting your eyes dart around over your conversation partner's shoulder, or back and forth in an article.

- To remember facts, fix them with scholarly techniques. Choose a quiet time and place with no interruptions. Sit up front to hear a speaker or to see a slide show. Highlight important words, take notes and do a brief outline.

- Repeat a new acquaintance's name after being introduced during your talk and when you say good-bye. Daniel E. Koshland Jr., professor of molecular and cell biology at the University of

California, Berkeley, calls learning through frequent repetition "habituation."

"The first time we telephone someone," Koshland explains, "we remember the number just long enough to dial; the second time, we find it easier. With frequent repetition, we go over a memory threshold and the number gets into long-term memory."

"We all have to work harder at remembering as time goes on," says NIMH's Mishkin. "Even if you keep active mentally and continue to learn and read in your special field of interest, you still lose some. But you have acquired so much knowledge over the years that you can afford to lose some."

Peters' article includes a number of suggestions that any writer should make use of:

- Observe with your senses
- Notice details, relax and concentrate
- Find a quiet place of recollection
- Mark books
- Take notes
- Make informal outlines
- Go over material several times.

Your memory is the key to unlocking the treasures of all your past experiences, remembering the people and events of your life.

## Exercise

Walk outside and observe a scene for five minutes. Now go inside and write down, as quickly as possible, everything you can recall from your observations.

Now inventory each of the five senses: sight, sound, touch, taste, and smell. Focusing separately on each sense, see what more you can remember from the scene, and write that down.

Now close your eyes. Breathe slowly and deeply for one minute, letting your arms and legs relax, clearing your mind of all thoughts. When you feel quite relaxed, focus your attention on the scene you observed. Recall any more details from the scene, and record them.

Compare your experience with that of a classmate. Which memory techniques worked best for each of you?

## Comparison: A Powerful Principle

An especially powerful principle used by thinkers—and thus one that must be understood by writers—is the principle of comparison. Reflective thinkers ask, "What is the same? What is different?" When you describe a man as "tall, dark, and handsome," you have contrasted him with a man who is "short, fair, and ugly." Writers regularly develop their ideas by comparisons, emphasizing what makes their idea different from what readers already know or believe. Notice how David Rosenthal used this principle of comparison in this extract from his article on television fathers found in Chapter 3 of this book:

> It was Jim Anderson, played by Robert Young on "Father Knows Best," who indelibly set the standard for all television fathers who followed. In fact, he set the standard for a lot of real-life fathers, too, even if he never intended to.
> "I always hated 'Father Knows Best,'" my own pop confided to me over the phone the other day, a revelation I'd never heard before. "He always made me feel inferior. Nothing ever threw him; he had all the answers. I never did and nobody I ever knew did, either."

The first sentence establishes a comparison between Jim Anderson of *Father Knows Best* and all other television fathers. Rosenthal claims that all TV fathers are compared to Anderson. His second sentence makes a second comparison, one between Anderson and real-life fathers. The third part of the quotation demonstrates that this comparison results in a contrast, as Rosenthal's father says he never felt he or any other real father could compare to Jim Anderson. As a reader, you should always be looking for the comparisons and contrasts the writer makes. Sometimes they are stated, as in the previous example. Other times, the contrast is implied, as in this sentence from James Baldwin's *Notes of a Native Son* from Chapter 4:

> He [the minister at the funeral] presented to us in his sermon a man whom none of us had ever seen—a man thoughtful, patient, and forbearing, a Christian inspiration to all who knew him, and a model for his children.

Notice that Baldwin expects his readers to work at understanding the contrast. We must understand that, contrary to the minister's portrayal, Baldwin's father was thoughtless, impatient, and unaccepting, being neither an inspiration or model to his family. Of course, Baldwin is just setting us up for another contrast when later he explains how he came to appreciate his father's good qualities.

# EXERCISE

To see how powerful this principle of contrast is, identify and write out at least one contrast in each paragraph of the excerpt from Baldwin's essay (Chapter 4, p. 117). Treat paragraphs 35–39 as one paragraph for this exercise. When you have completed the exercise, you should have a list of contrasts that Baldwin uses. Try to connect those contrasts to the point he makes in his final paragraph. If your instructor prefers, divide into groups in class, each group working on a single paragraph and then sharing the group's work with the class.

# CATEGORIZING: SORTING AND CLASSIFYING YOUR IDEAS

When a baby learns its first words, it begins to categorize the world in very simple terms. For instance, all adult males might be called "daddy," all small four-legged animals might be called "doggie," and all large four-legged animals might be called "horsie." As the child grows, he or she learns to make finer distinctions and learns new words to express those distinctions. Thus, by age five, most children can distinguish "dog" from "cat" from "rabbit." Children will recognize the differences among "horse" and "cow" and "reindeer." A child's growth in knowledge and language are intertwined. That remains true for you as an adult. As you develop more information about yourself and the world, you have a greater need to sort that information into categories so you can keep track of it and make sense out of it.

This act of sorting and classifying your knowledge will continue throughout your life. Much of the work you did in school and you now do in college requires learning new categories for information. Introductory courses in psychology and in linguistics consist mostly of learning how those disciplines categorize knowledge and, at the same time, learning the words used for naming the categories. Psychology may divide itself into categories such as experimental, behavioral, cognitive, and therapeutic. Each of those categories can be divided further, based on the knowledge of the mind that has been developed over the centuries. Linguistics (the study of language) includes such categories as historical, comparative, descriptive, and applied. Most college dictionaries include the results of comparative linguistics, namely a classification of the languages of the world. The result of this sorting into categories produces a chart of languages related to one another. In chemistry, the Periodic Table of Elements is another example of the result of many years of research establishing and describing relationships among basic chemical elements.

Whether you have thought much about it or not, you have been sorting and naming objects, people, experiences, and ideas your entire life. For the most part, you do this by accepting categories and names created before you were even born. In addition, each of you develops your own categories and your own systems of classification in some area of your life. You have some system for organizing your compact discs or tapes, the books in your personal library, the utensils in your kitchen, the tools in your toolbox, or the furniture in a room. Your system may be one that others could recognize easily, or it may be one so personal and idiosyncratic that only you understand the basis of your classifications.

What does all this have to do with writing? Simply this: a very common way to make a point involves sorting information into categories and explaining to your readers why those categories help them understand your point. For instance, you might find categories created by another writer who claims that athletes who become professional sports celebrities are either talented, hard-working, or lucky and offer your own examples to support that writer's categories. In effect, you are arguing that the other writer's categories are correct, or at least a useful way of thinking about professional athletes. On the other hand, you might disagree with the writer by modifying the other writer's categories or by creating categories entirely your own. This kind of reading, thinking, and writing is common in college, especially in course papers and written examinations.

## EXERCISE

Read Freda Garmaise's essay, "Shoppers of the World, Unite!" in Chapter 8 (p. 249). She develops her ideas by dividing all people who buy things into three categories. As an exercise, identify her three categories. Next, try to put each of your family members and three of your close friends into one of those categories. If you can put all the people you know well (including yourself) into one of her categories, then you could argue persuasively that her categories are correct. But if you find you have several examples that don't fit or that overlap, then you need to either modify her categories (and give them appropriate names) or create categories that she doesn't mention and name those new categories. In every case, you would have the basis for writing your own paper about the types of people that buy things, including the qualities that define each type.

# THIS IS A CAUSE, THAT'S AN EFFECT: WHAT'S THE CONNECTION?

Most scientific inquiry and experimentation focuses on either describing effects or finding causes. The history of medicine is filled with examples of identifying effects (symptoms) of some assumed cause (disease), then trying to establish how the cause produces the effects. When that is understood, medical researchers can then seek ways of altering the disease and reducing or eliminating its effects by actions we usually call treatment or therapy. Perhaps the most current dramatic example of this has been the work to recognize AIDS as a disease, to document the range of effects, and then to seek the underlying cause or causes. Because most organisms (including human beings) are quite complex, establishing clear connections between causes and effects can be quite difficult.

Not only in the area of health, but also in social, political, and economic areas, we are regularly engaged in the effort to link causes with effects. Teenage suicide rates have increased in the past few years. What can explain the increase? In other words, what are the causes? After an extended period of expansion of the American economy in the 1980s, an extended period of no growth or slow growth developed in the early 1990s. What caused the expansion? What caused the slowdown? Economists, politicians, talk-show hosts, and everyday citizens argue at length about what should be done to improve the economy. The nature of their proposals almost always depends on what they see as the causes of the problems as well as how significant they see the negative effects. Over the past thirty years, the rate of voter participation in American elections has declined significantly. What caused this decline? Has the electorate become less informed, or are voters more cynical about politics? Are people more preoccupied with themselves and their families and less with the larger community? Perhaps it's a combination of these causes. Perhaps the cause is something else altogether. You can see that identifying connections between causes and effects is quite complicated.

What does knowledge of causes and effects have to do with writing? Most of the arguments you will read in this text rely in part on cause-effect claims. Many of the papers you write will attempt to identify effects, establish causes, or claim some causal relationship between two facts or events. Thus, recognizing a cause and an effect is an essential part of critical reading. Arguing a relationship between a cause and an effect is the goal of most intellectual and scientific work. Learning to write about causes and effects is an important dimension of the work you will do in college.

## Exercise

Anna Quindlen organizes her article "The Legal Drug" (p. 149) around effects from drinking alcoholic beverages. To see how cause-and-effect analysis can be used in writing. make a list of all the effects Quindlen cites from alcohol use. Then, list any other effects (from whatever cause) she mentions in her article. For the second list of effects, try to identify the cause. Note whether Quindlen actually states the cause or leaves it unstated.

Once you have completed these lists, state, in a single sentence, Quindlen's argument about the effects of alcohol abuse.

# Focusing Your Ideas

We have already practiced several important techniques for understanding the key ideas in what you read: listing, comparing, categorizing, and identifying causes and effects. Making lists, finding the points of similarity and difference, sorting these points into categories, and establishing relationships among the points and the categories help you understand what a writer says. These activities serve another function. They provide you with material to consider in developing your own ideas and opinions. Making the leap from understanding another writer's ideas to coming up with your own ideas may be the hardest part of the reading-thinking-writing process. Understanding what you read, then deciding what you think about it, and finally putting that opinion into words can be an incredibly complicated process. So, if you find you are struggling with the process, don't get down on yourself. Everyone—even the most skilled writers— struggle as they first try to form their ideas into words. With regular practice, you can get better at this process. But good thinking is never easy. It is always hard work.

To bring your own thinking into focus, try writing a single sentence that states the most important point you want to make about what you have read. I find it useful to call this a *focusing statement*. Writing a focusing statement is harder than writing just any sentence because you are trying to do several things at once:

1. decide what is most important in what you have read
2. decide how you feel about those most important points
3. find words to express both 1. and 2.
4. create a sentence that shows the relationship between the different parts of your idea.

You can see this is something like juggling three balls while walking a tightrope—you need to keep focused or you'll drop the balls, or, worse, fall off the rope.

## EXERCISE

To practice writing a focusing statement, the following exercise will use some of the techniques already described:

1. Make a list of the qualities that Joyce Millman attributes to Vinnie, the main character in the TV show *Wiseguy*.
2. Watch some other cop show on television (e.g., *NYPD Blue, Miami Vice, Law and Order, Hunter, Magnum, P.I., CHiPs, Homicide, Cagney and Lacey, Street Justice*) and focus on one of the main characters. Make a list of that character's main qualities as a person and as a cop.
3. You now have two lists, which should provide the basis of some comparison. Make a third list describing the differences between the two characters—Vinnie and the one you watched on television.
4. Now try to write a single sentence—a *focusing statement*—in which you emphasize the most important differences between the two characters. At first you may have to write several sentences to state the

main ideas and then combine those ideas into a single sentence that gives the emphasis you are after. Don't be surprised if you rewrite this sentence several times. Thinking is not easy.

5. Finally, once you have written a sentence that you are satisfied with, use it as the first sentence in a paragraph in which you develop your ideas about the differences between the two characters.

# ORGANIZING YOUR MATERIAL: FOCUS, GROUP, ORDER

The hardest part of writing comes from the messy, confused, unfocused situation in which you find yourself after you have read and discussed and thought about some issue. A former student said this very well in the opening sentence of one of her essays: "I have a ragbag mind full of bits and pieces of useless material that I dare not throw away." We always have "stuff" in our heads, but finding ways to make sense out of that stuff, of putting it together so someone else can make sense out of it, is always difficult.

"Getting organized" is not one single act, but a very complex series of activities that probably cannot be fully described. Part of what happens in getting organized can be put on paper or put into words in conversation. Since much of what we consider (and reject and reconsider) goes on in our minds and never is made directly visible to others, it is not possible to neatly describe a series of steps for producing a perfect composition. We can describe some of the processes that must take place between the initial impulse to write (such as an assignment) and your finished paper. Three important processes of thinking and drafting (the writing you do to get your ideas on paper) are represented by these concepts: *Focus, Group, Order.*

*Focus* refers to the specific approach or emphasis in the material you are trying to write about. This focus should not be so general as to be meaningless (e.g., "Movies can be interesting.") and it should not be so specific that it leads nowhere (e.g., David Letterman is the star of *The Late Show with David Letterman*). The focus should make a promise to your reader that you plan to deliver in your paper (e.g., "David Letterman's off-beat humor makes him the best late night talk show host"). You've made two promises to a reader: you will show that Letterman's humor is off-beat and you will show why that makes him the best among all late night talk show hosts.

*Group* refers to the effort to find different aspects of your material that go together, points that are related or connected in some way. As you develop your ideas and your examples, keep them in short phrases so that you can easily move them around until you find the most sensible connections. You may find connections based on similarities, opposites, causes, or effects. Very often, after you make some connections, even better ones will occur to you. When that happens, *Regroup*. You may also find that as you group and regroup, that you find a better focus for your material than the one you started with. When that happens, *Refocus*. That simply means rewriting your focusing statement so it clearly connects to the new ideas you have developed on your subject.

*Order* refers to the sequence in which you present the material that you have grouped. In deciding on the best order for your material, consider whether you want to arrange it *chronologically* (the order in which it happened) or by *importance* (in order of strength of arguments) or by *impact* on the reader (in order of ease of understanding). You may want to try putting your arguments and examples in different orders until you find one that seems to work well for your paper.

## EXERCISE

To practice these ideas, read Barbara Karoff's article "Food Owes Him the World" (p. 141). Now, group each of the foods mentioned in the article according to the continent of origin (Europe, Africa, Asia, North America, South America). Next, group those same foods according to the continent where each became popular. Within each group, create an order that would make sense to a reader.

Looking at the results of your grouping and ordering, find a focus for the material and write a single sentence expressing that emphasis.

# YOUR OPINION IS ONLY AS GOOD AS YOUR SUPPORT

One of the great truisms in America states "Everyone has a right to their opinion." Like most truisms, it is true—as far as it goes. If you think the world is flat or that eating garbage prevents cancer or that short people are not as smart as tall people, you have a right to hold and express that opinion. But you don't have a right to have your opinion respected. You must earn respect for your opinion. The way we earn respect for our opinions is by the support we offer for them. This support comes in two related forms: arguments and evidence. The stronger our arguments and the more convincing our evidence the more likely others will respect our opinion. This principle holds true in everyday conversations, in courtrooms, on the editorial pages of a newspaper, and in papers you write for college classes.

In an earlier section, you practiced writing a *focusing statement*—a sentence which expresses the point you plan to develop in your paper. When such a statement expresses your opinion and is the key point in an argument, the sentence is usually called a *thesis statement*. Your thesis is simply an expression of the point you want to prove or the point you want to convince your readers to accept. Just stating your thesis and asserting your opinion, will not persuade readers. You need to give reasons and explain the basis of those reasons. Others will accept your reasons when they appeal to common sense, when they convey a sense of logic, and when they are supported by evidence. Depending on your opinion, your reasons may take the form of causes, effects, elements of a process, or aspects of an object (ideas we develop by comparing, contrasting, and classifying).

For instance, if a friend tells you the best apples can be found at a small country fruit stand, you may well ask how your friend arrived at this opinion. If his reason is "I've bought apples in three supermarkets and four fruit stands, and these are the best tasting of all," you might be impressed, but you also might wonder about nutritional value, cost, and the presence of pesticide residue. If his reason is "My grandfather told me," then you'll want to know more: what experience does his grandfather have? If his grandfather has worked his entire life growing and selling apples, then his opinion is worth much more than if his grandfather is allergic to apples but has invested money in this fruit stand. If your friend's reason is that the state Agriculture Commission sponsored a study by experts at the university which tested apples for food value, taste, and freedom from pesticides and identified these apples as the best overall, you might be persuaded. Notice that each kind of evidence has value for supporting an opinion (personal experience, the reported experience of others, the findings of experts), but that the strongest support comes when a writer can draw on all three forms of evidence.

In short, as writers, we always support our opinions from our personal knowledge. That personal knowledge may be gained from direct experience, from observing or hearing the experience of others, or from reading the systematically gathered data of researchers and experts. A reader will be most persuaded to our opinion when we can offer all three kinds of evidence to support our opinions.

## EXERCISE

To practice some of these concepts, read Joan Didion's essay "On the Mall" in Chapter 8 (p. 252). After reading the article follow the steps listed below.

1. Working in groups of three or four, agree on the main point Didion is making about shopping malls. Express that main point as a thesis statement.
2. List all the reasons that Didion gives for her opinion of the role of shopping malls. Which reasons are causes? Which reasons are effects? Are any of her reasons neither causes or effects?
3. For each reason you have identified, list the evidence that Didion gives for it. Label each piece of evidence as coming from her personal experience, from her personal observation, or from what she learned from her reading of experts' views.
4. Again working in groups, identify the connections between her evidence, reasons, and main point. If you can do all of this, then you have

a good grasp of the structure of her argument. Once you understand her argument, ask yourself, "How correct is Didion in her view of the role of shopping malls in contemporary American life?" Your answer to this question forms the basis of your own thesis about shopping malls. (Notice that her essay was published in 1979. You may have more recent knowledge about malls that adds to or modifies Didion's views.)

5. Based on your reading and analysis, write your own essay explaining the impact of shopping malls in your own community.

# Anecdotes: Using Little Stories

Telling stories is the most common and most powerful form of human communication. Every known culture and society conveys important ideas and beliefs through the telling and retelling of stories. Research shows that, by age nine, virtually all children have learned the rudimentary elements of story structure: plot sequence, character, and conflict. Because storytelling is so wide-spread and accessible, it is a powerful technique for writers as well as speakers and conversationalists. In the Christian Bible, Jesus would teach his followers by telling stories, called parables. In Africa, children are taught basic lessons through fables about animals. The Greeks explained the origin of the universe in a story form we now call a myth.

When a speaker or writer tells a brief story to help make a point, or to provide background for the point to be made, we call that story an *anecdote*. Anecdotes are extremely common forms in most cultures. We often draw on previous experiences or observations, often those of a dramatic nature, to explain dangers we face, fears we've developed, and triumphs and disappointments we experience. The usual form of conveying these experiences and observations to others is the anecdote. A well-chosen, well-told anecdote gives writing both clarity and vitality.

What constitutes an effective anecdote?

First, it must illustrate the point you are making or serve your purpose in preparing for the point you are making.

Second, a good anecdote contains all the necessary elements and details from the experience you are recounting so that its point is clear.

Third, an effective anecdote is brief, omitting details and elements that actually occurred in the event, but which don't contribute to your point or your purpose.

Fourth, good anecdotes use strong, lively language which further helps engage the interest of your reader.

Here are some examples of effective anecdotes:

Or what woman, having ten drachmas (coins), if she loses one drachma, does not light a lamp and sweep the house and search carefully until she finds it? And when she has found it, she calls together her friends and neighbors saying, "Rejoice with me, for I have found the drachma that I had lost." Even so, I say to you, there will be joy among the angels of God over one sinner who repents.

(Source: Luke, 13: 8-10)

## The Fox and the Grapes

A famished fox saw some clusters of ripe black grapes hanging from a trellised vine. She resorted to all her tricks to get at them, but wearied herself in vain, for she could not reach them. At last she turned away, hiding her disappointment and saying: "The Grapes are sour, and not as I thought."

(Source: *Aesop's Fables,* Tr. George Fyler Townsend. Doubleday: Garden City, N. Y., 1968, p. 154.)

## Why Wisdom Is Found Everywhere

Kwaku Anansi (trickster spider hero of the Ashanti of Ghana) thought himself wisest of all creatures. He could build bridges, make dams and roads, weave, and hunt. Deciding not to share wisdom with others, he went about collecting wisdom and put each bit he found in a large earthen pot. When it was full, he decided to hide it in a treetop where no one could find it.

Holding the pot in front of him, he began to climb. Anansi's son Intikuma, curious about his father's project, noticed that Anansi had difficulty in grasping the tree with the pot held in front. When the son offered a suggestion, the father scolded him for interfering.

Intikuma replied: "Excuse me, father, but I see you are having difficulty. If you put the pot on your back, you can climb easily."

Anansi tried it. With the pot on his back, he climbed swiftly. Stopping, he looked at Intikuma and was embarrassed. Though he carried so much wisdom in the pot, he had not known how to climb with it.

In anger, Anansi threw the pot to the ground where it shattered, scattering the wisdom in all directions. When the people learned of what happened, they came and took some of the wisdom Anansi had thrown away. So today, wisdom is not all in one place, but is everywhere.

This is the story Ashanti people remember when they say, "One head cannot exchange ideas with itself."

(Source: Retold from Harold Courlander, with Albert Kofi Prempeh, *The Hat-shaking Dance and Other Ashanti Tales from Ghana,* Harcourt, 1957.)

Mark Twain liked to recall that when he was 18 years old, he found his father to be stubborn, ignorant, and lacking in common sense. When Twain turned 21, he reported being amazed at how much his father had learned in three years.

An anecdote can be used anywhere in your writing. Sometimes it is a very effective way to begin an essay (as Gary Wills did in the essay in Chapter 1 on p. 15). It can be used to illustrate a point you have just explained in general terms (see the second paragraph of "Does Spelling Count?" in this chapter). You can use an anecdote to arouse feeling in your reader as in Elizabeth Glaser's speech to the 1992 Democratic convention when she told of the courage of her young daughter as she faced death from AIDS. You can use an anecdote to end your essay, to clinch your point, or to illustrate the implications of your point .

Though anecdotes are very powerful, they must be used judiciously and written effectively. Practice using anecdotes in your writing. Notice how others use anecdotes in conversations and formal presentations to get ideas of what is effective.

## EXERCISE

Anecdotes (in the form of testimonials) are frequently used on television shows that claim they have a product or method that will create good health or great wealth, especially the shows called "infomercials." Watch one 30-minute infomercial and list all the anecdotes that are used. Then, write a sentence explaining how effective each anecdote was for the purpose of the show. (If you cannot find an infomercial to watch, substitute five one-minute commercials that use testimonials.)

# WRITE TO WRITE

## START TO FINISH: THE PROCESS OF WRITING

Every other section of this chapter deals with a single aspect of the kinds of writing tasks you encounter as a college student. This section provides an overview of the entire process of writing a college paper, from start to finish. Every paper includes three main processes: thinking, drafting, editing. The thinking stage includes the planning you do in your head and on paper. Drafting refers to all the work you do in writing your ideas out. Editing refers to all the finish work you do making your paper accessible and acceptable to another reader, most often your instructor.

### THINKING AND PLANNING

You are always thinking and planning: when to leave for school, what to have for lunch, what to say to your boss at this afternoon's meeting, which movie you and your friend will see tonight. Just getting through every day requires you to do some thinking and planning. When you have a writing task, you need to be conscious of how you best think and plan. If you think best in the shower or while riding the bus or driving the freeway or late at night, alone in your room, use the thinking and planning methods that already work for you when you work on an assigned paper.

Begin your thinking and planning as soon as you receive an assignment. Though you may not write your paper immediately, you want to give yourself maximum time for thinking. Do not set the assignment aside, intending to return to it the night before it is due. It may be fine to write your paper the night before it is due, but if you don't think about it until then, you will have wasted valuable thinking time. Follow the steps listed before you sit down to write the first draft of a paper:

1. Read the assignment over several times, determining exactly what the task is. If you do this immediately, you will be able to think about the assignment whenever your mind is not occupied by more pressing matters. Students report doing this kind of thinking while jogging, doing laundry, driving, doing routine tasks at work, or cleaning the house. Recognizing times you can profitably think about a writing task allows you to do the most important work of planning: deciding on your focus and your main sources of evidence and examples.

2. When an idea or an example comes to mind, make a note—in your journal, in your text book, or anywhere you know you will find it. If you give yourself just 30 minutes per day for three days to do this kind of thinking and note-taking, you should be well prepared to write.

3. Reread the articles on which your assignment is based. Look for other written material in your everyday reading that may add to your ideas for the paper.

4. Consider at least three different ways of focusing your paper. Thinking of different approaches and choosing among them will give you greater confidence in the focus you decide on—and give you back-ups if you find your first choice doesn't work out.

5. Use one or more of the organizing techniques described earlier in this chapter: listing, clustering, nutshelling, outlining. These techniques will allow you to put your thinking on paper, giving some shape and organization to the thinking and planning you have done.

6. If you get stuck, do a free write or a blind write. Free writing can be used at any time to get lots of material on paper without worrying about how you will eventually use it. Blind writing is a technique primarily for those blocked from moving forward. (These techniques are described more fully on p. 68 of this chapter.)

## Drafting and Writing

Assuming you have a week to complete your paper, you should do your first draft after three days of thinking, leaving you several days before the due date. Even if you don't feel completely ready to write, it is better to get several hundred words on paper to see how much material you have and to see if you need to narrow your focus or expand your support material.

Think of your draft as a trial run. Mistakes are acceptable here. Getting your ideas on paper allows you to evaluate them more easily. Keeping everything in your head gets confusing. Once you have your focusing statement and your major examples on paper, you can think more about how to improve your work and how to make clearer connections between the parts of your paper.

One good drafting technique involves assembling key quotations from the reading you have done. It's best to copy these quotations onto paper or your word processor so that you can work with them separately from the original text. As you put them together on a page in an order that makes sense to you, you will be able to make connections among them more easily. Some writers put their quotations on index cards or sticky-back notes so they can easily move them around, deciding which order best helps make their point.

The heart of good writing lies in revision. Research shows that the most significant difference between novice writers and expert writers lies in the amount and kind of revision done on a first draft. Novice writers tend to stick with their first try, making only minor changes. Better writers regularly make major changes: moving whole paragraphs around, deleting whole sentences, writing new sentences, replacing a weak example with a stronger one, or finding a better quotation. As you improve as a writer, you will find more effective ways to revise your first version of a paper.

Always write a complete second draft of your paper, based on your review of all your planning material and your first draft. In the first draft, you are most focused on getting your ideas written out in an organized way. In the second draft, you should focus more on insuring that your reader will understand your ideas the way you intend. Here you want to make certain the connections between each part of your paper are stated clearly.

*don't generalize sentences*

## Editing

Editing your paper should be done only when your revision is complete. If you do a lot of editing on early forms of your paper, you are wasting your time. You may eliminate a sentence or paragraph that you spent ten minutes editing into correct form. Save your editing time for your finished paper.

Some writers make lots of text errors when they draft. There's nothing wrong with making mistakes as you get material down on paper. Mistakes are unavoidable. The good writer finds ways to ensure that mistakes are identified and corrected.

Having a systematic approach to editing works best for most writers. One approach involves focusing on certain aspects of your text and reading through it only for that purpose. For instance, you might check only for sentence punctuation, making certain every sentence ends in a period or question mark. Then, you might read for spelling. Then, you might read the paper aloud, listening for words that seem out of place or that don't really say what you mean. This approach to editing means establishing a routine, and applying it to the final version of each paper.

Another system focuses on what you know are your usual weaknesses. Keeping a list of editing errors from your papers allows you to look for those mistakes in your final draft. Some students keep a list of their personal spelling demons, the words they always have trouble spelling.

When you produce your final version, you need to be concerned with neatness and appearance. If your instructor specifies a format for final papers, follow those instructions. Use clean paper and blue or black ink if you write by hand. If you type, use a well-inked ribbon and use consistent margins. If you use a word-processor, be certain the paper is properly lined up in your printer. Find a stapler or paper clip before you get to class.

## EXERCISE

Review this section each time you have a writing assignment. Create your own checklist of elements of the writing process to ensure that you have made your best effort on the assignment.

# THE COMPUTER AS A WRITING TOOL

Computers have already made fundamental changes in the way writers work and the way writing is published. Every evidence suggests they will bring more and more changes to the ways we write. Because these changes develop so rapidly, new uses of the computer will be available by the time this book is published. In this section, some of the most useful applications of the computer for college writers are briefly described.

## WORD PROCESSORS

A word-processing program is the single most useful software a college student can have. Word processors allow easy production of text from a keyboard and provide numerous features for editing and formatting text. While early word-processors required learning complicated keystroke commands, all popular word-processors now include pull-down menus and icons (stylized graphics) for executing commands.

Word processors support the writing process described in the previous section. They allow you to put your ideas down as quickly as you think of them without regard to correctness or format. You can focus on your thinking and your material while drafting, since revising and editing are greatly facilitated by word-processors. Learning to use the "cut and paste" function and the "search and replace" function on your processor will prove valuable for all your college writing.

Most word processors include several other features that are useful in preparing your paper for presentation.

**OUTLINERS:**  Sometimes called "idea generators," these programs allow you to create lists and then refine those lists into increasingly detailed outlines. You as the writer actually generate the ideas. The software has various ways of organizing and displaying your draft ideas and notes that can be quite helpful as you try to *focus, group,* and *order* your material.

**SPELL-CHECKERS:**  The latest word processors routinely include a spell-checker. This feature consists of an extensive word list that follows the conventions of American spelling. It will identify any word in your text that does not match the spelling of the words on the program's list. This does not mean the word is misspelled. Most proper nouns (names of people, places, and organizations) are not included in the standard list. You must check the spelling of those words the spell-checker does not verify. If, however, you make a typing error that results in a real word, but the wrong word, the spell-checker cannot help you. If you type "in" but mean "is" or if you type "of" but you mean "if," the computer will not catch your error. You still need to proofread your final printed text.

**GRAMMAR-CHECKERS:**    These features are sometimes called style-checkers. In either case, they do only limited work and often have bugs (flaws that will give you misinformation). These devices survey your text for certain combinations of words that frequently are associated with errors in grammar or weaknesses in style. Some grammar checkers are wrong 50% of the time. They are not yet reliable. However, they may be useful in making you think about the verbs in your sentences, or the frequency with which you use particular prepositions or conjunctions, or the average length of your sentences. To the extent these grammar checkers help you reenter your text to consider how you might rewrite and improve your paper, they can be quite valuable. Remember, though, no computer can tell you how to write.

**ANNOTATION:**    Recent word-processing programs allow for both written and voice annotation of texts. This feature allows either your instructor or a classmate in a peer-editing exercise to leave comments in your text without marking it up. Having another person comment on your draft is always valuable. This feature makes that process easier, since the comments are placed directly in your text document.

**GRAPHICS:**    Full-featured word processors often include graphics and drawing capability, allowing you to place illustrations within your paper. If you anticipate taking courses where illustrating your text is important, this feature could be quite valuable.

**INTEGRATED PROGRAMS:**    Some software consists of a combination of word-processor, spreadsheet, database, and graphics software. If your studies will require you to work with tables of data, you might find such a program useful, since you can readily paste data from a spreadsheet or database into the text of your paper.

## NETWORKED COMPUTERS

Computers connected to one another greatly increase the resources available to any writer using a computer. The developing writer at the end of the 20th century will find increasing sources of information and ideas through networked computers.

Such connections permit the user to access the databases of both on-campus and off-campus libraries, as well as those of various public and government agencies, allowing you to search for material on whatever subject you are writing.

Increasingly, newspapers and magazines are creating electronic forms of their material, making them accessible through a networked computer. Some books, including the entire works of Shakespeare, are available on CD-ROM disks, which can be read by the latest personal computers.

The most powerful use of networked computers lies in those networks which allow the user to go on-line. Using either telephone lines or other cables, computer users can access the resources of numerous commercial services as well as the massive, global network of networks, The Net (or Internet). In addition to published materials, these on-line resources contain unpublished research and information databases, greatly increasing the source of ideas and documentation for any writer.

These on-line resources also allow users to contact other users directly, either through bulletin-board, electronic mail, or chat formats.

* Bulletin boards focus on specific topics and allow any user to write (called "posting") their own information and opinion on the topic. Extended discussions that last weeks and months are possible on bulletin-boards.
* Electronic mail (e-mail, for short) allows users to ask questions and send messages to any other user with an e-mail address. Some electronic mail systems are limited to a specific college or university or workplace, while others provide a system of access to The Net, which permits communicating with users all over the world.
* Chat lines provide users a way of conversing in writing in real time. Users must be on-line simultaneously. In some formats, as many as 25 people can "converse" in writing in the same chat-box at the same time. In this format, class "discussion" could take place without any class members being in the same place.

Each of these formats facilitates collaboration among writers. Student writers can trade drafts and critique one another's papers electronically. The formats also make it possible to gain access to experts who may be very distant or very hard to reach for some other reason. Instead of just reading an article in a magazine or a chapter of a book, it is possible to send questions directly to an author who has an e-mail address.

As new technology develops, your task as a student writer will involve learning and using the tools that best help you develop your skills as a reader, thinker, and writer.

# EXERCISE

While every student would benefit from having a personal computer, not all students will have a computer of their own. Even if you do have your own computer, its features may be limited. The goal of this exercise is to determine what computer resources are available to you through your college and the local community. As directed by your instructor, form groups for doing research on computer availability. Each group should seek out campus resources through on-campus computer labs, libraries, learning centers, and student centers. Other groups should document computers available to the public through community libraries, cities, and other public agencies. Each group should prepare a written report of their findings, including number and types of computers, software related to writing, and rules of access for students and community members. Sharing copies of each report with the entire class would allow every member to benefit from each group's research.

# Sentences: Making Them Better

Every good piece of writing builds on clear, strong sentences. The art of good writing comes down to writing good sentences and arranging them effectively. So, every writer must pay attention to the sentence. The scope of this book does not allow for a detailed treatment of writing sentences. Your instructor can direct you to grammar books, handbooks, workbooks, and computer programs that provide instruction and practice in sentence writing technique. However, you should understand why sentence work is important. As a writer, you want to improve your sentences in both fluency and flexibility.

## Fluency

*Sentence fluency* means that you can get your thoughts, feelings, and ideas onto a page with a certain amount of ease. Lack of sentence fluency is illustrated by a term used by Professor W. Ross Winterowd: *the scribal stutter.* Though most of us carry on conversations with fluency, some of us freeze up when it comes to writing. We may freeze up because of inexperience; we may freeze up because we are very nervous; we may freeze up because we don't want to make a mistake. Whatever the reason, the result is that sentences do not flow easily from our pencil, pen, or word processor.

Two exercises can help improve your fluency. The first exercise is called "free writing." In free writing, you write whatever comes to your mind on a subject. The only rule for free writing is that you cannot stop moving your pen across the page for some specified time period (try three or four minutes to start). If you get stuck, then you simply write "I am stuck" or "I can't think of anything" until another thought comes to mind. The key to free writing is that you keep going, no matter what. Often, students surprise themselves when they see what they produce in free writing exercises.

The second exercise might be called "blind writing." If you are using a computer, you simply turn the screen off so you cannot see what you are typing. If you are using pen and paper, cover your writing hand with a sheet of paper so that you cannot see what you have already written. You'll find you can't do this for very long, but if you are preoccupied with making mistakes, blind writing prevents you from seeing what you've done, so you can't go back to worry about it until you've finished. This last exercise should not be used routinely, but only as a way of breaking the habit of correcting every sentence as you write it.

## EXERCISE

Select a cartoon from the beginning of any chapter in this text. Focusing on the issues raised by the cartoon, free write for four minutes. Remember, keep writing whatever comes to mind, no matter what. Do not stop writing until four minutes have passed. Compare your results with those of a classmate.

## FLEXIBILITY

Sentence flexibility means developing a repertoire of sentence patterns so that you can always find another way to state your thought or idea. Every sentence must have a subject (some form of a noun) and a predicate (some form of a verb). But every sentence can be expanded by adding adjectives, adverbs, prepositional phrases, verb phrases, and various kinds of clauses. A writer develops sentence flexibility by experimenting with different ways of saying the same thing. For instance, I could write: "The girl ate the sandwich." I could restate it: "The sandwich was eaten by the girl." I could embellish it: "Because she had not eaten in two days, the dirty-faced girl rapidly devoured the thick, corned beef sandwich, which oozed with mustard and mayonnaise." Each of these sentences could have their place in a piece of writing. As a writer, you want to develop a variety of ways of expressing your thoughts and ideas, so that for a particular occasion and purpose, you can select the best way of getting your point across.

Listed below are two methods for improving your sentence flexibility.

1: Notice how other writers use sentences. Whenever you read, no matter what you read, take note of unusual, interesting, and effective sentences. You might keep a sentence notebook in which you copy out sentences you enjoyed reading or that you thought were especially effective. You could also include klunkers, sentences that don't work, as a reminder of the difficulties of writing good sentences.

2: Practice "sentence combining," writing exercises based on combining a series of simple sentences into more complex sentences. These exercises encourage flexibility since several combinations are possible. A number of research studies have demonstrated that regular practice with sentence combining exercises will bring improvement in sentence construction. Most developing writers can benefit substantially from sentence combining work. Many textbooks and workbooks provide exercises in sentence combining. Here's an example.

1. Columbus landed in the New World.
2. The landing was 500 years ago.
3. His landing set a revolution in motion.
4. The revolution was culinary.
5. The revolution changed the eating habits of the entire world.
6. The change was quick.
7. The revolution helped form cuisines.
8. We know these cuisines today.
9. The cuisines are national.

These sentences might be combined to read:

Five hundred years ago, Columbus landed in the New World, setting in motion a culinary revolution that quickly changed the eating habits of the entire world, a change that helped form the national cuisines we know today.

These sentences could be combined in many other ways, too. To see how the original author combined them, look at the opening sentence of Barbara Karoff's "Food Owes Him the World" (p. 141).

## EXERCISE

Combine the following five simple sentences into a single sentence. Create at least three different combined sentences. Decide which combination is best, then explain in writing why you think it best.

1. An officer chased a man.
2. The officer was uniformed.
3. The man ran away.
4. The running was frantic.
5. The man had a gun.

# DOES SPELLING COUNT?

"Does spelling count?" students often ask me. The question seems quite straightforward, but the answer is not simple. Ask yourself how you feel when someone misspells your name. If you are Jon or Patti, you don't want to be changed into John or Patty, do you? If your address is in Worcester, Massachusetts, or Wooster, Ohio, getting the correct spelling may be necessary to get your mail. Here's a true story about how spelling can make a difference.

In the 1950's, W. Ward Marsh was the movie and drama critic of the *Cleveland Plain Dealer*. He prided himself on his ability to spell properly and write grammatically correct. In fact, he didn't trust copy editors with his columns and reviews. He would send his material directly to the typesetter. But even the best of us can make mistakes, such as omitting a letter in a word. One day, Marsh wrote a movie review that contained this sentence: "Women love Rock Hudson, but Rock Hudson loves hores." The typesetter knew that the last word was misspelled, so he corrected it without checking with Marsh. His correction was to add a "w" to the front of the word. Now the sentence made sense, but not the sense Marsh intended. You see, the word was supposed to be "horses," not "whores." Sometimes changing just one letter in a word can produce a very embarrassing result. So, does spelling count?

During the 1992 presidential campaign, Vice President Dan Quayle was made fun of by commentators, comedians, and citizens when he directed a schoolboy to respell "potato" as "potatoe." Though the first spelling is correct and the second is not, no change in sense occurs. If you see either spelling, you still know the person is referring to America's most popular root vegetable. In many cases, misspellings cause no confusion in sense or meaning. But Mr. Quayle learned—at great cost—that in the public's mind correct spelling has become the mark of an educated person. Though there is no necessary connection between spelling and intelligence, many readers act as if there is. So, does spelling count?

Some people are more gifted than others in the detail of language. Just as some learn to play music by ear, others learn to spell by eye. But most people have ordinary talents and must work to produce an acceptable result, whether it be music or spelling. Some people are dyslexic and find spelling correctly is an extremely difficult task.

When you are taking notes that only you will read, correct spelling is not a big deal—unless you can't decipher your own notes. But as the previous examples illustrate, when you are presenting your writing in public, correct spelling is a very big deal. Since only a small portion of people are gifted spellers, most people have to learn some strategies for getting finished writing into the correct form. The following suggestions have worked for many students:

1. As you write, underline or put a question mark over any word whose spelling you question. Later, check a dictionary for correct spelling.
2. Read the draft aloud to yourself. Using both your ear and your eye can help you recognize a word that is incorrectly spelled.
3. Use the spell-checker in your computer program or one of the electronic spellers to identify misspelled words and find the correct spelling. (Remember, though, that computer programs can only verify that a word is spelled correctly, not that it is the right word. If you type "if" when you mean "is," your spell checker won't help you out.)
4. Keep a list of your personal demons. For instance, I'm always forgetting to double the "r" in "embarrassing. Then, double check

these words before you hand in your writing to a professor, publication, or an admissions committee.

5. Cultivate a friend who will read your text and point out misspellings, but always double check in your dictionary.

6. Study the rules for spelling in a handbook to learn the conventional
patterns for spelling that you have not yet mastered.

Finally, correct spelling is not a matter of intelligence or even of high
levels of education. It is a sign of sensitivity and courtesy to your readers.

## EXERCISE

Look up the word "homophone" in a dictionary. Then write five pairs of
English homophones. Homophones often pose spelling problems, but will
not usually be identified by a spell-checker.

# MANUSCRIPT, TYPESCRIPT, OR PRINTOUT?

"Do we *have* to type this paper?" This question comes up at the beginning
of every course I teach. Many students view the form in which they present
their work as meeting some irrational whim of a professor who is hopelessly
fascinated with requirements that make life tough for students. From a student's standpoint, the question is understandable. When you start school,
you are taught to print the letters of the alphabet. Just as you get fairly good
at it, the school curriculum declares you should learn cursive, the more
rounded, connected form of handwriting. A few years later, you are encouraged to learn typing or, more recently, keyboarding. By the time you have
graduated from high school, you've probably learned three different systems
for putting words on a page. From the writer's standpoint, usually the question is which form is easiest and most comfortable. When it comes to taking
notes, making lists, or writing plans or drafting papers, the writer's standpoint has a powerful argument: use the form that is easiest and most effective for the writer.

At a certain point, your writing will be put before a reader—or many
readers. Then, the writer must be concerned with making it easy for the
reader to decipher what the writer has produced. Thus, questions of legibil-
ity and neatness come to the fore. If you want your writing to be understood, you want your text to be highly readable. A reader that has to make
an effort just to figure out whether a letter is an "a" or an "o" can easily lose
track of your ideas and your argument.

If you are writing a paper or exam in class, handwriting (manuscript)
remains the common form, since most classrooms are not equipped with
typewriters or wordprocessors for each student. Then, the critical question
becomes "pencil or pen?" Again, this is usually a trade-off between concern

for the writer (pencil is easy to erase) and concern for the reader (ink usually provides more contrast, making it easier to read). In my classes, I require final exams to be written in ink, not because I want to make arbitrary rules for students, but because when I must read 50 to 75 handwritten exams, running from four to fifteen pages each, I need the papers to be as legible as possible.

Papers written out of class are usually typed or wordprocessed. Just as with spelling, the main concern here is respect and courtesy for your reader. If this entire text were printed in the original handwriting of each of the authors, most of you would find reading a much more difficult task. Good writers do not always have good handwriting. Some don't even have good keyboarding skills. If you aren't good with a keyboard, cultivate a friendship with someone who will prepare your final papers for you—or pay someone to do it.

Just as the pencil and the ball-point pen were enormous improvements over quill pens and inkwells, the word processor is an enormous improvement over the typewriter. Typists who were trained to transfer manuscript to typescript often developed accurate typing speeds of 60 to 70 words per minute. Yet, when we are composing our words in the first place, our minds can't work at much faster than 20 to 25 words a minute. So you don't need to be a speedy typist to use a word processor effectively. The real advantage comes in the rewriting and editing processes. If you handwrite or typewrite a page and make a glaring error (say, omit half of a sentence), you have to start over with a clean sheet and copy everything you already have done correctly. You may even make an error in a place that was perfectly correct in your first copy. But with a word processor, you change only what you need to revise or correct. If you forget half a sentence, you can move your cursor and reinsert the missing words. Everything else stays the same! What's more, most word processors have spell-checkers. Handwriting requires that you be your own spellchecker.

In general, using a wordprocessor is the best choice. But circumstances may dictate that you write by hand or on a typewriter. Whatever your writing tool, when you present your writing to another person, you are presenting yourself. Take the same care with that presentation as you do in preparing yourself for a first date with a person you want to think well of you. The principle remains the same: show courtesy and respect to your reader.

# REFERENCE WORKS: DICTIONARY, THESAURUS, HANDBOOK

No experienced carpenter or electrician starts a job without the basic tools of the profession easily available, on a belt or in a box. No skilled cook wants to prepare a meal without the utensils and equipment required to prepare food well. Just so, no one should plan to complete a piece of writing without ready access to the tools a writer needs. These tools are not limited to paper, pencil, pen, typewriter, or wordprocessor. Over the hundreds of years of written English, various conventions (forms) have developed for how sentences should be written down, including the use of capital letters, marks of punctuation, spacing, indenting, and selecting words for particular places in a sentence or for the exact meaning the writer has in mind. Because the language is complex, very few people keep this kind of information in their memory. Instead, they keep reference books handy when they are writing, especially during the revising and editing phases of a writing project.

## Dictionary

The writer's most critical reference work is the dictionary. Though an unabridged dictionary has the most complete list of words and meanings, most people go to the reference room of a library to use such a dictionary. But every student writer should have a desk dictionary, what is often called a "college edition." Such dictionaries include the most common words, names, and places that you are likely to encounter in your reading. Each dictionary has its own plan of organization; no two are exactly alike. In order to make effective use of a dictionary for reference, you should study the preface or front matter in the dictionary to learn how information is arranged in the book and how information is arranged in the entry for each word.

## Exercise

To check this out, copy out the entry for the word *nice* in a dictionary. Then compare your results with two classmates, both of whom has a different dictionary. You should find that the order of information will differ slightly from one dictionary to the other. You should also find that the word *nice* did not always mean nice as we know it today.

## Thesaurus

A thesaurus is a kind of limited purpose dictionary. A thesaurus, like a dictionary, is an alphabetical word list, but in this case each word is followed by a series of words that mean approximately the same thing as the entry word. Many writers use a thesaurus to find alternate ways of referring to their subject; others use a thesaurus to jog their memory for a word they can't bring to mind. This reference tool can be quite helpful, but you must know the meanings of the synonyms to be certain they will really work in your sentence. Sometimes, inexperienced writers use a thesaurus to find impressive sounding words, only to discover they have used them inappropriately. One legend says that a computer-based thesaurus turned the sentence "The spirit is willing, but the flesh is weak" into the sentence "The ghost is ready, but the meat is rotten." As you can see, not every synonym can be substituted in every sentence.

## HANDBOOK

A handbook is another valuable writer's reference tool. Most handbooks include extensive information about common rules of grammar, common errors in writing, common rules of usage and style, as well as glossaries and common forms for reports and research papers. Like dictionaries, each handbook has slightly different information and different ways of arranging the information. Your instructor may require you to purchase a handbook as one of your texts for this course. Even if a handbook is not required, you may want to buy one for your own reference collection. Though there are very few absolute rules about how to present a piece of written English, each discipline and field of study has established standards and forms for papers and articles to be presented at meetings or in journals. Thus, it is important that you learn what kinds of information a handbook can offer you and to use the handbook preferred by your college or by the field of study you plan to pursue. Some fields recommend a manual of style, which is a special purpose handbook, for published papers.

## OTHER REFERENCE SOURCES

Other reference works can be valuable for a writer, even if you don't own them. Encyclopedias are excellent places to begin research on almost any subject, since they provide brief overviews of a very wide range of concepts, places, substances, and historical figures, often illustrated with drawings, photographs, and charts. A dictionary of quotations can be extremely helpful to a writer, since they include an index of key words. Often an apt quotation can be an effective way of clinching a point in a paper. As with the thesaurus, you want to be certain the quotation really suits your purpose and subject. Finally, guides to usage can be helpful when faced with deciding among words and phrases that are more or less formal, considered desirable by some readers and inappropriate by others. Guides by Bergen and Cornelia Evans, Wilson Follett and Jacques Barzun, and H. W. Fowler are among the most widely used guides.

Regardless of which references you use, remember that you are the writer and you are ultimately responsible for what you say and how you say it. Reference works can give you an authoritative basis for the choices that you finally make.

## EXERCISE

Draw a pencil sketch of the reference room of your college or community library. Identify the locations of unabridged dictionaries, thesauruses, handbooks, and encyclopedias.

Play "Information Scavenger Hunt." Form into groups in class. Read the excerpt "Music" from Allan Bloom's *The Closing of the American Mind,* p. 229. Assign each group three of the names referred to by Bloom. The group that returns to class first with the correct identification of the name and a complete bibliographic citation of the source wins the hunt.

**What is the values conflict illustrated in this
8-year-old boy's cartoon monologue?**

# FAMILY

Every one of us has a family. No human being is born without a man and a woman cooperating to make a new life. Yet in a world of complex technology and fast advancing biochemistry, that man and woman who create a new life may never even meet one another. With the ease of travel and shifting cultural traditions, the man and woman who do create life through physical contact (still the overwhelming majority) may have little to do with one another after the conception of the child or after the birth of the child. These are among the factors that have caused "family" to be the focus of continuing controversy and often intense debate, in late twentieth century America.

The phrase "family values" has become a major theme in political campaigns. Educators, newspaper columnists, and religious leaders regularly declare the importance of "family values" and just as regularly disagree about what constitutes a "family" and what "values" should be honored in a family. Very often this debate pits an ideal (a mom, a dad, a boy, a girl, a house, a car, a dog, a cat) against some realities (a widow with three children, an unwed teenager with a baby, a father having custody of two children on weekends and two weeks in the summer). This contrast of ideal and real often leads to debate between what we say (children do best when raised in two parent families) and what we do (over half of all American children spend some of their childhood in one-parent families). Some feel their own family experience was wonderful and we judge others by that experience. Others feel some loss in their family experience and seek to correct that in their own marriages and families.

Many images of families come to us through media, especially television. One can still find reruns of *Father Knows Best* and *Leave It to Beaver* presenting idealized versions of family life. More recently, a vivid parody of that ideal has been portrayed on *Married ... With Children.* Practically every variation of parenting and caretaking has been presented on television dramas and situation comedies. Thus, any child growing up today in America has many models of what families are and what they can be: one's own family, the families of relatives and neighbors, or families seen in the news, portrayed in film and television, and presented on talk shows. The diversity and variation of these models guarantee that we will have differing views on what family is, what it should be, and what families value.

Closely related to one's model, or ideal, family are the roles of family members. In earlier times popular sayings suggested what those roles should be: "Father knows best." "A woman's place is in the home." "Children should be seen and not heard." Would you argue in favor of any of those sayings? If not, what would your response be to someone who did believe in one of those sayings? Can you think of other popular sayings that suggest what the roles of family members should be?

As you read the selections in this chapter, compare the opinions of each author to your own opinions of family, the values associated with family, the family model you favor, and the family roles you think are most appropriate. At the end of the chapter, you will find suggestions for reacting to and writing about family values, models, and roles.

◆

---

# GETTING AT THE HEART OF WHAT'S WRONG WITH THIS COUNTRY

AMI CHEN

---

◆

*Ami Chen, a writer in East Palo Alto, California, recently published a book on the relationship between the CIA and universities. She is also a teen program coordinator. Chen sees "family values" as an abstract phrase that, like an inkblot, can be interpreted differently by each person. How does her untraditional upbringing compare with yours?*

There's been a lot of talk lately about *family values.* Presidential candidates extol *family values* as the cure for everything from the budget deficit to inner-city riots to earthquakes and other acts of God.    1

I'm not sure just which family they're talking about, but I've got an increasingly uneasy feeling that it's not mine.    2

My mother was born in China. My father, who had an all-American 3
childhood, decided while in graduate school that the System needed fixing.

They were divorced when I was 3 years old. I saw my mother only dur- 4
ing summers and holidays. I was raised by a single father and an ever-
changing assortment of friends and housemates in various states and in
Canada.

Just guessing, but my childhood probably doesn't fit the *family values* 5
"proper parenting" model.

Which means, from what I've gathered, that I am part of a lunatic fringe 6
that, like the Shining Path in Peru, is out to destroy everything decent and
whole, every sacred *family value* that exists in this country.

Well, I don't know about your *family values*, but I'm beginning to feel a 7
little alienated.

In a backhanded way, the *family values* pundits suggest that the love I 8
received from those I grew up with doesn't count. The fact that I graduated
in the top 10 percent of my high school class and received my bachelor's degree from a well-respected university in the Midwest does not factor in.

What's important is that I didn't have a consistent mother model! I was 9
raised by experimental single people who walked the house naked! I used
my Campfire Girl beads as poker chips! My crucial developmental years
were spent in hot tubs, on road trips and at Jimmy Buffet concerts!

It's incredible that I can actually walk and chew gum at the same time. 10
Or hold a job. Or do volunteer work. Or have meaningful, long-term relationships. Or plan happily to have a child.

I must admit, there were moments in my early years when I yearned for 11
a family that fit the *family values* model a little better than mine did.

Like when my 10th grade English teacher told me it was time to start 12
wearing a bra. Or when I found out I was anemic because my diet at home
consisted mostly of frozen vegetables and tuna fish casserole.

Or when, in college, instead of receiving monthly gift baskets of cook- 13
ies, dried soups, tea bags and fudge, I got pickled bamboo shoots, dried
squid and seaweed. Sometimes I felt a little out of step.

But I wouldn't trade those moments for a lifetime loaded with *family* 14
*values*, because those moments came as a package with other moments that
I could never give up.

Like when I was 7 and everyone who lived at our house in Eugene 15
threw me a midnight party with balloons and a cake to celebrate my completion of the "Little House on the Prairie" books.

Or when Sima and her daughter Leah moved in and suddenly Christmas 16
came with Hanukkah too.

Or when I learned to milk a goat on a self-sustaining commune in rural 17
Oregon.

Or when I got suspended from junior high school and my father joked 18
about the vice principal's shiny green shoes and told me I could do better;
he knew it and was not worried.

If I had to guess whose *family values* our current, former and future    19
leaders are so pumped about, I might come up with the parents of those
people I met in the fraternities and sororities at my college.

Structurally, these folks were *family values* showcases. Working fathers    20
made millions in the free enterprise system on corporate mergers and
takeovers. Well-groomed mothers sent their sons and daughters gift baskets
of fancy jams, comforters and gourmet cookies.

Yet their children had the same problems we all do. Some were quickly    21
becoming alcoholics. A few dropped out or ended up in drug rehabilitation
clinics. Others were kleptomaniacs or pathological liars who cheated and
plagiarized.

Most were sexually irresponsible. Many suffered from guilt and shame    22
about their bodies, about their desires, about their parents, about their *family
values*.

The difficulty with all of this lies in the fact that the words family and    23
values do not need each other. Nor do they—by legal mandate or divine de-
cree—come as a package deal. We all know that a family may or may not
have worthwhile values, and values can lie outside of the family.

It's the content, not the structure, of one's life that dictates the integrity,    24
love and responsibility that one contributes to the world. Not everyone can
have a posse like George and Barbara Bush. But anyone can love.

The *family values* theme for this campaign, whether intentionally or    25
not, is exclusive. It doesn't get to the heart of what's wrong with this country. And it doesn't work for me and many others who suspect with discomfort that their families aren't included in the grand *family values* scheme.

If our presidential candidates are really talking about honesty, integrity    26
and responsibility, then that's what they should do. If they are talking about
a western, Christian, middle to upper class nuclear unit, then they should
practice some honesty and say so.

But most of all, they should stop hiding behind vague and misleading    27
phrases like *family values* and start talking like real people, with real values
like the people they are talking to.

## REFLECTING ON THE READING

In one or two sentences, write Ami Chen's definition of "family values."
Now write out your own definition of "family values." Compare the two definitions with those done by a classmate. Describe how they are similar and
how they are different.

◆

# A BIAS AGAINST WHITES

LISA TAYLOR SIMS

◆

*Lisa Taylor Sims, a graduate student in San Diego, has a view of parental responsibility that she perceives as different from the way other parents see their responsibility. As you read, identify Sims' view of a parent's role as presented in this article in the* San Jose Mercury News. *Compare her view to your own.*

I am the mother of a disadvantaged second-grader. I am young, single, working, financially strapped and live in the inner city. But none of these facts are why my child is disadvantaged. She is disadvantaged because she is white.

My daughter and I live in a tiny house in an older, modest San Diego neighborhood. When my daughter plays freeze-tag in the yard, it is with Hispanic, African-American, Vietnamese and Laotian children from the area. They all play identical games, live in similar homes and shop at the same stores that we do. These children seem no more nor less advantaged than my own child.

But while my daughter must attend the miserably inadequate and overcrowded neighborhood school, a bus, supported in part by my taxes, collects the children who live across the street to escort them to the finest public elementary school in the county. Their mom was able to check the "Hispanic" box on their school entrance forms. My daughter must remain behind to maintain "ethnic balance."

The two Asian girls next door attend a science "magnet" school that sweeps the science fair awards each year. Their father, a successful defense industry engineer, is pleased with his choice of schools. I may not choose; my white daughter is not eligible for "magnet" schools.

Is discrimination any more socially justified when it is a matter of policy, practiced by the government against such victims as my daughter?

One in four students in my daughter's kindergarten class could not speak English. Others had never held a pencil, could not tell a circle from a square. The harried teacher was forced to spend an inordinate amount of time teaching remedial skills.

What used to be the responsibility of the family has become the work of    7
teachers. My mother may have sent her children off to school in hand-me-down clothes, but we were fed, scrubbed and alert. When I was my daughter's age, it was not in our teachers' job description to provide for our basic personal hygiene or to ensure that we possessed rudimentary skills.

When my parents were children, they weren't taught in their own na-    8
tive French or German. They took pride in their growing fluency in English and worked hard for every success it brought them.

Does the whole current structure of federal assistance really provide an    9
advantage to the disadvantaged? Will a high-schooler who has never had to learn English ever score well on the SAT exam? More than that, are we not building a culture of dependence in which federal beneficiaries are taught from childhood to expect preferential treatment rather than learning to build on their own resources?

My income falls well below the average for the city where I live—    10
we're poor. My daughter comes from a "broken home"—a household headed by a single woman. To me, these conditions are not excuses for failure; they are challenges to be overcome. I don't look to the American taxpayer for a bailout.

My daughter's only real advantage is that she has a mother who reads to    11
her, sings to her, listens to her, guides her. A mother who has taught her that she can do well if she tries her best. This has nothing to do with the color of her skin or the adequacy of my bank account. It isn't something that can be legislated or bought with tax dollars.

Short-term, emergency programs will always be needed to cope with    12
catastrophes, but is it really to our advantage to allow "disadvantaged" to become a way of life?

## Reflecting on the Reading

Write out what Sims means by *ethnic balance* and *magnet schools*. Did you figure this out from context, or do you need to ask a person who is familiar with school desegregation plans? If one group at a school is treated differently than another group, is one group automatically disadvantaged? Write your definition of "disadvantaged" and "bias."

◆

# THE CASE AGAINST 'FAMILY VALUES'
## UNDEMOCRATIC AND SEXIST, THEY'RE A HINDRANCE TO HAPPIER HOUSEHOLDS

SHERE HITE*

◆

*What comes to mind when you hear the word "love"?*
*What kind of "love" do you associate with "family"?*
*Keep these thoughts as you read Shere Hite's argument*
*that new definitions of family are good.*

We constantly hear that "the family" is in trouble, that we must find
ways to strengthen it. We see headlines such as "Divorce on the Rise,"
or "Alarming New Figure on Child Abuse," or "Violence Against Women in
the Home Increases," and we conclude that we must do something about
"the breakdown of the family." The unspoken premise is that the ideal of the
family, as traditionally defined, is a worthy goal that immoral or selfish or stupid people have failed to achieve. In Washington this orthodoxy is now the
bipartisan conventional wisdom of politicians, policy makers and pundits.

Before the rest of us accept this premise, though, we need to consider
an alternative: that the breakdown of the family is a good thing, that the traditional family model has failed and that women especially (but not only) are
creating new living arrangements that are more democratic, fulfilling and
practical. It may be one of the most important turning points of the West,
the creation of a new social base that will engender an advanced and improved democratic political structure.[1]

The traditional family model can be beautiful, especially in its promise of
"true love." But its beauty should not disguise its repressiveness. The traditional hierarchical family, as it is celebrated in Western art and iconic imagery,
such as the holy family of Mary, Joseph and Jesus, teaches authoritarian psychological patterns and a belief in the unchanging rightness of male power. It
offers a hierarchy where love and power are inextricably linked, damaging
not only to all family members but to the politics of the wider society.

---

*Shere Hite is author-researcher of The Hite Reports and of "Women as Revolutionary Agents of
Change: The Hite Reports and Beyond," published by the University of Wisconsin Press.

Now that families are becoming different, we are seeing people question things in their upbringing that for centuries have not been questioned. We are beginning to see people ask themselves exactly what "love" is, and try to build families based on love that often do not exactly fit the old model.

The family, that is, human love and support systems for raising children, is not in danger of collapsing. What is happening is that finally democracy is catching up with the old hierarchical father-dominated family. The family is being democratized. We are all, many of us, taking part in the process; almost no one wants to go back to the days before women had (at least in theory) equal rights in the home, before there were laws against the battering of women, before the freedom existed for men and women to divorce if they can no longer form a loving unit. All these developments are advances over the "traditional family."

Yet, the phrase "preservation of family values" holds great appeal for most of us. Why?

Because it suggests that we will get more love than we are getting now. In a society beset by increasing violence, this idea is compelling. It bolsters the attractiveness of genderism and the old sex roles at a time when their appeal is otherwise fading. No sooner are social attitudes changed and new legislation passed about spouse abuse or rape or sexual harassment, then a certain hesitation sets in about letting go of the ideal of the traditional family. "Oh, everybody is equal now, aren't they?" people say. Such is the hope.

If those "who should know better" are still bringing up children who turn out to internalize many of the gender behaviors and stereotypes of the past, where are these stereotypes coming from?

When I began looking at the inner workings of the family several years ago, I found that many of the most rigid gender stereotypes seem to have their roots in mid-childhood, at the time we call "puberty." In fact, puberty, it seems to me, is as much an ideological as a biological category. Since control of reproduction is such a crucial issue in the social order, the age at which reproduction becomes possible is the time children are most heavily socialized. During puberty, the patriarchal values of our society put intense pressure on children to behave in gender-appropriate ways. When they do, we cite this as "proof" that gender behavior is clearly biological and hormonally based.

But if we listen to the individual psychological and sexual feelings children and young adults express, a significantly different—and more interesting—picture of "childhood" emerges. Boys in particular express a great deal of pain and distress at having to join the "act-like-a-man" system at this age.

The major crisis in boys' lives, I believe, comes during puberty, when boys are flooded with sexual feelings. At the same time, boys are pressured heavily by the culture to demonstrate toughness in sports, told to "Stay away from girls, don't hang around at home with your mother. Don't be a wimp!"

As boys' sexuality emerges, in the sense of full orgasmic capacity, it is tragically negativized. Boys are taunted by other boys and male relatives to see if they can "take it," urged to demonstrate that they are tough, "not like girls" and pressured to dissociate from all things female—in short, to "become men." This creates a lifelong psychosexual orientation in many men who come to associate eroticism with pain, in both their physical and romantic relationships with women.

For a century, psychological theory has provided a supposedly scientific rationalization for this process. Freud held that boys pass through two "Oedipal" stages, loving and desiring the mother—age 3 to 6 and then again age 13 to 16. Freud based his analysis of men mostly on his analysis of himself, a rather limited sample. Now it is becoming clear what causes pain for boys is not so much the mother's betrayal of the son for the father, as Freud surmised, but rather society's imposition of a narrow version of "masculinity" on the widening horizons of the young male. 13

Thus boys are taught that women are the power objects of desire, but also objects of contempt, leading to a lifelong love-hate relationship with women (the mother). This is Oedipus in Love, not an Oedipus Complex. Why should it be a "complex" if a boy loves his mother? Oedipus wants to love, but in patriarchy must dissociate, blind himself, to all that is female, leave that world behind and forever after refuse to grant it equal status or justice. 14

If men learn as boys that they should demonstrate contempt for the female world (and the mother they love), they can grow up to feel extreme ambivalence toward women. Men often desire power and control in a sexual relationship with a woman in order to avoid these feelings of confusion and "danger"; loving and identifying "too much" with a woman. (O.J. Simpson's overwhelming "love" for his ex-wife Nicole seems to be a classic example.) Much male violence is related to this identity learned through the trauma of what I term violent emotional dissociation. 15

Many men, like many women, have discovered that trying to copy one archetype of a personal life does not always permit them to relate honestly to the people around them or on the level they would like. So they are seeking to find in their own lives what does work, to put into place the values of democracy so long praised in public life. This in turn is leading to the diversity of choices we see today, and the new statistics on changing lifestyles all over the Western world. 16

What do the dire warnings from politicians really mean? The "alarming increase" in single-parent families is in fact a clear signal that more and more women cannot be bribed into traditional, Mom-as-servant, families. This preference of women needs to be respected and understood, not moralistically condemned. Many single-parent families are headed by divorced women who have opted out of the nuclear family because they found themselves drained by arguments and conflicts. They believe that giving love, warmth and stability to children is more important than preserving the outward appearance of normality. They do not feel that a higher level of material comfort compensates for an emotionally violent atmosphere. 17

There is every reason to think that many men are dissatisfied with the    18
family too. Men's idolization of lone male heroes in the movies since the
1950s—from "Shane" to James Bond to Clint Eastwood to Arnold
Schwarzenegger—is vivid testimony to their feelings about marriage and
family. Similarly, clichés about "nagging wives," and "needing to be free"
and "not being tied down" demonstrate men's desire to be free of the traditional roles of breadwinner and family disciplinarian. Most have come to
feel, on some level, that society sees fathers as fuddy-duddies.

Lack of economic support for children in families without fathers is a    19
real problem. Yet the solution is not for the government to entice—or
force—lower-income women into marriage. Rightwing social engineers may
imagine that they can reduce the incidence of single mothers by withhold-
ing welfare payments. Yet numerous welfare reform studies show that the
ability of policy makers to shape the behavior of single mothers on welfare
is modest to nonexistent. If most "welfare mothers" do not marry, it is not
because these mothers are recalcitrant but because whatever relationships,
if any, are open to them do not offer positive alternatives. Why can't we accept their belief that single-parent families (whether headed by welfare
mothers or Murphy Browns) are valid and good, one of the many possible
positive ways to bring up children?

A better solution to the low incomes of single-parent families would be    20
to encourage new forms of families that could provide more support for
children—female child-rearing partnerships, networks of friends and even
better, new relationships between mothers and children—and fathers and
children. Rather than scapegoat single parents as the source of social ills, we
should find ways to support them.

The solution to the widespread anxiety about the family is a version of    21
family values that is not nostalgic, rigid or hierarchical—a model of the family in which all the adults, not just women provide warmth, compassion, authority, and economic responsibility for children and one another. And this
is beginning to happen. Millions of people are trying to create more positive
and loving relationships with those around them. Why should we assume
that these emotional and practical choices are wrongheaded and inferior to
the abstract prescriptions of organized religion, the political parties and the
policy-making class? What we may be witnessing—and participating in—is
an overdue revolution in the family in which basic questions about the way
we live our lives, with whom and how, are being questioned and debated.

## REFLECTING ON THE READING

Hite mentions a number of males by name: Oedipus, Freud, Shane, James
Bond, Clint Eastwood, Arnold Schwarzenegger, O. J. Simpson. Identify each
of these males. Write a sentence stating the issue related to family illustrated
by these examples.

◆

# DO FATHERS STILL KNOW BEST?

DAVID N. ROSENTHAL

◆

*Sometimes it seems Ward Cleaver from* Leave It to
Beaver *has had more impact on American children
than real fathers have. Which TV father comes closest to
being like your own father?*

Here we are on the last Father's Day of the '80s, 40 years after the first TV  1
dad came on screen and the question is, does Father Still Know Best?

Probably not, which is why the most recent trend in television when it  2
comes to male heads of household is not one dad, but two or three. In other
words, safety in numbers, even if the total intelligence shown on "My Two
Dads" and "Full House" doesn't add up to one Bud Anderson, let alone pater Jim.

It was Jim Anderson, played by Robert Young on "Father Knows Best,"  3
who indelibly set the standard for all television fathers who followed.

In fact, he set the standard for a lot of real-life fathers, too, even if he  4
never intended to.

"I always hated 'Father Knows Best,'" my own pop confided to me over  5
the phone the other day, a revelation I'd never heard before. "He always
made me feel inferior. Nothing ever threw him; he had all the answers. I
never did and nobody I ever knew did, either."

But Jim Anderson did. Of course, it's easier when the script writers cre-  6
ate the problem and the solution. If they ever came up with a fix they
couldn't solve they probably just gave him a different one.

When I asked my dad what fathers he did like on television, his first re-  7
ply said a lot about his age and memory, if not his taste.

"William Bendix," he said, referring to the "Life of Riley" star who spent  8
most of his time grappling with revolting developments. "He was kind of
bumbling but in the end, everything came out all right."

Which must have been what a lot of other fathers liked about Riley, too.  9

When Bendix died in 1964, six years after Riley went off the air, his real-  10
life wife, Teresa, said a lot of his fan mail came from wives who said that
their husbands liked to identify with Riley because it helped them feel better
about their flub-ups.

With the exception of the saintly Jim Anderson, fatherly flub-ups have  11
almost always been part of the television landscape.

So has the sort of grumpy dad who barked first and asked questions   12
later. Riley was like that. So was Laverne's dad, played by Phil Foster, on
"Laverne and Shirley."

My favorite among this type was poor, put-upon Herbert T. Gillis (Frank   13
Faylen), father of Dobie Gillis. Herbert T. was a grocer whose son aspired
for better and whose schemes left dad muttering, "Just a darn minute" or
"Someday, I'm going to kill that boy," whichever was appropriate.

Archie Bunker (Carroll O'Connor) probably belonged to this class of fa-   14
ther, too, the kind who loved his kids but didn't know how to deal with them.

Despite the plethora of fathers on TV now, there is no equivalent.   15

Instead, there is—or was until the show's final episode last month—   16
"Family Ties," Steven Keaton (Michael Gross) the calm, well-reasoned father
whose biggest gripe was that he and wife Elyse had somehow, despite their
best intentions, reared a Republican for a son.

It wasn't that conservative son who drove my liberal father crazy. It was dad.   17

"He was a wimp," pop says succinctly. "A real goody-goody. I couldn't   18
stand him. He always wanted to reason everything out."

Today's most famous father, Cliff Huxtable (Bill Cosby), fares a little bet-   19
ter with my own.

"Oh, he's sort of nice," dad concedes. "Very moralizing."   20

If the truth be known, however, the sitcom characters who have always   21
bugged my father have not been dads, but rather kids.

"When you have kids on a show," he says, "they take over. Most of them   22
are so cute, I can't stand to watch."

Wait a minute, does this mean he always liked my sister and me because we   23
weren't cute? I don't think so. I think it was probably because we wrote our own lines.

Actually I think a dad whom dear old Dad would relate to is one on a   24
show he doesn't watch: "The Wonder Years."

Here, Dan Lauria plays Jack, a guy with three kids, a wife, a house in the   25
suburbs and a job he doesn't much like to pay for it all.

Like a lot of fathers in the '60s, when the show takes place, he is not   26
big on chat. He is a presence around the house but he doesn't really run
things. In domestic doings or disputes, he has a way of butting in about
halfway through and mucking them up, which, if you ask me, is a lot like
life, then and now.

That's a tricky thing on TV, getting that real-life resonance while still   27
making it entertaining.

"I don't want to watch a show with problems that would never come   28
up," my father says. "Of course, if the problems are too real, I don't want to
watch it because it reminds me too much of life."

Which is probably why he doesn't watch "thirtysomething," a show in   29
which all the problems seem real, although perhaps not to someone who's
sixtysomething.

But the prototypical TV father of the '90s is probably not Michael Stead-   30
man (Ken Olin) anyway.

It's John Goodman, the roly-poly mate of "Roseanne."  31

Unlike Cosby, from whom all wisdom flows, Goodman's Dan Conner is  32
the rock upon whom his wife and kids can depend.

He's not the brightest man in the world. He yells at his children and his  33
wife, but we know he loves them.

He's generally a good-natured chap, but he's certainly not a wimp. His  34
chief failing appears to be three whiny TV brats for kids, but that's not his
fault, since he didn't do the casting.

In contrast to Goodman, who seems like a lot of fathers I've known (al-  35
though not my own, who doesn't like to bowl or drink beer) is my least favorite television father, Alan Thicke.

That's not surprising, because he was my least-favorite talk-show host  36
when he did that. But Jason Seaver is just too wimpy for words, with kids far
too clever for their own good. Together they make "Growing Pains" a real pain.

As for the future, the networks appear to be offering us only a couple of  37
new dads, both on CBS.

There's "Major Dad," with Gerald McRaney as a sort of Great Santini  38
with laughs, and "The People Next Door," a kind of "My World and Welcome to It" without William Windom.

The two shows, "Father Knows Best" with epaulets and "Father Knows  39
Best" with an easel, will run back-to-back from 8 to 9 on Monday nights.

It's just a guess, but considering the network's recent track record in  40
that hour, no matter who knows best, I don't think we'll have to worry
about kicking either of them around by next Father's Day.

## Reflecting on the Reading

Make a list of all the TV fathers mentioned in the article. Then, make several
smaller lists, grouping the fathers that are most like one another. Now, try to
give labels to each of your groupings (e.g., traditional fathers, easy-going fathers, wimpy fathers). Now, think of TV fathers not mentioned in the article,
especially from recent programs. Try to fit them into your groupings (or categories). This may force you to develop new categories.

# REAL DADS DO NOT PLAY MOM

## NORMAN PODHORETZ

◆

*Norman Podhoretz, the editor of* Commentary *magazine, has very strong views on what a father is and
isn't. He seems to equate changing parental roles with
sexual confusion. What do you think?*

Another Father's Day has come and gone, but this one was different. 1
Among other things, the amount of gift-giving was greater than ever, with
much of the increase coming from skin-care and high-fashion products of
the kind that (as one retailer put it) were at one time sold only to women.
And why not? Instead of celebrating fathers as fathers, Father's Day this year
celebrated fathers as mothers.

A father—it is perhaps necessary to point out—is a man. As such, he can 2
sire but he can neither bear nor suckle children. Siring a child does not in itself force him to assume responsibility for it. But if he does choose to assume responsibility, it will (according to the consensus of the overwhelming majority of all the people who have ever lived) consist mainly of
providing food, shelter and moral authority.

Discharging these responsibilities (again according to what most people 3
throughout history and in most cultures have understood) is the natural
manifestation of paternal love, just as nursing, tending and consoling are the
natural expressions of maternal love.

Looking at the "nuclear" family in this elementary light, we can see why 4
it is so wondrous and irreplaceable an institution. No other conceivable system of rearing children can create so good a chance that every single human
being, no matter how insignificant in the eyes of the world, will be
supremely important to at least two other people, one of each sex.

Or so it used to be. But if things go on as they have been going, we may 5
reach a stage where American children will grow up without fathers at all.

Some of these children, of course, will be fatherless in the literal sense 6
of being physically abandoned by their fathers. Already this is true in a frightening number of black families. But the divorce rate among middle-class
whites is so high that we can speak without exaggeration of an epidemic of
fatherlessness in families belonging to that group as well.

Another form taken by the evasion of fatherhood is the spread, also in epidemic proportions, of homosexuality.

Now there is a good deal of controversy over the causes of homosexuality. But whatever they may be, the fact remains that a man who decides to live as a homosexual is abdicating his place as a father in the great chain of the generations. Indeed, it is entirely possible that this represents, either consciously or unconsciously, one of the main attractions of homosexuality.

The third major way of avoiding the responsibilities of fatherhood nowadays is more subtle than abandoning one's children or becoming a homosexual. It is to sire children and to remain with them, but without performing the duties of fatherhood.

If we had no evidence other than Jane Austen's portrait of Mr. Bennet in "Pride and Prejudice," we would know that such fathers are not an invention of contemporary America. Yet Mr. Bennet is judged with extreme harshness by Jane Austen for withdrawing as a moral force from his daughters' lives. The fathers of today, by contrast, are cheered on when they abdicate their paternal responsibilities—so long, that is, as they do so by playing at being mothers.

Unfortunately for these men, science has not yet overcome nature by equipping them with the capability of actually bearing children. But pending that great breakthrough, they attend courses on childbirth along with their pregnant wives, and they then join them in the delivery room where they time (though, to their great regret, they do not suffer) the labor pains.

Having done their best to bear the infant, these men now devote themselves to nursing and tending it. Here, science in the shape of bottles and formula and disposable diapers enables them to play the maternal "role" much more fully. In New York, as usual the cutting edge of cultural change, "new fathers are easy to spot," writes one of them: "They're the guys in the office corridor talking earnestly about Nuk bottle nipples, the ones rushing home at 5:15 with boxes of nursing pads."

Spending so much energy talking about and then nursing and tending to his children inevitably means that the "new father" will spend less on providing them with food and shelter. "I don't earn the money I would have if I had not taken some time off to be with our two boys," says a young professor who has become their "primary caretaker." Meanwhile his wife works full-time to bring home the bacon he has largely released himself from having to go out and get.

But what about moral authority? It is a safe bet that these maternal fathers—assuming their masculine natures do not rebel and drive them into the arms of other women who are still looking for husbands rather than wives—will become more and more wimpishly indulgent as their children grow older.

Paternal abandonment and abdication have already led to greater poverty, instability, delinquency and sexual confusion among American children. Yet the indications are that our society is bent on giving social, legal and moral approval to the means that so many men have hit upon in fleeing the responsibilities of fatherhood.

One such indication is the incentives to abandonment built into the wel-  16
fare system. A second is the passage of gay rights bills enshrining the idea that heterosexuality is no better than homosexuality. A third is the proliferation of books, college courses and programs denigrating men who want to be real fathers and celebrating those who would rather be surrogate mothers.

So influential have these programs become that Father's Day was ob-  17
served with an orgy of articles invidiously comparing the delights of ersatz motherhood with the brutishness of "the fathers of the '50s" who, poor dolts, were "satisfied with being known only as good providers."

God help the children—and the rest of us, too—if we do not soon begin  18
looking for ways of encouraging men to be fathers again.

## REFLECTING ON THE READING

Based on this article, list the roles that Podhoretz assigns to fathers and the roles that he assigns or assumes for mothers. Make a list of which roles in the family you think a father should play and which roles a mother should play. Where you do not agree with Podhoretz, explain why, using one sentence for each point of difference.

◆

---

# 'ORPHANS' SPEAK OUT

## HEY, IT'S TIME FOR MY GENERATION TO GROW UP

LADIE TERRY*

---

*Lisa Taylor Sims and Norman Podhoretz emphasize a parent's viewpoint on family issues. Here are four short pieces by young people who lived part of their childhood away from their families, in foster homes, in group homes, or on the street. Compare your home experience to theirs as you read.*

1

How do I feel about the Republican proposals for ending welfare? I thank them for making a wonderful choice. I believe it's time for my generation of young and poor black women to grow up and be indepen-

---

*Ladie Terry is a 21-year-old African-American who has lived in group homes or on her own since the age of 14.

dent. After all, I have been stripped, beaten, raped and killed, so explain to me why we can't survive this little battle!

On another level I think about how the system has always loved taking our children away from us. (Remember slavery days when our great, great, great grandmothers experienced the pain of watching their babies being taken away, sold to another plantation?) 2

Today, the system sees our children not as people, but as dollar signs. They say they'd rather give their money to orphanage homes or adoption agencies. Then they'll wonder why our children will grow up with hate, not love, in their hearts, never knowing the love of a real mother. 3

The only way to end this craziness is for us to stop having babies we can't handle. We need to stop being breeders to men who don't want to take on the responsibilities of being real fathers. 4

We are strong people. Once we took care of land and the village, of crops and animals, even of white people's children. So why is it so hard for us to be independent now? 5

Poor women like myself take pride in thinking, "I don't need a man to take care of my children." But that's because the system has been our man— the system took care of our kids for us. 6

It's time to put positive pressure on our men and force them to get the job that God intended for them to do. It's supposed to be man and woman helping each other out, not the government acting as man's substitute.[2] 7

◆

---

# JUST WHEN YOU TRUST THE COUNSELORS, THEY LEAVE

CHIH-HONG HSU*

---

◆

What I learned from growing up in group homes is that the key to succeeding is having someone you trust—a counselor who can help you come to terms with yourself, your parents, your past. The problem is that once you find such a person, he or she quits and you feel abandoned. 1

When I was 12, the city of San Francisco took me away from my mother. I was staying in a makeshift room made of two-by-fours and sheet rock next to the garage door. All the extra rooms in the house were rented 2

---

*Chih-Hong Hsu, a 20-year-old Asian-American, was raised in foster care and group homes from the age of 12.

to Chinese immigrants. I slept on a couch surrounded by storage stuff, and had access to a TV, phone, and a tiny kitchen and bathroom which were filthy. My father had left my mother the house after he divorced her.

My first placement was in a group home with six kids and two or three counselors. The worst part was the rules and regulations. You were expected to get up early, make your bed, keep the room clean, go to school, do homework, keep set curfews and do assigned chores. Your weekly allowance depended on completing the chores and behaving properly.   3

One counselor, Tony, took a special interest in me. He'd take me to McDonald's for breakfast before school. He'd give me big hugs of encouragement. Several times he even took us boogie-boarding.   4

But at some point Tony disappeared, which was no surprise. Counselors always come and go, often taking the job just to have a roof over their heads. And this is the downfall of these types of placements. As a kid, you bond and open up to a counselor who ends up disappearing. You experience the same sense of loss as when you were taken away from your home. As a result you close up and harden, giving up any future attempt to know yourself by sharing your feelings.   5

My life began to stabilize again only when I was fortunate enough to have three counselors who really cared. Thanks to them I was able to graduate high school and overcome the difficulties of a broken home. But I believe I'm an exception to the rule.[3]   6

◆

# INSTITUTIONAL LIVING IS LONELY, WITHOUT LOVE

LYN DUFF[*]

◆

When you live in an institution it's the loneliness that gets you. Institutions (group homes, hospitals—I've been in both) approach young people as if they're the problem. A friend of mine remembers getting a welcome packet from a group home that said, "Your goal while living in this facility is to work out your emotional problems and family issues with the end result of being sent home." But my friend's problem was that her parents were too sick to work or take care of her.   1

---

[*]Lyn Duff is an 18-year-old Caucasian who ran away from a psychiatric institution at 15 and lived in group homes, shelters, or on the streets for several years.

Most adults can't imagine what it's like to grow up in an institution—    2
what it's like to have your basic rights as a human being turned into "privileges." Basically all these places use behavior modification to get kids to behave. The idea is that they take everything away from you—food, TV, radios, free time, sleep—and offer it back only if you follow their rules that will teach you how to live in this society. To the adults who run these institutions, life and growing up is like a math problem kids have to solve and conquer.

What you get in return are three hots and a cot—three meals a day, a    3
snack before bed, classes, exercise, medical and dental care. No one sees "fun" as a necessity.

And you can forget about loving. All institutions young people live in    4
seem to have the same rule: No p.c. (physical contact). No touching. If nobody touches you at all for a long time, that begins to be all you think about.

When I lived in an institution, I used to hide in the bathroom and hug    5
myself. I was 15, but I felt after a while like I was four because I really just wanted somebody to hold me and touch me. When somebody did finally touch me it was a casual touch, on my knee, and it felt bad, like I was breaking the rules.[4]

◆

# ORPHANAGES AREN'T GREAT BUT BETTER THAN THE STREETS

WILLIAM JOHNSON*

◆

If an orphanage can provide a better environment than streets filled with    1
drugs and violence, go for it.

Although the group homes I was in weren't exactly kid heaven, they let    2
me go to school and be a 13-year-old boy rather than the 30-year-old man I had to be on the streets.

I didn't like the idea of being separated from my family and having to lis-    3
ten to strangers tell me what to do. I didn't like being in a town I knew nothing about. But after a while, I was able to make friends and go to high school and get into sports which every kid should be able to do. On the streets I

*William Johnson is a 19-year-old African-American who grew up in a variety of group homes and institutions. Johnson, Terry, Duff, and Hsu are writers for *YO! Youth Outlook,* a bi-monthly newspaper by and about teen-agers published by the Pacific News Service.

didn't have time for these things. I had to worry about things like where I was going to sleep and eat.

I know a family right now that has three girls and two boys. The mother is in recovery from drug addiction. None of the kids' fathers are around. Two boys are with their aunt who's getting foster care money for them. They're going to school and taking karate lessons and living like kids should live.

On the other hand, another relative has custody of the three girls and uses their welfare money for her drug habit. They're not in school. They're living in a ganged-out, drug infested neighborhood surrounded by prostitutes. Not good. Those three little girls don't have a chance unless they get out of that neighborhood and into a home where they can be cared for properly. .

After some women have kids it seems like they just give up on themselves and depend on the government to take care of them and their kids. If welfare were taken away from those who are capable of working, and the kids were put in a foster home, group home, or orphanage until the parent was able to parent, that might just give the parents the push they need to reunite with their families. If they choose to sit back and be a "lazy ass," at least their kids won't suffer with them.[5]

## REFLECTING ON THE READING

When parents cannot or will not fulfill their responsibilities to their children, who should be responsible? Other relatives? Churches? Charitable agencies? State welfare agencies? In separate sentences, describe the best alternative and the worst alternative. Use the articles by Ladie Terry, Chih-Hong Hsu, Lyn Duff, and William Johnson to find supporting reasons for your choices. List those reasons under the appropriate sentence.

◆

# DELIVERENCE

PETER DAVIS

◆

*In recent times, much has been written about child abuse and spousal abuse. In this incident, the issue is dealt with not by the legal system or the health system, but in a church. Had you been present in this church, how do you think you would have reacted?*

U p Bobmeyer Road off the Dixie Highway, between the motels and Hamilton's private airport, a small yellow wooden-framed house in advanced dilapidation wore a sign: "God's House of Deliverence, Pastor Dallis Alexander." The old house served as the church for a movement of intense, fundamentalist Christians whose theme, however they chose to spell it, was deliverance from Satan to God. Their devotion seemed to exist somewhere between the theaters of cruelty and the absurd, too well meant for the former, too real for the latter. 1

When the hymn about the blood of the Lamb ended, Dallis Alexander stepped to the lectern at the front of the dusty room that took up most of the house. Benches and a few chairs faced the lectern and were divided by an aisle. The House of Deliverence, well attended but not packed, had attracted about thirty of its members on a rainy Wednesday night. They were in overalls and cotton prints, and more than a few had some physical abnormality—a harelip, obesity, missing fingers, a blind eye. Pastor Alexander was very young and wore a plaid shirt. He was fresh-faced, sandy-haired, earnest, with wire rims framing his glasses. Briskly, he set in motion the episode that gave the service its axis. 2

"Even among those brought together by God to live in harmony, there can be affliction," Pastor Alexander said, "Jack and Rowena Clegg, there has been trouble in your home." Dallis Alexander did not ask and he was not accusatory; he simply asserted. He might have been talking about any visitation of external trouble, a burglary or a tornado. 3

"Drinking and beating," a high, trembling voice said from the middle of the benches on the right side of the aisle. 4

"Will you tell me what that means, Rowena?" Pastor Alexander asked. There was nothing challenging in his question, only tenderness and curiosity. 5

"He drinks ... " Rowena Clegg sat alone except for a small baby on her lap and another inside her. She was enormous, fat as well as pregnant, and she was beginning to cry " ... and I get beat." 6

Dallis Alexander watched Rowena Clegg while she sobbed and then, as though it were a spotlight, shifted his gaze to the other side of the House of Deliverence. 7

Jack Clegg sat, also alone, on a bench to the left of the aisle. He had chosen a seat to the back of the room, not directly across from his wife and accuser. He was tall and lean, with the look of a young man getting old fast. Even in a sitting position he seemed permanently bent from doing heavy physical work he was not really strong enough to do. His face and the back of his neck were deeply creased, and there were three moles, dark and heavy, on his cheeks. 8

"What do you say, Jack?" Pastor Alexander asked pleasantly. 9

Jack Clegg said nothing. He looked from the pastor down to the calluses on his hands. 10

"It seems like it's going to take both of you to keep your household together," Pastor Alexander said. "Come on now, and be delivered." 11

Jack and Rowena Clegg rose from their benches and shuffled toward the lectern where Pastor Alexander stood. Rowena Clegg carried her baby. Several other members of the church—friends or relatives—followed the Cleggs 12 to the altar space at the front of the room. By the time they reached Dallis Alexander, each was flanked by enough attendants to make this a wedding.

Most of the faithful, including those who did not follow the Cleggs to     13
the lectern, had drooping eyes and high foreheads, fat arms and thick legs, a prodigally extended family that appeared to have been inbred to preserve the trait that allowed them to load heavy things on carts and bear burdens over hilly passes. Only Jack Clegg was tall, and he was bent.

"Tell me the trouble we want to deliver you from," Pastor Alexander said.     14

Jack Clegg stooped lower in shame, Rowena Clegg clasped her baby and     15
looked up.

"Tell me Rowena," Pastor Alexander asked.     16

There was stillness until Pastor Alexander raised his hand as if he were a     17
conductor with a baton. Rowena Clegg began to blurt. "Friday night he didn't come home and when he come home he was off his melon and swingin'."

"Is that true, Jack?" Pastor Alexander asked.     18

But even if Jack Clegg had been disposed to speak which he was not, his     19
wife's flow had just begun. She wept as she talked. "His bottle was still with him and he roared out. I said, can I have the rest of your pay. He said, stick my pay. I said, be quiet for the neighbors. He said stick the neighbors. He come for me and I grabbed my baby from her crib, which he made her, I'll admit that. He commenced to beat on both of us till I screamed and she screamed. He hit me some more and some more, and I was afraid for my baby and the one I'm carrying. He drank a big lot and put his bottle down and pulled my baby out of my arms and held her over the stove."

Now, as Rowena Clegg tried to catch her breath, her husband uttered     20
one line in the direction of his feet. "I wasn't fixin' to hurt Ulalume, I just wanted you to shet."

"We come and hushed him then," said a squat older man with a grizzled     21
chin. He stood in back of Jack Clegg. "It wasn't no trouble."

Dallis Alexander raised both his arms high and stood on his tiptoes. He     22
could only have gone higher if he had taken wing, though he was still not as tall as Jack Clegg stooped. "Praise Him!" Dallis Alexander thundered. "Praise the living Lord!"

Rowena Clegg, huge and pregnant, with her baby in her arms, began to shake.     23

"All praise be to the Lord!" Pastor Alexander boomed again, still louder,     24
and Rowena Clegg shook harder. She stopped shaking for an instant, turned around and put her baby down on the lap of a friend in the front bench. Then she approached closer to Dallis Alexander's lectern.

Except for mumbling at his feet, Jack Clegg was silent, but he, too, shuf-     25
fled closer to Pastor Alexander. More self-conscious than his wife, his shame seemed mingled with some desire to bolt. He glanced at the door behind him as if it, not Pastor Alexander, were his means of deliverance. Pastor Alexander's attention was on Rowena Clegg.

He shoved his hand against her forehead and pressed down hard. She     26
trembled. As Pastor Alexander mentioned each of the Trinity, Rowena Clegg's abundant body shook more violently until it seemed she had been

struck by some wrathful disaster in nature, an earthquake or lightning. "Praise all, in the name of the Father, yes, and in the name of the Son, that's right, and in the name of the Holy Ghost! Hear me!" Rowena Clegg wailed and shrieked. She almost fell from shaking so hard.

In a corner of the church a few teenagers played with a collection bas-   27
ket. They paid no attention to what was happening at the altar. They used the small basket as though it were a hat or a ball or a frisbee, now wearing it on their heads and mugging beneath it, now throwing it to each other, now sailing it across the brief expanse of the House of Deliverence.

"I command the devil to go out!" When Pastor Alexander shouted at   28
Rowena Clegg, he was still pressing her forehead. She heaved and fell down, issuing a great moan. On the floor she still shook and shuddered. The pastor was serene. Jack Clegg stared at his downed wife, humiliated, triumphant. He looked up a Pastor Alexander, who had just accomplished what he, her own husband, had not been able to do—get Rowena Clegg on the ground in total submission. The pastor wanted to be sure. "Again, I command the devil to leave! Now!"

In his practice of repairing domestic relations through exorcism, Dallis   29
Alexander had not forgotten who the principal miscreant was. But it was not the pastor's way to force a parishioner to his knees who not so inclined, and Jack Clegg was not. In a test of wills with a doubter, especially a drinking and wife-battering doubter, Pastor Alexander could only lose. If Jesus could sponge all sin unto Himself for the sake of mankind, surely a wife could absorb some of it for her husband. "Rowena took on the devil for both of you, Jack," the pastor said. "Do you understand that, Jack?"

Could Rowena have beaten Satan for both of them? Could she have   30
shaken and trembled and wailed the devil away from the whole family? Jack Clegg began to mumble, and the words that came out were "Lord" and "forgive." He struggled a moment, seeming to search, then added "never, never," as if to ward off both the devil and John Barleycorn, who in the House of Deliverence were identical.

"Rise up, Rowena. Stand near, Jack," said Dallis Alexander. "Friends, we   31
have seen the devil leave this couple, but he'll be back. He always is. Now, Rowena and Jack, join hands."

Rowena Clegg was wringing wet when she clasped her husband's hand.   32
Jack Clegg was subdued and dry, drier, perhaps, than he had been in months. They stood together, facing their judge.

"When that devil comes back, Jack and Rowena, and he will, when he   33
comes back into your home, REBUKE HIM! You must REBUKE HIM! You must have nothing to do with him but to REBUKE HIM! You can do it. When he starts to happen in your home you both join hands, as you are now, and you pray and you pray, and you send that old boy off down the road. We don't want him, we don't need him, and we won't have him!"

Chastened, cleansed, Jack and Rowena Clegg retreated from the altar.   34
Rowena Clegg reclaimed her baby from her friend in the front row and marched proudly to her old bench. Jack Clegg followed, still not sitting be-

side his wife, but taking a bench only two rows back of her on the same side of the aisle. Rowena Clegg looked the more purified, her husband the more mortified, though it was not clear whether he looked this way because of his bout with the devil or because he had had to watch his wife shriek and moan and fall over in a public place. But Rowena Clegg was beatific, hugely beatific, as she rocked her baby against her bosom.

"All right now, we hope we've brought help to some people," Pastor   35
Alexander said. "Is there anyone else? Anyone else right now for deliverance?"

Jack Clegg looked at the door in back, appearing to measure the dis-   36
tance to it. Could he get out before the young pastor bellowed at him again? Should he ask his wife to come now? Could they get home in time for "The Waltons"? But an elderly man just in front of him had risen.

"My best friend has cancer, Pastor Dallis. He may not get deliverance in   37
time. Can we pray to the Lord for my friend, because he has had the cancer two years and it's a lot worse. Oh God, pray for him, can't we, Pastor?" The elderly man sat down.

"Of course we can. We will right now." Dallis Alexander closed his eyes   38
and cast them upward, but his spirit seemed still to belong in the exorcism of the Jack Cleggs. "Let us pray."

Pastor Alexander prayed silently, eyes shut, moving only his lips.   39
Rowena Clegg stood up, cradling her baby, and walked to the center aisle. When Jack Clegg joined her, she handed the baby to him. Together, quietly, they stole toward the rear door.

## REFLECTING ON THE READING

List three incidents in the story that caused strong feelings in you as you read. For each incident, write one sentence explaining why you felt the way you did.

# PUTTING IT IN WRITING

## RESPONSES

1. From any reading assigned, select a single sentence that attracts your interest or attention (positive or negative). Copy out that sentence. Write for three minutes explaining what attracted you to that sentence.
2. Select three words or phrases that seem important to the point being made by one of the writers. Write for five minutes trying to show the connections between those words and phrases.
3. Identify one statement you strongly disagree with in any of the readings. Write for five minutes explaining what your disagreement is and why you think that way.

# READING FOR MEANING

1. In any reading, select the single sentence that best expresses the writer's main point. Compare your selection with two classmates. If you disagree, look back at the reading to see what justifies your selection. You might consider that different sentences can state the same main idea in different words.
2. Reread the opening paragraph and the closing paragraph of any reading. Express in one sentence the main idea conveyed in those two paragraphs.
3. List the three most important values held by your family. Find the reading that most closely reflects those values. Copy out the sentences or phrases in that reading that come closest to stating the values you believe in.

# ORGANIZING YOUR IDEAS

1. Choose the idea of values, models, or roles as your focus. Find two readings that address the focus you have chosen. Make a list of the main opinions expressed in those readings about the idea you are focusing upon. Now, write a single sentence that states your opinion about that idea.
2. Choose either values, models, or roles as your focus. Elaborate your understanding of the term you choose by recalling three personal experiences from your own family life. Describe each experience in 100 words or less.
3. Think of the most unusual family you know other than your own. Write a short paragraph describing what makes that family unusual. After you have written the paragraph, try to decide whether the family is unusual in its values, the kind of model it presents, or the roles played by family members, or some combination of those elements.

# WRITING A PAPER

1. Identify one value that you learned from your family. Compare that value to one expressed in one of this chapter's readings. Write a paper explaining the importance of that value and how it affects you in your life today.
2. The Davis story portrays a family in crisis that is trying to live up to a model of family life. Compare some crisis or problem from your family life to those presented in the Davis article. Write a paper explaining what you learned from making the comparison.
3. Using the Sims and Podhoretz articles as a starting point, describe what you think are proper roles for the mother and father in a family.

Shere Hite

**What does Wasserman's cartoon assume about mothers and fathers?**

# PARENT AND CHILD

The first intimate relationship of our lives begins in the womb of our mother, usually lasting about nine months, and continuing several months, perhaps years, after birth. In most cases, we also establish close relations with our father when we are infants. Because these relationships begin when our lives begin, they are always powerful, whether extremely positive, extremely negative, or some complicated mix of positive and negative experiences. The bond between parent and child is considered "natural". Thus, when we learn of parents who harm children or children who harm parents, we are shocked, more so than in most other cases of violence and abuse.

In the past 25 years, the verb *parenting* has entered the English language. This new term suggests that parents can learn how to be parents through formal study. Adult schools offer courses in parenting; magazines regularly explore the subject. In the past, learning to be a mother or father was passed on from generation to generation, mostly by example and simple precepts such as the Christian commandment to "Honor thy father and thy mother." Some families also follow folk wisdom, such as the 19th century admonition: "Children are to be seen and not heard."

Today, new legal rights and new images of children challenge the traditional assumptions about the relationship between parent and child. In 1992, a 12-year-old boy was granted a "divorce" from his natural parents (he claimed they had neglected him) only to be adopted by another set of "parents." Adoption has produced its own controversy. Adults who were adopted as infants sometimes go to great lengths to discover and meet their natural parents. In the United States, the courts are increasingly called on to make judgments about the parent-child relationship, occasionally resulting in sensational cases, such as the 2 1/2-year-old girl who was returned to her birth mother, after the birth mother changed her mind although she initially agreed to an adoption. These cases create very lively and emotional debates, partly because each of us has in mind the ideal relationship between a parent and a child, though we would not agree on all the elements of that ideal.

Sometimes media images convey pictures of children out of control of their parents: children who steal, children who vandalize, even children who kill. In some communities, concern about "feral youth" leads to efforts to control children who endanger others. Curfew laws are passed. Special prisons and "ranches" for juvenile offenders are established. When some parents lose the ability to supervise their children, who should be responsible?

Communication between parents and children always has some emotional component. The so-called "generation gap" probably begins with the fact that parents do almost everything for a child during its first two years, none of which the child can remember. Then, as the child grows to adolescence and seeks independence from his or her parents, the child has experiences the parents know nothing about. These simple realities lead to a certain amount of conflict as both parent and child struggle with issues of authority, control, and power.

In this chapter, you will encounter three pieces dealing with mothers and children and four pieces dealing with fathers and sons. Though we experience many other important family relationships (brothers, sisters, grandparents, aunts, uncles, and cousins), the bond between parent and child always seems the most important and the most intimate. As you read, consider how you would compare your relationship with your parents to those portrayed in these readings.

◆

# THE TELEPHONE CALL

LYNDA BARRY

◆

*Have you ever made a prank phone call? Have you ever been caught by one of your parents in the act of doing a prank of any kind? Compare your experience to that of the two girls in "The Telephone Call."*

It turns out the whole thing would have never happened if my friend Judy Minter's dog Penny hadn't eaten the rotten baloney and then thrown it up on the sidewalk of Mr. Vicks. If it hadn't been for that, Judy would have never called up Mr. Vicks, said the thing about his balls, and then ended up having to go to Catholic school. When you think about it, that your whole life can be wrecked by a dog throwing up, it is pretty weird.

Mr. Vicks is a man who lives by Judy across the street and two houses down. A drunk guy who has Indian corn teeth and just sits on the front porch all day while his wife works double shifts up at St. John's Hospital. Everyone knows what a bum he is. He may do his yard nice and all but still he is a bum.

Judy did the phone thing to him because Mr. Vicks called Mrs. Minter to complain about the barf and Mrs. Minter called Judy and said Penny is your dog and you have to take responsibility, and she made her go over there and clean it up. Then while she was cleaning it the twins Brian and Billy Bano of course *would* have to walk by and now Judy has the nickname of "dog barf."

Every time she goes by Mr. Vicks's house she gives him the finger in her pocket. If I'm with her I do it too because that makes the power of it even stronger.

She got the idea to call Mr. Vicks from another girl we know, a snob we don't like that much named Toni Larson who has a yellow Princess phone in her room and when you go over there she shows off how cool she is by looking up the names of men in the phone book and then tells them her name is Debbie Haskelm and that she wants to screw them. Debbie Haskelm is this other snob at our school who Toni hates. The one thing Toni always says that really blows their minds is "I want to suck your balls."

Okay. So Judy's mom goes to the store and me and Judy go up to her mom's room and start messing with her miniature perfume bottle collection and looking at her jewelry and makeup and then Judy gets the idea to do a Toni Larson to Mr. Vicks. I watch out the window and see him sitting there while Judy calls information, gets the number, and then says, "Who should I say I am?" We decide Debbie Haskelm because then if Mr. Vicks tried to bust us we could just say it was really Toni Larson. "It's the perfect crime," Judy says, and then we both watch Mr. Vicks out the window as she dials the number. I about start peeing laughing when he gets up and goes into the house to get the phone. We squat down on the floor and then Judy says, "Hello darling." She holds the phone so I can hear Mr. Vicks saying "Who is this." Judy says, "What darling? You don't remember our passionate love? Is this Vernon Vicks of 3489 West Cranston?" I hear him go "Yes, who the hell is this." "It's Debbie Haskelm, darling," Judy says, "and I simply must suck your balls." And then we hear her mother yell "JUDY!" over the downstairs phone.

Judy throws the phone down and goes, "Oh god oh god oh god." We know we are dead. We hear the tiny voice of Judy's mom keep shouting her name from the phone and then Mr. Vicks's voice yelling something like he is going to fix some little son of a bitch's wagon and then we hear her mom's voice stop and hear her feet start coming up the stairs. "Oh god oh god oh god," Judy says, "she's going to kill me," and then she slams her mother's door shut and starts dragging the dresser in front of it. "Help me man!" she yells, and I push it and her mom starts trying to shove open the door and

Judy goes out the window and when Mrs. Minter gets the door open it's just me standing there with the sound of Mr. Vicks's voice yelling out in the background.

On the way home I try to imagine what I would do if my mom heard me talking like that to a guy. I guess I'd kill myself. Also, Judy was for sure busted by Mr. Vicks. He knew for certain it was her who said she wanted to suck his balls.

That night Judy's mom called my house about ten times. She couldn't find Judy and she was freaking out. She even called the police. She made me promise that if I saw Judy I would call her and I said I would.

I was asleep when I heard knocking on my window. It was Judy, who told me there was no use ever going home because she knew for a fact her mom was going to make her go to Catholic school. I told her to come in, and then my mom woke up and busted us and she called Judy's mom, who came over. Me and Judy had to sit at the kitchen table while my mom stared at us and smoked and Mrs. Minter asked us a hundred times could we please give her a reasonable explanation of why we would ever do such a thing.

She stood there with her arms crossed. "I'm waiting," she said.

## REFLECTING ON THE READING

Assume you are Judy's mother. How would you handle this situation? Write a short paragraph explaining why you would take the action you propose. If you were Judy, how would you feel about the action you took as her mother?

# MOTHERS AND DAUGHTERS

GWENDOLYN BROOKS*

*Usually, when parents and children have a conflict, they talk about it, perhaps even yell about it. Instead, Gwendolyn Brooks decided to write to her daughter about her opinion. Ask yourself how you would feel if you had gotten a letter like this from your mother.*

---

*Poet Gwendolyn Brooks has earned many honors, including a Pulitzer Prize and appointment as Poet Laureate of Illinois. The latest of her many books is *Children Coming Home*. Her daughter Nora Blakley is founder of Chocolate Chips Theater Company in Chicago.

A mother. A daughter. Today there are many complaints about relations between these entities. There are serious citations of cruelty, estrangement, misunderstanding, emotional assault.

How fortunate I have been! As a daughter, as a mother. I have written, in "Keziah" (Published by Tri/Quarterly) of the rich friendship between my mother and myself. Here I want to italicize the rich friendship between me and my daughter.

My daughter is now forty. As a child she was warm, sunny-spirited, forthcoming, intelligent. In all these years we have experienced only two story-worthy mother-daughter Explosions.

Number One: her refusal at the age of 17 to go to the dentist for tooth extractions, just before going away to begin college life. She was feeling her "wheat," hated dentistry and would, simply, have none of it. Since I could not pick her up and transport her, SHE WON.

Number Two: she wanted, *before* graduating, to "get an apartment." This idea powerfully upset me. Nora had been raised with meticulous care—protected. NOW she was going out into the World, with only the money I could give her for rent, food and DOUBLE-LOCKS. I suffered and suffered. I deliberated and deliberated. I yelled. Then I wrote this letter …

> Dearest Nora of Noras,
>
> I am setting this on paper so that I may not be accused of saying something I did not say and so that I may not be accused of not saying something I did say.
>
> I spent most of yesterday thinking very carefully about your concerns. The result of all that lengthy, clear considering mental activity is that I have decided *not* to sign my daughter out of her home.
>
> Although I have talked hard to and *at* myself, trying to convince myself that this is a *good* thing you're doing and that you know best—I have failed to *believe* myself. You do not need an apartment, even for the reasons of privacy and "being-on-your-own," that you advance—because you will BE alone most of the next two or three years in Champaign-Urbana; little of your time would be spent in the apartment, as very little of your time would be spent at HOME.
>
> In deciding not to accept the responsibility involved in underwriting residency other than my own, I considered that people your age, whether you choose to believe it or not, are rarely in hard control of their own emotions or minds. Things can happen in your apartment that you do not want to happen. It is not always easy to control yourself. It is not always easy to control other people.
>
> My distilled feeling is that you should settle your insides, keep your home as your springboard, STUDY, DREAM, get to know yourself better (without troops of people endlessly around to make this difficult) and plan to get an apartment of your own when college life is over. My distilled promise is that if you insist on leaving I shall pleasantly support you as we discussed—

but you will have to get the apartment ON YOUR OWN AND WITHOUT
ANY SIGNATURE OF MINE. NOW: one minute and a half for screaming.

**Then—s i l e n c e.**

**Then—a d u l t h o o d.**

**fini**

**Mama**

Parents—I recommend that *you* use pen and paper rather than tongues
and lungs. Well, my daughter read my letter, grinned, hugged me, said "I
hadn't thought about all that"—and called off that departure from home.

Nothing further has cut into the roots of our friendship.

And now?

My daughter is my best friend. We send notes to each other, we send
full-blown letters, we talk to each other on the telephone for a minute,
twelve minutes, half an hour, four hours. We advise each other, we scold or
semi-scold each other, we praise and honor each other.

When my mother died on March 14, 1978, two weeks after her nineti-
eth birthday, my daughter was a rich support.

I always regretted that I was not at my mother's bedside at the moment
she died. I was out of town that day, but Nora came, and spent a lovely time
with her on that, her last day alive. I was on a train, en route home. Nora
called me on the train. What a comfort was that Daughter—in the most trau-
matic time of my life. Subsequently, she was always available for those talks
which, to the bereaved, mean more than bread and water, more than head-
pats and consolation kisses. Nora wrote a fine and sensitive poem to which I
can refer when I need the nourishment it inevitably provides.

The poem, "For Mama," ends:

*she* lives
and chuckles and "pshaws" away—
as long as we light love candles
    of thought and times-when
as long as our regrettings are
    syncopated sadnesses
    with a happy beat
as long as you are of she
    and all are in me
and we laugh, and we straighten
and root ourselves
in the Here.

Today's media narratives, featuring woeful relations between mothers
and daughters, alarm us. They make us proud to call attention to a very different kind of story, and proud to announce that story "far and wide."

## REFLECTING ON THE READING

Imagine you are Gwendolyn Brooks's daughter and you have received the letter in this article. Write your response to the letter in no more than 150 words.

◆

---

# BOY CRAZY

WENDY HO IWATA

---

◆

*In the past, Chinese parents sometimes drowned baby girls, according to Wendy Iwata, who was born in Hong Kong and raised in San Francisco. Now, as the American-raised parent of two Chinese-Japanese-American sons, she is trying to find the right balance between her roles as a mother and as a woman. Are sons favored over daughters in your family? How does your family compare to Iwata's?*

It took me nearly 30 years to understand the demons and insecurities that shaped my Chinese father. Not that he didn't have any positive features, but as most psychological strategists say, it's one's vulnerabilities that drive the engine of heart and soul. Unfortunately, the shortcomings of my father are the same as those of my fatherland—women. Not as in "womanizing," but in the subtly debilitating, old sexist attitudes that still permeate the American landscape of 1990. I'm talking the subtle preference for boy babies over girls, about the higher divorce rates for families with daughters than sons, the boardroom business politics that advance men to top figurehead positions while female worker-bees sweat it out in the "pink ghetto."

I'm not blazing new territory here, only agonizing over the deep chasm that's allowed to exist in such a modern, advanced society. No, we don't drown baby girls anymore or bind young girls' feet so they can't run from their husbands. But as an affluent, young, pregnant attorney once wearily said to me, "I hope I have a boy ... because it's still a man's world out there."

The only reason I exist on this earth is because of my parents' faint hope that their fourth child would finally be a boy. It was a common attitude in China to rejoice over a boy and offer consolation over a girl. My poor mother just gave up after the fourth daughter and said, "No more." You'd give up too if you had four hungry little girls to raise with no help whatsoever from the father, and with society casting a condescending stare on a woman who could not bear sons. For some archaic reason, fathers in the old country at that time felt no obligation to lend a hand in raising daughters, although most men eagerly waited for their young sons to join them in daily walks in the village. And, of course, the blame for producing daughters

always fell on the mother, further alienating and reducing meaningful interaction with the female sex.

I grew up hearing this conversation play out a thousand times:

"And how many children do you have, Mr. Ho?"

"Four."

"Oh, how many boys or girls?"

"Four girls, no boys." (Accompanied by sheepish grin.)

"Oh" (Nervous laughter.) "Well, you can always try again." My mother
uttered those same lines by rote, always apologizing for having all daughters
and no sons. We four sisters grew up with a big chip on our shoulders, suffering under the weight of continuously proving our worth, our strength
and agility to do everything. As was typical of first-generation Chinese immigrant families in America, our family worked in grocery stores (guess who
performed all the duties of stockboy and warehouseman?), laundromats, dry
cleaners and restaurants. And so the girls grew physically strong, completely
self-reliant, always ready to take the initiative—traits we later found to be
quite threatening to men and which probably explain our feisty and somewhat argumentative relationships with them, even in marriage.

I rebelled under the authoritarian leash of my parents and struck out on
my own. No one told me that, in this society, all a girl really has to her name
is her pristine reputation. It made no sense to me that a boy could go out and
do incredibly wild and stupid acts, some of those acts to girls, and yet at
worst be dismissed for nothing more than juvenile behavior. But girls, who
are many times forced into compromising situations by boys, are forever
haunted by these episodes, always fearful that someone will bring up the
past to an attentive ear. I am still mortified that Vanessa Williams had to relinquish her hard-fought Miss America title—indeed, relinquish her whole future marketability and the promise of a charmed life, all because some male
photographer exploited her youth and inexperience for his dubious gain.

That sent a clear signal to me of the specious control I have over my life—
that all women (unless they're raised very strictly and properly by mothers
who could afford to dote on their daughters) have to constantly pay for the
sins of their past. This point hit hard in my college years when a young man
confided in me that he was mad at his girlfriend and he was going to tell everyone that she slept around and was unfaithful. I looked at him and asked why
he wasn't afraid that she could tell everyone something equally embarrassing
about him, like what a lousy lover he might be. He roared with laughter and
gave me one of those "you're-off-your-rocker" looks. I banished that thought,
and with it all hope that I as a girl would have as equal a shot at life as he.

As for the saga of the four daughters who brought shame to mommy
and daddy: My oldest sister, whose initial desire for children was not terribly
strong, became pregnant with the hope of giving my parents a grandson.
She delivered a beautiful baby girl which immediately prompted her in-laws
to declare defensively that it was OK to have a girl in America. She became
pregnant a second time in the same misguided hope of giving my parents a

grandson. Another beautiful baby girl resulted. My sister had her tubes tied and said, "No more." My two other sisters, for various reasons, probably cannot have children. That left me, and the pressure to deliver a boy after two generations of girls was as subtle as the U.S. dropping the atomic bomb on Hiroshima.

I remember the sigh of relief when a little boy wriggled out of my womb. The elation in my husband's voice as he yelled, "It's a boy," the admission of my Japanese mother-in-law that she had secretly prayed for a boy, my parents' immediate rush to the hospital upon news of a grandson. To be fair, I think everyone would have been delighted that I delivered a healthy baby of any sex, but the decibel level went through the roof with the boy-child.

True to my rebellious nature, I wanted a girl—not only because my Japanese husband, Chinese parents and American culture favored boys. It had everything to do with the pains of growing up female in a patriarchal society; of being bombarded with MTV images of vapid sex-kittens; of seeing women used as ornaments in booze and car commercials; of reading stories (fairy-tale and modern) of men coming to our emotional rescue. Just as war creates bonds between men, so does the unrelenting pressure of daily conformance to stereotype create empathy among women.

Perhaps that explains my deep desire for a daughter—someone to share the lessons I've learned of everyday coping, to empower with some streetwise skills for maneuvering successfully through society's maze.

But for all the gains women have made in recent years—the self-help magazines devoted to our advancement in society, the new breed of female political leaders, the contemporary media images of women as individuals instead of victims—the problems women still face are not actually women's problems. They're society's problems, passed from generation to generation, and they lie with the young lad who visits a bar for the first time and is surprised to meet "some really nice girls there," not at all what his mother had warned him about girls who go to bars. And here is where my responsibility lies: If I can't have a daughter to share womanhood with, I at least can instill in my sons a truly healthy respect for women. I have a duty to point out in bedtime stories that girls can be heroes sometimes, that playing with a gun doesn't arm one with power, that sensitivity to others is a wonderfully desirable trait. If I can open my son's eyes to the unlimited possibilities of women, then surely we cannot be far from the day we close our eyes to the color distinctions that still divide our society today.

It's finally my turn to say: "No more."

## REFLECTING ON THE READING

Make two lists, one of the traditional expectations of mothers indicated by Iwata and one of the modern expectations of a mother committed to women's equality. After you've made the lists, write a sentence that states your opinion of how traditional and how modern your own mother is.

◆

---

# SNIP, SNIP: TRADING HAIRCUTS IS A CHERISHED FATHER-SON TRADITION

JAMES E. BOUMAN

---

◆

*One of the defining aspects of a parent-child relationship
are the skills and traditions passed on from father to son,
from mother to daughter. As you read this account by
James Bouman, a Waukesha-based technical writer,
think of some skill you learned from a parent.*

It is a familiar scene in our clan: the son sitting in the bright backyard sun on a high stool, boosted to haircut height on the telephone books; the father doing his confident precision work with shears and a fine-tooth barber comb.

The father has been cutting this particular head of hair for more than 40 years, the son has been reciprocating more than 20. Trading haircuts.

The new element in the picture is my 3-year-old, Jesse, leaning against my knee, so close his arm and shirt catch some of the snipped hair. He is watching his grandpa, Bill Bouman, cut his daddy's hair, waiting his turn.

When the haircut is finished, the neck dusted with the same brush and talc used on the first haircut decades back—the scent triggers flashes of memory of haircuts in the '40s, the '50s—the son trades places, puts a drop of oil on the clipper blade and tries to size up what needs doing.

The son of the son shifts, now leaning on his grandpa's knee, now getting covered with hair that is all white instead of half and half. The clipper hums, slightly hot in the hand; this hand is competent enough, but slow, making amateur moves.

The clipper is a story in itself. In the mid-'50s the Andis Clipper Co. (now Andis Co.) in Racine received my father's clipper in the mail with a request for a tune-up. Six weeks later it came back to Cleveland in a new box, with new blades, a new switch and a ridiculously tiny charge for the work.

That service—and the fact that the clipper is in excellent condition after nearly 50 years—always has made me think of the clipper company as strictly top-drawer.

My father had professional tools from the start—the clipper, Wiss shears, an ancient but genuine barber chair, and a pair of bone-handled straight razors. The razors and a strop had been his father's; the razors—always in his tool box— somehow reach back to include a fourth generation in this quiet family portrait. Trading haircuts.

I tell my father as I begin cutting about a shop in Waukesha that caters to the impatient; they have a sign to update his bromide about the difference between a good haircut and a bad one—two weeks. They toot: "We repair Six Dollar Haircuts." He laughs, perhaps thinking about how he himself came to be giving haircuts.

He started after two younger brothers came home with barbershop haircuts for confirmation—skinned. Bad enough to get a lousy haircut, worse to have to pay for it with the Depression going on, worst to have to stand up in St. Ignatius in front of the bishop and the relatives, embarrassing their widowed mother. That was the beginning of trading haircuts.

Before I left home for college, he gave me my tools: a serviceable clipper someone had given him, one of his good shears and a few lessons. I gave haircuts in the dorm, flattops mostly, sometimes worth half-a-buck or two packs of cigarets.

Those were pre-Beatle days when a three-quarter-inch tonsure was the desirable collegiate look, and pretty easy to do. Perhaps my career total is 200 fair-to-good haircuts, nowhere near my father's 50-year total.

The haircut he just finished is only the latest of his serial opus that includes his brothers, my brother and me, scores of nephews and grandsons and others—all family. The ticket for a haircut is being in the family. And his specialty is first haircuts. Hundreds have been shorn first by this master-soother of the tearful, the wigglers, the cow-licked.

I gave my own son his first, but only because grandpa lives hundreds of miles away. His fine hair and writhing confounded my limited skills and patience. Grandpa arrived in time to give the second. Now, his mother has developed a liking for the layered look he gets at a six-dollar shop she takes him to.

Distance keeps my father and me from seeing each other more often than two or three times a year. I can be well on the way to shaggy, yet wait an extra week or two if I'll be passing through Cleveland, an overnight stay on the way to somewhere else.

He does the same, though not as often. He mostly trades haircuts with his brother, one of the confirmation kids, turned barber himself.

It would be easy to make more of this than it deserves. A haircut is a pretty ordinary thing, though some of the exotic haircut advertising I hear indicates otherwise: moderns singing, dancing, vamping about "hair care har-mo-nee."

But haircuts from my dad were more than his saving the six dollars a month it would have cost to send his boys down the street to Julius the barber. He did it because he could do it well and he wanted to take the time and effort.

My father is a gentle, careful, observant man; he raised his family on the money he earned in a not-very-stimulating occupation. He bought good tools and learned how to use them, barbering out of equal parts of necessity, avocation and craft.

Every haircut he's ever given me has looked as good as any—better than some—I've paid for in barber shops. If he hadn't been able to do it like a professional he'd have embarrassed both of us.

But he's not a barber; his craft, his profession is quintessentially family man. Cutting hair is one small part of what he taught me about being a father. When I'm 80 and my son is 40, I hope we'll be trading haircuts.

## REFLECTING ON THE READING

Reread "Mothers and Daughters" by Gwendolyn Brooks on page 106. Compare the Boumans' relationship to the Brooks'. What strengths do the two relationships have in common? Express your answer by writing a single sentence.

◆

# MEMORIES OF FATHER

YAACOV LURIA*

◆

*Some children feel the impact of a strong, dominant father in their lives. Other children grow up feeling the absence of a father. How does Luria deal with the fact of an absent father?*

Henry Adams' overquoted generalization about teachers, that they affect eternity, is probably truer of parents. Even where a parent is absent—increasingly commonplace in today's restless world—the influence continues. Memory and imagination join to fill the emptiness. My own experience, as a child and an adult, testifies to that.

All my life, I have been trying to escape my parents. I have wanted, as they say today, to be only me. I run, turn, rebel, hide from my memories, but I cannot shake them. If I forget them when I am awake, they return to me in dreams. There is nothing I can do; they are with me and within me.

Oddly—or, perhaps, not so oddly—my parents have not been with me for a long time. It's been 35 years since my mother died. I lost my father a month before my fifth birthday. Yet it's been my father who has had the stronger hold on me.

---

*Yaacov Luria lives in San Diego.

I can hardly remember my father as a physical presence, yet I have a composite picture of him limned in my mind from three experiences. These hold me fast to his realness ...

I am very small, and I am playing soldiers with a bunch of other kids. World War I is still on. We strut back and forth on the bridge that carried East 97th Street over the New York Central track below Park Avenue. A rhythmic ditty punctuates our march "Hip! Hip!" The Kaiser's got the grippe! Why? Why? Because he's gonna die! Where? Where? On the 'lectric chair! When? When? Half past 10!" In a surge of enthusiasm, I fling my vi-sored khaki cap into the air. A gust seizes the cap and takes it down to the railroad tracks.

I am bereft. All day long, I am inconsolable. When my father comes from work in the evening, he lifts me up and presses his face to mine. The bristles of his beard scrape my cheek. I don't remember any words. Somehow I am comforted ...

I am standing on sand, probably at Coney Island, watching my father floating on water. As he bobs up and down with the waves, I suddenly lose sight of him. I wail in terror. All at once my father is beside me again, drip-ping salt water and laughing. He wrestles me onto the sand and lies down face up, close to me.

My father luxuriates in the sun, but it is too hot for me. After awhile, his hair dries and stands up in spikes. I pour sand over him. Soon I have had enough of it, and I tell my father I want to pee. When he gets up, his black bathing suit is mottled with caked, brown sand. I don't like the gooky feel-ing of wet sand. He rubs my hands clean with his handkerchief.

On the long trip back to upper Manhattan on the subway, I have my fa-ther all to myself. He finds hazel nuts in his pocket and has me guess how many he has in his closed hand. If I guess right, he gives me the nuts. Above his beard, his usually pale face has taken on a ruddy glow. Feeling very close to him, I reach to touch his face. Gradually, I forget the fear that gripped me when he disappeared under the waves ...

It must have happened only a few weeks before he died during the flu epidemic in March 1919. I am in the midst of a great horde of people watch-ing a parade. I can see over their heads because my father has lifted me onto his shoulders. Forested by wind-whipped flags, ranks of soldiers march by with fixed bayonets. Others on horseback brandish sabers. Mounted on truck beds are cannon, field hospitals, submarines and airplanes. They pass by in an endless procession. Brass bands blare, drums beat, volleys of blanks fired from carbines overlay the air with the smell of gun powder.

Overwhelmed by the assault on my senses, I ask my father to put me down. I grip his hand as we push our way through the pack. My father shakes his head, sadly it seems. When I am older, I find out why. My father was a pacifist who opposed the war. Why did he take me to the victory pa-rade then? Perhaps because he thought it was something for me to remem-ber. More likely, he could not resist the spectacle ...

As I grew up, I put together a more complete portrait of my father from my mother's accounts. In her eagerness to provide me with a model, she exaggerated his virtues, giving me not a life story but a legend. My father made a meager living as a bookkeeper for a wholesale dry-goods merchant on the lower East Side. After working hours, he was an avid student of the vast compilation of Jewish learning called the Talmud. My mother insisted he was not just a scholar but a Talmudic genius. He was so generous that he went looking for people in need and shared his paychecks with them. He was so sensitive to other people's feelings that he never answered an insult. In time, I came to know my father's faults, which were predictable from his virtues. He often became so wound up in discussions with fellow Talmudists that he forgot to come home after work. The police were used to frantic telephone calls from my mother. He indulged his philanthropy at my mother's expense. My sisters and I were well fed only because my mother took in sewing.

For his gentleness, he suffered the universal penalty of pacifists; under their pretended admiration, more aggressive colleagues and relatives concealed contempt. Observing me, my mother often said, "You take after your father." I was never sure whether this was praise or blame.

My father's books and papers, even his Sabbath Prince Albert coat, which my mother couldn't part with for years, have disappeared long ago. I have saved a fading photograph in which he appears with my mother and an older sister.

There is just one more visible token of my father's presence on Earth. Each year, just before the High Holy Days in fall, I visit my father's grave in a cemetery in Queens, New York. Each time I reread the Hebrew inscription, "Our father feared God in truth, and was upright in all his works." It is a rather stilted tribute that echoes phrases from the Psalms. It is silent about his frailties. It is a proper epitaph.

Each year, the bed of my father's grave sinks lower. Ivy from nearby graves fling a mat of tangled vines over his. Someday the stone will crumble, but not in my lifetime.

As long as I live, my yearly pilgrimage will loop me to my father. The grass that grows among the ivy has a strangely sweet smell. As I weed the plot, I sometimes fantasize that the grass is emanating a message to me.

If my father in a world beyond is trying to communicate with me, he need not bother. Something of me is spread upon the stone. The earth that ground his bones has nourished me all the years since his death. Willy nilly, I have stayed his son.

## REFLECTING ON THE READING

Luria assumes his readers are familiar with certain names. Use a dictionary, encyclopedia, or other reference work to identify the following: Henry Adams, the Kaiser, the grippe, the Talmud, the Sabbath, and Prince Albert.

# NOTES OF A NATIVE SON

JAMES BALDWIN

*Often, children have conflicting feelings toward their parents. Baldwin focuses on what repels him from his father while he shows how much he admires his father. Try to understand both of Baldwin's views of his father.*

For my father's funeral I had nothing black to wear and this posed a nagging problem all day long. It was one of those problems, simple, or impossible of solution, to which the mind insanely clings in order to avoid the mind's real trouble. I spent most of that day at the downtown apartment of a girl I knew, celebrating my birthday with whiskey and wondering what to wear that night. When planning a birthday celebration one naturally does not expect that it will be up against competition from a funeral and this girl had anticipated taking me out that night, for a big dinner and a night club afterwards. Sometime during the course of that long day we decided that we would go out anyway, when my father's funeral service was over. I imagine I decided it, since, as the funeral hour approached, it became clearer and clearer to me that I would not know what to do with myself when it was over. The girl, stifling her very lively concern as to the possible effects of the whiskey on one of my father's chief mourners, concentrated on being conciliatory and practically helpful. She found a black shirt for me somewhere and ironed it and, dressed in the darkest pants and jacket I owned, and slightly drunk, I made my way to my father's funeral.

The chapel was full, but not packed, and very quiet. There were, mainly, my father's relatives, and his children, and here and there I saw faces I had not seen since childhood, the faces of my father's one-time friends. They were very dark and solemn now, seeming somehow to suggest that they had known all along that something like this would happen. Chief among the mourners was my aunt, who had quarreled with my father all his life; by which I do not mean to suggest that her mourning was insincere or that she had not loved him. I suppose that she was one of the few people in the world who had, and their incessant quarreling proved precisely the strength of the tie that bound them. The only other person in the world, as far as I knew, whose relationship to my father rivaled my aunt's in depth was my mother, who was not there.

It seemed to me, of course, that it was a very long funeral. But it was, if anything, a rather shorter funeral than most, nor, since there were no overwhelming, uncontrollable expressions of grief, could it be called—if I dare to use the word—successful. The minister who preached my father's funeral sermon was one of the few my father had still been seeing as he neared his end. He presented to us in his sermon a man whom none of us had ever seen—a man thoughtful, patient, and forbearing, a Christian inspiration to all who knew him, and a model for his children. And no doubt the children, in their disturbed and guilty state, were almost ready to believe this; he had been remote enough to be anything and, anyway, the shock of the incontrovertible, that it was really our father lying up there in that casket, prepared the mind for anything. His sister moaned and this grief-stricken moaning was taken as corroboration. The other faces held a dark, non-committal thoughtfulness. This was not the man they had known, but they had scarcely expected to be confronted with *him*; this was, in a sense deeper than questions of fact, the man they had not known, and the man they had not known may have been the real one. The real man, whoever he had been, had suffered and now he was dead: this was all that was sure and all that mattered now. Every man in the chapel hoped that when his hour came he, too, would be eulogized, which is to say forgiven, and that all of his lapses, greeds, errors, and strayings from the truth would be invested with coherence and looked upon with charity. This was perhaps the last thing human beings could give each other and it was what they demanded, after all, of the Lord. Only the Lord saw the midnight tears, only He was present when one of His children, moaning and wringing hands, paced up and down the room. When one slapped one's child in anger the recoil in the heart reverberated through heaven and became part of the pain of the universe. And when the children were hungry and sullen and distrustful and one watched them, daily, growing wilder, and further away, and running headlong into danger, it was the Lord who knew what the charged heart endured as the strap was laid to the backside; the Lord alone who knew what one *would* have said if one had had, like the Lord, the gift of the living word. It was the Lord who knew of the impossibility every parent in that room faced: how to prepare the child for the day when the child would be despised and how to *create* in the child—by what means?—a stronger antidote to this poison than one had found for oneself. The avenues, side streets, bars, billiard halls, hospitals, police stations, and even the playgrounds of Harlem—not to mention the houses of correction, the jails, and the morgue—testified to the potency of the poison while remaining silent as to the efficacy of whatever antidote, irresistibly raising the question of whether or not such an antidote existed; raising, which was worse, the question of whether or not an antidote was desirable; perhaps poison should be fought with poison. With these several schisms in the mind and with more terrors in the heart than could be named, it was better not to judge the man who had gone down under an impossible burden. It was better to remember: *Thou knowest this man's fall; but thou knowest not his wrassling*.

While the preacher talked and I watched the children—years of changing their diapers, scrubbing them, slapping them, taking them to school, and scolding them had had the perhaps inevitable result of making me love them, though I am not sure I knew this then—my mind was busily breaking out with a rash of disconnected impressions. Snatches of popular songs, indecent jokes, bits of books I had read, movie sequences, faces, voices, political issues—I thought I was going mad; all these impressions suspended, as it were, in the solution of the faint nausea produced in me by the heat and liquor. For a moment I had the impression that my alcoholic breath, inefficiently disguised with chewing gum, filled the entire chapel. Then someone began singing one of my father's favorite songs and, abruptly, I was with him, sitting on his knee, in the hot, enormous, crowded church which was the first church we attended. It was the Abyssinia Baptist Church on 138th Street. We had not gone there long. With this image, a host of others came. I had forgotten, in the rage of my growing up, how proud my father had been of me when I was little. Apparently, I had had a voice and my father had liked to show me off before the members of the church. I had forgotten what he had looked like when he was pleased but now I remembered that he had always been grinning with pleasure when my solos ended. I even remembered certain expressions on his face when he teased my mother—had he loved her? I would never know. And when had it all begun to change? For now it seemed that he had not always been cruel. I remembered being taken for a haircut and scraping my knee on the footrest of the barber's chair and I remembered my father's face as he soothed my crying and applied the stinging iodine. Then I remembered our fights, fights which had been of the worst possible kind because my technique had been silence.

I remembered the one time in all our life together when we had really spoken to each other.

It was on a Sunday and it must have been shortly before I left home. We were walking, just the two of us, in our usual silence, to or from church. I was in high school and had been doing a lot of writing and I was, at about this time, the editor of the high school magazine. But I had also been a Young Minister and had been preaching from the pulpit. Lately, I had been taking fewer engagements and preached as rarely as possible. It was said in the church, quite truthfully, that I was "cooling off."

My father asked me abruptly, "You'd rather write than preach, wouldn't you?"

I was astonished at his question—because it was a real question. I answered, "Yes."

That was all we said. It was awful to remember that that was all we had ever said.

The casket now was opened and the mourners were being led up the aisle to look for the last time on the deceased. The assumption was that the family was too overcome with grief to be allowed to make this journey alone and I watched while my aunt was led to the casket and, muffled in black, and shaking, led back to her seat. I disapproved of forcing the children to look on their dead father, considering that the shock of his death, or, more truthfully, the shock of death as a reality, was already a little more than a child could bear, but my judgment in this matter had been overruled and there they were, bewildered and frightened and very small, being led, one by one, to the casket. But there is also something very gallant about children at such moments. It has something to do with their silence and gravity and with the fact that one cannot help them. Their legs, somehow, seem *exposed*, so that it is at once incredible and terribly clear that their legs are all they have to hold them up.

I had not wanted to go to the casket myself and I certainly had not wished to be led there, but there was no way of avoiding either of these forms. One of the deacons led me up and I looked on my father's face. I cannot say that it looked like him at all. His blackness had been equivocated by powder and there was no suggestion in that casket of what his power had or could have been. He was simply an old man dead, and it was hard to believe that he had ever given anyone either joy or pain. Yet, his life filled that room. Further up the avenue his wife was holding his newborn child. Life and death so close together, and love and hatred, and right and wrong, said something to me which I did not want to hear concerning man, concerning the life of man.

After the funeral, while I was downtown desperately celebrating my birthday, a Negro soldier, in the lobby of the Hotel Braddock, got into a fight with a white policeman over a Negro girl. Negro girls, white policemen, in or out of uniform, and Negro males—in or out of uniform—were part of the furniture of the lobby of the Hotel Braddock and this was certainly not the first time such an incident had occurred. It was destined, however, to receive an unprecedented publicity, for the fight between the policeman and the soldier ended with the shooting of the soldier. Rumor, flowing immediately to the streets outside, stated that the soldier had been shot in the back, an instantaneous and revealing invention, and that the soldier had died protecting a Negro woman. The facts were somewhat different—for example, the soldier had not been shot in the back, and was not dead, and the girl seems to have been as dubious a symbol of womanhood as her white counterpart in Georgia usually is, but no one was interested in the facts. They preferred the invention because this invention expressed and corroborated their hates and fears so perfectly. It is just as well to remember that people are always doing this. Perhaps many of those legends, including Christianity, to which the world clings began their conquest of the world with just some such concerted surrender to distortion. The effect, in Harlem, of this particular legend was like the effect of a lit match in a tin of gasoline. The mob gathered before the doors of the Hotel Braddock simply began to swell and to spread in every direction, and Harlem exploded.

The mob did not cross the ghetto lines. It would have been easy, for example, to have gone over Morningside Park on the west side or to have crossed the Grand Central railroad tracks at 125th Street on the east side, to wreak havoc in white neighborhoods. The mob seems to have been mainly interested in something more potent and real than the white face, that is, in white power, and the principal damage done during the riot of the summer of 1943 was to white business establishments in Harlem. It might have been a far bloodier story, of course, if, at the hour the riot began, these establishments had still been open. From the Hotel Braddock the mob fanned out, east and west along 125th Street, and for the entire length of Lenox, Seventh, and Eighth avenues. Along each of these avenues, and along each major side street—116th, 125th, 135th, and so on—bars, stores, pawnshops, restaurants, even little luncheonettes had been smashed open and entered and looted—looted, it might be added, with more haste than efficiency. The shelves really looked as though a bomb had struck them. Cans of beans and soup and dog food, along with toilet paper, corn flakes, the risk of swelling up slowly, in agony, with poison. And the trouble, finally, is that the risks are real even if the choices do not exist.

"But as for me and my house," my father had said, "we will serve the Lord." I wondered, as we drove him to his resting place, what this line had meant for him. I had heard him preach it many times. I had preached it once myself, proudly giving it an interpretation different from my father's. Now the whole thing came back to me, as though my father and I were on our way to Sunday school and I were memorizing the golden text: *And if it seem evil unto you to serve the Lord, choose you this day whom you will serve; whether the gods which your fathers served that were on the other side of the flood, or the gods of the Amorites, in whose land ye dwell: but as for me and my house, we will serve the Lord.* I suspected in these familiar lines a meaning which had never been there for me before. All of my father's texts and songs, which I had decided were meaningless, were arranged before me at his death like empty bottles, waiting to hold the meaning which life would give them for me. This was his legacy: nothing is ever escaped. That bleakly memorable morning I hated the unbelievable streets and the Negroes and whites who had, equally, made them that way. But I knew that it was folly, as my father would have said, this bitterness was folly. It was necessary to hold on to the things that mattered. The dead man mattered, the new life mattered; blackness and whiteness did not matter; to believe that they did was to acquiesce in one's own destruction. Hatred, which could destroy so much, never failed to destroy the man who hated and this was an immutable law.

It began to seem that one would have to hold in the mind forever two ideas which seemed to be in opposition. The first idea was acceptance, the acceptance, totally without rancor, of life as it is, and men as they are: in the light of this idea, it goes without saying that injustice is a commonplace. But this did not mean that one could be complacent, for the second idea was of equal power: that one must never, in one's own life, accept these injustices as commonplace but must fight them with all one's strength. This fight begins, however, in the heart and it now had been laid to my charge to keep my own heart free of hatred and despair. This intimation made my heart heavy and, now that my father was irrecoverable, I wished that he had been beside me so that I could have searched his face for the answers which only the future would give me now.

## REFLECTING ON THE READING

This excerpt from a long essay is demanding to read, partly because the ideas are complex and partly because the sentences are complex. Choose three sentences you found particularly difficult to understand. Copy them out and then rewrite them in your own words.

---

# PICKING PLUMS

## FATHERS AND SONS AND THEIR LOVERS

BERNARD COOPER*

---

*Eventually, children grow to be adults. Then, parents and children alike are faced with the difficulties of reestablishing their relationship as two adults. Bernard Cooper gives a particularly vivid account of dealing with his father on the subjects of both age and sexuality.*

It has been nearly a year since my father fell while picking plums. The bruises on his leg have healed, and except for a vague absence of pigmentation where the calf had blistered, his recovery is complete. Back in the habit of evening constitutionals, he navigates the neighborhood with his usual stride—"Brisk," he says "for a man of eighty-five"—dressed in a powder blue jogging suit that bears the telltale stains of jelly doughnuts and Lipton tea, foods which my father, despite doctor's orders, hasn't the will to forsake.

He broke his glasses and his hearing aid in the fall, and when I first stepped into the hospital room for a visit, I was struck by the way my father—head cocked to hear, squinting to see—looked so much older and more remote, a prisoner of his failing senses. "Boychik?" he asked, straining

---

*Bernard Cooper's collection of essays, Maps to Anywhere (paper, Penguin), won the 1991 PEN USA Ernest Hemingway Award. His memoir "A Clack of Tiny Sparks" appeared in the January 1991 issue of *Harper's Magazine*. Cooper lives in Los Angeles.

his face in my general direction. He fell back into a stack of pillows, sighed a deep sigh, and without my asking described what had happened:

"There they are, all over the lawn. Purple plums, dozens of them. They look delicious. So what am I supposed to do? Let the birds eat them? Not on your life. It's my tree, right? First I fill a bucket with the ones from the ground. Then I get the ladder out of the garage. I've climbed the thing a hundred times before. I make it to the top, reach out my hand, and ... who knows what happens. Suddenly I'm an astronaut. Up is down and vice versa. It happened so fast I didn't have time to piss in my pants. I'm flat on my back, not a breath in me. Couldn't have called for help if I tried. And the pain in my leg—you don't want to know."

"Who found you?"

"What?"

I move closer, speak louder.

"Nobody found me," he says, exasperated. "Had to wait till I could get up on my own. It seemed like hours. I'm telling you, I thought it was all over. But eventually I could breathe normal again and—don't ask me how; God only knows—I got in the car and drove here myself." My father shifted his weight and grimaced. The sheet slid off his injured leg, the calf swollen, purple as a plum, what the doctor called "an insult to the tissue."

Throughout my boyhood my father possessed a surplus of energy, or it possessed him. On weekdays he worked hard at the office, and on weekends he gardened in our yard. He was also a man given to unpredictable episodes of anger. These rages were never precipitated by a crisis—in the face of illness or accident my father remained steady, methodical, even optimistic; when the chips were down he was an incorrigible joker, an inveterate backslapper, a sentry at the bedside—but something as simple as a drinking glass left out on the table could send him into a frenzy of invective. Spittle shot from his lips. Blood ruddied his face. He'd hurl the glass against the wall.

His temper rarely intimidated my mother. She'd light a Tareyton, stand aside, and watch my father flail and shout until he was purged of the last sharp word. Winded and limp, he'd flee into the living room, where he would draw the shades, sit in his wing chair, and brood for hours.

Even as a boy, I understood how my father's profession had sullied his view of the world, had made him a wary man, prone to explosions. He spent hours taking depositions from jilted wives and cuckolded husbands. He conferred with a miserable clientele: spouses who wept, who spat accusations, who pounded his desk in want of revenge. At the time, California law required that grounds for divorce be proven in court, and toward this end my father carried in his briefcase not only the usual legal tablets and manila files but bills for motel rooms, matchbooks from bars, boxer shorts blooming with lipstick stains.

After one particularly long and vindictive divorce trial, he agreed to a weekend out of town. Mother suggested Palm Springs, rhapsodized about the balmy air, the cacti lit by colored lights, the street named after Bob

Hope. When it finally came time to leave, however, my mother kept thinking of things she forgot to pack. No sooner would my father begin to back the car out of the driveway than my mother would shout for him to stop, dash into the house, and retrieve what she needed. A carton of Tareytons. An aerosol can of Solarcaine. A paperback novel to read by the pool. I sat in the backseat, motionless and mute; with each of her excursions back inside, I felt my father's frustration mount. When my mother insisted she get a package of Saltine crackers in case we got hungry along the way, my father glared at her, bolted from the car, wrenched every piece of luggage from the trunk, and slammed it shut with such a vengeance the car rocked on its springs.

Through the rear window, my mother and I could see him fling two suitcases, a carryall, and a makeup case yards above his balding head. The sky was a huge and cloudless blue; gray chunks of luggage sailed through it, twisting and spinning and falling to earth like the burned out stages of a booster rocket. When a piece of luggage crashed back to the asphalt, he'd pick it up and hurl it again. With every effort, an involuntary, animal grunt issued from the depths of his chest.

Finally, the largest suitcase came unlatched in mid-flight. Even my father was astonished when articles of his wife's wardrobe began their descent from the summer sky. A yellow scarf dazzled the air like a tangible strand of sunlight. Fuzzy slippers tumbled down. One diaphanous white slip drifted over the driveway and, as if guided by an invisible hand, draped itself across a hedge. With that, my father barreled by us, veins protruding on his temple and neck, and stomped into the house. "I'm getting tired of this," my mother grumbled. Before she stooped to pick up the mess—a vast and random geography of clothes—she flicked her cigarette onto the asphalt and ground the ember out.

One evening, long after I'd moved away from home, I received a phone call from my father telling me that my mother had died the night before. "But I didn't know it happened," he said.

He'd awakened as usual that morning, ruminating over a case while he showered and shaved. My mother appeared to be sound asleep, one arm draped across her face, eyes sheltered beneath the crook of her elbow. When he sat on the bed to pull up his socks, he'd tried not to jar the mattress and wake her. At least he *thought* he'd tried not to wake her, but he couldn't remember, he couldn't be sure. Things looked normal, he kept protesting—the pillow, the blanket, the way she lay there. He decided to grab a doughnut downtown and left in a hurry. But that night my father returned to a house suspiciously unlived-in. The silence caused him to clench his fists, and he called for his wife—"Lillian, Lillian"—as he drifted through quiet, unlit rooms, walking slowly up the stairs.

I once saw a photograph of a woman who had jumped off the Empire State Building and landed on the roof of a parked car. What is amazing is that she appears merely to have leapt into satin sheets, to be deep in a languid and absolute sleep. Her eyes are closed, lips slightly parted, hair fanned out on a metal pillow. Nowhere is there a trace of blood, her body caught softly in its own impression.

As my father spoke into the telephone, his voice about to break—"I should have realized. I should have known"—that's the state in which I pictured my mother: a long fall of sixty years, an uncanny landing, a miraculous repose.

My father and I had one thing in common after my mother's heart attack: we each maintained a secret life. Secret, at least, from each other.

I'd fallen for a man named Travis Mask. Travis had recently arrived in Los Angeles from Kentucky, and everything I was accustomed to—the billboards lining the Sunset strip, the 7-Elevens open all night—stirred in him a strong allegiance; "I love this town," he'd say every day. Travis's job was to collect change from food vending machines throughout the city. During dinner he would tell me about the office lobbies and college cafeterias he had visited, the trick to opening different machines, the noisy cascade of nickles and dimes. Travis Mask was enthusiastic. Travis Mask was easy to please. In bed I called him by his full name because I found the sound of it exciting.

My father, on the other hand, had fallen for a woman whose identity he meant to keep secret. I knew of her existence only because of a dramatic change in his behavior: he would grow mysterious as quickly and inexplicably as he had once grown angry. Though I resented being barred from this central fact of my father's life, I had no intention of telling him I was gay. It had taken me thirty years to achieve even a modicum of intimacy with the man, and I didn't want to risk a setback. It wasn't as if I was keeping my sexual orientation a secret; I'd told relatives, co-workers, friends. But my father was a man who whistled at waitresses, flirted with bank tellers, his head swiveling like a radar dish toward the nearest pair of breasts and hips. Ever since I was a child my father reminded me of the wolf in cartoons whose ears shoot steam, whose eyes pop out on springs, whose tongue unfurls like a party favor whenever he sees a curvaceous dame. As far as my father was concerned, desire for women fueled the world, compelled every man without exception—his occupation testified to that—was a force as essential as gravity. I didn't want to disappoint him.

Eventually, Travis Mask was transferred to Long Beach. In his absence my nights grew long and ponderous, and I tried to spend more time with my father in the belief that sooner or later an opportunity for disclosure would present itself. We met for dinner once a month in a restaurant whose interior was dim and crimson, our interaction friendly but formal, both of us cautiously skirting the topic of our private lives; we'd become expert at the ambiguous answer, the changed subject, the half-truth. Should my father ask if I was dating, I'd tell him yes, I had been seeing someone. I'd liked them very much, I said, but they were transferred to another city. Them. They. My attempt to neuter the pronouns made it sound as if I were courting people en masse. Just when I thought this subterfuge was becoming obvious, my father began to respond in kind: "Too bad I didn't get a chance to meet them. Where did you say they went?"

Avoidance also worked in reverse: "And how about you, Dad? Are you seeing anybody?"

"Seeing? I don't know if you'd call it *seeing*. What did you order, chicken or fish?"

During one dinner we discovered that we shared a fondness for nature programs on television, and from that night on, when we'd exhausted our comments about the meal or the weather, we'd ask if the other had seen the show about the blind albino fish who live in underwater caves, or the one about the North American moose whose antlers, coated with green moss, provide camouflage in the underbrush. My father and I had adapted like those creatures to the strictures of our shared world.

And then I met her.

I looked up from a rack of stationery at the local Thrifty one afternoon and there stood my father with a willowy black woman in her early forties. As she waited for a prescription to be filled, he drew a finger through her hair, nuzzled the nape of her neck, the refracted light of his lenses causing his cheeks to glow. I felt like a child who was witness to something forbidden: his father's helpless, unguarded ardor for an unfamiliar woman. I didn't know whether to run or stay. Had he always been attracted to young black women? Had I ever known him well? Somehow I managed to move myself toward them and mumble hello. They turned around in unison. My father's eyes widened. He reached out and cupped my shoulder, struggled to say my name. Before he could think to introduce us, I shook the woman's hand, startled by its softness. "So you're the son. Where've you been hiding?" She was kind and cordial, though too preoccupied to engage in much conversation, her handsome features furrowed by a hint of melancholy, a sadness which I sensed had little to do with my surprise appearance. Anna excused herself when the pharmacist called her name.

Hours after our encounter, I could still feel the softness of Anna's hand, the softness that stirred my father's yearning. He was seventy-five years old, myopic and hard of hearing, his skin loose and liver-spotted, but one glimpse of his impulsive public affection led me to the conclusion that my father possessed, despite his age, a restless sexual energy. The meeting left me elated, expectant. My father and I had something new in common: the pursuit of our unorthodox passions. We were, perhaps, more alike than I'd realized. After years of relative estrangement, I'd been given grounds for a fresh start, a chance to establish a stronger connection.

But none of my expectations mattered. Later that week they left the country.

The prescription, it turned out, was for a psychotropic drug. Anna had battled bouts of depression since childhood. Her propensity for unhappiness gave my father a vital mission: to make her laugh, to wrest her from despair. Anna worked as an elementary-school substitute teacher and managed a few rental properties in South-Central Los Angeles, but after weeks of functioning normally, she would take to my father's bed for days on end, blank and immobile beneath the quilt she had bought to brighten up the room, unaffected by his jokes, his kisses and cajoling. These spells of depression came without warning and ended just as unexpectedly. Though they both did their best to enjoy each other during the periods of relative calm, they lived, my father later lamented, like people in a thunderstorm, never knowing when lightning would strike. Thinking that a drastic change might help Anna shed a recent depression, they pooled their money and flew to Europe.

They returned with snapshots showing the two of them against innumerable backdrops: the Tower of London, the Vatican, Versailles; monuments, obelisks, statuary. In every pose their faces were unchanged, the faces of people who want to be happy, who try to be happy, and somehow can't.

As if in defiance of all the photographic evidence against them, they were married the following month at the Church of the Holy Trinity. I was one of only two guests at the wedding. The other was an uncle of Anna's. Before the ceremony began, he shot me a glance which attested, I was certain, to an incredulity as great as mine. The vaulted chapel rang with prerecorded organ music, an eerie and pious overture. Light filtered through stained-glass windows, chunks of sweet color that reminded me of Jell-O. My old Jewish father and his Episcopalian lover appeared at opposite ends of the dais, walking step by measured step toward a union in the center. The priest, swimming in white vestments, was somber and almost inaudible. Cryptic gestures, odd props; I watched with a powerful, wordless amazement. Afterward, as if the actual wedding hadn't been surreal enough, my father and Anna formed a kind of receiving line (if two people can constitute a line) in the church parking lot, where the four of us, bathed by hazy sunlight, exchanged pleasantries before the newlyweds returned home for a nap; their honeymoon in Europe, my father joked, had put the cart before the horse.

During the months after the wedding, when I called my father, he answered as though the ringing of the phone had been an affront. When I asked him what the matter was he'd bark, "What makes you think there's something the matter?" I began to suspect that my father's frustration had given rise to those ancient rages. But my father had grown too old and frail to sustain his anger for long. When we saw each other—Anna was always visiting relatives or too busy or tired to join us—he looked worn, embattled, and the pride I had in him for attempting an interracial marriage, for risking condemnation in the eyes of the world, was overwhelmed now by concern. He lost weight. His hands began to shake. I would sit across from him in the dim, red restaurant and marvel that this bewildered man had once hurled glasses against a wall and launched Samsonite into the sky.

Between courses I'd try to distract my father from his problems by pressing him to unearth tidbits of his past, as many as memory would allow. He'd often talk about Atlantic City, where his parents had owned a small grocery. Sometimes my mother turned up in the midst of his sketchy regressions. He would smooth wrinkles from the tablecloth and tell me no one could take her place. He eulogized her loyalty and patience, and I wondered whether he could see her clearly— her auburn hair and freckled hands— wondered whether he wished she were here to sweep up after his current mess. "Remember," he once asked me, without a hint of irony or regret, "what fun we had in Palm Springs?" Then he snapped back into the present and asked what was taking so long with our steaks.

The final rift between my father and Anna must have happened suddenly; she left behind several of her possessions, including the picture of Jesus that sat on the sideboard in the dining room next to my father's brass menorah. And along with Anna's possessions were stacks of leather-bound books, *Law of Torts*, *California Jurisprudence*, and *Forms of Pleading and Practice*, embossed along their spines. Too weak and distracted to practice law, my father had retired, and the house became a repository for the contents of his former office. I worried about him being alone, wandering through rooms freighted with history, crowded with the evidence of two marriages, fatherhood, and a long and harrowing career; he had nothing to do but pace and sigh and stir up dust. I encouraged him to find a therapist, but as far as my father was concerned, psychiatrists were all conniving witch doctors who fed off the misery of people like Anna.

Brian, the psychotherapist I'd been living with for three years (and live with still), was not at all fazed by my father's aversion to his profession. They'd met only rarely—once we ran into my father at a local supermarket, and twice Brian accompanied us to the restaurant—but when they were together, Brian would draw my father out, compliment him on his plaid pants, ask questions regarding the fine points of law. And when my father spoke, Brian listened intently, embraced him with his cool, blue gaze. My father relished my lover's attention; Brian's cheerfulness and steady disposition must have been refreshing in those troubled, lonely days. "How's that interesting friend of yours?" he sometimes asked. If he was suspicious that Brian and I shared the same house, he never pursued it—until he took his fall from the plum tree.

I drove my father home from the hospital, trying to keep his big unwieldy car, bobbing like a boat, within the lane. I bought him a pair of seersucker shorts because long pants were too painful and constricting. I brought over groceries and my wok, and while I cooked dinner my father sat at the dinette table, leg propped on a vinyl chair, and listened to the hissing oil, happy, abstracted. I helped him up the stairs to his bedroom where we watched *Wheel of Fortune* and *Jeopardy* on the television and where, for the first time since I was a boy, I sat at his feet and he rubbed my head. It felt so good I'd graze his good leg, contented as a cat. He welcomed my visits with an eagerness bordering on glee and didn't seem to mind being dependent on me for physical assistance; he leaned his bulk on my shoulder wholly, and I felt protective, necessary, inhaling the scents of salve and Old Spice and the base familiar odor that was all my father's own.

"You know those hostages?" asked my father one evening. He was sitting at the dinette, dressed in the seersucker shorts, his leg propped on the chair. The bruises had faded to lavender, his calf back to its normal size.

I could barely hear him over the broccoli sizzling in the wok. "What about them?" I shouted.

"I heard on the news that some of them are seeing a psychiatrist now that they're back."

"So?"

"Why a psychiatrist?"

I stopped tossing the broccoli. "Dad," I said, "if you'd been held hostage in the Middle East, you might want to see a therapist, too."

The sky dimmed in the kitchen windows. My father's face was a silhouette, his lenses catching the last of the light. "They got their food taken care of, right? And a place to sleep. What's the big deal?"

"You're at gunpoint, for God's sake. A prisoner. I don't think it's like spending a weekend at the Hilton."

"Living alone," he said matter-of-factly, "is like being a prisoner."

I let it stand. I added the pea pods.

"Let me ask you something," said my father. "I get this feeling—I'm not sure how to say it—that something isn't right. That you're keeping something from me. We don't talk much, I grant you that. But maybe now's the time."

My heart was pounding. I'd been thoroughly disarmed by his interpretation of world events, his minefield of non sequiturs, and I wasn't prepared for a serious discussion. I switched off the gas. The red jet sputtered. When I turned around, my father was staring at his outstretched leg. "So?" he said.

"You mean Brian?"

"Whatever you want to tell me, tell me."

"You like him, don't you?"

"What's not to like."

"He's been my lover for a long time. He makes me happy. We have a home." Each declaration was a stone in my throat. "I hope you understand. I hope this doesn't come between us." "Look," said my father without skipping a beat, "you're lucky to have someone. And he's lucky to have you, too. It's no one's business anyway. What the hell else am I going to say?"

But my father thought of something else before I could speak and express my relief. "You know," he said, "when I was a boy of maybe sixteen, my father asked me to hold a ladder while he trimmed the tree in our backyard. So I did, see, when I suddenly remember I have a date with this bee-yoo-tiful girl, and I'm late, and I run out of the yard. I don't know what got into me. I'm halfway down the street when I remember my father, and I think, 'Oh, boy. I'm in trouble now.' But when I get back I can hear him laughing way up in the tree. I'd never heard him laugh like that. 'You must like her a lot,' he says when I help him down. Funny thing was, I hadn't told him where I was going."

I pictured my father's father teetering above the earth, a man hugging the trunk of a tree and watching his son run down the street in pursuit of sweet, ineffable pleasure. While my father reminisced, night obscured the branches of the plum tree, the driveway where my mother's clothes once floated down like enormous leaves. When my father finished telling the story, he looked at me, then looked away. A moment of silence lodged between us, an old and obstinate silence. I wondered whether nothing or everything would change. I spooned our food onto separate plates. My father carefully pressed his leg to test the healing flesh.

## REFLECTING ON THE READING

"Picking Plums" is the longest essay in this chapter. Grasping "the whole" of a longer essay requires particular reading strategies. Divide Cooper's essay into separate sections based on different topic areas. Then, write a brief title for each section you have identified. Compare your results with the choices made by two classmates.

# PUTTING IT IN WRITING

## RESPONSE

1. Recall your very first memory of either your father or your mother. Visualize the place, situation, and actions. Now, write rapidly for five minutes recording all the details you can remember.
2. Describe the best prank you got away with when you were a child. If you never played pranks, describe an instance where you got in trouble for something you did or said. Be very specific, trying to recall names, places, objects, and actions involved in the incident.
3. Think of a word that describes a good parent-child relationship, e.g., "loving," "supportive," "disciplined," and then describe a specific experience you have had that illustrates the word you selected.

## READING FOR MEANING

1. Pick a reading that captured your interest. Write three questions you would like the author to answer. Pair up with a classmate. Each of you will pretend to be the author that the other person selected. Based on the reading, answer the three questions as though you were the author.
2. Find two statements, each from a different reading, that appear to contradict one another. Write out the statements and explain the contradiction you see.

3. Choose any reading (or one selected by your instructor) and copy out three sentences: one that best states the main idea in the article, one that best shows the author's attitude, and one that expresses the author's opinion most vividly.

## ORGANIZING YOUR IDEAS

1. List five qualities that you believe should be part of any good parent-child relationship. Next to each quality on your list, write the title of the article in this chapter that best exemplifies that quality.
2. Compare the parent-child relationships described in any two of the articles in this chapter. List at least three ways in which the relationships you compare are similar.
3. Often, silences and secrets are part of the relationship between parent and child. Find an example in one of the articles where silence or secrets affect the relationship. Then, write a paragraph comparing that example to an example from your own experience.

## WRITING A PAPER

1. Pick one of the parent-child relationships you have already read and thought about. Write a paper in which you show how that relationship is most like your relationship with one of your parents.
2. Write a letter to one of the authors, explaining why you admire the relationship they portray between parent and child or why you think the relationship they portray needs improvement.
3. Using the title "The Ideal _____ (father, mother, son, daughter)," write a paper developing your ideal, using examples from several readings and from your personal experience.

**What is the assumption Dave is making?**

# Food

*Food, Glorious Food,*
*Hot sausage and mustard,*
*When we're in the mood,*
*Cold jelly and custard!*
　—*Lionel Bart, Oliver!*

Food gives us joy and pleasure. That's the message sung by the mistreated orphans in the hit 60s musical based on Charles Dickens's novel, *Oliver Twist*. Of course, like air and water, we need food to live. Though asphyxiation and dehydration will do us in faster than starvation, we live in a world in which thousands of people starve to death every year. Somewhere between eating a subsistence level gruel and pigging out at an all-you-can eat buffet lies the desirable balance between good nutrition and pleasurable flavors.

We deal with food every day. We have slogans about food: "You are what you eat!" "Some eat to live, others live to eat," and "Life is short—eat dessert first!" We want "natural" foods and worry about chemical additives in and on our food. We want fresh food. And we want food that is fast and cheap. Sometimes these desires run up against each other. In order to have cheap food, we use chemical fertilizers for plants and growth steroids for animals. In order to have fast food, cooking time may be slighted and disease-causing bacteria may end up in our hamburger or chicken sandwich. As recently as 125 years ago, most Americans grew their own food—or most of it. Now, fewer than 5 percent of the total population work directly in food production. We now have farm and fishing factories, huge canning, freezing and packaging factories, large warehouses, distributors, and huge chains of supermarkets. Where once we selected our food for its feel and its smell, now we rely on its appearance. Or, more likely, we rely on the appearance of the package. Perhaps we are what we eat, but most of us have no idea where our food came from or how it was grown or packaged.

The economics and politics of food are subjects of great importance, as Frances Lappé argues in her book *Diet for a Small Planet.* Whether or not we think about those issues, we still devote considerable time and energy to preparing and consuming food and drink. While some of us still know how to make a cake "from scratch," most of us are more likely to use the defrost setting on a microwave oven to prepare our favorite dessert. For people who work long hours, meal planning now often means consulting the take-out menu of a nearby restaurant, calling in an order, and having the food delivered. For those with the money, a leisurely meal in a gourmet restaurant, featuring seafood flown from across the country, sun-dried tomatoes, fresh herbs, sauces using spices from all parts of the world, accompanied with a bottle of wine, has become commonplace. Anyone with enough money can eat like a king or queen.

Throughout history, food has been the centerpiece of celebrations, whether it's a simple family birthday party or a holiday barbecue for an entire community. The breaking of bread and the sharing of drink (wine, coffee, or simply water) is both the humblest of cultural activities and the most profound. Remember any special occasion and the smell and taste of the food will likely be a rich part of that memory. These associations of good-feeling and well-being with specific foods now even have a name: comfort foods. Comfort foods are those dishes we ate as children when we were sick or when we needed some kind of comfort. Ice cream is a common comfort food, but so is chicken soup, macaroni and cheese, tea and toast, vanilla pudding, mashed potatoes and gravy, or rice and warm milk. You might poll some of your classmates about what their comfort food is.

Everyone has an opinion about food. Some of us can't imagine why anyone would eat food with curry spices or hot peppers or a lot of garlic in it and others can't imagine why anyone would eat plain, bland food without salt, butter, ketchup or other condiments. The Romans had a saying, *De gustibus non est disputandum* or "Of taste there is no disputing." So if I like chocolate and you like strawberry, there's no point in arguing. We each have our own tastes. Yet, there's plenty of room for differing opinions regarding food. Should food be grown with or without chemical fertilizers and pesticides? Are commercial fishing ships damaging the oceans and endangering some species of fish, as various economic and environmental interest groups argue? Some people feel so strongly about vegetarianism that they proselytize others to give up eating meat. Other people so enjoy grilling meat on a backyard barbecue that they couldn't imagine a summer holiday without roasting some animal flesh over hot coals. While we need food just to stay alive, food also nourishes our spirits and helps make life worth living. M. F. K. Fisher, a noted essayist on the subject of food, explains that as well as anyone in the first reading in this chapter.

◆

# THE GASTRONOMICAL ME*

## M. F. K. FISHER

◆

*M. F. K. Fisher has written numerous essays and books on food, many of them collections of recipes, or simply "cookbooks." In food and drink, she saw cultural and spiritual importance. See if you get a sense of her philosophy about food from these two short forewords to books she published 35 years apart.*

People ask me: Why do you write about food, and eating and drinking? Why don't you write about the struggle for power and security, and about love, the way the others do?

They ask it accusingly, as if I were somehow gross, unfaithful to the honor of my craft.

The easiest answer is to say that, like most other humans, I am hungry. But there is more than that. It seems to me that our three basic needs, for food and security and love, are so mixed and mingled and entwined that we cannot straightly think of one without the others. So it happens that when I write of hunger, I am really writing about love and the hunger for it, and warmth and the love of it and the hunger for it ... and then the warmth and richness and fine reality of hunger satisfied ... and it is all one.

I tell about myself, and how I ate bread on a lasting hillside, or drank red wine in a room now blown to bits, and it happens without my willing it that I am telling too about the people with me then, and their other deeper needs for love and happiness.

There is food in the bowl, and more often than not, because of what honesty I have, there is nourishment in the heart, to feed the wilder, more insistent hungers. We must eat. If, in the face of that dread fact, we can find other nourishment, and tolerance and compassion for it, we'll be no less full of human dignity.

There is a communion of more than our bodies when bread is broken and wine drunk. And that is my answer, when people ask me: Why do you write about hunger, and not wars or love?

---

*Published in 1943.

◆

# Soup and Bread*

## One Hundred Recipes for Bowl and Board

### by Julia Older and Steve Sherman

## M. F. K. Fisher

◆

It is impossible to think of any good meal, no matter how plain or elegant, without soup or bread in it. It is almost as hard to find any recorded menu, ancient or modern, without one or both ... just as it is to read a book, or walk through a museum, without savoring one or both on the page, the canvas ... the mind's palate.

Of course bread and soup, being thus intrinsic to our survival, can be deeply personal things to the fortunate among us who are blessed with fearless memory. We read, for instance, about a soup served to an Egyptian princess or a Roman tyrant, or about bread broken long ago in the country called Israel—and then we taste, according to our cultural empathy and our gastronomical curiosity. But what we savor more keenly than these, if we are both lucky and honest, is a dusty soda cracker stolen from the pocket of a fat schoolfriend (shamed delight), or two bowls of a rich vegetable broth drunk lickety-split after a childhood fever (voluptuous satiety).

I have always been fortunate in this trick of recalling past pleasures, especially in times of inner drought and stress. They are food for the spirit. This is one reason why it is satisfying to find an intelligently compiled, sensitive, practical book called, with a simplicity that is reassuring, *Soup and Bread.*

It is evocative, as all good things should be ... on the page, the plate, the mind. It is well put together, so that a soup, and a good bread to go with it or even to follow it, face each other on the pages. Nobody need agree with how the authors have paired their recipes, for they can be used in any personal jumble. I myself would not like a Sally Lunn with Artichoke Soup; that is, my mental taste buds say that I would not. But I must think more about it ... try it....

The book evokes enjoyments, sensual memories. There is a good recipe for *Pan Dulce,* for instance, and reading, once more I am in the early market

*Published in 1978.

in a Mexican village, buying a warm sweet roll from a woman who walked for hours down the hills with the night's baking in a coarse cloth on her head. The bread was spicy, surprisingly rich for that spare country. I ate it from a piece of oily newspaper on the counter of a little open-front bar, and drank a local beer with it instead of the thick *sopa* suggested in this book, and it was a long time ago, but the taste of coriander and dark sugar and just-baked dough is still fresh.

It seems strange to me by now that when I was a child we were rescued by Sustaining Broths when we had been ill, and that the only real soup I remember eating with my parents was a rare Oyster Stew on the Sunday nights when Grandmother, our gastronomic mentor, was away. Of course, when I was drinking the invalid broths and downing the memorable Oyster Stews of my early days, the question of finding good bread was not yet dreamed of. Bread was good, that's all. The flour was good, and so was the water. If the current cook did not have a light hand with the dough, there was an excellent baker in town. Toast for breakfast, treats after school with strawberry jam, dried crusts for Bread Pudding stiff with raisins: we never *doubted.* We thrived.

Our gamut of baked breads was as limited as were our soups, almost: white, Graham, now and then hot baking powder biscuits or corn bread. The last two were "special" and served only at noon, but the others were ubiquitous. They were *there,* supposedly our right and privilege.

Once a very old woman told me what her even older grandmother had told her about Bread Soup. Across about a hundred and fifty years I heard again of the most comforting thing that could be eaten on this earth, at least in the days when the makings were unpolluted: broken pieces from yesterday's loaf, in a bowl, with a ladleful of boiling water poured over it and, on a feastday, a sprinkle of salt. This, the old, old woman told me through generations of gradually corrupted palates, was the best food in the world to comfort and bring sweet sleep.

Such a recipe is not found in a collection like this one. Indeed, its austerity is almost impossible to evoke with the mind's palate, so far are we from the child of 1830 who could find celestial what we would call prison punishment. Today's bread, today's water, even the iodized fluoridated salt? No.

That is another reason why this book is worth pondering. It nourishes us with simplicity, adjusted to our times, but also with many subtleties that are as amusing as they are plain. Why not put canned apricot juice in Cock-a-leekie Soup? It is logical, if you can read. And why not serve beer with one soup, milk with another, a Zinfandel here and a sparkling wine there? And the suggestion that sweet butter and wild grape jelly would do well with popovers! It is so sensuous that the scalp prickles ... centuries from a child's dream of bread-and-water....

We can be helped, in this less innocent world, to reach back a little in a book like *Soup and Bread.* Why not make something like Vegetable-Short Rib Soup, and some Wheat Germ Crackers ... find some good cold milk ... help a child of this century rise again?

## REFLECTING ON THE READING

Make a list of the foods that seem to nourish your spirit as much as your body. Describe one of those dishes in detail (aromas, textures, flavors, appearance) so that someone reading your description would feel the way you do about that dish.

◆

# DR. KELLOGG AND THE U.S. DIET

EVAN JONES

◆

*Most of you have eaten breakfast cereal at some time in your life. But you probably didn't know that it started as a health food developed by a religious group. See what else you learn in this article.*

Neither the Grahamites nor the Shakers carried matters of diet to the extreme espoused by a woman leader of the Seventh-Day Adventists, whose world headquarters had been established at Battle Creek, Michigan. She was Ellen White, wife of Elder James White, who had adopted Graham's ideas about food; Mrs. White was constantly receiving spiritual messages, and on Christmas Day 1865, she became convinced that the Adventists, who were frequently troubled by dyspepsia, should be treated in a sanitarium of their own. Not long after her vision became a reality, Mrs. White and her husband awarded a medical scholarship to a young Seventh-Day Adventist names John Harvey Kellogg, and the influence of Battle Creek on the American diet was set in motion.

While pursuing his medical studies in New York, young J. H. Kellogg breakfasted daily on seven graham crackers and an apple—once a week allowing himself a coconut as well, and occasionally including potatoes or oatmeal in the menu. Kellogg did his own cooking, and the chore increased his interest in developing a healthier diet for the patients he was being trained to serve back in Battle Creek.

"The breakfast food idea," he once recalled, "made its appearance in a little third-story room on the corner of 28th Street and Third Avenue, New York City.... My cooking facilities were very limited, [making it] very difficult to prepare cereals. It often occurred to me that it should be possible to purchase cereals at groceries already cooked and ready to eat, and I considered different ways in which this might be done." But it was two years later, after he had been put in charge of the Seventh-Day Adventist health sanitarium, that he hit upon a workable formula and, as he put it, "prepared the first Battle Creek health food which I called Granola." And in the following years, Kellogg told an interviewer, "I invented nearly sixty other foods to meet purely dietetic needs."

Granola may have been the first of the Battle Creek products that led to such twentieth-century breakfast items as Kellogg's Special K, but it was only one of the experimental precooked cereal products flooding the market before the turn of the century. Shredded wheat resulted from work done by Henry Perky, a dyspeptic who became an apostle of the wheat berry as the perfect food. He ran a vegetarian restaurant in Denver as well. His heart, however, was in the cooked grain product he developed and made famous as shredded wheat.[1]

Corn flakes are two words even better known internationally, and they acquired their specific meaning at the end of the century, when Dr. Kellogg and his brother Will perfected a method of flaking, which they first used on wheat kernels. Grape-nuts, so christened because the dextrose contained in the kernels was called grape sugar and because the new product had a nutty flavor, were developed by C. W. Post, who had come to the Battle Creek sanitarium as a patient of Dr. Kellogg.

In all their great variety, dry, precooked breakfast foods revolutionized menus for the morning meal. They helped to increase the consumption of milk and to minimize the high cost of living. Ironically, products that originated in the interest of improving health have undergone so many modifications to provide sweetness and other pleasant flavors that their once-vaunted nutritional values have been all but lost. A study conducted in 1970 indicated that forty out of sixty dry cereals may "fatten but do little to prevent malnutrition."

Still, many other uses have been found for breakfast foods since Mrs. J. H. Kellogg, author of *Science in the Kitchen* and *Every-Day Dishes,* published her recipe for "Cereal Pie Crust" made from her husband's products. Commenting on the "dietetic evils of Pastries," she said that "the very name

---

[1]It's unlikely that Perky imagined all the ways that eventually developed for using shredded wheat. Henry Wallace, who served as Franklin D. Roosevelt's least conventional vice president, seems to have relished a shredded wheat meal so unusual that it should, perhaps, remain unique: "The Wallace farm was an egg farm," Lillian Hellman wrote in *Scoundrel Time,* "and Ilo's dinner consisted of two poached eggs for Henry put on two shredded wheat biscuits, a horrid sight, made more insulting by one egg on shredded wheat for me and one for Ilo. It was the sight of this stingy, discourteous supper that made me say that I had already eaten and didn't wish anything else.... Ilo was undisturbed—what could disturb a woman who put eggs on shredded wheat?"

A woman who can make a baked pudding of two shredded wheat biscuits is in another category. Ruth Wakefield, who established a famous Massachusetts restaurant called the Toll House Inn, served her shredded wheat dessert with a hard sauce. Her recipe calls for crumbling the biscuits and mixing with a cup of milk, a slightly beaten egg, three-quarters of a cup of dark molasses, a teaspoon of cinnamon, and a little salt. The batter is dotted with butter and baked at 350°F. for three-quarters of an hour.

had become almost synonymous with indigestion and dyspepsia," and she worked out her recipe for a crumb crust not so much to increase sales as to steer cooks away from butter and lard. She stipulated one and a half cups of cereal crumbs in making a crust for a nine-inch pie; the crumbs, mixed with one to three tablespoons of sugar and six tablespoons of melted butter stick to the pie dish when pressed firmly against sides and bottom and should be prebaked at 325°F. for five minutes or a little longer.

Dr. Kellogg had said that the "original purpose in making the toasted flaked cereal was to replace the half-cooked, pasty, dyspepsia producing breakfast mush." In the considerable writing his wife did, she agreed, and she recommended that the newfangled flakes would provide "the very best capital upon which people who have real work to do in the world can begin the day." I would be surprised if she entertained the possibility of pancakes or waffles based on corn flakes, but such recipes were to come along nevertheless. For pancakes, corn flakes may be mixed with a buttermilk or sour cream batter and should be cooked at once to maintain their crunchy texture. Corn flakes also make interesting cookies. But Mrs. Kellogg might not have thought these innovations to be worthy enough. She was not one to gild the lily, for she advocated temperate eating in general. "A great variety of foods at one meal," she wrote, "creates a love of eating as a source of pleasure merely, and likewise furnishes temptation to overeat. Let us have well-cooked nutritious, palatable food, and plenty of it," she added, "but not too great a variety at each meal."

## REFLECTING ON THE READING

Read the list of ingredients on the side of a box of cereal. Write down all the ingredients that you are unfamiliar with. Try to find out why they are in the cereal. Answer the question "Is breakfast cereal still a health food?"

◆

# FOOD OWES HIM THE WORLD

BARBARA KAROFF

◆

*Almost anywhere you lived in the world in the Middle Ages, food was much more boring than it is today. Barbara Karoff explains how world exploration brought new foods and flavors to many parts of the world. As you read, look for information that is unfamiliar to you.*

*Barbara Karoff is a San Francisco native, food writer for national publications and author of "South American Cooking," published by Addison-Wesley.*

When Columbus landed in the New World 500 years ago, he set in motion a culinary revolution that quickly changed the eating habits of the entire world and helped form the national cuisines we know today. Columbus, of course, didn't set out to change the way everyone ate, but the enormous numbers of new foods discovered by him and those who followed did just that.

Now much of the world is involved in another culinary revolution, in which traditional ideas about cooking and ingredients are changing and evolving still further. This time we are experimenting and refining rather than adding large numbers of new foods to our diets.

In 1492, the world was poised and ready for the great Age of Discovery that marked the 16th century. Almost everywhere, people's lives changed rapidly as places as large as continents appeared for the first time on hastily drawn maps. Much of the world's population was about to receive a series of hearty and much needed flavor jolts right in the cooking pot.

Columbus, and the European explorers who followed him, returned from their overseas adventures with a wondrous variety of until then unknown foods. Quickly they turned the trade into a two-way process by returning to their new colonies with the staple food stuffs from the Old World.

The erudite and entertaining food writer, Raymond Sokolov, in his fascinating new volume entitled "Why We Eat What We Eat," argues convincingly against permanence in any country's food heritage. He believes that innovations in food are more important than tradition and that even the cuisines we think of as traditional are almost always cuisines in transition. It was true in 1492 and it is true today.

## A History of Exchanges

The Great International Food Exchange that took place in the 16th century was not, of course, the first time that cuisines and foods of different peoples mingled and merged, but it was the greatest and most full-scale example to date. It began as a deliberate effort of the Spanish crown, it continued of its own momentum and it involved most parts of the world and a far longer list of foods than at any time before or since. With the discovery of the New World, the great food exchange was under way in earnest and it soon moved into the fast lane.

Within 50 years, Spain established full-scale, European-style agriculture in her American colonies and was trading regularly with Asia via the Philippines. Her famed Manila Galleons crossed the Pacific from Manila to Acapulco, where the cargoes were hauled overland to Veracruz on Mexico's Atlantic coast and onto ships bound for Spain. The colonizers established farms in the New World and, according to official Spanish policy, planted wheat. By 1535 Mexico was in the wheat exporting business.

By 1500, slaves transported on Portuguese ships brought foods of West Africa to the New World colonies in what is now Brazil. Once there, the African foods and cooking methods (many of which had arrived on the African continent with the early Phoenician, Arabian, Persian and European traders) continued their travels throughout the Americas. They merged with indigenous foods and with the ones that continued to arrive from Europe and Asia. They helped to build foundations of today's South American Creole cuisines.

Individual foods, as well as many of the methods for preparing and preserving them, taken by the Spanish and Portuguese to the New World, were a legacy left to them by Moors who had occupied the Iberian Peninsula for 600 years.

wheat → Spain
oat → England
corn → main grain

## Setting the Table for the Future

By 1600, the food exchange between Europe and the Americas had created the essential ingredients of the cuisines in both hemispheres that we know today.

Exchange is the important word because, throughout the world, the shipments of food were never static or one way. It should also be noted that few of the foods that traveled from one place to another in the 16th century were mere exotic additions to fully established national cuisines because the national cuisines of the medieval Europe were undistinguished and virtually indistinguishable from one another. We simply would not recognize what we now think of as the national or traditional cuisines of Spain, Italy, France, Germany and Eastern Europe without the foods they have absorbed from the New World.

It would be just as difficult to recognize today's Mexican cuisine which, before the conquest, included no beef, pork or lamb, no oil, onions and garlic and no dairy products. Columbus brought most of these ingredients to the New World on his second voyage. How can we think of the Sechuan food of China, the curries of India and today's fiery dishes of Thailand and Southeast Asia without the chili peppers that are native to, and unknown outside of, the New World until the European discovery.

West African slaves were taken to Brazil and the Caribbean islands to work the sugar cane, which was brought to Spain and Portugal from India by the Moors. Columbus planted it in Cuba on one of his first voyages to the New World and the Portuguese introduced it (and the slaves) to Brazil.

The resourceful Africans brought with them seeds for food plants as well as long established cooking traditions and both flourished in the American tropics, where the climate and geography are similar to that of West Africa. These African contributions laid the foundations for the now world-renowned Bahian cooking and for a number of the Caribbean cuisines.

From these strongholds, many of the African foods and traditions eventually spread to the American South where they mingled again with other foods still arriving from Europe.

Taking a quick look at who and what contributed to this 16th century traveling food show emphasizes not only its diversity but its worldwide status as well.

*Foods travelled to Am*
*wheat beef pork*

## Guacamole Plus

Avocados, which we raise and eat throughout the year in California, are consumed in South America in far more innovative ways than they are any place else in the world. But they've had lots of time to experiment. Avocados were raised by both the Aztecs and the Incas long before the conquest. Seeds dating to 8000 B.C. have been found in what is now Peru, where they provided both protein and highly digestible oil to people who lacked both animal protein and oil in their diets. Today South Americans use avocados in appetizers and salads as well as in soups and stews (where they sometimes serve as thickeners), in frothy milk-based drinks and, whipped with a little sugar and lime juice, as a refreshing dessert.

Corn was also domesticated in Mexico and Peru as early as 7,000 years ago and, along with cassava, sweet potatoes and peanuts, was transported to West Africa. They have been raised in Peru since pre-Inca times and, after their introduction to Africa, they traveled back to the Western Hemisphere. This time they journeyed with the African slaves to North America, where, today, they are a multimillion dollar crop.

Cassava was a stapled food crop in the Amazon and Orinoco river basins by 2000 B.C. Although it has never been of much importance to most North Americans or Europeans, it is of major importance to the daily diets of 250 million people, most of them in South America and West Africa. It is a starchy root vegetable with little to recommend it in the taste and nutrition departments.

Sweet potatoes became popular in Europe almost as soon as they were introduced by Columbus. Within 100 years they appeared in China and from there, along with pineapple and papaya, they traveled to other parts of Asia and to the Pacific Islands.

Rice is native to India and was brought to the Iberian Peninsula by the Moors. From there, it traveled to the New World on Portuguese and Spanish ships where it became an important staple in Brazil and much of Latin America.

Chickens, pigs, cattle (and with the cattle dairy products), garlic, onions and olive oil were deemed essential and taken to the Spanish and Portuguese colonies almost as soon as the settlements became established. Today, or course, they are basic ingredients in all the Latin American cuisines. Later migrations of Germans and Italians to South America are responsible for much of the cheesemaking that often imitates Old World varieties.

Potatoes are native to the Andean highlands where they, too, have been raised since pre-Inca times. It was not, however, until the arrival of the Spanish and their cattle that cheese was first made on the continent. Today, many of Peru's most satisfying dishes combine potatoes and cheese in a heavenly marriage. They are, in fact, so well thought of in Peru they are often served as separate courses during a meal.

*Pilgrimage → 1603 → 'Turkey' fr. Spain*

## A Hill of Beans

Trade between Africa and the New World was eventually responsible for many of what are considered culinary essentials in both hemispheres. Kidney beans, okra, chickpeas, lentils and yams are all thought to have originated in Africa, although chickpeas (garbanzo beans) and lentils went to the colonies directly from Spain where they had long been popular.

Not only foods, but methods of food preparation traveled to the New World with the slaves. They introduced *dende* (palm oil) into Brazilian cooking. Despite the bad press it gets in North America, it is still considered essential in Brazil for its exotic orange color and elusive flavor. The black slaves were also responsible for introducing the techniques of wrapping and then cooking foods in banana leaves. It's a method still popular in parts of coastal South America, and, possibly, it translated into the tamales of Central America and Mexico.

The Europeans took corn, white potatoes, tomatoes and chili peppers to Africa, as well as to Europe, from the Western Hemisphere.

Chili peppers, one of Latin America's most important culinary gifts to the world, traveled many routes in the process of becoming established in cuisines around the world.

The Portuguese took the fiery capsicums to India and China via their trading colonies in Goa and Macao. They arrived in Northern Europe from the Balkans with the Ottoman Turks who had captured them during their siege of the Portuguese colony of Hormuz on the Persian Gulf. From the Balkans the chilies traveled to parts of the Holy Roman Empire, the former Byzantine Empire and to Russia. Right in the middle of this complicated exchange route was Hungary, which embraced the chili pepper and became Europe's largest grower and consumer. Hungary today is well known for its sweet and hot paprikas, which it exports to the rest of the world.

### South of the Border Birds

Turkeys, our very own Thanksgiving birds, are native to Mexico. From there they traveled to Spain, on to England and back to the New World, this time to North America.

Potatoes, most people now realize, did not originate in Ireland (despite how they shaped that country's history) but in Peru in the high reaches of the Andes. They were not widely accepted when first introduced to Europe, where they were regarded first as aphrodisiacs and later, by the food snobs of another era, as food for the poor.

The papaya was thriving in the New World when the colonizers arrived. It was transported about 100 years after the conquest, to Asia where it thrives today. Mangos, which had been growing in India for 4,000 to 6,000 years, were introduced to Europe via Portugal in the 16th century and taken by the Portuguese to the New World, possibly in exchange for the pineapple. Mangos are eaten today by more people in the world than any other fruit, and pineapples are widely cultivated in Hawaii.

Just for the record, chocolate and vanilla are also natives of Mexico. They were combined to create an exotic drink at the court of Montezuma. When it was served to Cortez, it made a lasting impression. When he returned to Spain with chocolate, it so impressed the Spanish crown that they kept it a secret from the rest of the world for many years. Chocolate was consumed only as a beverage before the Europeans finally devised the complex method of turning the raw product into confections.

This is far from a complete list. It only illustrates the exciting number and variety of foods that traveled around the world during the 16th century. This great exchange was responsible for establishing the foundations of the so-called national or traditional cuisines we associate with most of the countries of the world today. Once established, these cuisines continued to evolve and become more refined but changed very little until we entered the eras of refrigeration and jet airplanes.

Tradition and culture have always traveled with food, adding to and enriching the impact. Today, as we experience new and more subtle waves of culinary mingling, the cultural impact is no less important. Jet travel has shrunk the world but it has created nothing quite so enormous as what happened in the 16th century. Anything of such magnitude is not likely to happen again. Far fewer boatloads and planeloads of unknown foods arrive on our shores. What is happening today is far more subtle.

Goulash·· cowboy stew

### Identity in Cuisine

Most nations are frequently identified by their food. Because our country has from the beginning been a melting pot, and because of its sheer size and geographic and climatic variety, it is difficult for us to identify a truly national cuisine. Even dishes strongly identified with various parts of the country often originated in other parts of the world. Some, common to the coun-

coffe → South Africa

try as a whole such as our beloved hamburgers and hot dogs, fall increasingly into the fast-food category.

Rather than slowing down over the years, the arrival of new waves of immigrants to our shores has increased dramatically in recent times as our doors have opened to new people from Central America, the Caribbean, India, Southeast Asia, China and Japan, all places in the world with well-defined food traditions.

At the same time, we have reached a level of maturity that enables us to accept new ideas and new ingredients from the new arrivals. Especially along our Pacific and Atlantic coasts and along the borderlands of Texas and the Southwest, waves of new immigrants have had an enormous impact on what we eat. This impact will continue, spread to the hinterlands and become gradually more refined and more integrated.

This time around it is frequently the professional chefs, the food and cookbook writers, and others connected with the food industry who jump on the bandwagon and promote "new" food ideas, ingredients and trends.

In the Bay Area we see it happening every day. Restaurants, upscale deli and takeout operations and even the supermarkets help to promote the mingling and merging process. A San Francisco restaurant specializes in a mix of Asian and Italian cuisines. The spicy, fiery salsas of Latin America and the Caribbean light up restaurant menus with diverse ethnic heritages. As the strong and vital flavors and seasonings that distinguish the foods of the new immigrants become available, innovative and imaginative home cooks as well as professional chefs, hurry to adapt them to their own kitchens.

Change still fuels the fire. Food writer Sokolov's argument against permanence in any cuisine is still relevant. The great international food revolution that began in the 16th century is once again in the fast lane. In this country it is a continuation of our well established food heritage of accepting and adapting. Quite possibly, it is what makes "American" food the exciting experience it is today.


## REFLECTING ON THE READING

List the ingredients of a dish that is commonly prepared in your household. Using the information in "Food Owes Him the World," identify the original source of those ingredients.

◆

# THE GLORIFICATION OF ANOREXIC EMACIATION

*—unhealthy weight loss*
*—abnormally lean/malnutrition*

STEPHANIE SALTER*  *Bulemia —, eat & throw up.*
*Bulimia/Purging*

◆

*Anorexia and bulimia are two increasingly common*
*eating disorders, found especially among young women.*
*Think about your own attitudes about how you look*
*and how much you eat as you read Salter's article.*

Every day I pass it, and every day I get the same uncharacteristic urge: to take a big, broad, black ink marker and scrawl—in 3-foot-tall letters—FOR GOD's SAKE, HONEY, EAT!

"It" is a Calvin Klein underwear ad that occupies scores of Muni bus shelter advertising posters around The City. (Given that I consider graffiti a borderline felony, my desire to deface a billboard is no small deal.)

The ad features the super-hot model Kate Moss, reigning prototype of the popular just-liberated-from-Dachau look. In model jargon, it's called the "waif" or "gamin" look.

Actually, there are two versions: One shows Moss with her hand groping her own little breasts under her Klein T-shirt; the other is a straight-on frontal shot of Moss with one of her bony little legs bent and sticking out at an angle.

Lest anyone think this is about erotica in public advertising, understand: I've got no problem with the grope shot. In fact, I kind of like it. It's subtle enough. A kid would probably pass it by without a second thought. But it's suggestive enough to give a grown-up a little charge.

Even better, the grope shot is devoid of those rape fantasies that Georges Marciano and Guess Jeans made so dangerously mainstream in the '80s.

No, my problem is with the other ad, the one that shows so much of Moss' anorexic-looking frame. It is a painful sight. Whenever I get near it, I can almost smell the cultural sickness behind it.

As Canadian film maker Katherine Gilday pointed out in her 1992 documentary, "The Famine Within," the average North American adult female stands 5 feet, 3.8 inches tall and weighs 144 pounds. But as was also noted in the film:

"A collective delusion rules both sexes' perception of the female body ... Thin is 'normal' and everything else is an aberration."

---

*Stephanie Salter is a columnist for the *San Francisco Examiner.*

Consequently, at any given time, one out of two women in North America is on a diet, and 5-year-olds with eating disorders have begun to make their way into doctors' offices for treatment.

I don't know Kate Moss' vital statistics, but to say she resembles an 8-year-old boy who is recovering from tuberculosis is not to overstate the case. A grown woman with such a body is clearly the "aberration."

Yet, there she is. Emaciated, staring out blankly at all of us, the current female symbol of Calvin Klein, one of most talented and successful American clothing designers in history.

Look, I know we are talking about models here, and models have never been "real." The '80s were dominated by living Barbie dolls, models who were not only uncommonly tall and skinny, but who had uncommonly gigantic breasts.

And however grotesque things may be, at least women have not resorted to having a couple of ribs removed to achieve "the ideal figure," as they did in the last century.

Neither am I saying that Klein is a bad guy—just another heartless exploiter of women.

This week, Klein became the first person to receive both the Womenswear and Menswear designer-of-the-year awards from the Council of Fashion Designers of America. A hard-working, innovative and visionary craftsman, he seems most deserving of the unprecedented honor.

I'm not even saying that—my desire to deface aside—the public should be protected from Klein's glorification of scrawniness. Although it's getting harder to tell, the last time I looked, this was still a free country.

I'm just saying that Klein and the rest of us need to remember and give—you should excuse the term—weight to the effect that human symbols have on the population. Especially on impressionable girls and adolescents.

Journalist Caroline Miller, who chronicled her own struggle with bulimia in two books—"My Name is Caroline" and "Feeding the Soul"—recalled the first time she was seized with the compulsion to be thin.

At a restaurant with her family, she cringed when her father told the waitress, "The vanilla milkshake goes to the heavy one."

The next day, Miller began a diet. She was 8 years old.

## REFLECTING ON THE READING

Salter is irritated by the Calvin Klein underwear ad. Find a magazine ad, billboard, or TV commercial depicting a human body that really either irritates you or that you greatly admire. Explain what you find irritating or admirable in that depiction in five sentences.

◆

# THE LEGAL DRUG

ANNA QUINDLEN

◆

*Drinking beer has become just about as American*
*as eating apple pie. But in this article, former*
**New York Times** *columnist Anna Quindlen says*
*"beer is the dope of the quad." See what you think of*
*her argument.*

college students have more problem in substance abuse

For some it is a beverage, for some a habit, for some an addiction.

And those differences, perhaps more than anything else, explain why we have yet to come to terms with the vast damage that alcohol can do, with those it kills, those it harms, those who can't get loose from its sharp fishhook.

While even young children know that cocaine and heroin are nothing but trouble, while even young children know that cigarettes cause cancer, what they know and learn and believe about booze and beer and wine is different because it is the drug their parents keep in the refrigerator and use themselves. And that can be confusing.

The Center on Addiction and Substance Abuse at Columbia University quantified some of the results of that confusion this week. A commission report shows that "binge drinking is the number one substance abuse problem in American college life," far outweighing the use of drugs. The widespread use of alcohol at nearly every American school affects everything from the prevalence of venereal disease to the failure rate.

Ninety percent of all reported campus rapes occur when either the victim or the assailant has been drinking. At least one in five college students abandons safe sex practices when drunk that they'd use when sober. Two-thirds of college suicide victims were legally intoxicated at the time of death. Estimates of alcoholism range from 10 to 15 percent of the college population.

What's wrong with this picture? These statistics would normally be the stuff of vocal lobbies, calls for action and regulation. Instead alcohol manufacturers openly court the college market, advertising in campus newspapers despite the fact that many of the readers are too young to drink legally. In a 1991 report on alcohol promotion on campus, one marketing executive was quoted on the importance of developing brand loyalty in a student. "If he turns out to be a big drinker, the beer company has bought itself an annuity," the executive said.

"When parents visit, their concern is drugs," said one college administrator. "They're surprised if we want to talk about drinking. A few are even annoyed."

The demonization of drugs allows delusion about alcohol to flourish. There are 18.5 million people with alcohol problems and only 5 million drug addicts. More people who commit crimes are drunk than high. Illicit drug use on campus has decreased 60 percent in the last decade. Beer is the dope of the quad.

Colleges and universities are cautious in confronting alcohol use on campus; if they accept responsibility for policing it, administrators are concerned they will be held legally responsible for its effects. And for many parents, the legality of alcohol is a convenient excuse not to delve too deeply into the issues it raises for their kids, issues not only about drinking but about self-image. Research being done at Mississippi State University showed that many students drank to escape from anger and loneliness, to feel accepted and at ease.

College authorities and parents both have to find some way to communicate that using alcohol to anesthetize doubt and insecurity can become a lifelong habit as fast as you can say A.A. And that way lies disaster, disappointment, even death. The other day Betty Ford came with her daughter, Susan, to a symposium at the Center on Addiction and Substance Abuse so both could talk about how her family had to force her into treatment. "I suddenly found myself making excuses so that I wouldn't have to spend too much time over at the house," Susan said of the time when the former First Lady was addicted to booze and pills.

Cynthia Gorney, in an exquisite essay in The Washington Post last year, wrote of her mother: " ... she was a woman of curiosity and learning and great intelligence. She died in March, of cirrhosis of the liver, which is also what kills the men under blankets by the sewer grates."

But kids won't even begin to understand that until everyone starts to treat alcohol like what it is: a legal drug. That can be confusing too, since there are many who can drink with no ill effect and never come close to addiction. But just because many of us are safe drivers doesn't mean we don't acknowledge the existence of car accidents. And in the lives of many young adults, alcohol is an accident waiting to happen.

## REFLECTING ON THE READING

"Beverage," "habit," or "addiction"? Identify passages from the article that describe alcohol in each of these terms. Write a sentence stating your own opinion of alcohol.

◆

# DEMOCRACY AT STAKE

FRANCES MOORE LAPPÉ

◆

*Lappé argues strongly that some aspects of American agriculture threaten important American social values. Look for the evidence behind her arguments.*

I have talked of the resources and outright subsidies hidden in our cheap-grain-fed meat and how we are promoting this pattern of eating around the world. But I have left out perhaps the most critical lesson of all: how the production system that mines our resources also undermines social values we cherish. We have been taught that our production system rewards hard work and efficiency while providing abundant food for all, but it actually rewards waste, wealth, and size—and the hungry go without food no matter how much is produced. This is the most painful lesson I have had to learn in the last ten years.

## The Blind Production Imperative

In our production system, farmers' profits are in a continually tightening squeeze—between rising costs of production and falling prices for their crops. Their profits are squeezed because farmers are largely price *takers* who must confront price *makers* both when they buy what they need to make the land produce and when they sell their crops.

The first price makers are the manufacturers of farm inputs. Tractor manufacturers, for example, can pass on their rising costs to farmers in the form of higher prices, because farmers must have tractors and they are only a handful of manufacturers. The same holds true for fuel, pesticides, fertilizers, seeds, and other farming inputs. Farmers, however, cannot pass on their higher costs, because in selling their crops farmers meet the second price maker: the marketplace. Farm commodity sales may be the last truly competitive market, with thousands of units competing against one another. Farmers have to take whatever price they can get from relatively few major buyers. Going prices are determined largely by supply and demand, not by the farmers' costs of production.

Because they are at the mercy of price makers both in buying farm inputs and in selling their crops, farmers' profits per acre fall steadily. By 1979 profits per acre in real terms had sunk to one-half the level of 1945.[1] Because of their greater volume of sales, many large farms can survive these lower profits per acres, but smaller farms, *even if more efficient,* may not survive while receiving the very same price per bushel. Thus, ever lower profit margins favor size and force the smaller farms to try to become even larger. Moreover, simply to maintain the *same* income all farmers must try to increase production and lower production costs, regardless of the ecological or human consequences.

So Earl Butz's infamous "Get big or get out" was not a snide crack—it was sound economic advice. But who has the opportunity to "get big"? Only those farmers whose operations are already quite large, particularly those who have considerable equity in their land. They have the advantage when it comes to taxes, government payments, and marketing their crops.

But control of the land is key. Because of this incessant pressure to expand, the most limiting factor in production—land—steadily inflates in value. "Thus, simply owning land comes to be rewarded more highly than producing food on it," Marty Strange, co-director of Nebraska's Center for Rural Affairs, told me. "In other words, unearned wealth is a bigger factor today in farm expansion than earned income from farming." (For example, a typical farmer with 80 percent of his land paid for had an annual net income of $18,500 in 1978, but the value of the land itself increased by $34,600 that year, according to a 1979 government study.[2]) As the wealth of those with considerable equity soars, they have the collateral to buy out their neighbors down the road. By the mid-1970s almost two-thirds of all farmland sales involved the expansion of existing farms, a reversal of the 1950s, when two-thirds of farmland sales resulted in new farms.[3]

In this process, over four million farms have gone out of business in the last 40 years. Of those remaining, the top 3 percent now control almost half of all farm sales. By the year 2000, if trends continue, this 3 percent will control two-thirds of all farm output.[4]

In place of owner-run farms and widely dispersed control of our land, we see the possibility of what former Secretary of Agriculture Bob Bergland called a "landed aristocracy"; that is, more and more of the actual farming in this country will be done by tenants, sharecroppers, and day laborers.[5] Already in the "family farm" heartland of Iowa, more than half of the farms in some counties are operated by tenants or sharecroppers.[6] And those farms which are still owner-run will operate increasingly under contract to large export and processing firms. Newcomers, except the most wealthy, will be barred from entering farming.

The practice of better established, bigger farms gobbling up smaller ones is commonly defended on the grounds of more efficient production, yet already over half the value of all crops in the United States is produced on farms *larger* than can be justified on the ground of efficiency.[7] Moreover, costs of production on small to moderate-sized farms are often *lower* than on the biggest farms, according to the Congressional Research Service.[8]

Greater production and growing markets have always been held out to farmers as keys to their prosperity, but the most straightforward facts of our agricultural history deny this promise:

Our agricultural output has almost doubled in the last 30 years,[9] and agricultural exports have doubled just since 1970, yet the real purchasing power of an average farm family in 1978 was about the same as in the early 1960s.[10] And even this average masks the economic devastation of many (those unable to expand) and the meteoric rise of a minority. Eighty thousand dollars is the *average* net income of the 3 percent at the top, those who now control almost half of U.S. farm sales. The tiny group of 6,000 farms that captures 20 percent of farm sales now enjoys an average annual net income of roughly half a million dollars.[11] At the same time, if two-thirds of American farms tried to live off the sales of their crops alone, their income would fall below the poverty line. Their average income hovers close to the national median only because of increased nonfarm income.[12] And *that* average hides the continuing reality of rural poverty.

Thus, production itself, and efforts to dispose of it through livestock and exports (or, most recently, gasohol), can no longer be accepted as a solution to the plight of the farmer. For we can see where this blind production imperative has taken us—away from values that Americans have always associated with democracy, and toward a "landed aristocracy"; away from dispersed control over the land, and toward a highly concentrated pattern of control; away from a system rewarding hard work and good management, and toward one rewarding size and wealth alone. As I suggested earlier, ours is becoming the kind of farm economy that I have seen at the root of so much injustice and misery in the third world.

## Production Divorced from Human Need

We view our production system as rational, but what makes it go? It is motivated by this year's profits to the individual producer. We proudly cite abundant production as proof of the system's success. But "Does it produce?" cannot be the only question we ask. In judging our system, we must also ask, is it sustainable? Is it fair to its producers? I have already answered "No" to these questions. But the ultimate question which we must answer is, *does it fulfill human needs?* Production divorced from human need is not rational.

Our production is staggering: over four acres of cropland and pasture are producing food for each person in America. (That's the equivalent of about four football fields just for you!) We produce so much food that although roughly one-fifth is wasted altogether—simply plowed under or thrown out—we are still able to export the output on every third acre harvested. In fact, our production has been so great that one of the biggest government headaches over the last four decades has been the mountains of costly "surpluses."

Yet despite our abundance and the fact that our food prices do not reflect the true costs of production, middle-income families—$15,000 to $25,000 a year—must spend almost 29 percent of their income to eat a "liberal" food plan (as defined by the Department of Agriculture). Poor families must spend from one-half to two-thirds of their income just to buy a "low-cost" food plan.[13]

What's more, there is hunger in America.

"Hunger here?" The Dutch reporter interviewing me looked puzzled. "There can't be. I've never seen anything like your supermarkets. So much food. So many different kinds."

But I have learned that hunger can exist anywhere, within any society that has not accepted the fundamental responsibility of providing for the basic needs of its most vulnerable members—those unable to meet their own needs. And ours, sadly, is such a society. I found myself feeling ashamed when I learned that other societies with which we might compare ourselves—France, Sweden, West Germany—demonstrate by their welfare programs that they do accept this social responsibility. In a recent study of social benefits to needy families with children in eight major industrial countries, the United States ranked among the lowest. In France, a single, unemployed mother caring for two children would receive in benefits 78 percent of the average wage of that country. In Sweden, 94 percent. But in the United States she would receive only 54 percent—and in many parts of our country, much less.[14] (While benefits in other countries are uniform, in our system a person living in the South is likely to get as little as half the benefits of someone living in the Northeast, for example.)

Despite our staggering abundance, millions live in utter deprivation. Who are those denied access to America's abundance?

*They are the elderly.* Fifteen percent have incomes below the poverty line, and that percentage has begun to climb.[15] Forty percent of all unmarried elderly women in the United States live in poverty.[16]

*They are children, and the mothers who must stay home to take care of them.* Twelve million American children live below the poverty line, and poverty among inner-city children is climbing at a horrifying rate: between 1969 and 1975 poverty among related children under five rose, for example, 68 percent in Ohio and 49 percent in New Jersey.[17]

*They are the disabled and those unable to find work.* By the late 1970s, Americans were being asked to accept as normal an unemployment rate double that of a decade earlier.

In addition to the people who cannot work or cannot find a job, there are many Americans trying to support a family on the money they earn working for the minimum wage. You can work full-time for the minimum wage and still fall below the poverty line.

All told, 29 million Americans—about one in eight of us—live below the poverty line, which the government sets at about $8,400 per family of four.[18] Poverty-line income amounts to $583 a month, but family incomes of

$300 to $400 are more typical. To grasp how there can be hunger and other needless deprivation in our country, all I have to do is try to imagine meeting the needs of myself and my two children on $400 a month.

Many would like to deny that hunger and poverty exist in America. Just after Ronald Reagan's election as President, his chief adviser on domestic affairs declared that poverty had been "virtually wiped out in the United States." Since our system of government aid had been a "brilliant success," he added, it "should not be dismantled."[19] What irresponsible ignorance.

First, our welfare programs do not lift people out of poverty. *Even including food stamp benefits, in few states does welfare bring families even up to the poverty line.*[20] In half the states these programs do not bring families even to 75 percent of the poverty standard.[21] The second fallacy in this statement is that there could ever be a time when government welfare programs are no longer needed. This attitude reflects an unwillingness to accept responsibility for those who—in any society—cannot care for themselves, no matter how bright the economy looks.

But what about hunger. Even though poverty cannot be denied, haven't food stamps eliminated hunger? There is no doubt that food stamps have helped enormously, but they have not eliminated hunger. First, food stamps alone, at about 45 cents per meal, are not enough to supply an adequate diet.[22] The Department of Agriculture concluded that the diets of 91 percent of those families whose food spending is at the level of the food plan on which food stamp allotments are based are nutritionally deprived.[23] If they possibly can, most people supplement their food stamps with cash. But if you are trying to support a family on $400 a month, that means you'll probably have to squeeze some food money out of the rent or heating bill.

Other evidence exists to prove the reality of hunger in America. Poor children have actually been shown to be physically stunted compared to their middle-class counterparts. A Center for Disease Control study in the mid–1970s documented that up to 15 percent of the poor children examined showed symptoms of anemia and 12 percent were stunted in height.[24] Dr. Robert Livingston of the University of California at San Diego told us that "poor children have measurably smaller head circumferences than those in families with adequate income."[25]

Our infant death rate is another powerful indictment of our society. Because the infant mortality rate (deaths of babies less than one year old per 1,000 live births) in part reflects the nutrition of the mother, it is often used to judge the overall nutritional well-being of a people. Even though per person spending on health care has leapt tenfold in less than 20 years,[26] our infant mortality rate ranks 16th in the world, almost double that of Sweden or Finland.[27] In the United States, 14 babies die for every thousand born alive. This national average is "not enviable," the journal *Pediatrics* sadly notes.[28] But averages do not uncover the real tragedy. Among *nonwhite* babies the infant death rate is 22 per thousand, about the same as that of an extremely poor country like Jamaica.[29] Even assuming much better reporting of infant deaths here, this comparison should alarm us.

Even averages among nonwhites mask the extreme deprivation in some communities. In the Fruitvale area of Oakland, California, just across the San Francisco Bay from my home, the infant death rate is 36 per thousand. And in the capital of our nation the rate is 25 per thousand, approximately that of Taiwan.[30]

Perhaps the most convincing evidence of hunger amid abundant production comes from the few people who have the courage to go into our communities to meet and talk with those who are suffering from lack of food. One such person is a woman I met five years ago when we both participated in a Philadelphia "hunger radiothon," 24 hours of commercial-free radio in which all the breaks were used to tell people about hunger and its causes. Investigative reporter Loretta Schwartz-Nobel spoke about people starving in Philadelphia. As I was writing this book, I heard from Loretta again. This time she sent the manuscript that documented the hunger— even starvation—that she had witnessed. Her evidence includes many passages like this one, quoting an elderly former civil service worker in Boston:

> I've had no income and I've paid no rent for many months. My landlord let me stay. He felt sorry for me because I had no money. The Friday before Christmas he gave me ten dollars. For days I had had nothing but water. I knew I needed food; I tried to go out but I was too weak to walk to the store. I felt as if I was dying. I saw the mailman and told him I thought I was starving. He brought me food and then he made some phone calls and that's when they began delivering these lunches. But I had already lost so much weight that five meals a week are not enough to keep me going.
>
> I just pray to God I can survive. I keep praying I can have the will to save some of my food so I can divide it up and make it last. It's hard to save because I am so hungry that I want to eat it right away. On Friday, I held over two peas from lunch. I ate one pea on Saturday morning. Then I got into bed with the taste of food in my mouth and I waited as long as I could. Later on in the day I ate the other pea.
>
> Today I saved the container that the mashed potatoes were in and tonight, before bed, I'll lick the sides of the container.
>
> When there are bones I keep them. I know this is going to be hard for you to believe and I am almost ashamed to tell you, but these days I boil the bones till they're soft and then I eat them. Today there were no bones.[31]

If your reaction is that Loretta has simply ferreted out a handful of senile old people who refuse government help, read her book *Starving in the Shadow of Plenty* (Putnam, 1981). She is convinced that the people she met are only the tip of the iceberg. "It's happening all over the city," said a social worker in the community where this starving woman lived. "They can't get welfare; they're too old for the job market and too young for Social Security. What can we tell them to do? Tell them to go to the hospital and get treated for malnutrition?" In a Mississippi community, Dr. Caroline Broussard told Loretta, "Whole families come here malnourished. But what's worse is that we know for every hungry child or adult we see here in this clinic there are 20 to 30 others in the area we are not getting to." And in New York City, according to the Community Service Society and a number of public officials, 36,000 people are living on the streets. Again, we think of homeless street people as a third world tragedy. Yet their numbers are increasing right here in America.

### Illusion of Progress

Most Americans believe that since the late 1960s we've made steady progress in eliminating hunger and poverty, due to the introduction of food stamps, school lunch programs, and supplemental feeding programs for pregnant and nursing women. And it's true that these programs have had an impact. In 1967 the Field Foundation sent a team of physicians to investigate hunger in America. Their tour of depressed communities riveted national attention on hunger. Ten years later another Field Foundation team of physicians returned to the same localities. Their 1979 report noted "fewer visible signs of malnutrition and its related illnesses," although "hunger and malnutrition have not vanished." They attributed the improvement *not* to overall economic progress for the poor: " ... the facts of life for Americans living in poverty remain as dark or darker than they were 10 years ago. But in the area of food there is a difference. The Food Stamp Program, the nutritional component of Head Start, school lunch and breakfast programs, and to a lesser extent the Women-Infant-Children (WIC) feeding programs have made the difference."[32]

Clearly there was progress for those who received the benefits. But these benefits are totally inadequate. (A Texas family of four, for example, is expected to make do on $140 a month in welfare benefits.)[33] Moreover, poverty programs have never reached all those in desperate need of them. The food stamp program reached only half of those eligible for most of its life, reaching two-thirds of those eligible only after rule changes in 1977.[34] Programs for pregnant women and young children have served only one-quarter of those eligible.[35]

Moreover, the value of all our welfare programs has been declining over the 1970s because, except for food stamps, benefits are not tied to inflating prices. And now even food stamp benefits are falling behind. The poor are the worst hit by inflation because they spend a much larger share of their income on necessities, and the prices of necessities (housing, food, fuel, medical care) rose twice as fast as nonnecessities in the 1970s. Inflation has cost welfare recipients 20 percent of their purchasing power over the decade.[36]

In sum, if the lives of the poor have improved at all over the last two decades it has been, for the most part, not because of increases in job-related incomes but because of government programs, such as the grossly inadequate health and food assistance I've just discussed. And even these gains are being reduced by inflation and cut by President Reagan and the Congress elected in 1980.

As to the alleviation of poverty itself? New figures from the Census Bureau show that gains made since the mid-1960s had been virtually wiped out by 1980, even *before* the Reagan administration began to ax social-welfare programs. And in 1981 the nation experienced one of the biggest increases in poverty since the early 1960s, when the Bureau first started collecting poverty statistics. In early 1982, a county administrator in South Carolina told *The New York Times* how he experiences poverty's tightening grip: "The population of the jail has tripled, even though there has been no increase in serious crime," he said. "People get themselves arrested on some minor violation so they can get a meal or two, and I can prove that."[37]

"We're at risk of turning back the clock to a time when hunger and malnutrition were common in this country," Nancy Amidei told me. Nancy is director of the Food Research and Action Center in Washington, D.C. Over the last year she has talked throughout the country with low-income people who are already being affected by the Reagan budget cutbacks. What they told her can be summed up by 82-year-old Luisa Whipple who told a congressional committee, "I plead with you not to cut back the food stamp program, because as you cut back food stamps you cut back on our health and you cut back on our lives."

Every society must be judged as to how well it meets the basic needs of those unable to meet their own, and on whether it provides a living wage to all those able to work. Our society fails on both counts. How can we act on this judgment? First, we must keep alive in our minds the reality of hunger amid the massive squandering of food resources, for only a sense of moral outrage can keep us probing *how* our society evolved so as to divorce production from human need—and only a sense of moral outrage can force us to question our everyday life choices, asking just how each choice either shores up or challenges the economic assumptions and institutions that generate needless suffering. The "what can we do?" is then answered, not in one act but in the entire unfolding of our lives.

What we eat is only one of those everyday life choices. Making conscious choices about what we eat, based on what the earth can sustain and what our bodies need, can remind us daily that our whole society must do the same—begin to link sustainable production with human need. And choosing this diet can help us to keep in mind the questions that we ourselves must be asking in order to be part of that new society—questions such as, how can we work to ensure the right to food for all those unable to meet their own needs, and a decent livelihood for all those who can work? How do we counter false messages from the government and media blaming the poor and hungry for their own predicament?

Ironically, the notion of relating food production to human needs might strike most Americans as a "radical" idea. We know we're in trouble when common sense seems extreme! But maybe it hasn't gone that far yet.

"We've been going at it from the wrong end in the past," Agriculture Secretary in the Carter Administration Bob Bergland admitted. "This country must develop a policy around human nutrition, around which we build a food policy, and in that framework we have to fashion a more rational farm policy."[38]

1. General Accounting Office, Report by the Comptroller General of the United States, *An Assessment of Parity as A Tool for Formulating and Evaluating Agricultural Policy,* CED 81-11, October 10, 1980, p. 18.
2. U.S. Department of Agriculture, *Status of the Family Farm,* Second Annual Report to Congress, 1979, p. 3.
3. Marvin Duncan, "Farm Real Estate: Who Buys and How," *Monthly Review of the Federal Reserve Bank of Kansas City* (June 1977), p. 5
4. William Lin, George Coffman, and J. B. Penn, *U.S. Farm Numbers, Size and Related Structural Dimensions: Projections to the Year 2000,* Technical Bulletin No. 1625, Economics and Statistics Service, U.S. Department of Agriculture, 1980, p. iii.
5. Lyle Schertz and others, *Another Revolution in U.S. Farming?,* Agricultural Economic Report No. 441, Economics and Statistics Service, U.S. Department of Agriculture, 1979, pp. 300 ff.
6. Diocesan Coalition to Preserve Family Farms, *Fourteen-County Land Ownership Study 1980,* Diocese of Sioux City, Iowa, 1980.
7. U.S. Department of Agriculture, *A Time to Choose: Summary Report on the Structure of Agriculture,* Washington, D.C., January 1981. Table 24, p. 58, indicates that 100 percent of the economics of scale are, on average, reached when sales average $133,000. From Table 5, p. 43, one can calculate that roughly 50 percent of sales are from farms above this size.
8. Leo V. Mayer, *Farm Income and Farm Structure in the United States,* Congressional Research Service, Library of Congress, Report No. 79-188 S, September 1979, Table 11, p. 31. The lowest per unit costs of production—expenses per dollar of gross farm income—are found on farms with gross sales between $20,000 and $99,999 a year; the highest on farms with sales over $200,000.
9. *A Time to Choose,* op. cit., p. 56.
10. *Another Revolution in U.S. Farming?,* op. cit., p. 31.
11. *A Time to Choose,* op. cit., pp. 46-47, 144-45.
12. Ibid.
13. E. Phillip LeVeen, "Towards a New Food Policy: A Dissenting Perspective," *Public Interest Economics-West,* April 1981, Berkeley, California, Table 1.

14. Alfred J. Kahn and Sheila B. Kamerman, "Cross-National Studies of Social Service Systems and Family Policy," Columbia University, School of Social Work, 622 W. 113th St., New York, N.Y. 10025.
15. Warren Weaver, "House Unit Finds Aged Getting Poorer," *New York Times,* May 2, 1981.
16. National Advisory Council on Economic Opportunity, *Critical Choices for the 1980s,* 12th Report, August 1980, p. 15.
17. Ibid. pp. 16–17.
18. Census Bureau figures, as quoted in the *San Francisco Chronicle* of August 21, 1981.
19. Mike Feinsilber, Philadelphia *Enquirer,* December 24, 1980, quoted by Loretta Schwartz-Nobel, *Starving in the Shadow of Plenty* (G. P. Putnam's Sons, 1981).
20. Tom Joe, Cheryl Rogers, and Rick Weissbourd, *The Poor: Profiles of Families in Poverty,* Center for the Study of Welfare Policy, The University of Chicago, Washington office, March 20, 1981, p. iii.
21. Ibid.
22. Robert Greenstein, Director on Food Assistance and Poverty (former administrator of the Food and Nutrition Service, U.S. Department of Agriculture), statement before the Senate Committee on Agriculture, Nutrition and Forestry, April 2, 1981.
23. Interview with Robert Greenstein, May 30, 1981.
24. Nick Kotz, *Hunger in America: The Federal Response,* The Field Foundation, 100 East 85th Street, New York, N.Y. 10028, p. 13.
25. Interview with Dr. Livingston by research assistant Sandy Fritz, May 1981.
26. President's Commission for a National Agenda for the Eighties, *Government and the Advancement of Social Justice, Health, Welfare, Education and Civil Rights in the Eighties,* Washington D.C., 1980, p. 33.
27. M. E. Wegman, *Pediatrics,* December 1980, p. 832.
28. Ibid.
29. *Statistical Abstract,* 1978.
30. "Infant Mortality Highest in U.S. Capital," *New York Times,* December 13, 1981.
31. *Starving in the Shadow of Plenty,* op. cit.
32. *Hunger in America,* op. cit.
33. Robert Greenstein, testimony (see note 22).
34. *Access to Food: A Special Problem for Low-Income Americans,* Community Nutrition Institute, Washington, D.C., April 1, 1979, p. 17.
35. Interview with Nancy Amidei of the Food Research and Action Center, December 1981.

36. Greenstein, testimony, and Gar Alperovits and Feff Faux, "Controls and the Basic Necessities," *Challenge*, May-June 1980.
37. "Poverty Rate on Rise Even Before Recession," *The New York Times*, February 20, 1982.
38. *Dietary Goals for the United States*, Second Edition, prepared by the staff of the Select Committee on Nutrition and Human Needs, U.S. Senate, December 1977, reproduced by the Library of Congress, Congressional Research Service, March 31, 1978, p. xxxi.

## REFLECTING ON THE READING

Write out the sentence you most strongly agree or disagree with in Lappé's essay. Write a paragraph explaining specifically your reasons for agreeing or disagreeing with her statement.

◆

---

# WHAT IS A TACO, ANYWAY?

COLMAN ANDREWS

---

◆

*Colman Andrews sees a contradiction in American attitudes toward food. As you read, try to decide what he means when he writes "Americans eat badly" or "Americans eat well."*

*"I am looking rather seedy now while holding down my claim,
And my victuals are not always of the best...." ***

Americans eat badly. Our food is over-salted, full of sugar, full of fat. Much of it is highly processed to the point of being artificial—filled with emulsifiers, extenders, preservatives, and dyes—and even when it's not, it's often canned or frozen into insipid mush. Our bread is like cardboard, our cheese is like plastic, our fish is two weeks old. We care more for speed and convenience, both in our home kitchens and in our restaurants, than for flavor. Worst of all, we scarcely notice how bad our food is and probably wouldn't mind much if we did notice, because we have no real appreciation for the art and romance of gastronomy.

---

* "The Little Old Sod Shanty" (American Folk Song)

Contrast

basis

Americans eat well. We enjoy a variety and a quality of produce, meats, and other foodstuffs all but unparalleled in the world. We're learning to moderate our consumption of salt, sugar, and animal fats, and we're starting to demand (and get) good bread, fresh fish, organically grown fruits and vegetables. Our recent "culinary revolution," inspired by James Beard and Julia Child and led by Alice Waters, Wolfgang Puck, and their colleagues, has raised standards of both cooking and dining in this country dramatically, and promises to turn us finally into a nation of true gastronomes.

Who *cares* how Americans eat? We're all still here, aren't we? We must be doing something right. What more is there to say about it? Food is no big deal. It's just fuel—something you put in your belly when you're hungry. So what if it's processed? So what if it's organic? And what's all this crap about "gastronomy"? Why don't we all just shut up about food and get on with our lives?

There is something to be said for each of these positions. Each is, in a sense and to an extent, quite easy to defend. We eat badly, we eat well, and we probably worry too damned much about which is which.

What we don't do, however, is eat the way we used to. That "we" contains multitudes, of course. There is no single American diet, and no single American attitude toward food, or level of sophistication regarding it. We are a famously diverse people, and the way we eat (and think about eating) both reflects and reinforces our diversity. Still, no matter who we are or what we had for lunch today, our diet has changed significantly over the past twenty years or so.

minor details

The most obvious changes, because they're the ones that get written about the most in our magazines and newspapers, are those impelled by fad, or by fad's slower-but-surer cousin, trend. I'm thinking, for instance, of "California cuisine" and "designer pizza," and of the cooking of the "Pacific Rim" or the "New Southwest"—none of which anyone had ever heard of twenty years ago. In those days, too, food that was "blackened" got that way by mistake. (Now you can get blackened catfish in coffee shops.) Tuna came exclusively in cans—and it wasn't "dolphin safe" or packed in spring water, either. The jagged little greens we now refer to jauntily as "field salad" or "*mesclun*"—and buy, prewashed, for twelve bucks a pound—were thrown away as weeds. Salmon caviar was fish bait.

minor details

But other changes in our eating habits are more basic, and almost certainly more permanent, than any of our high-profile infatuations with individual ingredients or cuisines. I'm thinking, for example, of the marked increase in our consumption of seafood in recent years—and of the fact that, fad foods aside, our supermarket produce sections now carry more than twice the number of items they did ten years ago. And I'm thinking of the epic internationalization of American cooking—the way in which, on every level, it has so eagerly embraced and adapted the flavors of an entire world.

One day about fifteen years ago, as my father and I were driving down Santa Monica Boulevard in Los Angeles, we happened to pass a Mexican-themed fast-food stand with a banner reading "TACOS 25¢." My father turned to me and asked, "Just what *is* a 'taco,' anyway, son?" At that point in his life, he had lived in southern California for roughly forty years.

My father was not by any means an incurious or provincial man. In his heyday in Hollywood, he probably ate more dinners in restaurants and night-clubs than he did at home. Later in life, he traveled frequently to Asia and the Middle East, making more than twenty trips (as he liked to say) "east of Suez"—and presumably ingesting, of necessity, all manner of exotic and no doubt sometimes daunting dishes. Yet it had somehow never occurred to him, in all his years in southern California, to sample one of that region's most popular and widely available culinary specialties—a food item so typical of L.A.'s casual, Hispanic-flavored, eat-on-the-run culture as to be almost heraldic of the city. Apparently, he had never even wondered what it was before. It simply had no relationship to the life he lived.

If my father were alive today, I think he'd know very well what a taco was. The food not just of Mexico (and of Italy, France, China, and Japan—the basics), but also of Thailand, India, Ethiopia, Morocco, Central America, the Caribbean, Spain and Portugal, and more is represented amply in our cities today, offering us a seemingly endless menu of new culinary possibilities. This is true on the fast-food-and-frozen-dinner level (tacos and pizza have, after all, become as American as apple pie—and even dim sum and falafel have recently applied for citizenship), and it is certainly true in temples of the "new American cuisine." Dining in the present-day equivalents of the restaurants he used to frequent, my father would almost certainly be introduced, perforce, not just to tacos but to sashimi, paella, satay, and lots of other things he likely never tasted (although those tacos might well be filled not with fast-food ground beef but with duck breast, venison, or sea bass—say, just what *is* a taco, anyway?). The melting pot has found its ultimate metaphorical expression in the cooking pot.

I think all this is great. I think we're growing up gastronomically as a nation. We've certainly got more good restaurants than we used to have, more cuisines (both traditional and hybrid) to choose from, more food products with which to construct our meals, more good cookbooks, more good wines. We've also started paying more attention, finally, to the relationship between diet and health—and we're at least beginning to accept the possibility that good flavor and nutrition can go hand in hand.

That's the bright side of the American food story. At the same time, though, I think many of the apparent changes in our eating habits have been illusory, and even sometimes just plain phony. Whatever claims we may hold down, or victuals are still not always of the best.

If we've got more good restaurants today, we've also got more fast-food chains and "theme" eateries—apparently the theme of good food served well is not sufficient—and more dining "concepts" and contrivances (as if we needed to be *tempted* to eat, somehow, like children who will only take their vitamins if they're shaped like Yogi Bear). For every conscientious chef striving for purity and authenticity in his food, we've got a thousand—*ten* thousand—self-styled mass-feeders (who asked 'em?) cloaking precooked frozen entrees in sugary, salty premixed sauces. And, sure, our supermarkets offer ever-larger choices of fresh fruit and vegetables—but they also stock ever more varieties of frozen diet dinners, sugar-coated cereals, imitation eggs and butter, canned "pasta," and those mysterious powdered products that are said to be able to "help" tuna and ground beef (to do what?).

Almost half the $260 billion that Americans spend annually on food goes for highly processed items, and sales of snack foods (potato chips, etc.) alone have more than doubled in the last ten years. Indeed, the idea of "natural" food is such an anomaly today that our supermarkets have to have a special section for it—a section usually considerably smaller, it might be noted, than those devoted to the sugar-coated cereals and the frozen diet dinners.

Even our fresh fruits and vegetables aren't always what they seem. True, they're beautiful to look at—but do they have any flavor? Any aroma? Walk into the middle of your local supermarket produce section and inhale deeply. What do you smell? The damp, earthy scent of mushrooms and potatoes? The bright perfume of pineapples and melons? The frank, gassy odor of cauliflower or broccoli? Probably not. You're more likely to smell the disinfectant on the floor, or the produce manager's cologne. Meanwhile, our tomatoes are a well-known joke. Our strawberries are watery and pithy. Our garlic is old and dry. Our produce travels well, but it doesn't deliver.

A lot of this is our own fault: All too often, we take what we're given. We're gullible about food. We'll swallow anything. We believe those strawberries taste great because they *look* great. We believe (to appropriate the motto of one brand of precut freezer-bin fish fillets) that "frozen fish is fresher." We believe glossy magazines when they tell us that, for instance, basil is "out" this year and cilantro is "in"—as if the culinary validity of herbs that have been used for thousands of years was somehow affected by the capricious eating habits of a few thousand trend-conscious Americans!

And we're inconsistent: We might make much of bright young chefs and unusual cuisines—but at the same time we've somehow bought the lie that the only way to feed millions of people efficiently is with food that is processed, packaged, degraded. When we clamber onto airplanes, we obediently gobble down our tired, steam-soaked "flight-kitchen" dinners like so many starving sheep—as if *this* eating had nothing to do with the eating we do in restaurants and thus needn't be held to the same standards. And in our hospitals and schools, we accept without protest our canned fruit cocktail and our pressed turkey with instant mashed potatoes, as if this is the best that can be done under the circumstances.

Meanwhile, we pay lip service to unusual, well-written cookbooks, but make best-sellers out of aw-shucks TV chefs, and out of a culinary Barbara Cartland named Martha Stewart (whose evocative good-life reveries might almost have been penned by "Elizabeth Lane," the Barbara Stanwyck character in the original 1945 version of *Christmas in Connecticut*—except that Stewart, unlike Lane, apparently really leads the life she describes). We probably know more than ever about wine, and have access to an ever-greater choice of bottles, but we buy it by label instead of by taste. Anyway, our drinking-age young men and women seem to favor pallid beer, or cocktails made with Jell-O. And "health"? Let's face it: For all too many of us, the most significant nutritional event of recent years has been McDonald's debasing of its already sorry excuse for a hamburger with carrageenan, a gelatinous substance extracted from seaweed—*voilà*, the McLean burger.

Whatever tendencies we might have toward gastronomic sophistication as a nation, we ain't no gastronomes yet. Whatever we may like to tell ourselves while we're planting borage in the windowbox or buying our month's supply or Arborio rice and balsamic vinegar or ordering our American-eclectic carpaccio or tajine down at the local trenderia, we're still mostly just going through the motions. We haven't come to terms with food yet. We haven't accepted it as a natural and enjoyable part of normal life.

Something about food is eating us in America today, I think. Something about food unsettles us, makes us nervous. For some strange reason, and in many strange and senseless ways, I think we're afraid of food.

### Food Without Fear

*"It would seem that for thousands of years man has been eating all the wrong things! He has enjoyed the sense of taste that Nature has endowed him with, and all the time Nature was an ignoramus!"*[*]

When I say that Americans are afraid of food, I mean that we're afraid to buy it, because we're not sure how to pick it out or what it ought to cost; we're afraid to cook it, because we don't begin to understand the cooking process; we're afraid to eat it, of course, because we've heard about all the awful things it can do to us; we're afraid to utter its very name, for heaven's sake, because we'll probably pronounce it incorrectly.

Above all, we're afraid to *enjoy* food, or at least to let our enjoyment show—because, in this country, people who like food too much are objects of suspicion, likely to be branded by their peers as sissies, gluttons, or elitists, or held in pity and contempt for their obvious "self-destructive" tendencies. Somehow, we've managed to turn the primal act of eating—which ought to be appreciated as a glorious gift to humankind, a daily wonderment—into a sort of necessary evil, or at best a furtive pleasure. We don't *trust* food. We think it's out to get us.

---

[*]Pierre Andrieu, *Fine Bouche*

As noted, of course, a large and conspicuous portion of our fear is physical. Food—our very sustenance—is seen increasingly as something deleterious to health, something that threatens life as much as it sustains it. As any reader of the popular press has surely learned in recent years, our lettuces and apples now drip pesticides like venom; our poultry is laced with harmful hormones; the animal fats we eat so freely are pure poison (may as well drink arsenic-spiked lemonade or oleander tea!); raw eggs, even in the form of mayonnaise (or of ice cream!), are breeding grounds for salmonella—and raw oysters on the half shell are little more than bivalved petri dishes growing hepatitis cultures wholesale; caffeine causes cancer (or is it heart disease?), and so does the stuff they use to decaffeinate coffee; wine rots your liver and turns upright citizens into drunken butchers at the wheel.

Food also makes us fat. In this (theoretically) most diverse and individualistic of societies, we end up worshipping supposed ideal body types more reverently than did the most platonic-minded denizens of ancient Greece. We diet desperately and repetitively—becoming more obsessed with food in our avoidance or our measuring of it than we were when we just ate the stuff. In extreme cases, some of us literally starve ourselves to death, or purge our bodies violently, spewing back food gulped down in the first place not for nourishment or pleasure but in a vain attempt to fill an emptiness that, sadly, turns out not to have been attached to our digestive systems at all.

Physical fear of food is as ridiculous as it is sometimes tragic. Foods that people have been eating with impunity for centuries haven't suddenly turned deadly. Of course, it makes sense to limit our consumption of some foods—but maybe that's the whole point, the elegance of the design. Maybe we're not supposed to turn the best foods into commonplaces. Maybe we suffer from them, when suffer we do, because we've taken them for granted, gotten used to having them at whim. Only a fool or a glutton eats a pound of Stilton or a dozen scrambled eggs a day. On the other hand, some "bad" things are just *so good*—for instance, the fat-striated meat and sweet peripheral fat of good *jamoón jabugo* or prosciutto from Parma or San Daniele, the juicy cheeseburger with a pile of perfect French fries, the catfish rolled in cornmeal and fried in bacon fat, the fettuccine cloaked with concentrated butter and Parmigiano, the rich vanilla ice cream topped with toasted almonds and warm caramel or chocolate—that I simply cannot believe that we're not meant to enjoy them at least occasionally. (Those dieters who sport bumper stickers reading *"Nothing tastes as good as thin feels"* haven't been eating the right stuff.)

Why are we so susceptible to fear of food? I think there's a lot more to it than mere physical trepidation. I think the problem is fundamental. Somewhere along the line, and for whatever reasons, our innate ability as a national (as a culture) to understand and appreciate food has been bred right out of us.

Maybe it's our rigid sociopolitical underpinnings—what people tend to call our "puritanical" heritage (though I suspect that the average seventeenth-century Puritan emigré to the New World ate with a good deal more guiltless gusto than does the average urban secretary or construction worker today). Maybe we're too busy making money, making deals, making our own lives, to worry about just making stocks and vinegars and jellies. Maybe growing food ourselves and shopping for it enthusiastically and cooking it at home seem too much like corny old-country pursuits to us—things our grandparents did grudgingly, because they had to, but from which we have been liberated. Maybe the sheer abundance and variety of food available to us in America has overwhelmed us and finally anesthetized us to the keen, bright possibilities of the kitchen and the table. Maybe some of us are simply born incapable of appreciating food, in the same way that some of us are born without good hand-eye coordination or an ear for music.

Whatever the reasons, we're simply not connected with food anymore. We don't know where it comes from, how it gets from there to here, what it looks like whole—and mostly we don't want to know. We don't want to see food in its unfinished (i.e., fresh) state—dirty, bloody, raw, still in pods or shells. We want it washed, prepackaged, ready-to-serve. We don't want to take our time with food, to smell it, taste it, think about it, cook it with love or at least with wit. We just want to grab it, bolt it down, get it over with, hope it doesn't hurt us too much. We have no real investment in it to begin with, and so when we're told that it's not good for us, we don't fight back, we don't defend it. Can't eat Brie anymore or have that second glass of beaujolais? we ask. Who cares? Just pass the cheddar-flavored rice cakes and the kiwi-flavored mineral water.

(I was amused by the popular reaction to the announcement by a group of French researchers, late in 1991, that foie gras and other poultry fat might actually be beneficial to the human cardiovascular system: Everybody scoffed and tittered. A common response was something like "Oh, *sure*, the French *would* say that." Yet similarly, preliminary studies suggesting that this substance or that might be *dangerous* are taken as gospel. It's as if we want to believe the worst.)

I found what I'd call a positively emblematic example of our cultural disconnection from food in, of all places, the *Los Angeles Times* food section, as recently as late 1989: A column called "You Asked About" bore the headline, "Exactly What Is Meant by Phrase 'Leftover Chicken'?" The lead query itself read, "I would like to find out about getting chicken to the form requested in recipes that call for 'leftover chicken.'" The question stunned me. Was this a joke? No, it was apparently a legitimate, serious request for information, and it was answered seriously by the *Times*. ("When a recipe calls for 'leftover chicken,' any mildly seasoned roasted, broiled, baked or poached poultry may be used....")

Obviously, the person who made the request was someone to whom chicken was not a bird, but rather a series of neatly trimmed (and probably skinless, boneless) pieces of anonymous pale flesh, neatly portioned out and wrapped in plastic. If the supermarket didn't sell something called leftover chicken, I suppose, then leftover chicken was beyond this correspondent's ken. (One day soon, supermarkets probably *will* sell something called leftover chicken, precisely to satisfy the obvious demand for such a product.)

Here's another example of how divorced we sometimes are from the reality of food: One evening, over dinner at the Gotham Bar & Grill in New York, I happened to mention to one of my dinner companions that the potatoes in my fish stew—Yukon Golds, perfectly cooked—were some of the most delicious I'd ever tasted. "You mean there are different flavors of potato?" he asked, incredulous. We are a society that accepts without question the need for several dozen flavors of canned coda and forty or fifty kinds of cat food—but it never occurs to many of us that there is more than one kind of potato or apple or salmon, or that there might be any point in having more than one. (In fact, something like 400 varieties of potato were cultivated in the Andes in pre-Columbian times.)

On the positive side, I love this story told by landscape designer and writer Rosalind Creasy (author of *The Complete Book of Edible Landscaping* and *Cooking from the Garden*) in an interview in the Berkeley-based monthly *Bay Food:* A neighbor boy was waiting near Creasy's yard for his father to pick him up. Creasy asked him if he'd like to pull up a carrot while he waited. He looked confused. Could he find a carrot in her yard? she asked. No. That's because they grow underground, she said. "They do?" he asked. Creasy continues: "I showed him where it was and had him pull it out. He was so excited! He runs over to the car. 'Daddy, look at what I have! A carrot!' It's as if I had just given him some fancy toy from the store. He'll remember that carrot forever. Because in that instant, he realized that this stuff comes from the ground."

Even people who cook regularly and even rather well often betray a curious unfamiliarity with the nature of the materials they use, as well as a curious procedural rigidity, as if they're just going through the motions, making food by rote, with no idea of what they're really doing. Thus an outdoor cook who can grill New York steaks to perfection on the Weber has no idea what to do with T-bones. A mother cooking Thanksgiving dinner flies into a tizzy because she's out of powdered sage—even though there's fresh sage growing in the windowbox. A would-be baker rejects a recipe that calls for vegetable oil because all there is in the cupboard is peanut oil—and peanuts aren't really vegetables, are they? Some home cooks are reduced to indecision by recipes that list optional ingredients. "Well," they demand, "do I add the chervil or not?"

Don't misunderstand me: I'm not proposing that we all go sign up at the Cordon Bleu, or that we should all start making everything from scratch, churning our own butter, baking our own bread (even in Europe, it's mostly only show-offs or the poor who bake their own bread today), butchering our own calves. On the other hand, it probably wouldn't hurt if we all knew how to open a wine bottle, strip thyme leaves from their stalk, and maybe clean a fish. More to the point, I think we all ought to remind ourselves now and then that food is or was a living thing, a product of our environment—and that it deserves appreciation and respect as such. I believe, for instance, that when we eat vegetables, we ought to remember that they come from the soil and that the "dirt" we sometimes recoil from and wash down the drain has in fact nourished them and given them their character. I believe that when we drink wine, we ought to be aware of it both as an agricultural product and as a miracle of the benevolent decay known as fermentation. I believe that when we eat meat or fish or fowl, we ought to realize that we are consuming the flesh and blood of a fellow creature, which died to give us strength and pleasure.

I also believe that the way people eat and drink is one of the most vital and authentic things about them as a culture, linking them individually to their ancestral past and their communal present, and connecting them as a people, immediately and intimately, with the earth itself and its seasons and cycles. Thus I believe that betraying our culinary past, and even more so our culinary instincts—which is precisely what we do when we rely too heavily on processed foods, and shrink from food as if it were poison, and carelessly lose touch with the reality of food—is dead wrong, and very nearly unforgivable; and that a critical concern with food and drink—even a mild obsession with it—is, far from being somehow trivial or unhealthy, both sensible and admirable.

And I believe, above all, that we ought to learn to dine, or even just sit down and eat, not with fear or with the feeling that we're doing something bad, but with the happiness born of appetite and anticipation—with, if possible, sheer, ravenous joy.

## REFLECTING ON THE READING

What food do you eat even though "it isn't good for you"? Write a paragraph extolling the pleasures of some rich, fat, or sugary food that you especially enjoy. Make your readers wish they had the food you describe.

# PUTTING IT IN WRITING

## RESPONSES

1. List three of your favorite foods. Select one, describe how it is prepared, and explain what you like about it.
2. Draw a diagram of the store where you most frequently shop for food. Label the major sections of the store. Then formulate an explanation for why the store is organized as it is.

3. Some nutritionists say breakfast is the most important meal of the day. Describe your typical breakfast, both what you eat and the circumstances under which you eat it. Would you claim breakfast is your most important meal?

## Reading for Meaning

1. In the United States, the word "corn" has been applied to the native grain "maize." Check your dictionary to learn the original meaning of "corn."
2. Use the reference area of your library to learn what role the following organizations play in the growing, processing, labeling, and distributing of the food you eat: Food and Drug Administration, Department of Agriculture, Environmental Protection Agency, National Research Council, Center for Disease Control, Food Research and Action Council. You may want to form groups of six, with each group researching one of the organizations and then sharing your information.
3. Organize an "Information Scavenger Hunt" in your class. Form groups of equal size. See which group can be first to identify accurately the following names: Zinfandel, Sechuan, Bill Moyers, Ralph Nader, Henry Wallace, Lillian Hellman, Ralph Lauren, John Smith, Seminole, C. W. Post, Earl Butz, Yogi Bear, Barbara Cartland, Barbara Stanwyk, Brie.

## Organizing Your Ideas

1. Make three columns on a piece of paper. Put "tastes great" on top of one, "less filling" on top of the second, and "high nutrient content" on top of the third. Put all of the common foods and drinks you consume in a normal week in one of these categories. Now try to form a general statement that describes your results.
2. Use the ingredients listed on your three favorite packaged foods and determine which contribute to nutrition, which contribute to taste, and which contribute to preserving the food. If you have trouble determining the role of an ingredient, explain how you would get that information.
3. One version of a balanced meal would call for meat (or protein), vegetable, starch, and dairy ingredients. Identify typical meals from Italian, Chinese, Mexican, and Indian restaurants. Now put the ingredients of each meal under one of the four food groups listed in the first sentence.

## Writing a Paper

1. Check your local newspaper for a restaurant review by a food critic. Using that review as a model, write a review of a fast-food restaurant you frequent.

2. Based on the reading in this chapter, identify a problem in food production, processing, or distribution. Find at least one source outside of the textbook that provides more information about that problem. Now write a paper in which you attempt to convince your classmates of the importance and significance of solving this problem. Explain the problem in some detail and show the negative results of not solving the problem.

3. Identify a controversy regarding food, such as vegetarianism vs. meat-eating; dieting for social reasons vs. dieting for health reasons; using pesticides on crops vs. organic farming. Take one side of the controversy and present at least three arguments to support your opinion.

VEGAN / OVA LACTO VEGAN
↓
VEGGIE BURGER
↓
BUGGING
↓
PROCESSED FOODS

There are enough vegetables that vegetarians can at. This is according to the Dept. of Agriculture, that we are producing so much food in the croplands, that ⅕ of it just go to waste. Besides, being a vegetarian is not easy, I am a vegetarian myself

Lotus STJo  .. Macintosh HD
open up          Application
click File c     NetApps
open file open loc
↓
http://www.yahoo.com
click (Aspects) (work of) (line) (network)
(type name) (Join)

Frank & Ernest, as couch potatoes, are told to lower their standards. What on television does not meet your standards?

# Television

Television pervades our lives. The car, the airplane, and the electric refrigerator changed American lives in the first half of this century, but the box with moving pictures has become the defining technology of the second half of the century. Newton Minow, chairman of the Federal Communications Commission during the Kennedy administration, reports that, in 1961, Americans watched television an average of 2.2 hours per day. By 1990, the average had risen to 7.3 hours—per day! Thus, if the average person works 8 hours, sleeps 8 hours, and watches television 7.3 hours, we must do everything else in 45 minutes everyday. That doesn't seem quite right, but the whole subject of television watching is quite tricky. Many people say they never watch television. One survey found that people who say they never watch television actually watch an average of 8 hours per week. Obviously, anything that human beings spend so much of their time with must be fairly important.

Critics worry about the effects of television watching, as well as the content of the programs. What do people actually experience when they watch television? Is it a vast wasteland? Or is it the major cause of violence in American society? Or is it a cornucopia of entertainment and informational delights? Or is it a habit-inducing drug that contributes to the moral decay of our culture? Or is it just a box with pictures that some people make too much fuss about?

When people discuss television, they often don't even mean the same thing. To some, "television" means only the prime-time programs produced by the major networks. To others, it means only that programming intended as pure entertainment. Still others include only the act of watching programs as "television." But, the term applies to all of that and more: cable programming; public service and news programming; programming on local public access channels; home videos; movies viewed through a video cassette recorder; information services provided through the television; video games played on your home television set.

The readings in this section have been selected to give a range of perspectives on the role of television in our culture. You should find many opinions with which you agree and disagree. Before reading any material in this section, make an inventory of your own television watching pattern. List programs you watch regularly and those you watch occasionally, note the times when you watch whatever is on, and figure out the total number of hours you watch in a typical week. Because one popular opinion says that watching a lot of television is bad, many people underestimate the actual amount of time they watch it. Try to make an accurate assessment of your own practices.

◆

# HARRIED WITH CHILDREN: TV's BAD SCENES FOR KIDS

KATHLEEN PARKER*

*Kathleen Parker uses a dramatic anecdote to illustrate her point. In making her point, she assumes a relationship between television viewing and its effects on children. State the assumption Parker has.*

She wears gold lamé.

A sparkling, thigh-high dress that leaves her muscled thighs free to roll rhythmically as she belts out a sound best described as … primeval.

Stage right: Enter Generic Muscle Man. In leather.

He strides across the room, undulating like the floor of snakes in Raiders of the Lost Ark. He pulls the mesmerized girl, in a hip-swiveling, snake-and-bird ritual, to the top of a staircase.

Are we panting yet? Stick around.

There, he binds her torso in a straitjacket. Yes.

Then he pulls out, you got it, The Chain.

Roughly, as though wrestling a young bronco to the ground, he wraps the cold links around her delicate ankles.

---

*Parker writes a lifestyle column for the *Orlando, Fla., Sentinel*.

The music escalates, the bass deepens to a heart-stopping thud. The girl suddenly begins to struggle as she realizes that Prince Charming is, in fact, Mr. Goodbar.

Her eyes shift frantically, hopelessly looking for someone, anyone, willing to save her.

As the music reaches a crescendo, the leather-clad man, who looks like Arnold Schwarzenegger's worst nightmare, pushes the helpless girl down a, what's this? A slide.

Yes, it's a slide. Like a serpent, it slithers—gleaming and inevitably—into a pool of water. There, the girl, now surely doomed, writhes and wriggles—not only helpless, but, yes! Wet!

Cut!

That's a wrap, as they say in show business. What we've just witnessed is not real. It is an MTV-type vignette being made within the television show *MacGyver*, which airs at 8 p.m. on Mondays.

MacGyver, who seems like a nice guy, ambles over to the singer and sums up the action: "I'm impressed," he says. "Catchy tune."

How's that? Catchy tune?

We've just witnessed the Marquis de Sade's wildest fantasy on prime-time television, during which an innocent girl is seduced, then bound and murdered to a drumbeat to resurrect King Kong, and all MacGyver can say is "Catchy tune"?

How about, "That was bizarre"?

This show, while perhaps common fare for Monday nights, took me by surprise. I flipped to this station quite innocently, as might any child with a remote-control box in his hot little hands. This was my first evening in front of the tube in about two years.

We banned television a couple years ago not because we're smarter than or morally superior to the rest of America, but because our children argued incessantly about who was in control of the idiot box.

After carefully considering the matter for 30 seconds or so, the grown-ups decided we were in control and put the TV set in the basement.

Lo and behold, the arguing stopped. And the grown-ups began to sorely miss television. The news, of course.

So last month I bought a small 7-inch television for my husband's birthday so we could watch the news while fixing dinner in the evenings.

This is significant for the following reason. When one is unfamiliar with something—whether a football game, a hurricane or prime-time television—one tends to be more objective about it.

To say that I was shocked by this programming, which any young child could have watched, is like saying childbirth can cause some discomfort.

Objectively speaking, such programming borders on the pornographic. While there may arguably be a time and place for some pornography, depending upon one's definition, that time and place is certainly not during prime-time family television viewing hours.

So the girl doesn't really get seduced or murdered. She doesn't really get wrapped in a straitjacket and bound with a chain. Adults would know that, if they paid attention.

But young children, who watch television at 8 o'clock on Monday nights, might not. The line between fantasy and reality is barely discernible for most young children. In the cartoons, on television and in the movies, nobody ever really dies.

In the end, it doesn't matter whether the girl gets away. The message is clear: Large, powerful men seduce and murder pretty young women while shrewish sexual sirens lure them with their songs.

Fantasy or reality.

## REFLECTING ON THE READING

Parker's example is dramatic, but is it common? Sample the programming from 7 P.M. to 9 P.M. in your viewing area. Compare notes with your classmates. How many "bad scenes" can you identify?

◆

---

# PASS THE CHIPS

MARK LEYNER

---

◆

*Mark Leyner takes a humorous approach to a technology that may solve part of the problem identified by Kathleen Parker in the preceding article. Decide whether you think his proposal is worthwhile.*

I was excited to read recently about a new technology that enables parents to automatically block out television programs that they consider deleterious to their kids. This technology utilizes an unoccupied portion of the television signal which can serve to transmit a ratings code for shows that feature excessive violence, nudity, sexuality, and naughty words. So we'd have "V" for violence, "N" for nudity, "S" for sex, "O" for obscenity, etc. And your TV set or cable box could then be equipped with a computer chip that could be programmed to block out shows with any or all of these ratings.

Now, you probably think I'm about to hoist the oriflamme of the First Amendment and wage a holy battle against any gadgetry that facilitates censorship in any form. Sorry, I have a brand-new daughter, and I'm already aware of the grim reality: technologically speaking, it's us against them—us, the parents, against them, the kids. My kid, Gabrielle, is only five weeks old, and somehow she has already learned how to manipulate the signal from her baby monitor so as to jam my microwave and VCR when she's cranky. Her mother and I have just hired a pediatric counter-insurgency expert from the Rand Corporation to assist us in eavesdropping on and, if necessary, interdicting some of the electronic communication that our daughter is involved in. So I applaud the new technology—it gives us a critical new weapon in our parental armamentarium.

I'm disappointed, though, in the selection of targets at which the lock-out chips are being aimed. A "V" chip for violence? An "N" chip and an "O" chip for nudity and obscenity? Come on! On any given promenade through New York City, Gaby's going to encounter the brutal economic disparity between rich and poor, which is more profoundly violent and, over time, more morally inuring than any shoot-'em-up or love-in-the-afternoon flesh fest she'll ever see on the tube.

I'd like to make the following recommendations to the Federal Communications Commission for further televisual exclusion. How about a "J & L" chip that will enable me to lock out *John & Leeza from Hollywood*? Have scientists sufficiently studied the neurological effect of this kind of stultifying pabulum on the developing brain? Until they do, I want it scratched from little Gabrielle's television *carte du jour*. What about a "KL" chip, a "PS" chip, and a "B" chip—Kathie Lee, Pauly Shore, and Barney? I don't want that sludge clogging up the Gabster's synapses, any more than I want lead-paint flakes in the girl's Lucky Charms. And I'll be the first to call the local Nobody Beats the Wiz to order an "AH" chip. There's no way I'm going to permit the unctuous, sycophantic repartee of *The Arsenio Hall Show* to etch itself upon the tabula rasa of my little G's mind. I'll also be at the front of the line for a "CRC" chip—a Charlie Rose Condensing chip—which will automatically modify Charlie's obtrusive and verbose interview style. I'd like to be able to get a word in edgewise at the breakfast table when Gab starts talking. And I'm sure I'm not the only parent who will opt to install an "MT" chip—*Masterpiece Theatre*. I'm sorry, but I just don't think it's healthy for Gabrielle to be exposed to Edwardian bachelors who resemble the members of Duran Duran discussing the assassination of the Archduke Ferdinand week after week. And I propose an "SV" chip—Single Viewing. It's fine to watch *It's a Wonderful Life* once, but not fifteen, twenty, forty times. Such obsessive viewing habits can foster a dangerous confusion between knowledge of trivia and erudition. Young people can come to believe that knowing the derivation of "Zuzu's petals" is as valuable as knowing which countries were the Axis powers during the Second World War. As a teen-ager, my sister Chase watched *Funny Girl* in its entirety some seventy times. She came to regard Fanny Brice as a spiritual icon and prophet, like Joseph Smith. Today, Chase is a loving mother and an accomplished actress, but not without having had to undergo a fortnight of rather harrowing deprogramming in a New Brunswick motel room when she was twenty-one.

Lest you think that I'm some kind of hyperintellectual anti-television snob, let me assure you that I'm quite the TV addict. Give me a turkey club, a Scotch-and-soda, and some ESPN, CNN, QVC, C-SPAN, *Kojak* reruns, scalp-paint infomercials—whatever—and I'm a contented man. I've even met with my local-cable-company president about the feasibility of a twenty-four-hour Thesis Defense Channel. But we'd be naïve not to be concerned about the effect of the hegemony of television over, for instance, our kids' literacy. Just the other day, I was interviewed by the young editor of a very hip magazine, and she asked me what I was reading, and when I said George Eliot's *The Mill on the Floss* she immediately assumed that it was a book about dental hygiene.

It's time for us parents to draw a line on our television screens that our kids cannot cross. We owe it to the little ones to show some guts, take a stand, and let the chips fall where they may.

## Reflecting on the Reading

Some might call this blocking chip a "bozo filter." What five programs or commercials would you want blocked on your TV set? Write a one-sentence explanation for each of your choices.

◆

---

# Blest be the TVs That Bind

## Matt James

---

◆

*Matt James is communications director of the Kaiser Family Foundation in Menlo Park, CA. In contrast to the preceding writers, he discusses several beneficial results from television. As you read, think of additional examples of good effects from television.*

When I was a kid, the show was *All in the Family*. Before that, *Laugh-In* and *The Smothers Brothers Comedy Hour*. Predating these was *The Ed Sullivan Show;* in later years, we all saw *Roots*.

These shows sparked national debates on issues that crossed generational, cultural, educational or class lines. When Archie Bunker's idol, a former pro-football player, revealed he was gay (tame stuff today, but a real shocker in the early '70s), it was written about in the newspapers, hashed over on talk shows and discussed at dinner tables across the country.

Likewise, Alex Haley's *Roots* helped educate America. Growing up near Detroit, we were unaccustomed to lengthy discussions about slavery and its consequences.

For the past 40 years, television has helped Americans share experiences. Many shows dealt with controversial moral and ethical issues facing society. Many more were just entertainment, from sporting events to sitcoms. In the simpler days of three networks, PBS and a smattering of independent stations, television served as a national sounding board for ideas, news and information.

Cable television began to change this. For the first time, television consumers could control more of what they saw and, coupled with VCRs and pay-per-view, when they saw it.

Now comes the information superhighway. It soon will provide us with 500-channel cable systems and countless ways to interact with one another as well as with services, government and schools.

The opportunities are restricted only by the imagination of programmers. A brave new world, right?

Hardly. There are major questions that surround this new technology, from how much consumers will have to pay to whether equal access will be provided to less-powerful groups. Still, most industry experts expect that in the near future, television viewing will operate like this: You will be provided with menus of viewing (such as sports, comedy, drama, music) and within these groups will be subgroups (the basketball channel, the rap-music channel, the Muslim channel) for you to choose from.

More diversity. Empowerment of viewers. But what of shared experiences?

Will there still be a place for a ground-breaking show or revealing documentary for the general populace?

It hardly seems likely. Instead, it appears programmers will continue the current trend of designing programs for narrow interests. With the problems that advertisers will face with this system (who are going to watch ads when they can scan 500 channels?), we may end up with a system where viewers are charged for what they watch. This means they will only watch what directly appeals to them.

Thus, the cross-pollination of cultures, ideas and opinions may actually be affected by a megachannel system. The system that many hope will ensure diversity may instead ensure that individual groups will tune out others' opinions and experiences.

Ten years from now, perhaps 20 channels will be available to "born-again" Christians, five channels to the gay community and 10 for the black community.

What are the odds that black or gay communities will engage in constructive discussions of family values with "born-again" Christians? If dialogue and exchanging points of view are the keys to constructive debate, how does that debate begin without debaters?

This is not to defend the past practices of networks. Far from it.

Shows like *Sanford & Son* presented white America with a glimpse of the black community that was untroubling and unrealistic. But then there was *The Cosby Show, Harvest of Shame* and other shows that helped weave minority voices and experiences into our national fabric.

By contrast, a recent, provocative episode of *Nova* focused on the Tuskegee syphilis experiments. It may have been seen by a wide audience when there were just three major networks and PBS. But of the people I know, it was seen only by a black doctor and a black journalist.

Our multichannel future is inevitable. The changes will be profound.

But as we head down this new information superhighway, we need to realize that television is a unique tool to educate us about each other. Let's hope the information superhighway will ultimately teach us more about each other and not further isolate us.

## REFLECTING ON THE READING

List five television programs or commercials that have affected you positively. Write a one sentence explanation of the good effect from each example on your list.

◆

---

# KILL YOUR TELEVISION

JAMES A. HERRICK

---

◆

*James A. Herrick is an associate professor and chair of the Department of Communication at Hope College in Holland, Mich. He wrote this article for the Scripps Howard News Service. Herrick will offer you five reasons for eliminating television from your life. Look for each reason as you read and see if you agree with those reasons.*

People sometimes ask why I, a professor of communication, do not have a television in my home. When I try to explain this apparent inconsistency, the usual response is something like: "I admire that decision, but I don't think it would work for me."

Television presents a dilemma: Many of us find that it does not represent a productive or enriching use of time, but we nevertheless find it attractive as a source of entertainment and information.

So how can a thoroughly modern American choose to get rid of the tube without committing cultural suicide?

Eliminating television from your life can be a perfectly reasonable decision. Here are some of my reasons for taking the cultural path less traveled.

First, I object to the system that drives television. Commercial television in America today must be understood, not principally as a medium for delivering entertainment and information, but as an enormous industry centered on garnering viewers of commercials. Entertainment and information are bait in television's great fishing expedition for audiences. And television seeks audiences for only one reason—to sell those audiences to advertisers. Commercials are the point of *commercial* television, and programming is a means of securing attention to those commercials.

When I watch television, I am investing uncompensated time as a "commercials viewer"—my time is being sold to an advertiser by a network.

No, thanks. I've got better things to do.

Second, television viewing is a gigantic waste of time. The typical American family has the television on for five or six hours each day, and in many households it's on considerably longer than that. The only other activities to which most of us devote that much time are work and sleep. Our reward for that investment of time is a meager one—a heavily edited view of world events through "news" programming and the shallow comedies and tragedies of prime time. Given the choice, I would rather spend that time reading, taking a walk, talking with a friend. Which brings me to my third point.

Television robs relationships of time. Relationships among friends and family members take time to develop—quantity time. Marriages, for example, are nurtured on communication, and this communication takes time—lots of time, regular time. Television steals the time it takes to build and enjoy real-life relationships, which are a lot more satisfying than sitcoms.

Doesn't time spent watching television together build relationships? No. Television does not usually encourage communication, either while people are watching it or afterward. I am an advocate of conversation, and thus an opponent of television.

Fourth, let's face it: Television programming is mostly vacuous, noxious or both. Need I elaborate? Does television programming typically set a high standard for personal conduct? Does it ask me to think hard about what I ought to value, and why? Does it provide insights into the intricate issues that face any citizen of this increasingly complex and diverse society?

Television seldom does any of these things. And even when it inadvertently does accomplish a worthwhile goal, there are any number of surer paths to these ends. Most of us need more, not less, incentive to live humanely, think broadly, and engage relationships emphatically.

My final reason for turning off the tube is that involvement with it is often based on an unexamined concept of entertainment. Television is usually justified as a means of entertaining ourselves, of relaxing from the demands of work. But many of us have accepted uncritically the Hollywood notion of entertainment as "amusement without boundaries," whether those boundaries are of time or subject matter. I am not arguing against the fatigued duo of sex and violence. Rather, I am asking: How much time should go to entertaining myself, and which activities are really relaxing? Maybe I'm missing something here, but I don't find television viewing relaxing at all.

Finding better sources of entertainment, information and relaxation is not difficult. People freed from the tube find a lot of imaginative and satisfying ways to fill newly discovered time.

Each of us has precious little time to use as we wish. Why should so much of that time go to television?

## REFLECTIONS ON THE READING

List each of Herrick's reasons for not having a television. For each reason, write a one sentence reason that counters Herrick's argument.

◆

---

# THE TIES THAT BIND 'WISEGUY'

JOYCE MILLMAN

---

◆

*Most major newspapers have one or two television critics, writers who try to look deeper into television programs. Joyce Millman's article is an example of a critic's effort to go beneath the surface of a popular, prime-time series. Compare what Millman says about Wiseguy with a "cop show" that you have watched.*

On cop shows, there are good guys and there are bad guys, and then there are good guys pretending to be bad guys. *Miami Vice* was the fist series about undercover detectives to suggest that good guys might actually get a thrill out of playing bad. But as the sun sets on that increasingly tapped-out show, the stars are rising for CBS's *Wiseguy,* executive producer Stephen J. Cannell's finest hour since *The Rockford Files.*

*Wiseguy* follows the adventures of streetwise federal agent Vinnie Terranova (Ken Wahl), who was trained by a supersecret FBI branch for long-term infiltration of organized crime; to authenticate his cover as a mean operator, he served two years in a federal pen—it looks good on a resumé when you're trying to get hired by the mob.

Vinnie is so deep undercover as a syndicate thug, he has trouble remembering which side he's on. "You live with these guys who are supposed to be the black hats and you realize they're not much different from us," he confesses to his brother Pete the priest, the only person outside the Bureau who knows that he's really not a hood. "They worry about puttin' on weight. They take the garbage out at night. They love their kids." Except, unlike Vinnie, the black hats live by a code of honor. They don't betray their friends.

As its growing cult knows, this show is really about friendship, betrayal and hypocrisy. Like *Mean Streets* and *The Godfather*, *Wiseguy* is layered with religious metaphors and pungent Italian-Catholic guilt.

Vinnie is tormented by the fact that he makes a living upholding a system that isn't concerned with the human details. "I took down a guy, a black hat. At least he was supposed to be," Vinnie tells Father Pete in their mother's kitchen in Flatbush. "And I could hardly hear myself think about him because of the 30 pieces of silver in my pocket. And I'm supposed to be a white hat.... I turned friendship and loyalty into an obscene joke."

But Father Pete is also having a hard time living up to the orders of the Home Office: "When a girl walks by in a halter top, don't you think I get a twinge?" he snaps at Vinnie. The show's message is clear: Cop, priest, or gangster, anyone who says one thing and does another is an undercover agent of sorts, a living lie, a walking ghost.

Cannell, who created *Wiseguy* with partner Frank Lupo, has always been fascinated by the idea of undercover—he also created *Baretta, Toma* and *21 Jump Street,* and with *Stingray,* he attempted to make his own edgy, cool version of *Miami Vice.*

But with *Wiseguy,* he takes "Vice" a step further. On "Vice," Crockett and Tubbs are largely voyeurs. Except for the fluky episode (based on Michael Mann's film *Manhunter*) in which Crockett develops a weird empathy with a psycho killer, Crockett and Tubbs always know who they are, always stop short of succumbing to the temptations of their job.

But Vinnie is in over his head because, to maintain his cover, he has to do whatever is asked of him, even kill people—or seem to. It doesn't matter that in the show's corniest plot device, Vinnie always manages to phone home to get his chief, Frank McPike (played with deadpan sarcasm by Jonathan Banks) to equip the would-be victims with bulletproof vests and memberships in the witness protection program.

What matters to Vinnie is that, staged murder or not, he *did* pull the trigger. And what gives him nightmares (and in one episode, sent him to group therapy for undercover cops) is that he's not sure if he did it to save his skin or to fit in.

You can't have betrayal without friendship. And the most intriguing part of *Wiseguy* is the mutual affection that develops between Vinnie and the richly characterized villains who appear in seven- or eight-week cycles.

Vinnie's beefy Stallone-ish looks are his ticket to the inner circle. He stays alive by appearing to be a stupid muscleman who surprises his underworld bosses with his ambition and smarts; he reminds them of their hungry young selves. Vinnie lets them think they've discovered a diamond in the rough. And they trust him more than their yes men.

*Wiseguy* takes male bonding, a staple of cop shows from *Starsky and Hutch* to *Miami Vice,* to delirious, often hysterical heights. You have to laugh sometimes at the show's heterosexual heroes going through their brawny rituals (roughhouse, sexual bragging, sports talk) because the show keeps veering, without irony and apparently without intention, into homoeroticism—just as Vinnie's and his buddies' banter keeps edging into self-conscious send-ups of love talk.

Face it, this show is *weird.*

Take the series-opening "Sonny Steelgrave cycle" (which has achieved cult status for Ray Sharkey's performance-of-a-lifetime as Sonny). The first meeting between Sonny and Vinnie (Vinnie was planted in the Steelgrave family after Sonny's brother killed a federal agent) turned into a bare-knuckles boxing match that played like both courtship and test of manhood.

Soon, Sonny was making Vinnie his righthand man, turning to him for help as rival families plotted his demise. Vinnie was spellbound, and why not? Like Vinnie, Sonny was just a cocky kid from the old neighborhood making it big. "We're businessmen, entrepreneurs," Sonny tells Vinnie. "The difference between us and Iacocca is that when he's successful, he gets his picture in the paper. When we get it right, they put our pictures in the Post Office."

When it came time to reel in Sonny, Vinnie stalled—Sonny had only killed other gangsters. What was so terrible about that? But in the frantic final episode of the Steelgrave cycle, "No One Gets Out of Here Alive," Vinnie did his job.

After a long chase, Vinnie and Sonny ended up in an abandoned movie theater, in another knock-down fist fight. They finally stop brawling because their hearts aren't in it—they like each other too much. Instead, in Sharkey's tour de force final scene, Sonny offers Vinnie a quaff from his bottle of whiskey, slaps the jukebox upside the head and they start jawing about girls, fathers and lost dreams.

In the big windup, Sonny asks "How will you remember me?" and their eyes lock just as the Moody Blues' "Nights in White Satin" gets to the part that goes, "I love you, oh how I love you."

Yow! No wonder tough guy Vinnie had to take a couple of months off to sort things out. The FBI shrink quaintly called Vinnie's problem, ahem, "identity confusion."

Anyway, our boy is now back at work, and this time he's after drug-and-arms dealers Mel and Susan Profitt (Kevin Spacey and Joan Severance). To get to them, he cultivated a weak link, their underling Roger Lococco (William Russ).

Still in his cover as a Steelgrave wiseguy, Vinnie came on to Roger like a seasoned coquette; knowing he was a munitions freak, he struck up a conversation about the relative capabilities of their, uh, guns, and before you knew it, Vinnie was a Profitt employee.

Cannell and company may have painted themselves into a corner by offing the commanding, lovably flaky Steelgrave. He's a tough act to follow. But Roger, the Sonny figure of this cycle, does have a hint of a conscience and a tormented hang-dog look, and he's winning Vinnie's sympathy. Besides, they're both afraid of the Profitts.

Psychotic incestuous geniuses from the backwoods of Tennessee, Mel and Susan are more calculatedly decadent inventions than Sonny. For instance, despite his round, choirboy face and snide, puckish superiority, Mel is a drug addict. And after sister Susie tenderly shoots him up in the feet, he purrs contentedly, "Only the toes knows."

In one episode, Vinnie and Roger were sent to Tennessee to oversee a drug operation run for Mel by a farm couple, had the hallucinatory quality of a Norman Rockwell painting reflected in a funhouse mirror. Vinnie and Roger, in leather jackets and muscle shirts, lurked around the farmhouse saying "please" and "thank you" and sleeping in bunk beds, like a steroid-pumped version of Ricky and David Nelson. Preparing to bunk down for the night, Roger tossed Vinnie a joky warning not to get the wrong idea, and Vinnie cracked, "I had you pegged for a homophobe the minute I met you."

Maybe *Wiseguy* is so intriguing because the show, like Vinnie, is unsure of what (who) it is. There are mundane Cannellisms aplenty, like leaden anti-drug messages and flashy car chases. But then, there are moments when it seems like a sympathetic gay version of the pernicious Al Pacino film *Cruising* (an undercover cop is "turned into" a homosexual by his investigation of the murder of gay men). Delving as deep as it can go into male friendship, it finds impulses it would rather not think about in prime time, and brushes them off with a nervous laugh.

## REFLECTING ON THE READING

Think about the ways Joyce Millman characterizes *Wiseguy* to help you ask questions of similar shows. Choose a crime or detective show currently on television and describe in a paragraph the relationship between the main characters. Use Millman's descriptions of Sonny and Vinnie as a model. (To work on the vocabulary of this article, see the exercise in Chapter 2, p. 37.)

◆

# IT IS REALLY TELEVISION'S JOB TO FAN FLAMES OF UNREST?

TODD GITLIN

◆

*How should live news coverage of events in progress (wars, riots, accidents, natural disasters) be carried out? Todd Gitlin, a professor of sociolgy and director of the mass communications program at UC-Berkeley, seems to say that television doesn't cause these problems, but it does magnify them. Does your experience confirm what he says? How does what he says apply to the televising of the Los Angeles Police Department freeway pursuit of O. J. Simpson and the coverage of the bombing of the federal building in Oklahoma City?*

The murderous riots spread from city to city. On the streets and in quiet neighborhoods, angry mobs attacked innocent civilians, killing and wounding many. Arson spread. Cars full of blacks fired randomly on white residential districts.

The year was 1919. There was no television. Neither was there radio broadcasting. In that case, the riots began in Charleston, S.C., then spread to Washington, Chicago and other cities. In that case, the killers who started the cities boiling were white mobs looking for blacks to lynch. In that case, the riots took months to spread.

Without question, television fans flames, accelerates time, spreads alarm, invites terror and revulsion—and fellow-feeling. Especially so, given commercial television's obsession with electric immediacy, in-your-face confrontation, melodrama with plenty of climaxes. Live battlefield coverage and instant replay stoke up public juices of all flavors. Saturation riot coverage quickens the pulse of TV news directors and gladdens the hearts, if that is the right word, of the business office.

But the effect of this saturation is tricky to gauge. Only one thing is sure: The fires will go out—this time. Depending on circumstances, those fanned flames will have led to moral revival or to race war; to a reminder that multicolor, polyglot America is wired together for good or for ill, or to recurrent flare-ups, under control for a while, out of control for a while—cycles of aimless rage alternating with repression, unending cycles in which urban hulks are reduced to battlefields for warlords of every color and description, with everyone who can afford to leave getting out to the malled suburbs.

It has happened in our benighted time that saturation coverage of nightmarish violence can transfix the country and help build a moral consensus for social change—as happened in 1963, when millions of people of all races, watching Birmingham, Ala., Chief Bull Connor's police dogs and water hoses against civil rights demonstrators, made the civil rights cause their own and demanded federal action. Or it can help polarize the population—as happened in 1968, when live coverage of Chicago's confrontation and police riot at the Democratic Convention helped split the country in two, 60 percent siding with the police, 40 percent with the demonstrators, the subsequent victory going to Richard Nixon, setting the stage for a virtually uninterrupted quarter century of Republican rule.

Television is collective conscience. It is also collective frivolity and evasion. It rubs ugliness in our eyes, it rubs blinding cream into our faces. It appeals to voyeurism—and samaritanship. It drains the collective will, it amplifies demagoguery. Now this.

Likely, the endless replay of George Holliday's video of the beating of Rodney King in March, 1991 and since, helped educate much of the white population that "excessive force" is no idle phrase. (Note—it wasn't the routine reporting of eyewitness news that enlightened and sickened Americans; it was a camera in the hands of an amateur.) Those same replays in the courtroom may have numbed the easily numbable jurors of Simi Valley, refuge for retired police and the Ronald Reagan Presidential Library, but they also aroused many African and other Americans to righteous indignation, spurred them to rise up any way they could think to do and throw something at someone and get something for nothing. Thursday, helicopter live shots of drivers being beaten by enraged mobs inspired fear and loathing. One of those shots also inspired an unemployed black aerospace worker in south central L.A. to drive to the scene and help a severely beaten white truck driver to the hospital in time to save his life. "One more minute, just one more minute, and he would have been dead," said a paramedic, according to the Los Angeles Times.

Everyday television is also a riot machine. It tells you that your dignity depends on rushing out to the store for the most up-to-date appliances and shows. And then it offends your dignity by showing you what the police might do to you if you look like Rodney King. It yells fire, murder, drugs—and before we get around to some serious talk about what our whole nation needs to be a whole nation …

We'll be right back.

But television, easy as it is to blame for this week's riots, is only the fanner of the flames. There will be calls for censorship—as there were in the aftermath of 1968 riots. Then, the networks complied with federal "requests" for "restraint" in news coverage. They phased down coverage of militants—militants whom they had made household names in the first place. But the riots didn't stop—and most important of all, the wounds in the social body didn't stop festering.

Here we are, a quarter of a century later. The breadth and quality of rage so destructively manifest on the streets is a measure of how long the looting has been going on. For decades, it is the cities that have been looted—by businesses shutting down factories, moving their operations south or offshore, festively picking up tax breaks, while clucking about how undereducated the city kids are; by real-estate speculators, aided and abetted by tax abatements, trashing affordable housing; by the best and brightest products of our business schools (not much "political correctness" there) teaching conglomerates how to cut corners and pile up debt; by multinational drug syndicates; by a federal government using that debt as a rationale for lopping aid to the cities. Looters all.

So what's the effect of television? Yet to be known, yet to be *created*. People are not the inert material into which television sends its hypodermic needle. One way or the other, people will decide—will act either to sustain or to transform the appalling system of economic misery, political race-baiting, and legal default that has broken the cities in half and driven virtually everyone to fear and trembling.

The crimes are numberless. The cruelty is no longer unusual. The punishment is perennial. The replays are only beginning. The jury is every color in the rainbow. So are the defendants. This time, each member of the jury had better think twice about what it is like inside another skin.

## Reflecting on the Reading

Perhaps the Rodney King beating and the television coverage of the trial of the Los Angeles police officers was an unusual case. Briefly describe a case in the past two years where television coverage created tension or contributes to violence in some community? Discuss your findings in small groups with your classmates.

# Television:

## How Far Has It Come in 30 Years

Newton N. Minow

*In 1961, Newton Minow, President John F. Kennedy's newly-appointed Chairman of the Federal Communi-*

*cations Commission, gave a speech to the National As-
sociation of Broadcasters which became famous for his
assertion that television had become a "vast wasteland." In the speech that follows given thirty years later,
Minow reviews what has changed in television programming and what has not.*

*Minow is now the Director of the Annenberg Wash-
ington Program in Communications Policy Studies of
Northwestern University and Counsel, Sidley & Austin
in Chicago. The speech was delivered at the Gannett
Foundation Media Center at Columbia University in
New York City on May 9, 1991.*

After finishing that speech to the National Association of Broadcasters
(NAB) thirty years ago today, I remained near the podium talking with
LeRoy Collins, a former governor of Florida who was serving as NAB presi-
dent. A man from the audience approached us and said to me,

"I didn't particularly like your speech."

A few moments later the same man returned with,

"The more I thought about it, your speech was really awful."

A few minutes later he was back a third time to say,

"Mr. Minow, that was the worst speech I ever heard in my whole life!"

Governor Collins gently put his arm around me and said,

"Don't let him upset you, Newt. That man has no mind of his own. He
just repeats everything he hears."

Thirty years later I still hear about that speech. My daughters threaten to
engrave on my tombstone "On to a Vaster Wasteland."

My old law partner, Adlai E. Stevenson, loved to tell a favorite story
about the relationship between a fan and a fan dancer: There is really no intent to cover the subject—only to call attention to it. Like a fan dancer, it is
not my intent today to cover every part of that speech, but rather to use its
anniversary to examine, with thirty years' perspective, what television has
been doing to our society and what television can do for our society.

Thirty years cannot be covered fully in thirty minutes, but let us begin
by reminding ourselves of the times, circumstances and optimistic spirit of
the Kennedy administration in the early '60s. What was broadcasting like at
that stage of development?

President Kennedy started off with a dream of a New Frontier, but made
a major blunder on April 17, 1961, at the Bay of Pigs. A few weeks later, on
May 5, there was a great triumph: the successful launch of the first American
to fly in space, Commander Alan Shepard. Commander Shepard returned
from his flight to meet President Kennedy and Congress on May 8. On the
same day, President Kennedy was to speak to the National Association of
Broadcasters and invited me to accompany him when he gave his speech. I

was to meet him outside the Oval Office in the morning and to ride with him to the Sheraton Park Hotel.

As I waited there, President Kennedy emerged and said,

"Newt, how about taking the Shepards with us to the broadcasters?"

Of course, I said, and the president went back into his office to make the arrangements. He returned to say,

"It's all set. Now come with me, I want to change my shirt. And what do you think I should say to the broadcasters?"

Although I had known Jack Kennedy before he was president, it was the first time that I was in the bedroom of the president of the United States watching him change shirts and being asked to advise him on what to say. Nervously, I mumbled something about the difference between the way we handled our space launches compared to the Soviets: that we invited radio and television to cover the events live, not knowing whether success or failure would follow. On the other hand, the Soviets operated behind locked doors. President Kennedy nodded, took no notes, and led me back to his office, where Commander and Mrs. Shepard and Vice President Lyndon Johnson were waiting. We went out to the cars. The vice president and I ended up on the two jump seats in the presidential limousine, with the president and the Shepards in the back seat in an ebullient mood as we rode through Rock Creek Park. After we arrived, President Kennedy gave a graceful, witty, thoughtful talk about the value of an open, free society, exemplified by the live radio and television coverage of Commander Shepard's flight. The broadcasters responded with a standing ovation.

The next day I returned to that same platform for my first speech as chairman of the Federal Communications Commission. Many people think I should have asked President Kennedy to watch me change my shirt and give me advice on my speech because, as you know, the audience did not like what I had to say.

In that speech, I asked the nation's television broadcasters

"To sit down in front of your television set when your station goes on the air and stay there without a book, magazine, newspaper, profit-and-loss sheet or rating book to distract you—and keep your eyes glued to that set until the station signs off. I can assure you that you will observe a vast waste-land....

"Is there one person in this room who claims that broadcasting can't do better? Your trust accounting with your beneficiaries is overdue."

That night, at home, there were two phone calls. The first was from President Kennedy's father, Joseph Kennedy. When I heard who was calling I anticipated sharp criticism; instead Ambassador Kennedy said, "Newt, I just finished talking to Jack and I told him your speech was the best one since his inaugural address on January 20th. Keep it up; if anyone gives you any trouble, call me!"

The second call was from Edward R. Murrow, then director of the U.S. Information Agency. He said, "You gave the same speech I gave two years ago. Good for you—you'll get a lot of heat and criticism, but don't lose your courage!"

Those two calls gave me the backbone I needed.

What was the situation at the time? In the late '50s, scandals damaged both the FCC and the television industry. President Eisenhower had to replace an FCC chairman who had accepted lavish entertainment by industry licensees. Broadcasters had to explain quiz show and payola scandals in congressional hearings. Television was still new—in its first generation of programming. The word "television" did not yet appear in the Federal Communications Act.

While at the FCC, we followed two fundamental policies: 1) to require that broadcasters serve the public interest as well as their private interest, and 2) to increase choice for the American home viewer. In the long run, we believed that competition was preferable to governmental regulation, especially where a medium of expression was involved. So we worked to open markets to new technologies, to help build a noncommercial television alternative and to provide educational opportunities through television. Satellites, UHF, cable—we encouraged them all.

Today that 1961 speech is remembered for two words—but not the two I intended to be remembered. The words we tried to advance were "public interest." To me, the public interest meant, and still means, that we should constantly ask: What can television do for our country? for the common good? for the American people?

Alexis de Tocqueville observed in 1835:

"No sooner do you set foot on American soil than you find yourself in a sort of tumult, all around you everything is on the move."

What would Tocqueville have said about the explosive expansion of telecommunications, particularly the electronic media, during the thirty years between 1961 and 1991?

In 1961 there were 47.2 million television sets in American homes; by 1990 that number had more than tripled, to 172 million. Fewer than 5 percent of the television sets in 1961 were color; in 1990, 98 percent of American homes receive television in color. Cable television, which started by bringing television to people who could not receive signals over the air, now brings even more television to people who already receive it. In 1961, cable television served just over a million homes; now it reaches more than 55 million. Between 1961 and 1991, the number of commercial television stations in America doubled, from 543 to 1102. Noncommercial, now called public, television stations quintupled from 62 to 350.

Americans spend more time than ever watching television. Since 1961 the U.S. population has risen from 150 million to 245 million, and the amount of time Americans spend watching television has skyrocketed from 2.175 hours a day to a staggering 7.3 hours per day. In 1961, television viewers spent more than 90 percent of their viewing time watching the three commercial networks; today that figure is around 62 percent.

While the U.S. government slipped from a $3 billion surplus in 1960 to a deficit of more than $161 billion today, total advertising revenues for the television industry rose sevenfold in the same period, from $3.2 billion to $24 billion. In 1961 cable advertising revenues were zero; in 1988 cable advertising revenues were $1.16 billion. And cable subscribers, who paid an average of $4 per month in 1961, today pay around $25 for cable service. Cable subscriptions accounted for revenues of $51 million in 1961; now they amount to almost $20 billion.

Video revenue in the movie industry, which was zero thirty years ago, is now $2.9 billion—more than $700 million larger than current movie theater receipts. VCRs, unavailable commercially in 1961, are now in more than 58 million American homes.

Children today grow up with a remote control clicker, cable and a VCR, says former NBC President Bob Mulholland, who now teaches at Northwestern University's Medill School of Journalism. These children don't remember the days when television signals came to the home through the air to an antenna on the roof as God and General Sarnoff intended. My children used to say, "Is it time for the 'Mickey Mouse Club,' yet?"

My grandchildren say, "Can I watch the tape of *Peter Pan* again?"

Today, new program services like CNN, C-SPAN, HBO, Showtime, Disney, Nickelodeon, Discovery, Lifetime, Arts and Entertainment, ESPN, USA, TNT, Black Entertainment TV, Bravo, Cinemax, TBS, Home Shopping, Weather Channel, Univision, CNBC, Galavision, Nashville, MTV, FNN, American Movie Channel, and even more, enter the home by wire for those who can pay the monthly cable bill. Choice has skyrocketed. The VCR means you can watch a program when you want to see it, not just when the broadcaster puts it on the schedule. If you are a sports fan, a news junkie, a stock market follower, a rock music devotee, a person who speaks Spanish, a nostalgic old-movie buff, a congressional-hearing observer, a weather watcher—you now have your own choice. The FCC objective in the early '60s to expand choice has been fulfilled, beyond all expectations.

Yet, to many of us, this enlarged choice is not enough to satisfy the public interest. There are several reasons. Although some viewers have gone from a vast emptiness to a vast fullness, others have been excluded. Choice through cable comes at a price not all can afford, and cable is still not available to the entire nation. (Where I live in Chicago, we did not receive cable service until last year, and of course many parts of New York City and Washington, D.C., do not have cable either.) And as CBS President Howard Stringer said in a speech at the Royal Institution in London last year, "We see a vast media-jaded audience that wanders restlessly from one channel to another in search of that endangered species, originality, more choices may not necessarily mean better choices."

One evening as I watched, with my remote control in hand, I flipped through the channels and saw a man loading his gun on one channel, a different man aiming a gun on a second, and another man shooting a gun on a third. And if you don't believe me, try it yourself. I think the most troubling change over the past 30 years is the rise in the quantity and quality of violence on television. In 1961 I worried that my children would not benefit much from television, but in 1991 I worry that my grandchildren will actually be harmed by it. One recent study shows that by the time a child is 18 he has seen 25,000 murders on television. In 1961 they didn't make PG-13 movies, much less NC-17. Now a 6-year-old can watch them on cable.

Can this be changed where television is concerned? My own answer is yes. If we want to, we can provide the American people with a full choice, even if the marketplace does not meet the demands of the public interest. I reject the view of an FCC chairman in the early '80s who said that "a television set is merely a toaster with pictures."

I reject this ideological view that the marketplace will regulate itself and that the television marketplace will give us perfection. The absolute free market approach to public good has been gospel in our country in the case of the savings and loan industry, the airline industry, the junk bond financing industry, and in many other spheres of commerce and common interest. If television is to change, the men and women in television will have to make it a leading institution in American life rather than merely a reactive mirror of the lowest common denominator in the marketplace. Based on the last thirty years, the record gives the television marketplace an A+ for technology, but only a C for using that technology to serve human and humane goals.

Bill Baker, president of Thirteen/WNET here in New York (and like me a veteran of both commercial and public television) said it all in two short sentences: "To aim only at the bottom line is to aim too low. Our country deserves better."

Felix Rohatyn, a star of the marketplace, was on target when he said, "Though I believe the marketplace knows best most of the time, I am skeptical that it should always be the ultimate arbiter of economic action, and I am more than willing to interfere with it when it becomes a distorting rather than a benign influence."

In the last thirty years, the television marketplace has become a severely distorting influence in at least four important public areas. We have failed 1. to use television for education; 2. to use television for children; 3. to finance public television properly; and 4. to use television properly in political campaigns.

First, education. Suppose you were asked this multiple-choice question: Which of the following is the most important educational institution in America? (a) Harvard, (b) Yale, (c) Columbia, (d) the University of California, (e) none of the above. The correct answer is *e*. The most important educational institution in America is television. Most people learn more each day, each year, each lifetime from television than from any other source. All of television is education; the question is, what are we teaching and what are we learning? Sometimes, as in the case of the splendid Annenberg/CPB-sponsored educational course on the Constitution (created here at Columbia by Professor Fred Friendly), we see what television can to do stretch the mind and the spirit. In Ken Burns' brilliant programs about the Civil War, millions of Americans learned more about that terrible period in American history than they ever learned in school. We are slowly doing better each year in using television for education, but too much of the time we waste television's potential to teach—and viewers' to learn.

Second, television for children. Bob Keeshan, our Captain Kangaroo for life, has seen how television for children all over the world is designed to be part of the nurturing and educational system. But "in America," he says, "television is not a tool for nurturing. It is a tool for selling." True, there are glorious exceptions like Joan Cooney's work, starting with *Sesame Street.* But far too often television fails our children. And it fails them for more hours each day than they spend with a teacher in a classroom.

Competition, it is said, brings out the best in products and the worst in people. In children's television, competition seems to bring out the worst in programs and the worst in children. Children lack purchasing power and voting power, and the television marketplace and the political process have failed them. Cooperation instead of competition, among broadcasters and cable operators, could do wonders for children. Congress last year and the FCC this year have finally started to address these issues, and the attention is long overdue. If they would give the same time and attention to policies for children's television as they give to industry fights about the financial interest and syndication rules, our children would begin to receive the priority concern they deserve.

Third, public television should become just as much a public commitment as our public libraries, hospitals, parks, schools and universities. Yet it is a stepchild, struggling to provide outstanding public service while remaining in the role of a perpetual beggar in the richest country in the world. We have failed to fund a strong independent alternative to commercial television and thus failed, Larry Grossman's words, to "travel the high road of education, information, culture and the arts."

There are many ways to establish a sound economic base for public broadcasting. For example, Congress could create a spectrum-use or franchise fee for all commercial broadcast and cable operators to fund public broadcasting on a permanent basis. If this were set in the range of a 2 percent annual fee on broadcasting and cable's $50 billion total annual revenues, it would produce about $1 billion a year. Even at that figure, we'd still be behind Japan. If we added $5 as a tax on the sale of new television sets and VCRs and earmarked the funds to match private contributions to public broadcasting, we could catch up to Japan—which now spends twenty times as much per person for public broadcasting as we do!

Finally, the use of television in political campaigns. Studies of the 1988 campaign show that the average block of uninterrupted speech by a presidential candidate on network newscasts was 9.8 seconds; in 1968 it was 42.3 seconds. As Walter Cronkite observed, this means that "issues can be avoided rather than confronted." And David Halberstam adds, "Once the politicians begin to talk in such brief bites, they begin to think in them."

A United States senator must now raise $12,000 to $16,000 every week to pay for a political campaign, mostly to buy time for television commercials. A recent United Nations study revealed that only two countries, Norway and Sri Lanka (in addition to the United States) do not provide free airtime to their political parties. If we are to preserve the democratic process without corrupting, unhealthy influences, we must find a bipartisan way to provide free time for our candidates and stop them from getting deeply in hock to special interests in order to pay for television commercials.

More than twenty years ago, I served on a bipartisan commission for the Twentieth Century Fund which recommended the concept of "voters' time" for presidential candidates. Voters' time would be television time purchased with public funds at half the commercial-time rates and given to candidates. In exchange, we would prohibit by law the purchase of time by the candidates. And while we're at it, we should institutionalize the presidential debates, make them real debates by eliminating the panels of journalists. And we should clean up our political campaigns, once and for all.

In these four areas, the television marketplace has not fulfilled our needs and will not do so in the next thirty years. These four needs can be met only if we, as a nation, make the decision that to aim only at the bottom line is to aim too low. If we still believe in the concept of the public interest, we can use television to educate, we can stop shortchanging our children, we can fund public broadcasting properly, and we can provide free television time for our political candidates. My generation began these tasks, and the time has now come to pass the responsibility on to the next generation, the first generation to grow up with television.

What will happen in television in the next thirty years, from now until 2021? As Woody Allen says, "More than any other time in history, mankind faces a crossroads. One path leads to despair and hopelessness. The other to total extinction. Let us pray we have the wisdom to choose correctly."

In the next thirty years, four main forces, globalization, optical fiber, computers and satellite technology will illuminate the crossroads.

Today's able FCC chairman, Al Sikes, is wisely trying to keep public policy in pace with rapidly changing technologies. As Al observes, "Today we can see the new world, in it, tomorrow's communications networks will be dramatically improved. Copper and coaxial cables are giving way to glass fibers, and wavelengths are being replaced by digits...."

Well before 2021, I believe there will be convergence of the technologies now used in telephones, computers, publishing, satellites, cable, movie studios and television networks. Already we see tests of optical fiber demonstrating the future. In Montreal tonight, a home viewer watching the hockey game on television can use his remote control to order his own instant replay, order different camera angles, and become his own studio director. In Cerritos, California, a viewer today can participate in an experiment to summon any recorded show at any time, day or night; and he can stop it, rewind it, or fast forward it.

Here in New York City, Time Warner is building a two-way interactive cable system with 150 channels. People will be able to order any movie or record album every produced and see and hear it when they themselves want to see and hear it. We see 400- and 500-channel systems on the horizon, fragmenting viewership into smaller and smaller niches, and we need to remember that for all their presumed benefits these developments undermine the simultaneous, shared national experiences that comprise the nation's social glue.

At the Annenberg Washington Program of Northwestern University, we are developing a blueprint for the future of optical fiber. As this new technological world unfolds, the risk remains that we will create information overload without information substance or analysis, of more media with fewer messages, of tiny sound bites without large thoughts, of concentrating on pictures of dead bodies instead of thinking of human beings. Henry Thoreau warned us more than 125 years ago: "We are in great haste to construct a magnetic telegraph from Maine to Texas; but Maine and Texas, it may be, have nothing important to communicate."

When we launched the fist communications satellite in 1962 we knew it was important, but we had little understanding of its future use. I did tell President Kennedy that the communications satellite was more important than launching a man into space, because the satellite launched an idea, and ideas last longer than human beings. The last thirty years have taught us that satellites have no respect for political boundaries. Satellites cannot be stopped by Berlin Walls, by tanks in Tiananmen Square or by dictators in Baghdad. In Manila, Warsaw and Bucharest, we saw the television station become today's Electronic Bastille.

Thirty years is but a nanosecond in history. If President Kennedy were alive today, he would celebrate his 74th birthday later this month. He would be seven years older than President Bush. He would be astonished by the technological changes of the past thirty years, but he would be confident that the next thirty years will be even more advanced.

Before he was elected president, John F. Kennedy once compared broadcasters and politicians in these words,

> Will Gresham's law operate in the broadcasting and political worlds, wherein the bad inevitably drives out the good? Will the politician's desire for reelection, and the broadcaster's desire for ratings, cause both to flatter every public whim and prejudice, to seek the lowest common denominator of appeal, to put public opinion at all times ahead of the public interest? For myself, I reject that view of politics, and I urge you to reject that view of broadcasting.

I went to the FCC because I agreed then and agree now with President Kennedy's philosophy of broadcasting. As I think back about him, and also think of our future, I propose today to the television and cable industries: Join together to produce a unique program to be on all channels that will have enduring importance to history. Seldom in history have we had five living American presidents at the same time: Right now, Presidents Reagan, Carter, Ford and Nixon [since this speech was delivered, Richard Nixon has died] are with us, in addition to President Bush. You can bring all of them to the Oval Office in the White House to discuss their dreams of America in the 21st century, and you can give every American the opportunity to see and hear this program and to share a vision of our future.

The '60s started with high hopes, but confronted tragedy and ended in disillusion. Tragically, our leaders—President John F. Kennedy, Reverend Martin Luther King, Jr. and Pope John XXIII, left too soon. We cannot go back in history, but the new generation can draw upon the great creative energy of that era, on its sense of national kinship and purpose, and on its passion and compassion. These qualities have not left us—we have left them, and it is time to return.

As we return, I commend some extraordinary words to the new generation. E.B. White sat in a darkened room in 1938 to see the beginning of television, an experimental electronic box that projected images into the room. Once he saw it, Mr. White wrote:

> We shall stand or fall by television, of that I am sure. I believe television is going to be the test of the modern world, and that in this new opportunity to see beyond the range of our vision, we shall discover either a new and unbearable disturbance to the general peace, or a saving radiance in the sky.

That radiance falls unevenly today. It is still a dim light in education. It has not fulfilled its potential for children. It has neglected the needs of public television. And in the electoral process it has cast a dark shadow.

This year, television enabled us to see Patriot missiles destroy Scud missiles above the Persian Gulf. Will television in the next thirty years be a Scud or a Patriot? A new generation now has the chance to put the vision back into television, to travel from the wasteland to the promised land, and to make television a saving a radiance in the sky.

## REFLECTING ON THE READING

Minow identifies four areas that he feels television has failed the American public. Pick one of those areas and list three examples of your own that either agree or disagree with Minow's opinion.

# PUTTING IT IN WRITING

## RESPONSES

1. Pick one of the readings in this chapter. Map the article to show its main points. (See Chapter 2, pages 39–40 for an explanation and

example of mapping.) Now write one sentence that explains how the title connects to the article's point.

2. Read only the first and last paragraphs of an essay you have not yet read. Based on reading only those two paragraphs, write a paragraph that could connect the other two. Now read the whole essay and compare your paragraph to the original article.

3. Write for five minutes explaining what you think television will be like in the year 2020.

## Reading for Meaning

1. Find a reading that includes a number of unfamiliar words. Before reading the whole article, skim the article and make a list of ten words whose meanings you don't know. Look them up in the dictionary. Then read the article.

2. Several of the articles in this chapter use anecdotes to develop their point. Pick one of those articles and write a brief statement explaining how the anecdote supports the writer's point.

3. Several of the articles in this chapter use comparisons to support their point. Pick one of those articles, describe the objects or concepts compared, and explain how the comparison supports the main point.

## Organizing Your Ideas

1. Make a list of television's positive and negative effects on you. Now, write a thesis statement using one point from each list.

2. Based on your television viewing for the past year, list the three best programs you have watched and then list the three worst programs you have watched. After you complete the two lists, write a single sentence that explains what you mean by "best" or "worst."

3. Write a nutshell of one of the readings in this chapter. (See Chapter 2, page 42, for an explanation and example of nutshells.) Then think of another point that would support the writer's thesis and add that to your nutshell.

## Writing a Paper

1. Assume the president has named you Czar of Television for the United States. Write a paper explaining three changes you would make in television programming. Be certain to be specific and to give your reasons for the changes.

2. Several of the writers in this chapter argue that television has various harmful effects on people. Choose one of those articles and write a paper that argues those harmful effects are not caused by television, but by something else. Use your material from #1 in "Organizing Your Ideas."

3. Using Joyce Millman as your model, write a review of a television program you really like or one you think is really terrible. Use several examples from the program and vivid language to support your opinions. Draw on your work from #2 in "Organizing Your Ideas."

In this "Doonesbury" cartoon, the humor derives from the assumption that the music of a teen-ager represents opposition to "adult" values. Was that true for the music you listened to most as a teen-ager?

# Music

"And she shall have music wherever she goes." So says the fantasy ending of an eighteenth century nursery rhyme. But in the late twentieth century, the fantasy has become reality. An in-line skater can skate down the street to the rhythms of music only she or he hears, on a radio or tape headset. Virtually every automobile has a radio, and usually a tape deck or a CD player. We can listen to music while watching music videos, available 24 hours a day. Computers are now designed to play music from CDs. Whether at home, at work, in the car, or at the beach, we can have music wherever we go.

The pervasiveness of music in our culture raises debates about the value of music and especially about the relative values of particular styles and types of music. You can make a quick enemy simply be insulting a person's favorite music or musician.

Plato saw music at the lowest end of the hierarchy in his Republic because it appeals so powerfully to the passions. In the early eighteenth century, William Congreve wrote that "music has charms to soothe the savage beast," a sentiment that parents of today's teenagers might quibble over. Human beings are rhythmic animals. We float in fluid for nearly a year before we are born and then seek rhythmic movement the rest of our lives. We find that movement in many forms: dance, games, sports, worship services. Often, that movement is accompanied by music. And very often the music has words, in the form of a song, that adds the rhythm of language to the rhythm of the music.

Every culture develops its own music, often borrowing elements from earlier or neighboring cultures. The basic instruments are drums, whistles, bells, horns, strings, and keyboards, though the exact form those devices take depends on the local materials and the tradition of the culture. Today, we've added the capacity to record music and to manipulate it electronically, so that the combinations we can produce are limitless.

Singers and musicians have always played an important role in culture. Those gifted with beautiful voices and those who can make the sounds that enthrall the rest of us have always been honored in some way. In Homer's *The Odyssey*, the hero Odysseus says of the singer: "Among all the men on the earth singers are sharers in honor and respect." Today, the singer earns not only honors, but also celebrity status and great sums of money. Some become icons—like Elvis Presley, the Beatles, Madonna, and Michael Jackson. Because we place such high value on music, entrepreneurs can make great business enterprises from music. Record companies and tour promoters use all the devices of modern advertising and modern technology to get us to pay for the music we want with the quality of sound that we desire.

Because music is so pervasive and so close to the emotions, we argue about it. The old usually prefer the music of their own youth to whatever is currently popular. The young seek rhythms that reflect their own distinctiveness and sense of self. Some like it loud; some like it soft; some like it cool; and some like it hot. When loud and hot encounter soft and cool in the same space, conflict often develops. The headset has allowed people to share the same space while listening to different music. But the headset separates people, while the concert brings them together. At a concert, the audience often becomes part of the performance as performers and listeners respond to one another. Not only do we debate styles of music, but we disagree about the volume at which music is played. Most communities have adopted noise ordinances that restrict the places and levels at which music may be played publicly. Often these ordinances lead to local controversy.

Before you read the articles in this chapter, do a short inventory of your own musical preferences. Try this exercise. Make lists of your three favorite songs or musical pieces and your three favorite performers when you were in your early teens (13–15). Then, make lists of your current five favorite songs or pieces and your five favorite performers (ones you would pay to hear in person, for instance). Compare your lists with several other students in your class. Now see what you think of the opinions expressed by the writers in this chapter.

◆

# TEEN'S MOM HORRIFIED BY FIRST ROCK CONCERT

## ANN LANDERS

*Recall the last musical concert you attended. Think about the behavior of the performers and the reaction*

*of the audience. Then compare that experience to the one described in this letter to Ann Landers.*

Dear Ann Landers: A few days ago I took my 15-year-old daughter and three of her friends to a rock concert. I decided on the way out that instead of fighting the traffic both ways I would buy a ticket and stay and see the show.

I consider myself fairly open-minded but I was shocked senseless by what I saw and heard.

The language of the kids around me was unreal. Every other word started with F or S. When one of the rock stars appeared in a G-string the crowd went wild. That fellow was 99 percent naked.

The audio was turned up and the audience went crazy. My eardrums began to pop but no one else seemed to mind, in fact they loved it. Then the kids around me started to light up joints.

People all over the place began to toss firecrackers. I swear, Ann Landers, I have never been so petrified in my life, not only for me but for every person in that building.

There were broken bottles all over the place and several fights going on. The police were nowhere to be seen.

I lost track of the number of people who had to be carried out. Some were unconscious. Others were hysterical. I saw two couples having sex right out in the open. Others were taking off their clothes all over the place.

When the concert ended, there was an incredible stampede. I was afraid if I fell I would be stomped to death. I prayed for strength to stay on my feet.

On the way home (still shaking) I told my daughter that she would not go to another rock show as long as she lived in my house, no matter how old she was. And I am going to stick to it.

Here is some advice to every parent who is reading this: Don't ask your kid what goes on at these performances. Go see for yourself.

I am signing my name but please do not use even my initials.

My daughter says she was embarrassed by my outburst in front of her friends and she would never forgive me if my identity became known. You may say, however, that this letter came from

- Madison, Wis.

Dear Madison: I am at a loss to comment on your letter because I have been to only one rock concert in my life (seven years ago) and it was nothing like the one you described. I do know, however, that last December two teen-agers were crushed to death and 29 were hospitalized following a show in Nashville.

May I hear from some of you parents? Is this mother's letter an accurate account of what goes on at most rock concerts? Do you want your teen-agers to patronize such performances? I'd like to know.

## REFLECTING ON THE READING

Based on your own experience at concerts, write a short response to "Madison," providing your own version of Ann Landers-type advice.

◆

# 'SGT. PEPPER'S LONELY HEARTS CLUB BAND,' THE BEATLES, CAPITOL, 1967

JEFFREY MOSER

◆

*What is your father's or mother's favorite piece of music? Compare it to Jeffrey Moser's description as you read his letter from Rolling Stone.*

My dad loved three things: my mother, the army and *Sgt. Pepper's Lonely Hearts Club Band.*

Christmas Day, 1964: Saigon blast kills two americans, screamed the headline of the *Washington Post.* "A terrorist bomb knocked out the main U.S. Officers' billet in downtown Saigon last night." Among the injured was Lieutenant Colonel Dewey F. Moser, my dad. After having been rocked by the Cong on Christmas Eve, he came back to the States, Purple Heart in hand, a different man. He was forty-one, disillusioned, vulnerable, and he loved John Lennon and the Beatles.

On Saturday nights, he would invite fellow officers and their wives over to play cards. One of those nights, I was mucking around in the kitchen when I heard him silence the room and stop the game. I walked to the edge of the stairs and peered down where everyone was gathered. Colonels, majors, captains – Dad was standing in the middle. He waved his arms, said, "Listen," walked over to the stereo, cranked up the volume and cued up "A Day in the Life." It was his favorite song from his favorite record. It's the thing I remember most about him. He died in 1975.

## REFLECTING ON THE READING

What piece of music is most memorable to you? Why? Write a short letter to *Rolling Stone* explaining the connection between the music and your experience.

◆

# ICE CUBE: BUCKWHEAT WITH A GUTTER RAP

L· liHle rascal, dumb

## DERRICK Z. JACKSON

◆

*Derrick Jackson, an African-American journalist for the Boston Globe, criticizes the values implied in the lyrics of Ice Cube, an African-American rap singer. Try to identify the reasons for Jackson's criticisms as you read.*

DEAR ICE CUBE: Freeze!!! Against the wall! Stick out your tongue. Open wide. Choose your poison, child. Dove, Dial or Camay. You get sassy and spit, you'll find yourself walking through a car wash with your clothes on. If I ever catch you sampling Malcolm X on a gutter album again, you're going to eat Ivory until you gag on your trashy-ass blackness.

I hear that your new album, "The Predator," entered the Billboard 200 this week at No. 1. That is the first time a rap album began as No. 1 for all music. You sold 200,000 copies in your first week. I assume that you are toasting yourself with St. Ides malt liquor, the booze you claimed in ads was "guaranteed to get a big booty undressed."

On the album cover, you condemn "white America's continued commitment to the silence and oppression of black men. "In the opening rap you ask, "Will they do me like Malcolm?" Before the last rap you insert Malcolm speeches. One of them said, "Whenever a black man stands up and says something that white people don't like, then the first thing that white man does is run around to try and find somebody to say something to offset what has just been said."

It is a pity that you spend nearly the whole album oppressing yourself. Homicide is searing African-Americans, and here you come with more assault rifles. You praise Africa, but your lyrics are full of nigger. Nearly all women are bitches and whores. All others are faggots and muthas (and you know that's not the whole word).

Cube, either you have not seen the Malcolm movie or you have a vacuum chamber for a head. In the movie, when Malcolm was in jail an inmate told him that people who cuss do so because they cannot find the words they really want to use. In his autobiography, Malcolm said of an inmate named Bimbi:

"What fascinated me with him most of all was that he was the first man I had ever seen command total respect … with his words…. That ended my vicious cursing attacks. My approach sounded so weak alongside his, and he never used a foul word."

Since I often defend rap as a harsh but important window of rage and alienation, I tried to find something positive about your album. You said you had not sold out because "a black woman is my manager, not in the kitchen."

But what can that manager be thinking when you brag about showing women "your meat" or "breaking" their vaginas. When you yell "don't trust no bitch," I know you did not see the Malcolm movie. Or did you fall asleep when Malcolm broke with the Nation of Islam after he learned about Elijah Muhammad's adultery?

Your wit effectively drills police brutality. But you seem equally intent on impressing everyone with your ability to "Wet'cha," spraying more African-American men with bullets. With carnage like yours, who needs genocide?

Cube, you say on your album cover, "Ice Cube wishes to acknowledge the failure of the public school system…. Without its role in the conspiracy, the Predator album might not have been made."

"They once had blaxploitation movies. Now it's blaxrap. Cube, you are part of a conspiracy to make African-American men look dumber than fiction. At the same time Cincinnati Red owner Marge Schott is under fire for calling players "million-dollar niggers," you are No. 1 with 73 utterances of nigger. At 200,000 albums, that is 14.6 million utterances floating among young people.

Malcolm said, "You can cuss out colonialism, imperialism and all other kinds of isms, but it's hard for you to cuss that dollarism. When they drop those dollars on you, your soul goes." By that standard, Cube, your soul is at the bottom of that 40-ounce bottle of St. Ides. You are the fool doing the racists' work, turning hate into self-hate.

Ice Cube, you love to quote Malcolm, but you cuss at everyone and everything but dollarism. Instead of 18.6 million references to bitches an ho's, why not rap about how the homies need jobs in Los Angeles? Until you do, you are nothing more than Buckwheat with an AK.

## REFLECTING ON THE READING

To understand Jackson's views, you must know who Ice Cube, Malcolm X, Elijah Muhammad, and Buckwheat are. Imagine you are Ice Cube's publicity representative. Write a short letter to Derrick Jackson defending your client.

◆

# Mozart, the IQ—and music sales

Javier B. Pacheco*

◆

*Researchers have been trying to prove that music has "soothing" qualities, ones that relax us or allow us to think more clearly. What kind of evidence does this article cite in support of that idea?*

Researchers at the Center for Neurobiology of Learning and Memory at UC-Irvine report that 10 minutes of listening to a Mozart piano sonata temporarily raises the measurable IQ of college students by as much as nine points.

Confident headlines proclaimed Mozart can make you smarter.

This should spur brisk sales of classical music.

No? Who cares! We're overdue for healthy doses of musicality, Right? Whoa, horse!

For pre-exam cramming I'm sure Mozart melodies are more tart than hip hop or heavy metal, but let's qualify our assumptions.

First, controversy over ethnocentric bias in IQ tests has not died. Questions remain unresolved about intelligence measurement and the person being measured. Individual and cultural traits need to be factored.

Second, is the listener musically illiterate, musically educated or musically semi-smart? What about tone-deaf people or those with perfect pitch?

How is the music perceived? How does it affect us?

We're often touched in quite different ways by the same experience.

Does listening positively to Mozart produce emotion, tranquillity, empowerment, love, joy or reverence?

Unfortunately, the test used only one Mozart work, *Sonata for Two Pianos in D Major*. The subjects scored higher on spatial reasoning tests than those who heard a relaxation tape or worked in silence, but the IQ boost lasted only 10 minutes.

The researchers did not attempt to test the effects of other kinds of music. Tsk, tsk.

Degree of familiarity and affectation are big variables in music tests. We're still not sure how deeply music affects us. Examples abound of music that induces short-term meditative states or enhances abstract thinking.

---

*Javier B. Pacheco, a composer-pianist and poet, is working on his doctorate in ethnomusicology at UCLA.

Most music lovers can cite examples. I've found a number of strains that inspire, including Bach, Ponce, Revueltas, Debussy, a bolero, Jobim samba and Afro-Latin jazz.

To ensure more scientific control in a study involving music, the UC-Irvine researchers would have profited from ethnomusicological survey methods.

But that may not have been their intent. Curiously, the researchers themselves admitted their findings were inconclusive and open to misinterpretation by "over-anxious parents and educational hucksters."

Lo and behold, the study was funded by the National Association of Music Merchants.

## REFLECTING ON THE READING

The idea that listening to certain kinds of music would raise your IQ has real appeal. List three reservations that Pacheco has about the particular study discussed in this article. Based on what you read, write one sentence stating the cause-effect relationship between music and IQ.

◆

---

# STILL HOT, STILL SEXY, STILL DEAD

## TWENTY YEARS LATER, JIM MORRISON AND THE DOORS STILL LIGHT OUR FIRE.

### BARRY WALTERS

---

◆

*In the folk song "Martin, Abraham, and John," one line reads "the good they die young." Does that apply to singers like Janis Joplin, Jimi Hendrix, Jim Morrison, and Kurt Cobain? What does Barry Walters think about singers like them?*

One of my earliest nightmarish childhood memories involves the Doors. It left a lasting impression, one that would forever temper my feelings about what many have considered to be the greatest American rock band of all time.

It happened where key suburban rock'n'roll experiences are likely to occur—in the basement. In 1967, ours had been freshly remodeled but was no less terrifying to my 6-year-old imagination. For the basement was the dwelling place of my much older brother, a hippie/biker-type possessed of a sadistic streak as wide as his white-boy Afro.

Like many older siblings, my brother had a bent for discovering new ways of tormenting a younger sibling—me—and then explaining them to appear as innocent fun in our parents' eyes.

I was quite the rock tyke, one who collected 45s the way other brats collected marbles or dead frogs. I could do the dances on Shindig, I stayed up late every Monday night to see The Monkees, I knew all the words to "Sgt. Pepper"—I was cool. But my brother one day found the limits of my first-grader taste.

It was nighttime. No one was in the house except me and the subterranean sibling, who had called me into the cellar. The lights were off and I had to feel for the steps in my descent to what had become hippie hell. Biker mags and books on Eastern religion were strewn all over the linoleum floor. The flicker of red candles danced across my brother's face, making him look even more satanic than usual. Incense burned, mingling with another smell I'd probably now recognize as pot.

I'm absolutely sure of what was playing—"The End." It was the first time I'd heard anything by the Doors besides the poppy "Light My Fire," which I loved. This was something else entirely. There was an organ, church-like but ominous, creepy. Drums rolled and crashed. And this man whispered, growled and then screamed through a story I was too young and too scared to understand.

Now I'm older and still can't understand what Jim Morrison was going on about for nearly 12 minutes. But back then, it terrified me and that's what mattered. I remember running toward the stairs and my brother grabbing me and pinning my sobbing body to the floor until "The End" was over. Like every nightmare, it seemed to last forever.

Just like many pop listeners who came of age musically years after Morrison had died in 1971, I bought the Doors reissues, read about the members' lives, listened to the radio wear out the grooves of "Break on Through," "Love Me Two Times," "Roadhouse Blues," "L.A. Woman," "Riders on the Storm" and at least a dozen more Doors tunes.

I've grown to admire these FM rock staples, but at a distance. The joys of the music have become difficult to separate from the marketing of the Morrison myth.

The best of the Doors' songs have done what all great pop music does: both reflect and transcend the time in which it was created. You can't hear them without your head filling up with memories (or at least impressions) of the late '60s and early '70s. And they've aged better than many FM classics not half as old. The Doors' debut album—containing both "Light My Fire" and "The End"—still sounds more "progressive than much of the new stuff that makes it onto today's oldies/heavy rock radio playlists.

The Moody Blues, Procol Harem, Jethro Tull and other "progressive rock" bands may have changed rock language by adding instruments. The Doors did it with less: drums, guitar, keyboards, voice. Unlike almost every rock band throughout the '50s, '60s and '70s, the Doors' lineup did not include a conventional bass player. Although a bassist was hired for *L.A. Woman* (the band's last album with Morrison), the majority of the bass parts were supplied by Ray Manzarek on keyboards.

This technique has become commonplace in contemporary dance, rap and soul music, but it was a breakthrough in 1967, one that slashed the Door's connections to traditional R&B. This less-is-more philosophy created a sound entirely their own.

Rock drumming is centered in the snare and bass drums. Jazz percussion concentrates on the cymbals. Few rock drummers put as much emphasis on the cymbals as the Door's John Densmore, who filled the sonic space unoccupied by a traditional bassist with swinging syncopation, not funky beats.

Guitarist Robby Krieger also had a non-rock orientation: flamenco. You could hear it most obviously in "Spanish Caravan," but also in "Light My Fire" and many others. Whereas Jeff Beck, Jimi Hendrix and Eric Clapton broke new rock ground with speed, distortion and tone, Krieger made his mark with melody and economy. Neither his rhythm playing nor his solos overwhelmed the Door's arrangements.

The band's primary instrumental voice was supplied by Manzarek, a keyboardist more essential to his band than most guitarists. His mix of jazz, R&B, garage-band rock, classical and religious music (both Western and Eastern) made him one of rock's first and few keyboard players with a recognizable style all his own. In his own way, Manzarek was the Doors as much as Morrison was.

As for Morrison, his remains one of rock's signature voices. Bitter and seductive, it was characterized by his sliding from note to note, a technique that furthered his mostly self-created mystique as the "Lizard King." He wasn't the first to slink through songs—Elvis did it, though not as boldly or excessively.

If it's difficult to distinguish the Doors from the Morrison myth, it's even harder to distinguish Morrison the man from that myth. Much has been said about Morrison's connections to Dionysian poets like Verlaine and Rimbaud and heroes of experimental theater like Artaud and Brecht—possibly too much. When Morrison was ambitious, he was often pretentious. To these ears, Morrison was never as good a "poet" as he was a rocker. I still prefer a simple plea like "Love Me Two Times" or "Touch Me" to rambling ruminations such as those that weigh down "The End."

Morrison had it all – he was sexy, smart, spiritual. He was the right guy at the right time, when brainy rock needed a new sex symbol. Of course, he was ultimately self-destructive, but this trait only encouraged much of his audience to romanticize his life and lyrics. His death gave listeners the opportunity to reinterpret every line for personal meaning that would make sense of his deterioration and untimely demise. His songs were no longer songs. They became *statements*, even suicide notes.

The Doors arrived on the rock scene when the idea of progressive rock was a new concept that did not rule out pop appeal. Indeed, most of the bands that pushed rock's lyrical and musical boundaries in the mid- to late '60s—the Beatles, the Stones, Dylan, the Band, Jefferson Airplane, the Kinks, the Who, the later-day Beach Boys—were also among the most popular.

By the time Morrison died—only four years after the release of the Doors' debut album in 1967—a huge gap had grown between rock's avant-garde and its biggest sellers. The masses bought the Carpenters, not the Stooges. It was years before early '70s cult heroes like Roxy Music and David Bowie—superstars in Britain—got significant American radio exposure. In the '70s, one was more likely to read about challenging rock than hear it on the radio.

This fact set the stage for the huge expansion of the Doors' audience in the '80s. Elektra, the Doors' record label, sold more of their albums in the last 10 years than it did when Morrison was still alive. Danny Sugerman's Doors bio, *No One Gets Out Alive,* became a must-read for outlaw teens. Francis Ford Coppola set battle scenes in *Apocalypse Now* to "The End," the first of many war-film epics to unite Vietnam and rock. Oliver Stone's upcoming movie about Morrison will undoubtedly inflate the myth even more. A whole new generation has been primed to become followers of a band that no longer exists. Morrison could come back to Earth just like Elvis.

Ironically, the Doors commercial explosion occurred at exactly the same time that several bands that bore the Doors' influence—X, Echo and the Bunnymen, Joy Division—were making an impact on the alternative "new wave" circuit with little American sales or radio exposure. The same album-rock radio stations that were playing Doors oldies wouldn't touch the band's stylistic stepchildren. Even Manzarek's role as producer of X's earliest (and best) albums couldn't get them on mainstream radio. "Progressive" radio ceased being progressive at exactly the same time that bands like the Doors started hogging all the airplay.

Indeed, if the Doors themselves first appeared in the '80s, chances are the same radio stations that put them in prime oldies rotation wouldn't have played their records until they had proven "demographics." MTV, on the other hand, would probably have latched onto Morrison, turning him into an '80s icon to rival Prince, Michael Jackson and Madonna. But the overnight success created by the immediate Top 40 and FM rock acceptance of "Light My Fire" undoubtedly would have taken years to happen.

What was progressive about the Doors' music became overwhelmed by the ahistorical way it was marketed after the fact. Nowhere on a 1985 "best of" album is there any mention of the years—even the decades—when this music was recorded. In his liner notes, Sugerman ignores the cultural upheaval that shaped the Doors' creativity. Morrison is instead characterized as an "artist" following his "muse," sacrificing himself to create art "of the highest caliber." In short, the mythology that has grown up around Morrison romanticizes his "artistic lifestyle"—the very thing that cut his artistry and life short.

Funny how things have changed. Today's rock stars are not martyrs or saints. Substance abuse is seen for what it is, not as a means to create. It's the music—and, perhaps more insidiously, the image—that matters, not the mythology. Rock hero-worship is by and large a thing of the past: Now, in the age of MTV and sophisticated marketing, people worship not mad, bad, dangerous heroes but pure images. Which is one of the reasons Morrison retains his cult: Images are ephemeral, and people get tired of new bands much more quickly.

But for those who need a romantic rock legend, Morrison is alive and well—and near-perfect. He's got a great gig. He doesn't have to make anti-drug public service announcements. He doesn't have to worry about warning stickers on his albums or contracting AIDS from his groupies. He doesn't even have to keep his stage clothes on to avoid arrest.

He doesn't have to "just say no." He can say "yes" to everything today's rock idols and fans can't. He can say it for us.

## Reflecting on the Reading

Walters states that, in rock today, "music" and "image" matter much more than "mythology." Test his claim by writing a paragraph about a current rock star or other music celebrity in terms of "music," "image," and "mythology."

◆

---

# Sinéad Speaks

Alan Light

---

◆

*Pop music stars get exposed to very large audiences. Many of them use that forum to express their opinions about social, moral, and political issues. Sinéad O'Connor has been particularly outspoken. Look for opinions you agree or disagree with as you read the interview published in* Rolling Stone.

H er face goes blank, and everyone in the room knows what's coming. Things were moving along smoothly during Sinéad O'Connor's public debut of material from *Am I Not Your Girl?*, her first album since her 1990 breakthrough *I Do Not Want What I Haven't Got.* The risky new record is a collection of pop standards that were family favorites in her youth: "These are the songs that made me want to sing," she explains in the album credits. She's spent all morning in front of a forty-piece orchestra at Kaufman Astoria Studios in Queens, New York, singing Loretta Lynn's "Success Has Made a Failure of Our Home," in preparation for a television broadcast on the BBC's *Top of the Pops.* As show time approaches, she's told she only needs to answer one brief introductory question before going into the song.

But when the host beams in from London over Sinéad's headphones, the singer flinches. She doesn't want to say what she's been doing lately. "It's such a boring question," she says. "What do you *think* I've been fucking doing?" Then she's off—can't he ask her something specific, like was there really a potato famine in Ireland? No, it's explained, that would confuse the listeners. Finally, she agrees to answer. "I've been getting as far away from being famous and materially successful as possible," she snaps, a response that—surprise—never makes it to the airwaves.

As she starts to sing, her voice sounds great, fuller and more dramatic than on the album, but what everyone will remember about Sinéad this day is that she was *difficult.* It's a split-second paradigm of her career. After *I Do Not Want* rocketed up the charts, powered by a haunting, unforgettable version of the Prince-composed "Nothing Compares 2 U," and established her as both one of the most revered and most despised new stars in recent years, she commenced a series of moves that alienated a large percentage of even her most devoted fans.

In rapid succession, she pulled out of a *Saturday Night Live* appearance because shock comic Andrew Dice Clay was that week's host, refused to allow "The Star-Spangled Banner" to be played before a concert of hers in New Jersey (Frank Sinatra said she deserved a "kick in the ass"), boycotted the Grammy Awards to protest the materialism of the music industry (Hammer offered to pay her way back to Ireland) and moved to Los Angeles but soon returned to London, claiming that "there isn't any American culture." Last year she continued growing up in public, giving painful accounts in the press of the childhood abuse she suffered at the hands of her mother.

As she curls up barefoot on a sofa in her mid-Manhattan hotel, smoking Camels and slamming espresso through two intense marathon conversations, it is clear that the twenty-five-year-old O'Connor continues to regard interviews as an opportunity for public therapy, a way to confront her current twin obsessions—God and child abuse. Her whispered words swing from moving to loopy in seconds. She asserts ideas and opinions that are still essentially unformed and, more curious than strident, is passionately sincere even when directly contradicting herself. And talk about wearing your hang-ups on your sleeve: Her ripped oversize T-shirt reads RECOVERING CATHOLIC.

*What is it like to go back and sing songs familiar from your childhood—such an unhappy time in your life?*

Without me noticing it, it became a kind of a journey inside myself, to rescue myself. To go in and have fun and be who I am, which is just a girl who wants to have fun and sing. The songs on the first two albums were all about me working things out. These songs are about having worked a lot of those things out.

I'd say it's the closure of a phase and therefore the opening of another one. I have to let go of some things so that I can become whoever it is I'm supposed to be. I'm only twenty-five. I'm not going to be who I'm really supposed to be till I'm fifty or sixty. I think I'm becoming a woman. I'm growing up, but I've been finding it hard to let go of being a girl.

*Were the songs selected for specific memories?*

A lot of them were. "Don't Cry for Me Argentina" is very emotional for me because my mother used to really like me to sing her that song. It was the first song that I ever sang outside of school. Later, I used to run away, and to make money I would sing that song in talent competitions. "Scarlet Ribbons" links up with my father because he used to sing me that song, I was staggered by the idea of these ribbons just appearing because this girl asked God for them.

*Are you afraid of people looking at "Don't Cry for Me Argentina" and thinking you're being presumptuous, trying to emulate Eva Peron or present yourself as a martyr?*

I don't know anything about Eva Peron. It's just one of the most beautiful songs that I've ever heard. I can hardly sing it, it makes me feel so much. That's the only reason I've ever done anything.

Actually, that's the song that a lot of people have picked out because they said they thought it was just crap, but then when they heard it, they said they heard the song for the first time in their lives. They could hear it as a song and not just some bollocks.

*What was it like singing in front of an orchestra?*

I felt like they must look at me and think: "Who is this upstart? Why is she pretending to be a singer?" I felt so intimidated because they just walk in off the fuckin' street and play. That's how they spend their whole lives. I just felt like such a bluffer.

I was really fucking paranoid about it. I was walking in where people like Ella Fitzgerald and Julie London had been. I just kept saying to myself, "Shit, you're nothing, you don't deserve to be here, who do you think you are?" But after I was done, I ended up feeling that I'd like to get into that side of it, "cabaret," for want of a better word. I'd like to do things like musicals or things like what Liza Minnelli does.

*Most of the artists you usually talk about—rappers, Dylan, Van Morrison—break so many of the rules of songwriting, whereas these songs defined many of those rules.*

No, I don't think they do at all. I think that pop music these days is all along defined lines, but this music isn't. Cole Porter was an enormous chance taker. In an age where there was such a lot of censorship, he was able to very cleverly write rude things but say them in the most beautiful way. They did it in a much more pure and honest and truthful way. They went for reality then.

We don't really write about real feelings, 'cause we don't know how to talk about them anyway. We don't make love anymore, we *fuck*, and we write about fucking. We don't feel, we don't feel. These people felt, and the songs still feel now. They wrote fifty or sixty years ago, and it's exactly the same as it is now, whereas sixty years from now "I Want to Sex You Up" is not going to be in any way connected to what anybody feels. These people had it right. And after them it died.

*Did you try to record anything that you had written?*

No, I had no interest in putting out another Sinéad O'Connor record. Just not interested. I needed to have some fun and get away from it for a while, 'cause it went somewhere that I wasn't planning for it to. It's not that I was displeased by that; I'm pleased with being successful, but now I need to leave that alone. Besides, I'd like to be happy for a while.

But I'm a singer as well as a writer. I think of myself much more as a singer than a writer. The only reason I ever wrote songs was because I was so fucked up in my head that I had to figure things out for myself, and so I wrote songs to figure things out.

*"Nothing Compares 2 U" was an interpretation of a song you didn't write, too.*

Well, exactly. And I think that that's what I enjoy doing. I enjoy doing other people's stuff better because it's like acting. It's a chance to use someone else's words for a change instead of having to expose yourself. It's a chance to let out the other parts of myself and not just the angsty young thing. Now I want to be a woman.

*How do you look back on those crazy months after 'I Do Not Want What I Haven't Got' came out?*

Well, it's all one thing to me. "Nothing Compares 2 U" was just the herald, so it's all one big conglomeration of experiences to me. I feel I was very lucky to have the experience. It was very frightening, and it was also good fun. And I got completely and utterly fucked up by it. I felt lost, I didn't know who I was, I had a total identity crisis. I practically broke down. But if it wasn't for having got to that point, I never would have been put in a position where I had to find that out quickly, or else I was going to die.

*Is there anything you would handle differently now?*

No. Well, a lot personal things, not public things. As far as any of the things I've done in public, no. Except before the second album came out, my having said that I would support the IRA. Apart from that there's actually nothing I regret.

On a personal level, I regret relationships that I got into where I didn't have my armor on. But if it wasn't for those things, I would never have had to ask myself why I did these things, why I attracted these people, why I couldn't protect myself emotionally. Now I have my armor as a result of not having had it. So you've got to be grateful to the people that fucked you up. It's actually something to thank them for.

*What got you back on track?*

I had been stopped at a very young age and really hadn't grown at all. So then when I became famous, all these things happened to me, and I was so broken down that I had to be helped. That's when I met someone who became a very good friend—Peter Gabriel—who had been through a lot of the same things himself and recognized them in me.

*There was talk of a romance between the two of you.*

People always assume that if a man and a woman are great friends, that they are lovers. I would say the Peter Gabriel and myself are very, very, very, very close, and he's one of my best, best friends, and beyond that I don't have any comment. We're a man and a woman who happen to be very good friends, and we have a lot in common.

I'd say actually that most people who are influential in my life are grown men, men with a lot of experience and a lot of life. When men get to that age, they think about their lives a lot, they analyze their lives, and they're very wise. Men really come to fruition when they're about forty. Women, I think, more when they're around thirty. It takes a long time to become a man.

*What do you think of the "men's movement"?*

I love it. I love it. I love that book *Iron John*. It's very accurate, what (Robert Bly) says in that book. I wish he would do a book that was the equivalent for women. I'd love it if he analyzed the story of Joan of Arc, wrote *Iron Joan*. I think women are not very understanding, and I think it's our own fault. Women are in control, whether we see it or not, because we have the babies, we raise the sons and the daughters. So if we don't like how we're being treated, we've got to see that it's our own fault because we're not allowing our sons to be men.

*You have said that you are not a feminist.*

I'm not an anythingist. I don't belong to anything.

*What does feminism mean to you?*

I have a very deep love and respect and understanding for men. I have a love and understanding for women, too, but sometimes I feel more compassion for men because of the pain they're in. I don't feel that men are bastards, and I don't think it's right to frighten them by trying in a conglomeration to act against them. It's very difficult to be a man, far more difficult than being a woman. That's not to make little of what women are saying, because women are being treated abominably by some men, but it's only because they don't know what to do.

*Do you have any female role models?*

Joan of Arc is my biggest. My influences have been men, which is curious. I haven't felt as safe with women. I've never been close to them. Obviously, because of my mom. My singing has been influenced by people like Etta James or Barbra Streisand. But Joan of Arc is definitely the one, because she fought for what she knew was the truth. She took literally what God told her, and she listened to the voices inside her and died for it. Died a most horrific death.

*Is the reason for these feelings about women entirely due to your relationship with your mother?*

I think probably inside myself I've been quite frightened of women. Not that I don't like them—I love them. But because of my mother, I'm very sensitive to how women look at me. The most frightening aspect is the way their faces look when they actually look at me. I've been treated quite badly by women, like the girls at school. They hated me because I was very quiet, and I had long hair, and I would brush it in front of my face, and I would sit in the back of the class, and never used to speak to them. They thought that I was very full of myself. They thought I was very beautiful and thought that I thought I was great and that's why I wouldn't talk to them. So I feel safer with men.

*It seems you've gotten more focused on religion.*

There's no such thing as religion, there's only God. Which is truth. Organized religion is a lie. It's designed to take you away from God, particularly the Christian church. People must learn about the history of the popes, the people who are running the world. 'Cause whether we like it or not, whether we practice Christianity or Catholicism or not, we've got to realize that those fuckers are running the world, they're running every government in the world. They are the World Bank. I don't have proof of that, but I know that it's true.

We're living in hell as far as I'm concerned. The existence of child abuse means that the devil is winning. The devil to me is not a little red guy with a fork, he's a guy with a collar and a big red hat on that goes round saying, "Young people of Ireland, I love you," when the young people of Ireland are sitting on the streets, on heroin.

*Your spirituality sounds almost obsessive.*

It's from direct experience. I lived in hell for a long period of time. The only thing that saved my ass was God. I suppose it sounds like kind of an obsession, but it's the only reason I survived. It was the only way I could come out of a pretty grim situation and have a decent relationship with myself and my family. I'm still angry, but I'm alive, and that's because of God. If I hadn't believed in God, I would be dead now, I would be drunk, I would be on drugs. God gave me a voice, and that's what saved my ass. What got me through hell was my voice.

They don't know what God is; they're the Roman Empire, the people who invented child abuse. All you have to do is look at their history to know that this is true. That's why they killed Joan of Arc, that's why they killed Jesus Christ, that's why they killed Martin Luther King, that's why they killed John Kennedy, that's why they killed (Pope) John Paul I. That's why they killed Malcolm X. It's why they've locked up Mike Tyson.

Poor Mike Tyson. I mean there is an example of a man who was treated abominably as a child; all his ancestors have been abused as children. He's only a little tiny baby, and all of these people are trying to fuckin' kill him. And they have killed him to a certain extent. They all have a great time saying what a monster he is. Lay off, because there but for the grace of God goes every single one of us. Poor man. He has had the most miserable up-bringing. If he looks for solace in the arms of lots of women, what do you expect him to do? And that woman that is suing him is a bitch. I don't care if he raped her; he should learn about himself and why it is he behaves like that, et cetera, et cetera. But equally she should look at herself and look at the disgrace that she is making of women. Look at what she is doing to him by trying to get money off him, going around doing chat shows. She's used him, you know. It's disgraceful, and she's a disgrace to women as far as I'm concerned.

*You say we need to counter that with love. How do we get to that point?*

It takes forgiveness. Forgiveness is the most important thing. We all have to forgive what was done to us—the Irish people have to forgive, the African peo-ple, the Jewish people—all have to forgive and understand. The only way to stop the cycle of hate and abuse is not to allow ourselves to get caught up in it.

*What did you think about the riots in Los Angeles?*

I thought it was great. I really did. I thought it was time something hap-pened and that people had some expression at last. I think it's a shame that some people went so far as to kill other people, although I understand that people are in so much pain that they don't know how to stay in control. But I think those people have a perfect right to go into shops and take anything they wanted to take. Absolutely. I admire that, I'm very glad. It was a cleans-ing experience, and a lot of good has come out of it.

*Still, it doesn't seem the most forgiving response.*

They have to defend themselves. Jesus says that as well: "Woe to the na-tion that doesn't defend itself against the invader." You don't have the right to kill, but you have the right feed and clothe your family. You don't have the right to go and break into a shop, but if the shop is fucked up and your children are starving and they don't have anything to wear or they're sick, then you have every right to take what you want. I think that obviously it's awful for the people who do business and whose stores were destroyed, but in the end it's a good thing that serves everybody. There'll have to be a lot of chaos for us to sort ourselves out.

*When you moved from L.A., it was said that you felt a lot of anger to-ward America.*

Well, that was a lie. I did not leave the country for anything to do with that. I left because I missed home, and I missed my husband, and I missed red buses. I was lonesome. Being in Los Angeles was very tricky. I thought that the people would be so used to celebrities that it wouldn't be a prob-lem. In fact the opposite is true because all the celebrities there really love being celebrities. I hung around with a couple of those people for a day or two, and they frightened the shit out of me. It's like a hotel people check into for material success at any cost.

*Do you think people will be surprised to see the album dedication to New York?*

I never said I had a problem with America. People told you that because they want you to think that I'm a liar and that I'm full of hatred. They distorted what I was doing. People like me are scapegoats, people who point out the fact that those people are living a lie, and they want to shut us up. That's why they've assassinated everyone throughout history that ever spoke the truth.

*Why do you think there was such a backlash when you started speaking out so much?*

I think that was mainly because I was at a stage in my life where I had not yet the energy to be understanding of other people's feelings, and therefore I expressed my own feelings in an aggressive way. I wouldn't change my feelings or not express them. But now I try to be considerate of what other people out there hear. I wouldn't be so aggressive and angry and pointing blame—I regret that—but that all came from a lack of understanding.

*Do you think the changes you've gone through can happen on a larger scale?*

I can see it happening. I can see Axl Rose, myself, Roseanne Arnold and other people talking about their experiences. We can see the role models coming out now and giving hope to other people giving a sense that you can survive. That's what Axl Rose is in the process of doing right in front of our eyes. Really, we're just the same as everyone, we just happen to be so angry about it that we got ourselves famous so we could tell our stories.

*Are you comfortable presenting yourself as a role model? Lots of rappers, for instance Ice Cube, say that they never signed up to be role models just because they make records.*

I used to say that, too, but I think you've got to accept the responsibility. With Ice Cube, that's his low opinion of himself because of the upbringing he's had. He doesn't necessarily see how wonderful he is; really he's afraid to accept that he is the greatest poet that America has ever had. I would rank Ice Cube on an equal level with Bob Dylan in terms of being the voice of a generation. He's possibly the most powerful person in this country, but he's afraid to see that.

*Were you bothered by any of the controversial stuff on Ice Cube's last album?*

That doesn't mean that he's not a good writer. The point that everybody's forgetting is that art is the use of language, the means of expressing feelings. We all know what he's talking about and he's making us feel. Also, he's created a conversation where there has been silence. He's created that debate, and that's what art is for.

*Do you still listen to a lot of rap?*

I think it's had its day. I think its age is over because it's done everything it can do. It will continue, but it can't go any further, musically. Now something else will happen. Rap was the most influential form, the thing that most brought people together in the last ten years and that saved our asses, but it's over.

Rappers are all young men, and they're angry, and that's why it's brilliant. They're angry, and they've all been fucked around by their fathers. They were abused as children, and now that is why they're making themselves heard. It's also why Axl Rose is famous, Roseanne Arnold—it's why I'm famous.

*Because of a need to be heard?*

Because of wanting help, because we want help. We want our stories told. We don't understand what's happened to us, and we're in a lot of pain.

*When Axl talks about his childhood abuse, you're very aware of his being in therapy.*

My therapy is my belief in God.

*Have you tried formal therapy at all?*

I tried it, yes, but it didn't speak to me. I tried one of the twelve-step programs—adult children of alcoholics-dysfunctional families, but I didn't like the clinical shrinks so much. I didn't get off on that, but I got off on the twelve-step thing.

*Is one-on-one therapy just too detached or too structured?*

It's too much by the book. There's rules they apply to everybody. They seem very concerned with money and are always looking at their watch. It just didn't speak to me. Whereas the first time I walked into the adult child of dysfunctional families group, I was home. But it's my belief in God that's got me through.

*You've talked about your fondness for smoking dope and also about your belief that crack imprisons the population of the inner city. By buying any drug aren't you helping finance the destructive part of the drug trade?*

I don't buy marijuana off anybody that sells any other kind of drug. As far as I'm concerned, selling marijuana is one of the most respectable things anyone could do. I think everybody should smoke it.

*Why?*

Because it teaches you a lot about yourself. It forces you to feel. You cannot avoid being aware and getting in touch with yourself. People say you get really paranoid when you smoke, but it's not that; it's that you were feeling that way the whole time. You can't run away from your feelings; it forces you to face them.

*What do you make of the elections?*

I'm shocked at how the stars in the entertainment industry allow themselves to be used. I'm shocked that Aretha Franklin sang the national anthem at the convention, for example. I don't know anything about Bill Clinton; I can't really say except that his speech at the convention was more sad than anything else.

*You don't think stars should choose sides or they shouldn't be involved at all in the process?*

Being involved in politics, which is designed to take you away from the truth. Those people are only interested in getting into power and getting a good salary.

*What if a celebrity feels that since they get this kind of attention, they should use it to help a cause they believe in?*

That's fine, they should do that—but why not do it through the truth? Don't go through the liars to give your truth. Just give it.

*But as long as this country is in a situation where, say, access to abortion is controlled by the political process ...*

No, as long as you're in a situation where you're controlled by people who want money, it doesn't matter who you vote for. George Bush said that he wouldn't ban abortion. Bill Clinton will probably do the same thing. I wouldn't trust any of them. I wouldn't trust anyone who would hold a convention like that, who would hold it as if it were a gig, a big show, balloons and bands and flags and TV screens. It's got nothing to do with anything but the publicity and the pomp. It has nothing to do with people who are starving. It's all a lie.

*Should people vote?*

I've never voted, and I will never vote in my life, because I realize that there's absolutely no point. Because they're all fucking liars, they all want the same thing, they're all after one thing, which is money. They are not the way. Politics is there to take you away from truth.

People should just not vote, they should stop going to work, they should screech this whole fucking sham to a halt. Put the fuckers out of business and start all over again. Have the faith to go through the chaos that will result from doing that, realize that's the only thing to do. Look at what happened in Los Angeles. That has to happen on a larger scale without the destruction of people's property or lives. If we're all together, we can fuck it up.

## REFLECTING ON THE READING

Write the three statements by O'Connor with which you most disagree. Now state your opinion on those subjects in equally strong and direct terms.

◆

# THE MAKING OF A GREAT AMERICAN BAND

THEY CAME OUT OF THE EAST L.A. BARRIO, PLAYING TRADITIONAL MEXICAN MUSIC AT CINCO DE MAYO PARTIES AND WEDDINGS. BUT OVER THE PAST TWO DECADES, LOS LOBOS HAS WOVEN TOGETHER EVERYTHING FROM JAZZ TO ROCKABILLY TO NEW ORLEANS STOMP TO CREATE THE RICHEST MUSICAL TAPESTRY IN AMERICA.

ELENA OUMANO

◆

*If you are not familiar with music by Los Lobos, what reason explains your lack of familiarity? If you know*

*their music, try to recall when you first heard it. See
what new information you learn in Oumano's article.
Elena Oumano writes about music for the* Los Angeles
Times, LA Weekly, *and the* Village Voice.

A phosphorous-like glow rims the tall firs that encircle the Greek Theater
in Los Angeles. The moon has risen and stars peep through the haze of a
smog-choked late summer sky as the five members of Los Lobos take the stage
for their annual homecoming performance. Against a backdrop of gently
swaying gauze panels back-lit by an empyreal hue of lavender—a nod to its latest album, *Kiko and the Lavender Moon*—the band chooses to begin by paying homage to its Mexican roots. A roar surges up from the crowd of 6,000 as
Los Lobos breaks into a rollicking acoustic folkloric number. They follow with
a popular *Norteño*, a sweetly exuberant melody bearing a bleak tale of survival
on the wrong side of the border, in North America's garbage heap.

The night air is filled with ecstatic coyote yodels from an audience heavily populated by the denizens of East L.A.'s strictly segregated barrios. But
this band of lifelong buddies is more than an emblem of Mexican-American
pride, more even than the soul-stirring musical fusion of the American and
Chicano experiences. As far back as 1987, the late blues master Willie Dixon
declared Los Lobos "the best band in the country." Producer-musician T-
Bone Burnett has classed them with the Beatles, the Who, the Rolling Stones
and U2. With the release of *Kiko and the Lavender Moon* this summer, it
became official: The critics proclaimed the arrival of a great American
band—some would say *the* greatest band playing today.

Music reviewers were moved to exalted heights, describing *Kiko* as an
"epic" and a work of "genius." Because the album draws upon a variety of
musical traditions—including rockabilly, jazz, Mexican folk, blues, Afro-
Caribbean and New Orleans "stomp"—comparisons have been made to Paul
Simon's *Graceland*. But while Simon merely scavenged the deep riches of
South African music to heat up his tepid soul, in *Kiko* Los Lobos has effort-
lessly absorbed the sounds and rhythms of the global present to create
something original. The only other American bands that come close to
achieving this rich a musical stew nowadays are the Neville Brothers and the
Grateful Dead, and neither of these bands has ever produced a masterpiece
like *Kiko and the Lavender Moon*. Lyrically and musically, the bands's seventh album reaches deep down into the bruised heart of America, and from
that secret place, Los Lobos has created a true and loving sonic portrait that
not only reflects our present but suggests our future as well.

It has been almost two decades since David Hidalgo, Conrad R. Lozano,
Louie Pérez and Cesar Rosas, four rock'n'roll-playing teens from East L.A.'s
Garfield High, gathered in Mr. and Mrs. Rosas' backyard to figure out how
they could make a living gigging at Cinco de Mayo celebrations and Mexican-
American weddings. "It was different at the beginning," says Lozano, who
plays bass and sings back-up, in an understatement of gargantuan propor-

tions. For eight years the band performed acoustic folkloric music, such traditional barrio favorites as "Mil Amores." The name Los Lobos (The Wolves) originated as "a kind of a joke," recalls Lozano, who, like all the band members, is gregarious and completely without pretension. "Here we were these rock'n'roll musicians turning around and playing this Mexican stuff. 'What can we call ourselves for the next weekend's gig?' we wondered. We used to make fun of a band called Los Lobos de Norte because we thought their music was Mexican bubble gum. So we said, 'Let's call ourselves Los Lobos de Este,' which means East L.A. We thought it was funny, and the name stuck."

Money was scarce in the early days, but the band members received strong support from their families. "David (Hidalgo, who sings lead vocals and plays a variety of instruments) grew up with his mom in a little stick-and-cardboard house by the railroad tracks near the freeway," lyricist and drummer Louie Pérez recently told journalist Karen Essex. "We brought in drums, guitars, other stuff. Little by little, we kind of moved her out. She was left with a small corner of the house and a black-and-white TV. She would put in earplugs and say, 'Have at it.' The ceiling was so low, we used to bash out the light fixtures on a regular basis with our guitar necks. And luckily she worked at Newberry's, so she could replace them right away."

Pérez's dad had died when he was 9 years old. He grew up with his working mom and sister in a barrio peopled by female survivors: the little old lady who ran the corner store, the women hunched over sewing machines in sweatshops, the teens pushing baby carriages. Conrad Lozano's parents were divorced. His father, a punch press operator, spent money he didn't have to buy his only son his first amplifier. A few years later, in 1969, he went into debt so Conrad could own a state-of-the-art amplifier.

For several years, Los Lobos earned a respectable living gigging at universities and other culturally minded venues. With the help of friends, they managed to buy enough time at $30-an-hour studios to record an album, which they distributed from the trunks of their cars, charging $1, if anything at all. But by the 1980's, campus entertainment funds were drying up and Mexican restaurants like the Red Onion, where they were hired to play five hours a night, five nights a week, provided a humbler but steadier income. "Finally we ended up in a place in Anaheim called Los Lomos, a cool little Mexican bar-restaurant," Lozano recalls. "It was packed every night with people listening to us play the traditional forms. Pretty soon they began yelling out, 'Hey, man, do you know any Beatles songs?' So we played Beatles songs and early '60s stuff from the East Coast; we'd just remember them out of the blue and try them. Everybody would get a kick out of it because we did them with traditional instruments."

As the band added rock classics to its repertoire, it began relying more on electric instruments. "Pretty soon," Lozano says, "someone asked for a Hendrix song. 'Sure!' It got to the point where we had a full kit, bass amps, guitar amps, and we were giving them two hours of folk music and two hours of dance music and rock'n'roll. Then we got fired because it got too loud."

Los Lobos wound up in a garage, the venue occupied at some point by nearly every other early '80s L.A. band. There was nothing to do but rehearse—and write. "We thought if we came up with some original stuff, we could play on the west side of town," says Lozano. The Blasters, stars of the Sunset Strip scene at the time, became Los Lobos' ticket west. After listening to a tape, the Blasters invited them to open their gig at the fabled Whisky A Go-Go.

That Westside debut "knocked everybody out," says Steve Berlin, who was playing saxophone and keyboards with the Blasters at the time. "They asked if I wanted to learn some of their songs to jam with them," he recalls. "It started from there." For a time, Berlin bounced back and forth between the two groups, until the inevitable scheduling conflict presented itself and he opted for the ever-expanding musical universe of Los Lobos. "The Blasters, God love them, were a wonderful group, but they had defined their territory with 40-foot-high walls," he says. "There was room to grow but it was more or less focused inwardly within a fairly narrow range, albeit very much of their own and pretty cool. Los Lobos was including a wide open range of possibilities. Even then you could see they were pushing things. There was a lot of freedom and willingness to experiment back then, but within the scene's own set there was a lot of parochialism. X and Los Lobos were the only (Los Angeles) bands trying to stretch every boundary they could."

The Blasters, who were signed to Slash Records, persuaded the label to take on Los Lobos. In 1983, after a year and a half or so of playing for beer and peanuts, the band released … *And a Time to Dance,* a seven-cut EP. The budget was minuscule, says Berlin, but there was the simple pleasure of "getting something on tape, having it come back, and realizing more or less what the band sounded like."

Los Lobos toured Europe and America twice before returning to the studio in the summer of 1984 to record the anthemic *How Will the Wolf Survive?,* one of those albums that announced to the world there was something new and vital bubbling up from the L.A. underground. "In some ways, *A Time to Dance* was a postcard, but *How Will the Wolf Survive?* is more like a letter," says Berlin. "We had more time in the studio, the Olympics was going on at the same time, so a lot of focus was on the city, and they'd be running a marathon right on the street. There was a great vortex of activity, and we were able to bring something a little deeper to the marketplace."

The electricity that galvanized *Wolf* misfired on 1987's *By the Light of the Moon,* an album marred by an absence of focus. The beckoning light, that glimmer of some overarching inspiration that led the group before and since, was missing. "That one was kind of strange," says Berlin, who has doubled as producer on most of the band's albums. "We started the process with about five songs written, and we recorded those songs in about a week. Then the next five songs took a year. We learned how not to make a record on that one and how easy it is to waste thousands and thousands of dollars if you don't have a clue about what you're doing. That record is probably the hardest one for me to listen to and get into just because it was not fun to make. I remember a sense of relief just at having been done with it, rather than 'Wow, it's great, let's go tour and play these songs!' The same magic that happened with *Kiko* was the inverse on *By the Light*."

Before leaving hearth and home to slog dutifully around the country in support of *By the Light*, Los Lobos ducked into the studio for two weeks to record the soundtrack to the Ritchie Valens biopic, *La Bamba*. The Valens family had informally adopted the group after it had played its hometown of Santa Cruz, and it insisted its *carnales* (friends who are like family) be given the job of interpreting the late singer's music for the screen. As soon as Los Lobos wrapped up *La Bamba*, the band headed out on tour, confident that the movie would go straight to cable. The stars were unknown, it was only director Luis Valdez's second film venture, and the subject was Mexican-American—not exactly a formula for box-office success. "It wasn't like you rubbed your fingers together and thought, 'Oh, boy, this is going to sell 4 million records!'" Berlin says. "If anything, we thought it would sell four records."

But much to the band's surprise—and chagrin—the *La Bamba* soundtrack flew to the top of the charts and nested there for months. "There we were, with everyone singing this stupid song everywhere we went, all summer long," Berlin says. "To have all that adulation for something that was really not much of a part of us was discomforting. It's not that I'm whining about selling all these records. It's just mildly surreal that it was about a favor to Ritchie's family more than anything else, and it didn't necessarily reflect the breadth and depth of the work we had come up with at that point and since.

"It was really more about Columbia and Paramount Pictures and Coca-Cola and a lot of money moving around the Earth. The producers of the movie saw fit to sell the rights to the song to virtually anyone who had 50 cents to rub together, so the song was used to push all these other pathetic things, like popcorn and tanning oil. That kind of got to me, because people thought we sold out. 'God! They had a hit record and now they're selling popcorn.'"

Drastic measures were taken, in the form of 1988's corrective (albeit lovely) *La Pistola y El Corazon,* essentially a re-release of their independently produced 1978 folkloric LP plus three new songs. Sung entirely in Spanish and played on acoustic instruments, the album was a crystal-clear statement that Los Lobos had not watered down their music in search of filthy lucre. "It was a way to reclaim a perspective on what we were doing," says Berlin.

This time the band toured for the hard core only; *La Bamba* fans were effectively warned off by advertisements for "an evening of acoustic folkloric music with Los Lobos." "A lot of people couldn't figure out what we were doing and thought we should have chased after all this momentum that *La Bamba* built," says the warm and boyish-looking Pérez. "But, in a way, we had to put a stop to it."

Four years later, Los Lobos found their way back to their unique rock'n'roll juju with 1990's *The Neighborhood*. But when they went out to tour, America was at home, too broke from the deepening recession to go out. Besides, the Gulf war, the year's biggest spectacle, was keeping people riveted to their TVs. Though it seems no one heard *The Neighborhood* at the time, it contained the seeds of the inspired musical genre-crossing that would bloom two years later in *Kiko*. By the album's completion, the band had found its true voice. The studio was no longer an alien environment. Los Lobos had learned, says Berlin, "how to make a record that reflects (the band's) complexity and musicality, how to have it make sense and come from a deeper place. In some ways, *The Neighborhood* came from the same experimentation (as *Kiko*), but with less self-trust, less of the idea that whatever happened was going to be OK. I remember mixing a lot of the songs six, seven, eight, nine times, beating the life out of them, not really sure and not really trusting ourselves to say, 'OK, it's done now. This is as accurate a reflection of where we're at as it could possibly be.' That was what we did with *Kiko*."

The progression from *La Bamba* to *La Pistola* to *The Neighborhood* to *Kiko* has a natural logic, according to band members. "*La Bamba* left us wondering, 'Who are we?' says Pérez. "That was a real reassessment time, and it took us two records to get to this one, the one that we've been wanting to make for a long time. But there was so much we had to get out of our system that I don't see how we could have made this record without going through the process of ridding ourselves, of letting it all go. We had to do those records, and in the process we found things, and we had to be brave."

Before *Kiko,* the band had been all over the musical map. There was really only one place left to go. "That was inside—it was an inside job," chuckles Pérez. "We had to close our eyes, turn ourselves away from everything outside, and plumb deep to do something completely, totally from us."

By going deep within, Los Lobos was able to crash through musical barriers and create their "breakthrough" album. But in arriving at this great musical synthesis, have the band members left the barrio behind, or have they brought it to the world? "We've gone beyond what people expect from a Mexican-American band, even what our own people expect from us," says Pérez. "We defied a lot of elements of our own culture, because there's no reason to feel any limitations. I grew up in that kind of insular environment in East Los Angeles; it becomes real safe. 'Well, this is it, my whole world. I'm Mexican-American.'

"Everything about us has been trivialized—our music, our dance. So everybody has preconceived notions about who and what we are. The only reference points are Cheech and Chong movies or old Westerns with the *banditos* with the big mustaches. It's amazing, but the media has perpetuated that for many decades. It's 1992 and we have so far to go."

A man in the audience at the Greek is calling loudly and repeatedly for "Anselma" from … *And a Time to Dance*. He'll finally get that gritty ballad about life on the border, but not until the audience has been treated to a set structured largely around *Kiko*'s intoxicating dreamscape—16 songs with gorgeous arrangements blending sleek strains of jazz, boisterous Mexican *cumbia*, feverish Bourbon Street beats and Afro-Cuban polyrhythms, mournful country and western, gristly Chicago blues and straight-up rock'n'roll. Told in brilliant bursts of images reminiscent of Latin American magical realism, *Kiko's* tenderhearted tales of human wretchedness shimmer with numinous meaning. Loss is redeemed, though, by faith in a heavenly reality that barely takes note of this one.

The band launches into the cool Ellingtonian samba-swing that introduces the album's title track, and David Hidalgo's warm, plaintive tenor floats seraphically through the warm night air. Like Aaron Neville, Hidalgo is tall and sturdily built, and his impassive macho persona mysteriously produces the same pure voice of an angel. Then it's "When the Circus Comes to Town," set to the dragging tempo of a rundown carousel, a tune that evokes The Band at its most haunted best. Los Lobos follows this with the aching, bittersweet "Just a Man," the kind of blues that either comforts or sends depressed listeners out the nearest open window. Lest disconsolate souls in the audience drift away on a sea of reverie, Cesar Rosas, the yang to Hidalgo's yin and the bands's goatee-and-shades-wearing hipster, brings the show back to earth with his full-throated rendition of "That Train Don't Stop Here." These *hombres* are definitely ethereal, but they also come in the name of funk.

Much has been made of the time songwriters Pérez and Hidalgo spent with former members of The Band in Woodstock. But while "Circus" does conjure up memories of the early Band, the period the two songwriters spent in upstate New York just before writing *Kiko* merely served to get their creative juices flowing. "There wasn't much but David and myself in this little house in Woodstock under 5 feet of snow," recalls Pérez. "It could have been anywhere and any situation. Work on our record didn't happen until we got back, although there were a couple of things we started there that we decided to keep for ourselves. When we got back to L.A. sometime in February (1991), we already knew we had opened up a can of worms."

Pérez and Hidalgo decided to move the 25-year conversation that had begun in the little room in Hidalgo's mother's house to another little room that they rented behind a bookstore in Whittier, the tree-lined bedroom community where they now live with their wives and children. "We would drop the kids off at school, show up there every day and hang out until it was time to pick them up," says Pérez. "It was unusual for us to set up shop somewhere, but it was a place for us to sit down and exchange ideas. We could have gone on forever. Mitchell Froom (*Kiko's* co-producer) said we had to stop sometime, so we put a lid on it after 16 songs. As far as we're concerned, David and I are not done yet. We get together where and when we can, in a hotel room or when we have a chance to talk."

"When we wrote *Kiko*, we felt we had healed or cleansed ourselves," Pérez continues. "We're not writing for anybody but ourselves. That's when you leave things wide open and become a kind of receptor; everything starts to come in and go out."

This same spirit of openness and spontaneity held firm in the recording studio, where the entire group agreed to make room for magic by keeping the production process as simple as possible. "We tried to get first takes as much as we could," says Berlin, "to get the first idea that popped into our heads when we heard a chord sequence. More times than not it would work; it was pretty amazing."

Pérez and Hidalgo would sing or play a four-track tape of a chord sequence, or a groove, or the idea of an approach. The rest of the group would listen three or four times, Berlin says, then "run to an instrument and start banging on it. We would record right away, and usually something would happen. We weren't sure if it would become part of the record or just a map, but usually the first idea was pretty powerful. We would grab it, and get something within three takes, be it the drum track or most of the drum track, or a sound. We used a lot of '60s and '70s technology like fuzz boxes; we used very little digital equipment. The older technology is definitely warmer and odder."

Modern digital processing would have undermined the spontaneity in the studio. "What we wanted was to find other stuff that perhaps wasn't as trendy," says Berlin. "A lot of the trouble with the modern technology is you have to program it; you have to figure it out, you have to stare at it for a while. Whereas the way we wanted to use the older (instruments) was plug them in and fly. For a couple of weeks we were competing to see who could top who by bringing in the weirdest-looking, weirdest-sounding devices to the studio. David, Chad Blake (the studio engineer), and myself all collect that stuff. We would bring something in, everyone would stare at it like at the monolith from *2001,* then plug it in and start playing with it. It was all old, outmoded, out-of-work devices."

"Mitchell likes the idea of creating a band," Berlin continues. "We'd hear a song and he'd say, "Why don't we put together a band with accordion, harmonium, bongos, fuzz guitar and penny whistle?' In other words, what would happen if you just played the song naturally but on these wacky instruments? He likes to put together odd combinations—not necessarily play songs oddly—but just play them and see what happens. It was one of those cases where we all had a very similar idea of what kind of record we wanted to make, which, oddly, is not often the case between producer and band."

Another element that distinguishes *Kiko* is its fulsome and melodically sensitive polyrhythms, thanks in part to Pérez's co-drummer, Pete Thomas, who expanded his instrument's role beyond mere rhythmic foundation to something less parochial and more atmospheric. "Pete worked hard at developing an idea that would work and be different," says Berlin. "His wacky approach, as much as almost anything, pushed us in interesting directions."

Even the artwork for *Kiko* reflects the music's aura of childlike wonder and exploration. One side of the CD booklet pictures a low-angle view past a child's yellow wooden chair (labeled "Kiko" in wobbly print), and through a half-opened window to a dark lavender sky. The other side, also set in the child's moonlit room, pictures a white and pink birthday cake covered with candles flickering in the breeze.

"When you finally get rid of a bunch of ghosts, you find a real pure place in yourself," says Pérez, reflecting on how the various band members' personal evolution led to the making of *Kiko*. "Not that we've approached some kind of nirvana-like enlightenment, but when you finally can exorcise yourself of some of those (ghosts), then things naturally become very innocent and childlike. We all wish we could get back to that place. As we grow older, we get so calloused and tough-skinned. For the most part, we're tanks running around trying to protect our vulnerability. Every now and then a little something leaks out, and that's when we paint and write and love."

## REFLECTING ON THE READING

Music critics have developed their own language, such phrases as "fulsome and melodically sensitive polyrhythms." Identify three phrases like that from Oumano's article and explain their meaning in everyday language.

◆

---

# MUSIC

## ALLAN BLOOM

---

◆

*The late Allan Bloom was a distinguished professor of philosophy at the University of Chicago. As you read, decide whether or not you think Bloom is qualified to discuss rock music.*

Civilization or, to say the same thing, education is the taming or domestication of the soul's raw passions—not suppressing or excising them, which would deprive the soul of its energy—but forming and informing them as art. The goal of harmonizing the enthusiastic part of the soul with what develops later, the rational part, is perhaps impossible to attain. But without it, man can never be whole. Music, or poetry, which is what music becomes as reason emerges, always involves a delicate balance between passion and reason, and, even in its highest and most developed forms—religious, warlike and erotic—that balance is always tipped, if ever so slightly, toward the passionate. Music, as everyone experiences, provides an unquestionable justification and a fulfilling pleasure for the activities it accompanies: the soldier who hears the marching band is enthralled and reassured;

the religious man is exalted in his prayer by the sound of the organ in the church; and the lover is carried away and his conscience stilled by the romantic guitar. Armed with music, man can damn rational doubt. Out of the music emerge the gods that suit it, and they educate men by their example and their commandments.

Plato's Socrates disciplines the ecstasies and thereby provides little consolation or hope to men. According to the Socratic formula, the lyrics— speech and, hence, reason—must determine the music—harmony and rhythm. Pure music can never endure this constraint. Students are not in a position to know the pleasures of reason; they can only see it as a disciplinary and repressive parent. But they do see, in the case of Plato, that that parent has figured out what they are up to. Plato teaches that, in order to take the spiritual temperature of an individual or a society, one must "mark the music." To Plato and Nietzsche, the history of music is a series of attempts to give form and beauty to the dark, chaotic, premonitory forces in the soul—to make them serve a higher purpose, an ideal, to give man's duties a fullness. Bach's religious intentions and Beethoven's revolutionary and humane ones are clear enough examples. Such cultivation of the soul uses the passions and satisfies them while sublimating them and giving them an artistic unity. A man whose noblest activities are accompanied by a music that expresses them while providing a pleasure extending from the lowest bodily to the highest spiritual, is whole, and there is no tension in him between the pleasant and the good. By contrast a man whose business life is prosaic and unmusical and whose leisure is made up of coarse, intense entertainments, is divided, and each side of his existence is undermined by the other.

Hence, for those who are interested in psychological health, music is at the center of education, both for giving the passions their due and for preparing the soul for the unhampered use of reason. The centrality of such education was recognized by all the ancient educators. It is hardly noticed today that in Aristotle's *Politics* the most important passages about the best regime concern musical education, or that the *Poetics* is an appendix to the *Politics.* Classical philosophy did not censor the singers. It persuaded them. And it gave them a goal, one that was understood by them, until only yesterday. But those who do not notice the role of music in Aristotle and despise it in Plato went to school with Hobbes, Locke and Smith, where such considerations have become unnecessary. The triumphant Enlightenment rationalism thought that it had discovered other ways to deal with the irrational part of the soul, and that reason needed less support from it. Only in those great critics of Enlightenment and rationalism, Rousseau and Nietzsche, does music return, and they were the most musical of philosophers. Both thought that the passions—and along with them their ministerial arts—had become thin under the rule of reason and that, therefore, man himself and what he sees in the world have become correspondingly thin. They wanted to cultivate the enthusiastic states of the soul and to re-experience the Corybantic possession deemed a pathology by Plato. Nietzsche, particularly, sought to tap again the irrational sources of vitality, to replenish our dried-up stream from barbaric sources, and thus encouraged the Dionysian and the music derivative from it.

This is the significance of rock music. I do not suggest that it has any high intellectual sources. But it has risen to its current heights in the education of the young on the ashes of classical music, and in an atmosphere in which there is no intellectual resistance to attempts to tap the rawest passions. Modern-day rationalists, such as economists, are indifferent to it and what it represents. The irrationalists are all for it. There is no need to fear that "the blond beasts" are going to come forth from the bland souls of our adolescents. But rock music has one appeal only, a barbaric appeal, to sexual desire—not love, not *eros*, but sexual desire undeveloped and untutored. It acknowledges the first emanations of children's emerging sensuality and addresses them seriously, eliciting them and legitimating them, not as little sprouts that must be carefully tended in order to grow into gorgeous flowers, but as the real thing. Rock gives children, on a silver platter, with all the public authority of the entertainment industry, everything their parents always used to tell them they had to wait for until they grew up and would understand later.

Young people know that rock has the beat of sexual intercourse. That is why Ravel's *Bolero* is the one piece of classical music that is commonly known and liked by them. In alliance with some real art and a lot of pseudo-art, an enormous industry cultivates the taste for the orgiastic state of feeling connected with sex, providing a constant flood of fresh material for voracious appetites. Never was there an art form directed so exclusively to children.

Ministering to and according with the arousing and cathartic music, the lyrics celebrate puppy love as well as polymorphous attractions, and fortify them against traditional ridicule and shame. The words implicitly and explicitly describe bodily acts that satisfy sexual desire and treat them as its only natural and routine culmination for children who do not yet have the slightest imagination of love, marriage or family. This has a much more powerful effect than does pornography on youngsters, who have no need to watch others do grossly what they can so easily do themselves. Voyeurism is for old perverts; active sexual relations are for the young. All they need is encouragement.

The inevitable corollary of such sexual interest is rebellion against the parental authority that represses it. Selfishness thus becomes indignation and then transforms itself into morality. The sexual revolution must overthrow all forces of domination, the enemies of nature and happiness. From love comes hate, masquerading as social reform. A worldview is balanced on the sexual fulcrum. What were once unconscious or half-conscious childish resentments become the new Scripture. And then comes the longing for the classless, prejudice-free, conflictless, universal society that necessarily results from liberated consciousness—"We Are the World," a pubescent version of *Alle Menschen werden Brüder,* the fulfillment of which has been inhibited by the political equivalents of Mom and Dad. These are the three great lyrical themes: sex, hate and a smarmy, hypocritical version of brotherly love. Such polluted sources issue in a muddy stream where only monsters can swim. A glance at the videos that project images on the wall of Plato's cave since MTV took it over suffices to prove this. Hitler's image recurs frequently enough in exciting contexts to give one pause. Nothing noble, sublime, profound, delicate, tasteful or even decent can find a place in such tableaux. There is room only for the intense, changing, crude and immediate, which Tocqueville warned us would be the character of democratic art, combined with a pervasiveness, importance and content beyond Tocqueville's wildest imagination.

Picture a thirteen-year-old boy sitting in the living room of his family home doing his math assignment while wearing his Walkman headphones or watching MTV. He enjoys the liberties hard won over centuries by the alliance of philosophic genius and political heroism, consecrated by the blood of martyrs; he is provided with comfort and leisure by the most productive economy ever known to mankind; science has penetrated the secrets of nature in order to provide him with the marvelous, lifelike electronic sound and image reproduction he is enjoying. And in what does progress culminate? A pubescent child whose body throbs with orgasmic rhythms; whose feelings are made articulate in hymns to the joys of onanism or the killing of parents; whose ambition is to win fame and wealth in imitating the drag-queen who makes the music. In short, life is made into a nonstop, commercially prepackaged masturbational fantasy.

This description may seem exaggerated, but only because some would prefer to regard it as such. The continuing exposure to rock music is a reality, not one confined to a particular class or type of child. One need only ask first-year university students what music they listen to, how much of it and what it means to them, in order to discover that the phenomenon is universal in America, that it begins in adolescence or a bit before and continues through the college years. It is *the* youth culture and, as I have so often insisted, there is now no other countervailing nourishment for the spirit. Some of this culture's power comes from the fact that it is so loud. It makes conversation impossible, so that much of friendship must be without the shared speech that Aristotle asserts is the essence of friendship and the only true common ground. With rock, illusions of shared feelings, bodily contact and grunted formulas, which are supposed to contain so much meaning beyond speech, are the basis of association. None of this contradicts going about the business of life, attending classes and doing the assignments for them. But the meaningful inner life is with the music.

## REFLECTING ON THE READING

Bloom seems to argue that rock music's primary effect is to arouse sexual feelings in young people. What evidence does he offer for this opinion? Do you agree or disagree with him? What evidence do you have to support your opinion? Summarize your answers to these questions in a paragraph of about 150 words.

# PUTTING IT IN WRITING

## RESPONSES

1. List your five favorite musicians and/or singers. Try to write a single statement that explains the appeal of all five for you.
2. Watch three TV commercials or three music videos you have not seen before without the sound. In a short paragraph, describe your response to viewing without the sound.
3. Listen to any one of the songs mentioned in one of the chapter's readings, preferably one you have not heard before. Describe your reaction to the song in a short paragraph. Then, write one or two sentences explaining why you reacted that way.

## READING FOR MEANING

1. Using a reading selected by your instructor, copy out the single sentence that best states the author's main point. Then copy out two other sentences that support that main point.
2. Using a paragraph selected by your instructor, list all the words that convey the author's emotions or feelings. Then, in one sentence, state what the author's feeling is.
3. Using the article by either Walters or Oumano, list five references unfamiliar to you and look them up in an appropriate reference work. Explain each reference in a single sentence.

## ORGANIZING YOUR IDEAS

1. Find the lyrics of a song you really like and the lyrics of a song you really dislike. List the phrases from each song that support your opinion of the song.
2. Listen for an hour to a popular local radio station (one that features music). Based on the music you hear, describe the type of music and the format of that station.
3. Look at the kinds of questions asked of Sinéad O'Connor in the *Rolling Stone* interview. Now, assume one of your classmates is a celebrity.

Formulate a series of questions that would help reveal his or her values and character. Bring the questions to class and interview your classmate. After the interview, try to write a brief introduction that would summarize the main points you learned about your classmate.

# WRITING A PAPER

1. Find an opinion about music that you agree with from one of the readings. Compare that opinion to the one you developed in #1 in "Organizing Your Ideas." Now, write a paper based on comparing your opinion with that of the author you selected.
2. Several of the articles in this chapter assume a cause-effect relationship between listening to certain kinds of music (rap, rock, classical) and particular behaviors by those who regularly listen to that music or those lyrics. Write a paper in which you analyze the evidence cited by the writer for the cause-effect connection. Evaluate the writer's claims based on your own experience. (The work you did on #2 and #3 in "Responses" may be helpful in developing your material.)
3. Find two articles in this chapter that express conflicting opinions about some aspect of music. Explain each opinion, summarizing the writer's main arguments, and then express your own opinion, supporting your differences with the two writers you analyze.

**CATHY** • Cathy Guisewite

**Choosing clothes to wear can be difficult, depending
on the situation and the impression you want to make.
What's the irony in Cathy's situation?**

# CONSUMING

Growing up in the 1940s and 1950s, I never thought of myself as a "consumer." The word has very recent, modern connotations for me. So, I thought I would check out my intuition. In the reference room of my college library, I consulted several unabridged dictionaries until I found one that provided dates for when words first entered the English language. I knew I could check in the *Oxford English Dictionary*, but my belief that the word was quite new led me to a more recent source. *The Random House Dictionary of the English Language, Second Edition*, copyright 1987, provided me with the information I wanted—and a surprise. "Consumer," used in the sense of "squanderer," went back to the time of Chaucer, entering English some time between 1375 and 1425. In its more current meaning ("a person that uses a commodity or service"), entry into English is dated at 1525–1535, a few decades before Shakespeare was born. So, the word is quite old.

Why did I think the word was so recent? Well, I scanned the column of related words in the dictionary until my eye fell upon "consumerism." This term carried the dates 1940-1945 and was defined, in part, as a movement to protect consumers against "useless, inferior or dangerous products, misleading advertising, unfair pricing, etc." That word did come into English during my lifetime and is the connotation I most often have when I think of being a "consumer." This sense relates to a much older piece of advice for purchasers of goods and services: *caveat emptor*, or "let the buyer beware."

The first "consumer protection" practice I can recall is one my mother taught me. She would often send me to the corner store with a note and my wagon to buy such items as bread, milk, or potatoes. Once in a while, she also asked me to go to the butcher shop next to the grocery store to buy some meat. Her instructions were very specific: "Ask the butcher for one pound of round steak. After he has cut and weighed it, say 'grind it, please.'"

This practice was intended to guard against a butcher who might substitute some lesser grade of ground beef. I can't imagine myself doing that now!

Today, being a consumer has many dimensions. We shop for necessities such as food and clothing. We shop for luxuries such as jewelry and sports cars. We are encouraged to buy through advertising. If we buy too much too quickly, economists worry that we'll cause inflation. If we don't buy, government and business leaders worry about recession and a lack of "consumer confidence." When we shop, we may be mostly concerned with value, getting the greatest quantity or the highest quality for the least money. We also may be concerned with status, owning an object that will impress others as well as serve some function (such as, designer clothing or gourmet food). We may shop out of some emotional need, buying things because we are depressed or being waited on by salespeople because we need attention. Modern shopping centers and malls, like the marketplaces of old, provide places to meet people, as well as places to see and be seen. Modern packaging, chemistry, and manufacturing methods have all created new challenges for consumers. As you will see in the readings in this chapter, the act of "consuming" is rarely only the act of a person using a commodity or service.

As a way of activating your thinking, make two lists before you read any of these articles. The first should list the three largest purchases you have ever made in your life. The second should list the goods and services that you buy routinely (on a daily, weekly, or, at most, monthly basis). After you have made your lists, think about your methods and reasons for buying these goods and services. Then, as you read, compare your experiences to those described by the authors of the articles in this chapter.

◆

---

# SORRY, FRIEND, MY HOME IS A NO-SELLING ZONE

## MARTA VOGEL

---

◆

*When you go to a car dealership, you expect to get a sales pitch. But Vogel finds she gets sales pitches in unexpected places. What's the most unusual situation in which someone tried to sell you something?*

An ex-neighbor whom I don't often talk to comes by on what I think is a friendly call, perhaps to invite us to dinner or to thank me for the baby present. When I ask, "How do you manage with three kids? I'm tired just from one," he seizes the opportunity and tells me that he's been taking a nutritional supplement that really works. Would I like to hear more about it?

Within the same week, a writer who comes to the screenwriting group at my house says, "Oh, by the way, I'm going to bring along a water filtering system I thought you might be interested in." And the babysitter's teen-age daughter wants to tell me about NuSkin.

Everybody is selling something these days, and they're doing it up close and at home. With telemarketing oversaturated and mail boxes indiscriminately crammed with junk mail, marketers are on the lookout for cracks in the consumer's life that haven't been sealed against selling. Friends and acquaintances fit the bill.

According to Success magazine, "Experts predict that in the '90s 'network marketing'—sometimes called multi-level marketing or just MLM—will fuse Americans from coast to coast into one gigantic, pulsating sales amoeba."

Please. Leave us somewhere without a commercial. Some friends without a pitch.

Marketing people are scared, and I guess they should be. Chris Whittle, the "innovator" of commercial TV in the classroom, estimates that more than 40 percent of Americans rarely see commercials, even the biggest campaigns.

So Whittle, who markets "place-based TV," and network marketing people are out to get you where you can't turn them off and you can't say no.

At my former pediatrician's office, a Whittle Communications video asks teen-agers, "What bugs you most about your parents?" Another patient in the reception area, looks at me and asks, "Are you watching this?" No. And then he does something that he had never given a second thought to but which he assumed to be his right as a watcher of TV: He attempts to change the channel. He can't.

Gotcha. "Captive audience" was never more aptly applied.

And while I could have said no to my friend flogging nutritional supplements, this is a person I like and whose friendship I would like to keep. He's in my living room making his pitch. Gotcha.

Is no place or person sacred from selling?

Let's designate no-selling areas. In the same manner that we now have no-smoking areas, it's time for "no advertising zones." Homes, schools, hospitals, parks—and friends—should be the first candidates.

We need places in our immediate environment where we can say no, turn the dial, turn the ad off. We also need places where the mind can roam without being forced to contemplate whether to buy something.

## REFLECTING ON THE READING

Which form of selling in your home (telemarketers, junk mail, door-to-door salespeople, friends with a sales pitch) offends you the most? Describe one such incident and suggest one way to deal with intrusive sales approaches.

◆

# ARE WE LOSING OUR WAY IN $150 SNEAKERS?

ELLEN GOODMAN*

◆

*Can you recall a situation in which you and your parents disagreed about a purchase you wanted to make? What was the situation? What was the basis of the conflict? How did it get worked out?*

We are talking about sneakers. Big sneakers. Size 12 sneakers. The new ones that are currently located on my friend's son's feet, which are currently located on a high school floor.

The sneakers, which loom even larger than a size 12 in her mind's eye, came into her life all pumped up with hostility. Parent and child had wrangled over them for weeks.

This woman did not approve of the purchase. She and her husband regard $150 sneakers as proof of warped values, rip-off materialism, not to mention the decline and fall of Western civilization. Her son regards them as a necessity, an object of desire, proof of his need to make his own choices.

At the end of the family wrangling, the boy played his trump card or, more specifically, his paycheck. This what he said: "I'll use my own money." He went into the store with a portion of his summer earnings and walked out with scientifically designed, engineered and marketed ego-building shoes.

The woman and her husband were silenced by his declaration. And bothered by it.

This is what we talk about in the shadow of these sneakers, this woman and I: Our parents, ourselves, our children. Money and independence and family.

Our parents who were young during the Depression used to bring money home, put money on the table. Those were the expressions they used. The assumption was that whatever they earned went into the family pot for distribution. Little went directly to their own pockets.

Now half a century later, teen-agers earn "their own money." They are much less likely to "bring it home." In some families, that money may ease pressure on the family budget. In others it may be designated for college as

---

*Ellen Goodman is a *Boston Globe* columnist.

well as compact discs and sneakers. But it is usually described and circumscribed as "theirs." To do with as they will.

Immigrant families still seem to pool their resources. But American parents who depend on a teen-ager's earnings for groceries or rent are more likely to feel ashamed of themselves than proud of their children.

Is this an economic piece of the heralded breakdown of the American family? My friend thinks so.

We count the many ways in which the marketplace treats us as individuals rather than members of families. Most adults are employed on our own as workers who now earn single wages, not family wages. We are subdivided as consumers with separate wants—sneakers and Walkmen—not shared needs. Even preschoolers have their Saturday morning TV market.

Increasingly each generation is on its own, liberated and isolated in and by the economy. We appear less like a permanent family unit than like temporarily connected individuals, currently cohabiting.

It happens up and down the age spectrum. On the turnpike this summer, I passed an elderly couple in a car decorated with a bumper sticker that read "If you don't go first class, your children will." My friend remembers laughing at a boat named "My Children's Inheritance."

We both know parents of our age wrestling with the costs of college. Should they borrow money on their house or have their children borrow? Should they invest in their children's future or their old age? Will helping their dependents leave them dependent?

What do they expect of their children later in life? The assumptions of family—I will raise you and you will care for me—have been replaced by the assumptions of independence. A reluctance to ask, a fear of needing.

Even divorce laws are now infused by the idea that husband and wife are separate economic units. The goal is to achieve independence, self-sufficiency as quickly as possible.

My friend's paycheck is, of course, not entirely her own, nor is her husband's. It is owned by the bank, the supermarket, credit card companies. They don't ask their children to pay room and board, although in rancorous wrangling over these shoes, an ugly reference was made to this expense.

But in the aftermath of the Sneaker Affair, her family has done a great deal of thinking about money earned and shared. The pros and cons of our famed American self-reliance. About economic rights that belong to an individual and responsibilities that belong to a family.

This is not a simple talk. The mess of economics and emotions do not lend themselves to a bottom line. But this is what my friend has learned: It has become far too easy to run away from family in a pair of $150 sneakers.

## REFLECTING ON THE READING

Should parents have some say in what teenagers do with the money they earn? When should a child living at home begin contributing money to the support of the household? Develop your opinion in no more than a 150 word paragraph.

◆

# IMELDA IN ALL OF US

KATHARINE MACDONALD

◆

*The term "conspicuous consumption," as well as the
phrase "compulsive shopper," have become part of popular vocabulary. What do you think are the reasons for
this kind of buying behavior?*

Imelda Marcos' shoes have been starring in Johnny Carson's recent mono-
logues. It's funny stuff. It's also sort of interesting, given the fact that, in
Carson's most recent divorce, his ex-wife Joanna asked for, among other
things, $37,065 a *month* for jewels and furs and $88,000 a month for personal expenses.

The evening news has shown us rooms in Malacanang Palace looking
like nothing so much as a warehouse in the garment district. The palace is a
study of pathological consumerism, a shrine to Imelda Marcos' avarice.
Everyone who sees it is shocked, and that's got me confused.

Oh, I understand the shock of the Filipino people, many of whom live in
unspeakable poverty. The grief on the faces looking at the evidence of what
the Marcos regime did to them is clear, and it's understandable. What's not
so understandable is how it came to be so fashionable among residents of
Los Angeles' affluent west side to talk about "that *terrible* woman, Imelda
Marcos." Because the same avarice that drove Marcos to buy, buy, buy is
much in evidence here.

I know a woman who is said by many to have married for money. I suspect, but don't know for a fact, that that's true. What I do know is that, once
she married money, she set about spending it with fervor that makes one
suspect the act of acquisition is to her a religious experience. She just *loves*
money, and the things it will buy: cars, clothes, jewels, useless doo-dads,
whatever. She has raised shopping to an art form. Now and then, the constant shopping in Los Angeles creates a certain ennui. So she goes to other
cities, sometimes other countries, and when she comes back she talks, not
about museums or beautiful vistas, but the adorable little boutiques.

These days, in between trips to stores, this woman has taken to talking a
lot about "that awful, awful woman" Imelda Marcos. It's hard to keep a
straight face, listening to all this, because the only difference I see between
the Filipino shopper and the American shopper is quantitative. The American hasn't an entire country to plunder, just one man's bank account.

There is a television show called "Lifestyles of the Rich and Famous." I've never seen this show, but I'm somehow certain it slobbers, awestruck, over evidence of obscene levels of spending.

There is a magazine called "People," which is not so much about people as it is about rich and famous people. Oh, every once in a while they throw in a piece about a scientist who has made a real contribution, or an article on homelessness, but it is still pretty much an ode to the rich and famous, and the rich and fatuous among us.

One issue, in a profile of a Texas socialite, showed us pictures of the socialite's closet—well, it wasn't really a closet, it was an entire room where the clothes were hung on racks, just like in a department store, just like (dare I say it?) in Malacanang Palace.

What we are shown by that television show and that magazine is offered to us in the spirit of "gee, gosh, golly, isn't this wonderful? Isn't this the height of human success? Isn't this the best there is?"

The Princess of Wales is said to be not terribly bright, under-educated, and ill-read. She is also wonderful looking and beautifully dressed. Shopping is reported to be her favorite activity. And she is about as famous as a person can be. For all this, her name appears regularly on lists of the most admired women. (Speaking of the English royal family, Diana's mother-in-law is said to have a personal fortune in the billions. This money was not obtained through hard work or through a democratic process. It is the fruit of plunder, hung onto through sufficient generations to legitimize it.)

The fact is, we celebrate acquisitiveness in this society. We honor it. We lust after not just money, but the tangible symbols of money. One might say that Imelda Marcos just sort of took an idea and ran with it.

Of course, an argument can be made that what is shocking about the Marcos spending is that all that money was stolen from the poor, and that in the stealing, a public trust was violated. But it's a specious argument. To be shocking, information needs to carry an element of surprise. Is it really so surprising to any of us that the Marcoses stole from the poor?

Imelda Marcos has been living lavishly for a long time now. And while we hadn't before seen her closets, we'd certainly seen her wearing some of the things that hung there: we saw pictures of her wearing them in New York, in Europe, wherever there was a party, whenever it took her fancy to go. What did we think all those years? That she financed the trips and the clothes by judicious expenditure of the housekeeping money given to her by her husband, who made $5,700 a year?

There is no question, Imelda Marcos deserves our scorn. The question is, are we in any position to bestow it?

## REFLECTING ON THE READING

Think of a person you know who fits the "shop till you drop" category. Describe their shopping behavior in concrete detail. List at least five things the person says or does to qualify for the category.

◆

---

# In Minnesota, the Biggest Megamall Under the Moon

David Sarasohn

---

◆

*Malls have become a sort of community center in many parts of America. Do you remember when the first mall came to your town or neighborhood? What kinds of people frequent the mall you know best? If you don't shop in malls, what's your reason? David Sarasohn writes for The Oregonian in Portland.*

Twenty years after man first landed on the moon, people are whining that Americans have lost the capacity for grand achievements of will, creativity and technology, the kind of projects that a generation can proudly bequeath to its grandchildren.

But abandoning challenges is not what America is about. And this summer we've seen the opening of the world's most expensive domed baseball stadium and the groundbreaking for the world's largest shopping mall.

That's one small step for man, one giant leap for Mastercard.

Back during the late 1960s, people used to say that the space flights were our cathedrals, the great messages we were sending out to posterity about what kind of people we were and what we could achieve when something was important to us.

The Megamall fits the parallel exactly.

And while the Sky Dome in Toronto is actually outside our borders, the whole idea of domed stadiums originally came from Houston, back when that city had just become the capital of the American space exploration program. As they tell you in south Texas, the first word uttered by man on the surface of the moon was "Houston."

The Megamall—formally called the Mall of America, meaning that burning it will be constitutionally forbidden—will be twice the size of any existing shopping mall and 10 times the size of the average one. It will be located in Bloomington, Minn., although it will also cover most of South Dakota.

At last month's groundbreaking, a squadron of F–14s flew overhead, underlining the patriotic meaning of a mall the size of 78 football fields, with an indoor amusement park, 100 restaurants, a miniature golf course and four electoral votes.

"I know of no other mall anywhere in the world that even comes close," said John E. Riordan, executive vice president of the International Council of Shopping Centers. "This will be a colossus and an extraordinary event. A lot of people are saying, 'How can it be?'"

That is, of course, exactly what people used to ask about the Taj Mahal, the landing on the moon and other great accomplishments of man. And like all the others, it shows what man can do with a dream, determination and a friendly zoning board.

Actually, the Sky Dome and the Megamall are coming along just in the nick of time: For a while there, it looked as if the only legacies of the 1980s would be bankrupt savings and loans and an Indiana Jones lunchbox.

For the rest of this week, a lot of people are going to be watching the television tapes of Neil Armstrong landing on the moon, and asking what happened to the drive of a society that could achieve such a thing. Through-out the 1970s, Americans would cite the landing as a benchmark: If we could put a man on the moon, they would ask, why couldn't we (fill in the blank)?

Nobody asks that anymore. For one thing, the system has been taken apart, and today we not only can't do any of those other things, we can't put a man on the moon. For another, we no longer believe that our power can be used successfully for anything except creating more and bigger places to buy frozen yogurt.

Once, we went to the moon.

Now, we go to the mall.

## REFLECTING ON THE READING

Make two lists. In one, write down the kinds of items that you usually buy in a mall near you. In the other, write down the kinds of items you cannot buy in that same mall. Write one sentence generalizing what you learned from making the lists.

◆

# IN A SHOPPING MALL, A VISION OF THE FUTURE

RICHARD RODRIGUEZ*

◆

*For Rodriguez, the shopping mall provides evidence of an important cultural development in the United States. He makes a great deal out of the pronoun "I" versus the pronoun "we." What's his point?*

Quivering like hounds, demographers point at the growing non-white population of America, of California particularly. By the turn of the century, half of California's population will be non-white.

Recently I had my vision of the future. I found myself at Serramonte Shopping Center in Daly City. I had gone in search of the North Pole, for toys for my 6-year-old nephew, my 3-year-old niece. Instead, I discovered new California—the warm ocean of faces from Asia and Africa, from Samoa and Latin America and the Philippines. The rarest complexion was white— the blond girl—but her boyfriend was black.

As we ended the decade, we noticed the newspapers were filled with the drama of Europe discovering itself. As Europe moves toward unification and tribalism, perhaps it is America's destiny to discover the world in a California shopping center.

In the past, America for most immigrants was a rejection of Europe. Americans, nevertheless, have been accustomed to thinking of the United States as a European discovery, a European idea. People escaped fathers or kings or the inevitable poverty of the village by sailing away to America. What vision does that incantation conjure now?

While Europe fashions its new coherence and gathers optimism, America is faced with classrooms where students come from everywhere in the world and speak 40 or 50 languages, only one of which, Spanish, derives from Europe. Europe now boasts of her cumulative wealth—the Marshall Plan has paid off— and her high level of education. America fears the burden of a non-white future.

For obvious racial reasons, there will be Americans who will resent the new non-white look of this country. At some more complicated level of culture, Americans must wonder about the coherence of a country where not

---

*PNS editor Richard Rodriguez, author of "Hunger of Memory" and "Days of Obligation" (Viking), is also a contributing editor of the *Los Angeles Times*.

everyone looks like an astronaut; where astronauts do not look like John Glenn, where we no longer mean the same thing when we speak of God or founding fathers or even "the West." The controversy of American education in coming years will be one of shared knowledge. Are there facts, dates and scarlet letters we can teach students in common?

In the mid–19th century, the nativist argument against Irish immigration to America was a religious argument. America was about to go to war with Catholic Mexico. The fear was that the Irish would conspire with Mexican papists to overturn the Protestant state. The question was whether America would be diminished by allowing Catholics—historical enemies of Protestant individuality—to share in the fledgling Protestant creation.

But America's Protestant tolerance, our faith in individualism, could not, after all, exclude the outsider. The Irish came. America was truest to itself when it risked dissolution. The Irish became Americans.

Many decades later Americans wonder if America risks too much, if America will remain a European idea, if America can allow so many non-Europeans into the country without losing some necessary "character." To remain true to itself, America has no choice but risk.

All the while, Americans regard the advent of a new Europe with envy and unease, being accustomed to thinking that only we can make the new. Cutting loose from Europe is our creation myth. It is unsettling to watch Europe turn its back on America.

Americans ought to feel a sense of triumph and the flattery of history. Americans took from Europe the 18th century first-person pronoun—the model "I." Americans polished that pronoun; we invested it with the myth of our invincibility. No state in America advertised the American "I" as relentlessly as California has done—in our music, our movies, with our freeways and our two-car garages.

Now we hear the American "I" proclaimed by masses in the Eastern European square. The "I" is whispered in the villages of Latin America. The American "I" is the reason why so many want to come here. And yet Americans begin to fear the passing of our influence. If every city becomes Los Angeles, then our influence must seem to be diminished.

Last spring, Americans watched in awe as Chinese students—clothed in the armor of conviction we had made—drew the Excalibur "I" from its stone in Tiananmen Square while American elected officials wrung their hands and tut-tut-tutted.

Are Americans afraid of history? Or is it that we have entered a post-American phase? As the rest of the world grasps the American "I," Americans seem unable to wield it any longer. We are afraid of 50 languages. Americans are wary of variety.

Perhaps we should be. Americans (like Western Europeans) speak a new environmentalism—the grammar of global "we"—even as Latin Americans hack down their jungles, clearing a path to the future the way Americans did in the 19th century. Now Americans speak of protecting the "quality of life."

Maybe Americans have traveled too long on that American freeway—our only counsel the voice of the traffic reporter. We are lonely. The most important psychological drama of our day is movement, the commute from one point to another. Americans, Californians especially, are willing to submit to three-hour commutes to uphold the American ideal of the little house on the prairie. But when we get back to our houses in the evenings, home is without any reassuring embrace of "we." Exhausted, we watch TV. We set the alarm for 5 o'clock. Our kids go to the mall out of boredom or despair, seeking the communal.

The new immigrants do not please us for wanting the American "I." They annoy us for the assurance of their "we." They always speak of themselves in the plural.

"Let one in and they bring the whole damn family."

The toys I found at the shopping mall were tawdry and without charm. And I regretted the passing of innocence. But they were what my nephew wanted.

America's destiny will be to join its traditional "I" to some post-modern "we." Or is the "we" an ancient return?

I stopped for lunch at a new Chinese restaurant that used to be a chuck wagon. A San Francisco joke is that every 10 seconds a new Chinese restaurant is born. Was that the demographer's prediction printed on the congratulatory red ribbons flapping in the draft from the door?

I surveyed the customers, only half of them Asian. Yet the entire congregation easily negotiated the menu. The young waiters took English orders in Chinese characters. My vision was of two epic pronouns meeting. I could hear only the clicking of chopsticks.

## Reflecting on the Reading

Although this essay is short, it is difficult to comprehend without careful study. Rodriguez assumes readers are familiar with the fact that the United States has been formed out of three major migrations: Europeans and Africans crossing the Atlantic and moving west, Asians crossing the Pacific and moving east, and Latin Americans moving north. Observe the people in a mall near where you live. In a short paragraph, describe the mix of people in terms of national origin and ethnic background.

◆

# SHOPPERS OF THE WORLD UNITE!

FREDA GARMAISE

*[handwritten: Read (do Reflecting) do pg 257 → WRITE 5 questions about shopping experiences MEMORABLE]*

◆

*For Freda Garmaise, the distinction between "shopper" and "consumer" is significant. Explain how her distinction is important to the point she makes. Do you agree with her?*

To take the measure of a person, I have often asked: Do you dance? Do you vote? Do you like Graham Greene? But in the future I intend to ask: "Do you shop?"

I imagine myself at a party directing this inquiry to someone (an economist, critic, editor) whose epic sweep of mind can be seen in his contemptible ties and shoes. He will answer that no, he does not, and offer the fact that he hates to shop as yet another credential of his superiority. Asshole, I will say, if I am feeling bold; how can you deliberately deprive yourself of means to exercise your ability to select, bargain, experience the new, relive the old, and give your life the rich detail that the thoughtless cut of your suit and hair shows you are severely lacking? Get out there and shop, I will say to him, and then come back and talk to me about price structures or the future of publishing.

We all shop (even he does). But less than fifteen percent (my figure) of the earth's inhabitants do it well. And doing it well is to be *mindful* of it; to be aware at all times that as a daily activity it is uniquely constituted to make us aware of ourselves and the world around us.

But because we do it automatically, resentfully, indifferently, impatiently, excessively, nervously, hysterically, and, above all, thoughtlessly, we deprive ourselves of shopping's real benefits. Our willful indifference has far-reaching results, bringing us trade deficits and wars as well as cheeseboards and sheets we detest. Yet great shopping ("Where did you get this unbelievable egg timer?") is only acknowledged in private circles.

"Neither Bush nor Dukakis recognizes shoppers," I complained to a shopper.

"Shabbas? Dukakis recognizes Shabbas. Kitty makes him."

When I told her I'd said "shoppers," she said: "Oh, you mean consumers." Well, no I don't. Consumers are interested in getting value for their money and may not even *like* shopping since, for them, it may be a tedious quest in search of quality, fair play, and honesty. Shoppers may care about those things, too, but not necessarily. They may tolerate inferior quality for some other attribute (cuteness, for example), they may indulge in foul play and cheat in pursuit of the prize on the bargain table, but to them shopping is a path of discovery, the route to enlightenment—whether it leads them to the magic lamp in a dusty corner of the shop or not. Shoppers shop for its own sake—as a means to be out and about, to check up on the world, to renew themselves—not just to find something to buy.

But if the word *shopper* has a bad name, it is because those to whom it is usually applied are considered greedy and ridiculous. The Nancy Reagans and the Imelda Marcoses have discredited the term, but they are not shoppers. They are spenders. They do not browse, poke around, snoop, pounce, discover. They order. They acquire. They could just as well shop from a catalog or TV screen. Unlike true shoppers, they must have money. True shoppers like to have money too (no denying that), but they can shop without it.

I fell in with a bunch of true shoppers in California. Living by the skin of their teeth, they buy everything at the thrifts—furniture, household articles, books, clothing, major appliances. Being with them was like being in several different decades at once and simultaneously experiencing the Depression dinette set, the couch from the forties, and the edition of *The Great Gatsby* issued while F. Scott Fitzgerald was still alive. Particularly thrilling to me, in these cholesterol-conscious times, was the opportunity I had to extract lettuce and fish from the big, fat fifties fridge built to house dry martinis and three-inch steaks.

Of course you can be an enterprising, imaginative, indefatigable, even prophetic shopper and never go near the thrifts; but unlike the fan in the Deanna Durbin frock and ankle socks, who puts into perspective the sea of jeans at the rock concert, you will never be able to offer those around you that remembrance of things past that brings the present into focus. And that's what makes the thrift shopper the greatest on earth.

I am not a good shopper. I am too timid, too unsure, too lazy. I am touched by the packages of panty hose fanned out to lure me into the neighborhood lingerie store, but I am afraid to go in for fear of being bullied into buying something. If I were a great shopper, I would risk getting stuck with a pair of cocoa knee-highs to preserve that greatest of all shopping traditions—contact between buyer and seller. Similarly, when I am in the mall and feeling guilty because I should be doing more than buying a packet of pins (in order to justify all the fountains and flowers and marble resting places), I shall remember that even the purchase of pins is unwarranted in this place, with its pseudomarket air that defiles everything the ancient practice of shopping is about.

For years I thought I *was* a great shopper because I had great clothes. But that was when I was a fashion editor and my wardrobe consisted of the liveliest of the manufacturers' samples rejected by middle-of-the-road store buyers as too original, too avant-garde for general consumption. I congratulated myself on my taste and smart buying habits, forgetting that what buyers refuse is usually the best the manufacturer has to offer. When I had to buy my clothes in stores like everyone else, my wardrobe quickly became a reflection of the numbing selection made on my behalf. I became a dull and listless shopper. Or perhaps it would be truer to say I was revealed as the dull and listless shopper I always was. Up until then, my wardrobe distracted from my substandard level of shopping. Now, it joined my other purchases, confirming the insulting opinion most stores have of me—that I am not interested in the new, the beautiful, the original, or even the sensible.

Thanks to the substandard performance I and millions like me give, stores keep getting more and more boring. Perhaps Bloomingdale's *would* be like no other store in the world if its buyers were encouraged by lively, aware shoppers who continually challenge them to be different by refusing merchandise that could be found elsewhere. As it is, Bloomingdale's is indistinguishable from other stores, despite those spectaculars when the store is transformed for China month. To the true shopper, these extravaganzas seem no more than an elaborate ruse to sell the dragon-stenciled tote bag.

In an effort to improve, I have decided to shop even when I do not need anything, even when I am broke. (Note: I do not say buy; the practice of buying things one cannot afford is a degradation of shopping. No, I talk of scouting the shops, studying the trends, quizzing the clerks—in short, observing the rituals.) I will also ignore the rule that certain things may be inspected only by those who can afford them and I shall insist on examining the Rei Kawakubos. And finally, I will try not to hasten the death of the hunt by buying bargains only in discount stores.

And then perhaps one day I will reach the point where I can look at the teakettle or bathrobe I own without my spirits sagging because it is proof not only of the way I shop, but the way I do most things.

How often have I believed that something outside my life (a bout of Buddhism, regular exercise) could change it, when all the time shopping—already an integral part of existence—was the answer!

Now do you see why I did not account it progress when I read of a man who did shopping for his wife? He wouldn't think of jogging for his wife, would he? No, everyone must shop for herself. For himself. Buying and selling are basic; none of us can afford not to be part of the process. The world is undoubtedly in the shape that it is because men believed themselves above shopping, relied on surrogates to do it, and used the time instead to get into mischief. (Hitler, I am convinced, never shopped. And if there is hope for the Eastern block, it is in the fact that, I believe, Gorbachev does).

Throughout the entire 1988 presidential campaign, no one saw fit to ask the candidates, "Do you shop?"—although the subject was broached with their wives.

So, Bush went into the White House with nothing known of this vital aspect of his character. There is still time to remedy the situation. Let's get the measure of the president by asking whether he actually went out and bought Barbara's birthday present.

For all we know, he could lead us into a future where, having succumbed to labels, we move as automatons from one corporate outlet to another in a grotesque parody of shopping. And as the kinder, gentler nation becomes a duller, meaner, more standardized place, we will remember dimly, perhaps, a happier time—a time full of color and variety, before we betrayed our destiny and the singular fact that we were born to shop.

## REFLECTING ON THE READING

Based on Garmaise's article, write definitions of "consumer," "spender," and "shopper."

◆

# ON THE MALL

JOAN DIDION

◆

*Didion, a noted essayist and novelist, asks more of her readers than most writers. Her essay consists of several parts that are not explicitly connected to one another. As you read, find the connections among the parts. This more complex arrangement requires more careful rereading. As you read, think of changes in shopping malls since this essay was published in 1979.*

They float on the landscape like pyramids to the boom years, all those Plazas and Malls and Esplanades. All those Squares and Fairs. All those Towns and Dales, all those Villages, all those Forests and Parks and Lands. Stonestown. Hillsdale. Valley Fair, Mayfair, Northgate, Southgate, Eastgate, Westgate. Gulfgate. They are toy garden cities in which no one lives but everyone consumes, profound equalizers, the perfect fusion of the profit motive and the egalitarian ideal, and to hear their names is to recall words and phrases no longer quite current. Baby Boom. Consumer Explosion. Leisure Revolution. Do-It-Yourself Revolution. Backyard Revolution. Suburbia. "The Shopping Center," the Urban Land Institute could pronounce in 1957, "is today's extraordinary retail business evolvement.... The automobile accounts for suburbia, and suburbia accounts for the shopping center."

It was a peculiar and visionary time, those years after World War II to which all the Malls and Towns and Dales stand as climate-controlled monu-

ments. Even the word "automobile," as in "the automobile accounts for suburbia and suburbia accounts for the shopping center," no longer carries the
particular freight it once did: as a child in the late Forties in California I recall
reading and believing that the "freedom of movement" afforded by the automobile was "America's fifth freedom." The trend was up. The solution was
in sight. The frontier had been reinvented, and its shape was the subdivi-
sion, that new free land on which all settlers could recast their lives *tabula
rasa*. For one perishable moment there the American idea seemed about to
achieve itself, via F.H.A. housing and the acquisition of major appliances,
and a certain enigmatic glamour attached to the architects of this newfound
land. They made something of nothing. They gambled and sometimes lost.
They staked the past to seize the future. I have difficulty now imagining a
childhood in which a man named Jere Strizek, the developer of Town and
Country Village outside Sacramento (143,000 square feet gross floor area, 68
stores, 1000 parking spaces, the Urban Land Institute's "prototype for centers using heavy timber and tile construction for informality"), could materi-
alize as a role model, but I had such a childhood, just after World War II, in
Sacramento. I never met or even saw Jere Strizek, but at the age of 12 I imagined him a kind of frontiersman, a romantic and revolutionary spirit, and in
the indigenous grain he was.

I suppose James B. Douglas and David D. Bohannon were too.
I first heard of James B. Douglas and David D. Bohannon not when I was
12 but a dozen years later, when I was living in New York, working for
*Vogue*, and taking, by correspondence, a University of California Extension
course in shopping-center theory. This did not seem to me eccentric at the
time. I remember sitting on the cool floor in Irving Penn's studio and reading, in *The Community Builders Handbook*, advice from James B. Douglas
on shopping-center financing. I recall staying late in my pale-blue office on
the twentieth floor of the Graybar Building to memorize David D. Bohannon's parking ratios. My "real" life was to sit in this office and describe life as
it was lived in Djakarta and Caneel Bay and in the great chateaux of the Loire
Valley, but my dream life was to put together a Class-A regional shopping
center with three full-line department stores as major tenants.
That I was perhaps the only person I knew in New York, let alone on
the Condé Nast floors of the Graybar Building, to have memorized the distinctions among "A," "B," and "C" shopping centers did not occur to me (the
defining distinction, as long as I have your attention, is that an "A," or "regional," center has as its major tenant a full-line department store which carries major appliances; a "B," or "community," center has as its major tenant a
junior department store which does not carry major appliances; and a "C,"
or "neighborhood," center has as its major tenant only a supermarket): my
interest in shopping centers was in no way casual. I did want to build them.
I wanted to build them because I had fallen into the habit of writing fiction,
and I had it in my head that a couple of good centers might support this

habit less taxingly than a pale-blue office at *Vogue*. I had even devised an original scheme by which I planned to gain enough capital and credibility to enter the shopping-center game: I would lease warehouses in, say, Queens, and offer Manhattan delicatessens the opportunity to sell competitively by buying cooperatively, from my trucks. I see a few wrinkles in this scheme now (the words "concrete overcoat" come to mind), but I did not then. In fact I planned to run it out of the pale-blue office.

James B. Douglas and David D. Bohannon. In 1950 James B. Douglas had opened Northgate, in Seattle, the first regional center to combine a pedestrian mall with an underground truck tunnel. In 1954 David D. Bohannon had opened Hillsdale, a forty-acre regional center on the peninsula south of San Francisco. That is the only solid bio I have on James B. Douglas and David D. Bohannon to this day, but many of their opinions are engraved on my memory. David D. Bohannon believed in preserving the integrity of the shopping center by not cutting up the site with any dedicated roads. David D. Bohannon believed that architectural setbacks in a center looked "pretty on paper" but caused "customer resistance." James B. Douglas advised that a small-loan office could prosper in a center only if it were placed away from foot traffic, since people who want small loans do not want to be observed getting them. I do not now recall whether it was James B. Douglas or David D. Bohannon or someone else altogether who passed along this hint on how to paint the lines around the parking spaces (actually this is called "striping the lot," and the spaces are "stalls"): make each space a foot wider than it need be—ten feet, say, instead of nine—when the center first opens and business is slow. By this single stroke the developer achieves a couple of important objectives, the appearance of a popular center and the illusion of easy parking, and no one will really notice when business picks up and the spaces shrink.

Nor do I recall who first solved what was once a crucial center dilemma: the placement of the major tenant vis-á-vis the parking lot. The dilemma was that the major tenant—the draw, the raison d'être for the financing, the Sears, the Macy's, the May Company—wanted its customer to walk directly from car to store. The smaller tenants, on the other hand, wanted that same customer to *pass their stores* on the way from the car to, say, Macy's. The solution to this conflict of interests was actually very simple: *two major tenants*, one at each end of a mall. This is called "anchoring the mall," and represents seminal work in shopping-center theory. One thing you will note about shopping-center theory is that you could have thought of it yourself, and a course in it will go a long way toward dispelling the notion that business proceeds from mysteries too recondite for you and me.

A few aspects of shopping-center theory do in fact remain impenetrable to me. I have no idea why the Community Builders' Council ranks "Restaurant" as deserving a Number One (or "Hot Spot") location but exiles "Chinese Restaurant" to a Number Three, out there with "Power and Light

Office" and "Christian Science Reading Room." Nor do I know why the Council approves of enlivening a mall with "small animals" but specifically, vehemently, and with no further explanation, excludes "monkeys." If I had a center I would have monkeys, and Chinese restaurants, and Mylar kites and bands of small girls playing tambourine.

A few years ago at a party I met a woman from Detroit who told me that the Joyce Carol Oates novel with which she identified most closely was *Wonderland*.

I asked her why.

"Because," she said, "my husband has a branch there."

I did not understand.

"In Wonderland the center," the woman said patiently. "My husband has a branch in Wonderland."

I have never visited Wonderland but imagine it to have bands of small girls playing tambourine.

A few facts about shopping centers.

The "biggest" center in the United States is generally agreed to be Woodfield, outside Chicago, a "super" regional or "leviathan" two-million-square-foot center with four major tenants.

The "first" shopping center in the United States is generally agreed to be Country Club Plaza in Kansas City, built in the twenties. There were some other early centers, notably Edward H. Bouton's 1907 Roland Park in Baltimore, Hugh Prather's 1931 Highland Park Shopping Village in Dallas, and Hugh Potter's 1937 River Oaks in Houston, but the developer of Country Club Plaza, the late J. C. Nichols, is referred to with ritual frequency in the literature of shopping centers, usually as "pioneering J. C. Nichols," "trailblazing J. C. Nichols," or "J. C. Nichols, father of the center as we know it."

Those are some facts I know about shopping centers because I still want to be Jere Strizek or James B. Douglas or David D. Bohannon. Here are some facts I know about shopping centers because I never will be Jere Strizek or James B. Douglas or David D. Bohannon: a good center in which to spend the day if you wake feeling low in Honolulu, Hawaii, is Ala Moana, major tenants Liberty House and Sears. A good center in which to spend the day if you wake feeling low in Oxnard, California, is The Esplanade, major tenants the May Company and Sears. A good center in which to spend the day if you wake feeling low in Biloxi, Mississippi, is Edgewater Plaza, major tenant Godchaux's. Ala Moana in Honolulu is larger than The Esplanade in Oxnard, and The Esplanade in Oxnard is larger than Edgewater Plaza in Biloxi. Ala Moana has carp pools. The Esplanade and Edgewater Plaza do not.

These marginal distinctions to one side, Ala Moana, The Esplanade, and Edgewater Plaza are the same place, which is precisely their role not only as equalizers but in the sedation of anxiety. In each of them one moves for a while in an aqueous suspension not only of light but of judgment, not only of judgment but of "personality." One meets no acquaintances at The Esplanade. One gets no telephone calls at Edgewater Plaza. "It's a hard place to run in to for a pair of stockings," a friend complained to me recently of Ala Moana, and I knew that she was not yet ready to surrender her ego to the idea of the center. The last time I went to Ala Moana it was to buy *The New York Times*. Because *The New York Times* was not in, I sat on the mall for a while and ate caramel corn. In the end I bought not *The New York Times* at all but two straw hats at Liberty House, four bottles of nail enamel at Woolworth's, and a toaster, on sale at Sears. In the literature of shopping centers these would be described as impulse purchases, but the impulse here was obscure. I do not wear hats, nor do I like caramel corn. I do not use nail enamel. Yet flying back across the Pacific I regretted only the toaster.

Return of

## REFLECTING ON THE READING

Draw a diagram of a large shopping mall you are familiar with. Identify which features of mall design that Didion describes are incorporated in the mall you have diagrammed.

# PUTTING IT IN WRITING

## RESPONSES

1. You often hear people say "That's a rip-off!" Write for three minutes, without stopping, about the biggest rip-off you know.
2. Think of a food store that you go to frequently. Make a quick sketch of the store's layout. Is it organized for convenient access to what you purchase most often? Where do they keep the bread, milk, and soft drinks? Where do they put the magazines? In one or two sentences, write your opinion about why the store is organized the way it is.
3. Write down the first three brand names that come to your mind. Write a sentence for each name that explains why you recalled those particular brand names so quickly.

## READING FOR MEANING

1. Writers often exaggerate to dramatize their point. Find a paragraph or short passage in one of this chapter's readings in which the author exaggerates. Explain what the exaggeration is and how you reacted to the exaggeration when you read it.
2. Writers often use the opening of their piece to get you interested as a reader. Find one article in this chapter that "hooked" you in its open-

ing and one that didn't. Explain, in a few sentences, why one opening was better than the other.

3. Writers frequently repeat key words to emphasize their point. In Ellen Goodman's article "Are We Losing Our Way in $150 Sneakers?" count the number of times the words *sneakers* and *family* or *families* occur in the article. Do any other nouns occur as frequently? How does Goodman manage to connect the two key terms?

## Organizing Your Ideas

1. Pair up with a classmate and interview each other on the subject "My Most Memorable Shopping Experience." Prepare for the interview by writing three to five questions that you think will get the most interesting responses from your classmate. Write down the main points of your classmate's answers to your questions. When you have finished interviewing one another, give your questions and your notes to your classmate for use in writing a paper.

2. Choose a product or service that you have found very valuable. Make a list of all the good qualities of that product or service. Then write the opening you would use to convince a friend to buy that product or service.

3. Using television commercials, magazine ads, or newspaper ads, make a list of deceptive words and phrases used to sell products or services. Based on your list of words and phrases, write one sentence that generalizes about that kind of language.

## Writing a Paper  *Next Paper Thursday draft*

1. Using the notes from the interview in #1 in "Organizing Your Ideas," write a paper on the subject "My Most Memorable Shopping Experience." Add details you have thought of since the interview. Make certain your paper contains a sentence that conveys your idea of what made the experience "memorable."

2. Based on an actual experience in which you have received defective products or ineffective service (consider using the experience you wrote about in #1 in "Responses"), write a letter to the company explaining the problem and describing what you think they should do to correct the situation. If you have time, send the letter and report the results back to your classmates and instructor.

3. Richard Rodriguez and Joan Didion each write about malls as important places in American culture. Select one opinion from either Rodriguez or Didion and state it in your own words. Then agree or disagree with that opinion, supporting your view by using examples from your own experience with malls.

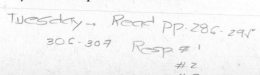

*Tuesday — Read pp. 286-295*
*306-307  Resp #1*
*#2*
*#3*

What effect does putting a phone number on the back
of a commercial vehicle have on its driver?

# Driving and Riding

As a young person approaches adulthood, he or she faces some test to demonstrate readiness to take on adult responsibilities. Anthropologists call this sort of test a "rite of passage." In the United States, for most young people, qualifying for a driver's license marks the rite of passage to adult responsibility. The automobile was invented just about a century ago, but, in that time, cars, highways, freeways, driving, and riding have become part of the fabric of our culture. American children ride in cars practically from birth. Some less fortunate families even live in their cars. Some more fortunate, retired people purchase recreational vehicles and live part or all of the year in these houses on wheels. One of the stock scenes in both comedy and action films is the car chase.

The passenger car has made the people of the United States the most mobile in history. Anyone with an auto in good repair and some money for gasoline can take off in almost any direction, to see other cities, to visit the countryside, or even move to another part of the state or the country. The car has also become an integral part of our dating and courtship rituals. Where once young couples talked and smooched on the front porch, not far from parents' watchful eyes, the teen who has a car can take a date to any viewpoint or secluded spot accessible by automobile. A stock image following a wedding shows the newly married couple entering an automobile (sometimes a limousine) while well-wishers throw confetti.

The car has also become a central element of our economy. Steel makers, rubber manufacturers, and glass companies supply materials to automobile manufacturers, all of them employing large numbers of people. Add in the people who transport cars, the people who sell them (both new and used), the people who repair them, and the people who drive for a living, and you can see just how large a role the car has in our economic system. At the individual level, after food and housing, our cars usually represent the next largest part of our monthly budgets. In fact, many of us spend more on our cars than on our food.

Though cars provide mobility and independence, they also have considerable effects on our environment. Studies show that, in some cities, more than 60 percent of the land surface is devoted to automobiles (streets, driveways, garages, gas stations). The gas, oil, and kerosene that makes cars run can contaminate both land and water. The exhaust from car engines contributes about 50 percent of the air pollution in urban areas. The car not only contaminates our air, land, and water, but it poses a serious threat to our safety and physical well-being. Despite continuing safety improvements, tens of thousands of people die every year in car accidents. Thousands more are seriously injured, and sometimes permanently disabled. Because modern cars have such power and speed, the qualifications of drivers, especially the very new driver and the very old driver, remain a concern of state motor vehicle agencies and local police.

Cars have also come to mark social status. Driving a Cadillac, Mercedes-Benz, Jaguar, or Lexus suggests the owner has good taste and, probably, a healthy bank account. Convertibles suggest sex appeal; Jeeps, Range Rovers, and other utility vehicles suggest a rough and tough outdoors type; the Volkswagen bug, Honda Civic, Yugo, and Hyundai have suggested low-cost, no-frills transportation.

Before you read the articles in this chapter, try to recall all the cars your family owned while you were growing up. List the make and model of each car, and then, next to that, write a strong memory associated with that car. If you own your own car, make a list of the features that led you to buy it. If you don't own a car, list the features you would want in a car you owned. If you object to automobiles, list the features that serve as the basis of your objections.

◆

# IMPATIENT MOTORISTS AND THEIR MIDDLE-FINGERED SALUTE

## SUSAN MACLEOD

◆

*Susan MacLeod, a mother of two and a resident of Orange County, CA, does a lot of driving. Though we have laws and rules of courtesy governing our driving, most of us encounter frustrating situations. How do you handle those occasions, either as a driver or a passenger?*

Idaho has been constructing its part of I-90 for a long, long time, so it was not surprising to be traveling on a winding, mountainous part of that freeway with only one lane.

Alone with my small son, I was clutching the steering wheel with white knuckles and traveling as fast as I dared, 25 mph.

The driver behind me, obviously a local guy, was not amused.

He tailgated me so closely that I could read the words on his T-shirt:

"I Jumped over the Snake River with Evel Knievel."

When the road widened, he sped by me and gave me an unfriendly big-fingered-salute, as did his passenger.

A few years later, I was driving along a busy road looking for a turnoff. I was speeding up and slowing down, when a guy in a red sports car sped around me, stuck his finger in the air and turned down a side street.

Maybe I deserved it, but still it stunned me. For a long time, I thought about driving up that street just to take a closer look at him.

As I grow older and wiser, I still don't always know where I am going and probably perturb some drivers. I can almost tell when someone might use the big finger, so I turn my head. If I don't see it, I don't feel its hostility.

For drivers, the hostile gesture of choice is the finger, the bird, the one-fingered nautical gesture, the flipping off of someone.

They aim it for many reasons—at drivers speeding up and slowing down, unsafe lane changes, PMS and maybe bad vanity plates.

They know they can do this with anonymity and be quickly gone. That is why we don't see many walkers giving each other rude middle-fingered gestures.

Sometimes the finger-takers don't take the finger-givers too graciously. Things can get ugly.

It wouldn't be wise to gesture at a pickup truck with a gun rack over the back seat, bikers, police officers or cars filled with gang members leaving local bars.

On the other hand, a woman with a carload of children would be a safe choice.

I was talking to a woman neighbor who complained about another, a big blonde in a white Lexus who had been speeding and giving rude gestures almost daily. It was driving Cathy, in her Ford Astro, crazy.

"She lives here and someday she's going to hurt someone the way she drives," Cathy said.

One day, they both were detained in an intersection at the same time. Again the blonde was in a hurry. The middle-fingered gesture followed.

Cathy volleyed a return gesture, in this case a clenched fist, and then yelled, "I want to talk to you."

The blonde rolled up her passenger window and made a little sweep-away gesture that implied, "Oh don't bother me."

Knowing it was a long light, Cathy got out of the car. She ran up to the drivers window and started lecturing:

"You are dangerous!"

"You are going to kill someone someday the way you drive!"

"Try AA! Get some counseling! Go to Jenny Craig!"

"Become a brunette! Move out of the state!"

The woman, looking straight ahead but getting a little nervous, rolled up her window and drove her car through a small space between the median strip and a beat-up Toyota pickup.

Metal scraped metal. Suddenly the pickup was in hot pursuit of the Lexus, honking the horn and waving her to stop.

As the woman drove away, Cathy, now looking oddly like Mona Lisa, offered a final gesture—a wave goodbye.

And she shouted to the Toyota, "I'll be a witness."

My husband commutes daily so I asked him if he ever gives anyone the finger.

"No, I never do," he said. "Never have. Oh, maybe when I was in high school."

That sounded about right. Apparently a lot of people haven't gotten beyond that stage.

## REFLECTING ON THE READING

Try to think of an alternative to the "middle-fingered salute" for letting another driver know you do not appreciate their rudeness. Share your ideas with a group in class and decide together which alternative would be most effective.

◆

# TIMMY'S ROOM

ANONYMOUS

◆

*The scariest aspect of driving and riding lies in the possibility of an accident. Recall a close call you have had with injury in an automobile or other vehicle. Compare the emotions you felt with those of Timmy's father.*

Timmy's room. It's a lot like any other kid's room—a private place for all the things that are a part of growing up. Beside his bed is a well-worn baseball glove creased by backlot wins. There are comic books and photos of his family and friends. Model cars and souvenirs clutter the shelves his father built. Timmy's room is a special place, just like your son's or daughter's room. The only difference is that his room is silent.

Timmy's father, Robert Tiernan, lives in Bethesda, Maryland and practices law in the District of Columbia. He is now a USAA-CIC policy-holder. The compelling testimony he gave during recent Senate and Department of Transportation hearings on automobile safety standards explains why Timmy's room is silent. Here is Tiernan's story:

I am the father of three children. Two are living and one is dead. Timmy, the youngest of the three, died a year ago January at the age of 15. He was irreversibly head-injured in an auto accident that left him in a coma for a year and a half. The accident happened on the night of August 15, 1981. Timmy was then 13.

We were on our way with two of his friends for a weekend of fun at our cottage in Mt. Storm, West Virginia. Mt. Storm is about an hour's drive west of Romney, the largest town in that area. I was driving the car—a late model front-wheel drive Chrysler K car.

We stopped in Romney to pick up groceries for the weekend. We put the groceries in the rear seat with Anne, the 18 year old girlfriend of my other son, Bob. Timmy and his 11 year-old friend, Danny, were sitting up front. I was driving, Danny was in the middle—he had fallen asleep—and Timmy was sitting on the far side in what is known as the death seat.

None of us were belted. I'm sorry to say that we were not in the habit of using seat belts. I don't know how much difference seat belts would have made for Tim. They might have, but we were not belted.

It was a rainy, foggy night. About 10 miles west of Romney on U.S. 50, a winding narrow road, the car went off the pavement onto the shoulder. At first I thought nothing of it, but when I tried to bring the car back onto the pavement, it did not respond. Suddenly, I realized we were in serious trouble. I couldn't stop the car or bring it under control.

The next thing I remember was seeing trees. It seemed like there were trees everywhere—like I was in the middle of a forest.

I recall trying my best to avoid hitting a tree to my immediate right. Apparently, I sideswiped that tree and ricocheted off it. The next thing I saw was another tree dead ahead. I could not avoid it. The car hit head on. According to the authorities, we hit at a speed of about 15 miles per hour.

Just before impact, I think Timmy yelled to watch out for the tree. I do remember turning toward him. What I remember was grisly. Thinking about it sends shivers up my spine. When the car hit, the seat on Timmy's side ran down off the end of the track under the dash. Timmy went with it and crashed into the dashboard face first. Apparently, the car door then flew open and Timmy fell out. When I got out of the car and went around to his side, he was lying half in and half out of the car. His legs were caught between the seat and the door post. I could tell, just by looking at Tim, that nothing would ever be the same again.

I am not a technical expert, but I know that an air bag would have helped. Had there been an air bag between the seat and the dash to act as a buffer or brake, I don't think Timmy would have been hurt at all. At least I'm sure he would not have been badly hurt.

Danny, who was riding in the middle of the seat, suffered serious breaks in both of his legs midway between the knees and thighs. His recuperative process was extensive, but he's a normal, healthy teenager today. In the backseat, Anne rode out the accident with only minor cuts and bruises.

The next year and a half were pure torture—every minute, every hour, every day that Timmy lay in a coma. First there was despair, then hope, but mostly the total helplessness of waiting and waiting. Timmy was operated on several times, including an emergency operation that took ten hours. There were breathing machines and tubes in Timmy's skull to relieve the pressure of blood and fluids on his brain. A tube was inserted into his windpipe so he could breathe. And every hour of every day—over 12,000 times—a nurse stuck a suction tube down his throat to remove fluid from his lungs. He would tense up and convulse.

Timmy deteriorated slowly but inexorably through two bouts of deadly gram negative spinal meningitis. It was a horrible experience. I was worried about how to pay the tremendous medical expenses and wondered what would happen if, God forbid, he outlived me. Seeing the grief of his mother, his brother, his sister, his friends and all those who loved him, I wondered whether Timmy was also aware of his horrible situation and, if so, how terribly frustrating that must be.

The nightmare lasted for eighteen months. I couldn't concentrate on the practice of law and, ultimately, left the firm I had been with for twenty years. My daughter, Amy, dropped out of college. Tim's mother was with him almost every day at the hospital. She had no time for herself nor could she give our other son, Bob, the attention he needed. To make matters worse, there was not an adequate facility in the Washington, D.C. area to care for Tim once his medical condition stabilized. He had to be taken to Erie, Pennsylvania, where he remained for over ten months until his death.

Timmy died the evening of January 24, 1983. The doctor called to say that Tim had stopped breathing and that his eyes no longer dilated, meaning he was brain-dead. The doctor asked whether we wanted Timmy put on a respirator. We said no. So Timmy died with neither of us at his side. Although there was grief over Tim's death, we also saw it as a blessing. He was finally released from the body that had become a prison.

Timmy's case is not unique. It happens hundreds, probably thousands of times each year. I do not understand why the automobile industry refuses to use the air bag technology available to it to save these people. And I cannot understand why our government does not require it. This is not a debate about states' rights or anything esoteric like that. It just has to do with being responsible, being compassionate. It's not enough to say that Timmy "should have" been belted. He wasn't. Neither are many other children. They are innocent victims. If air bags had been phased into cars years ago, Timmy would be here today, healthy and smiling.

In 1977 the Department of Transportation estimated that air bags would save 9,000 lives each year and prevent 65,000 moderate to serious injuries. It's now 1984, 72,000 lives later. What are we waiting for? It's a national calamity and we sit here and talk about surveys—are air bags acceptable to the driving public? We talk about cost and we talk about hardship on the auto industry.

Who ever heard of conducting a survey to determine if action should be taken to save one child's life, much less thousands, when the means is clearly at hand? The cost, $125 per car. That or less than that is the Department's estimate for air bags. Show me a person who says that's too much to save our children. Hardship on the auto industry? The only hardship is that the government would require the industry to do something it can do, and should do.

Believe me. If you want to see hardship, go to a care facility and see the children injured in auto accidents. Look at their pictures on the wall—the pre-accident photos. Then look at them now. You can hardly tell the resemblance. Before, they were handsome, beautiful, active children. Now they are atrophied, dumb-looking and helpless. Their brains are like scrambled eggs. Think of the hardship they and their families must endure.

We can't do anything for Timmy now, but I hope and pray that some way will be found to make air bags in automobiles mandatory. I have two other children I worry about.

## REFLECTING ON THE READING

This article was published in 1984. What is the current status of law and practice regarding seatbelts and airbags? What evidence now exists regarding injury prevention and reduction as a result of seatbelts and airbags? Research these questions and report your results in a paragraph.

◆

# BEWARE THE BOY WHO ASKS, 'MAY I BORROW THE CAR KEYS?'

T.T. NHU

◆

*Conflict over the car seems inevitable between parents and children. What form did that conflict take for you?*

It's a triangle involving the family car, a 15-year-old boy and his parents. Actually, there are four in this situation, but I am counting the parents, my husband and me, as a single voice.

Here's what happened. Our oldest son, who was a high school freshman last year, developed a compelling interest in car care. I was delighted. At last, someone in the family who had a pragmatic grip on life. On back-to-school night, his father and I visited the auto-shop teacher who pumped our hand vigorously in greeting and told us we had a fine boy who was going to be a good mechanic. They only other parent there, a professorial type, said to us: "If my son wants to be in car care, I'd be very glad."

We all laughed. We knew what he meant.

Sometime this spring, my son asked, innocently enough, if he could borrow the car keys. This routine usually meant that he wanted to retrieve something from the car. I thought nothing of it. The next morning, I went to the car, a station wagon which has faithfully served the family since 1976, and turned on the ignition. A horrible shriek pierced the air, followed by the sound of disintegrating metal.

"Don't dismember him," Fred, our mechanic urged when we had the car towed to the garage. "It could happen to anyone. When I was a kid, just to see what would happen, I put sugar in the gas tank. I can still feel the whipping today," he said ruefully rubbing his backside. "The car may have been on its way out and what the kid did, or didn't do, might not be related."

Of course the kid denied it. Even before we had said a word, he launched into his deathless alibi: "I didn't do it."

I swear, "I didn't do it" is going to be his epitaph. He said that he had simply taken the keys out to the car where he met Neil, the student who assists us in the domestication of our tribe. Neil was engaged in the perpetual tinkering with his lemon motorbike. Our son claims that he got in the car and asked Neil what would happen if he put the key in the ignition. "You turn it clockwise," Neil answered, not looking up.

"OK," our son admits, "I turned it clockwise. I did it, but Neil told me to do it."

We suspect that he turned the key, and held it awhile in the starting position. This is where I have trouble remaining calm. "Let me handle this," my husband, the great conciliator, said.

Even as I write this, my blood is boiling. I can see why the English send their children to boarding school so they don't have to deal with this kind of homicidal feeling. I didn't speak to my kid for weeks.

First the flywheel had to be replaced. $800. I don't know what a flywheel is, but it is not as insignificant as it sounds. The car worked for a few days. Then it wouldn't start. It turned over all right, but wouldn't budge.

Sometimes, if we went away for 15 minutes or more—say to make a desperate phone call to Fred at the garage—when we came back, it would start again. More often than not, after it was towed dangling at a 45 degree angle, it would start as if nothing were wrong. We thought we might be losing our sanity.

The costs mounted. We had the sparkplugs changed ($59); it was given a carbon bath ($59); an air exchange part had to be purchased and installed ($150). By now the figure was running into the down payment of a new car. Foolishly, out of attachment to the car, we kept authorizing more work.

Obsessed, I once spent an afternoon quizzing a man at a luncheon who had unwittingly said he was a mechanic. After listening to the litany of woe, Hank told me, in a kind but final sort of way: "Y'know, this is the beginning of the end of the car. Sooner or later, you're going to have to junk it. Fred (the mechanic whom he knew and pronounced honest) is trying one thing after another, but the problem keeps eluding him." No kidding.

He graphically describing the terminal throes of a dying car. I knew he was right. The car's days were numbered.

I am still barely speaking to my son. I guess in another era, he would have been whipped and sent into the cruel world. He is supposed to help pay for the damage but somehow has not been able to find a job this summer in spite of constant hectoring. His solution was to sell his bicycle to fulfill some of his obligation. Although he continues to "accept" the responsibility for wrecking the car, he also claims that "Neil"(read, "the devil") made him do it.

I worry about the kid. Because we have bent over backward not to inflict justifiable pain and pin the blame on him, he has managed to maintain an ambiguous innocence. We can't prove that by keeping the key in the ignition too long he doomed the car, but at the same time, if he hadn't had the key turned in the ignition, the car probably wouldn't be in its sorry state.

Yes, it's back in the garage. This time the computer module (I didn't even know a car had one!) is being replaced. Don't ask. I don't want to talk about it. This is the last chance for the trusty family wagon.

In the meantime, relations between the teen-ager and his parents are tenuous. It has something to do with being 15, I'm sure, and the car is certainly symptomatic of the anger and ambivalence of being at each other's throats. It's terribly hard to maintain perspective and balance in dealing with a young man who transformed from a falsetto to bassetto just this year.

I'm struggling with forbearance and patience, when what I need really is a restraining order. We are now bracing ourselves for the prospect of three kids to go, only one car left and a negative balance in our bank account.

## Reflecting on the Reading

What do you think about the way Nhu handled the situation with her son? Write a paragraph describing how you would handle a similar situation with a child of yours.

◆

---

# GET OFF THE ROAD

GLEN MARTIN

---

◆

*Every state has a minimum age to qualify for a driver's license. Should there be a maximum age? How would the state decide? See if this article changes your view.*

I thought I was going to die, and it wasn't as I expected. Scenes from my life didn't flash before my eyes. Time didn't slow down and attenuate, giving me ample opportunity to contemplate possible courses of action. On the contrary, time accelerated; death lunged for me hyperkinetically, like a crazed Daffy Duck in an old Warner Brothers cartoon.

Thirty seconds before, everything had been just dandy.It was a gorgeous spring day. I got on my motorcycle, hankering to feel the wind in my hair, the sun on my face, even the bugs in my teeth.

Ten minutes into my run, I found myself confronted by the Grim Reaper in the guise of a little old lady in a large Buick. I was going north; she was waiting to turn across my two lanes of traffic into the two southbound lanes from a supermarket parking lot. I slowed down. I could see her look in my direction. The Buick started to ease out, then stop. It was apparent she had seen me. Just as I started to accelerate, however, she lurched out into my lane, obviously oblivious to everything around her. That's when I knew this little gray-haired grandma was going to kill me in a horrible and bloody fashion.

My first reaction was to put the bike down and hope for the best. Yet even as my mind reacted one way, my body reacted in another. I pulled in the clutch with one hand, revved up the RPMs to the max with the other, downshifted with a great grinding of metal, popped the clutch and shot forward like an F-15. I cleared the old lady's front fender with inches to spare, almost swerved into the concrete lane divider, nearly plowed into the rear end of a Toyota in front of me and finally decelerated and pulled over to the side of the highway. I looked back. The Buick putted up the road, its driver either unaware or unconcerned about her near brush with vehicular manslaughter. Right then I wanted to kill, and I mean KILL, that old lady. That's because this kind of thing has been happening a lot to me lately.

Two weeks before, I had watched a car driven by an elderly woman crash through shrubbery bordering a parking lot into a lane of traffic, lurch over a concrete divider (which ripped off her muffler) into another lane, jump a curb, careen in circles around a plowed field, then dive swan-like into an empty irrigation ditch, the two rear wheels of her car spinning freely. When another bystander and I helped her out, she expressed irritation that her groceries were spilled all over her back seat.

Some time before that, my wife watched in grim disbelief while an elderly man inexorably drove into the rear of her Mazda while she was filling it with gas. Fuel spewed everywhere. "I saw him pull into the station, and he didn't slow down, he just kept coming until—POW!" she told me later. "He said there was something wrong with his brakes, but the gas station manager checked them. Everything was fine."

And before that I had spent 10 minutes one rainy afternoon with several other people trying to coax an old lady out of her car, which she had managed to wrap around a telephone pole. Smoke was seeping from under her hood. We had no access to a fire extinguisher, and we had fears that she would be immolated. But she had rolled all her windows up and wouldn't come out. She wouldn't even look at us; instead she stared down into her lap and shook her head at all our importunities. It took a no-nonsense police officer who was not afraid to loudly broach the possibility of arrest before she finally unlocked her door.

Now, I honestly don't have it in for old people. I like them. Hell, I downright love some of them; my parents are old. But I have to admit that I'd appreciate some reciprocal concern on their part, at least when they're in their cars. It may not be politically correct, but my empirical take of the situation is that they're out to get me. Whenever I see the tell-tale signs of an elderly driver—a large, older car, a slow rate of speed, side-to-side swerving—my palms get sweaty and the hackles rise on the back of my neck. You think I'm paranoid? You think I'm nuts? Wrong. Insurance statistics indicate that elderly drivers have one of the lowest accident rates of all age groups. But those statistics are deceptive.

"Overall, it's true that the accident rates for drivers over 65 are low," says Judy Ludwick, the coordinator of the California Traffic Safety Project for Older Adults. "But things change completely when you base the rates on the number of miles driven. Older people drive far less than younger drivers. By this evaluation, older drivers have one of the highest accident rates for all age groups."

Peggy St. George, the deputy chief of program and policy administration for the California Department of Motor Vehicles, is even more specific. "Our stats indicate that the accident rate by miles driven for people over 70 most closely resembles the rate for drivers in the 20-to 30-year age group—and they're only slightly less accident-prone than teen-age drivers."

## Looking at Statistics

St. George says that the accident rate for miles driven points to a 33 percent increase for drivers in the 70-plus age category.

The federal government breaks down age categories a little differently than the state, but the numbers tell the same story. Statistics released by the National Research Council indicate that drivers between the ages of 16 and

24 had the highest accident fatality rate; right behind them were drivers in the 70-to-84 bracket.

Ludwick observes that the problems older drivers face are both physical and cognitive. "Vision is probably the greatest problem," she notes. "Vision is really about 80 percent of successful driving. Older drivers have far less in the way of visual acuity than younger drivers. Most also have deteriorating peripheral vision, and their night vision is usually severely compromised as well."

Compounding the difficulties of failing eyesight is a diminution of physical mobility. "Basic movements that younger people take for granted—like looking over a shoulder or from side to side—can be very painful for older people," Ludwick says. "So we've found that older drivers don't tend to check out oncoming traffic to as great a degree as younger drivers. Strength can also be a problem. It can be difficult for older drivers to turn the steering wheel quickly and precisely, especially if the car doesn't have power steering."

## Mental Deterioration

Some older drivers also suffer from mental as well as physical deterioration. "There's no doubt that some older drivers are confused, lacking in mental acuity just as some may be lacking in visual acuity," Ludwick says. "Age affects different people in different ways, but it's obvious that physical skills aren't necessarily the only powers that deteriorate as we get older."

Not only do older drivers bring diminished physical and mental capacities to the driver's seat, but a good many of them drive under the influence of prescription drugs.

"Many of the drugs commonly prescribed for the elderly have a great effect on reflex reactions and mental clarity," says Suzi Haywood, the occupant protection coordinator for the California Office of Traffic Safety. "When you combine that with physical or mental capacities that are already diminished, you have a real problem."

## The Aging Population

It's a problem that's going to get bigger. There are about 19 million licensed drivers in the state; about 4 million of them are 55 or older. The national demographic trend toward older drivers is inexorable. By the year 2020, more than 17 percent of the population will be 65 or older.

"People are living longer, and they're healthier during their retirement years than they ever have been," St. George says. "Cars are as representative of freedom and mobility to old people as they are to younger people—more so, in fact. Seniors often feel that their cars are essential for their independence. Driving has become a very crucial part of our culture, of the way we view the quality of our lives. People will fight to keep their driving privileges."

## Monitoring Drivers

The solution isn't getting old people out of their cars. Rather, it's getting some old people out of their cars, and testing and monitoring the rest on a regular basis.

Though the matter is constitutionally sticky and a political bombshell, many traffic safety experts would like to see a designated age after each testing prior to license renewal is mandatory—55 seems to be a favorite target age among pundits, since it's right around then that various physical powers begin to wane markedly.

Age cannot be used as a criterion in determining testing standards in California. This has been the case since the late 1960s, when pressure from the American Association of Retired Persons crushed a legislative drive in that direction. Considering the growing power of the gray lobby, it's unlikely that any attempt to change this situation would be successful.

## Toughening Tests

There is a logical alternative. Require all drivers to take written, visual and driving tests prior to license renewal, and toughen the tests themselves, particular those that deal with visual acuity, mobility and motor reflex.

"The current visual and reflex exams don't come close to measuring the crucial deterioration which can occur in an aging driver," says Ray Peck, the director of research and development for the Department of Motor Vehicles. "They're really pretty crude. All the vision tests determine is basic acuity. We need to check for peripheral vision and glare response as well. Basically, the tests just don't address the kinds of physical declines that can occur. That's one thing that we're determined to change in the DMV, one way or the other. It's a difficult and controversial process, however."

Peck, St. George and their colleagues are interested in the various mature driver improvement programs that are now flourishing in the state. Programs of this sort have long been sponsored by the American Association of Retired Persons. A bill passed in 1987 by the California Legislature has greatly enhanced interest in the programs, however. The bill by Assemblyman Richard Katz, D-Los Angeles, certifies a curriculum for mature driver improvement courses, making drivers who take them eligible for substantial discounts on their automobile liability insurance.

## Driver Improvement

Peck is hopeful about the trend, but has some reservations.

"Critics of the mature driver programs have pointed out that the problems mature drivers have are basically physical," he observes. "Their strength and mobility may be gone, or their eyesight may be very poor. Even most of their problems with mental acuity are the result of organic disorders. It's not like it is with teen-age drivers—they basically have the wrong attitude. Older drivers tend to be very law-abiding, given their physical limitations. The question remains, then—how can you adequately address physical problems with an attitudinal program? The jury is still out on this, though we're all hoping the programs will demonstrate positive results."

### Cut Costs

If Peck is not completely convinced of the efficacy of the mature driving programs, however, Dorothy Labernik is a true believer. The San Jose resident is the California coordinator for 55 Alive, the officially sanctioned mature driver program for the American Association of Retired Persons.

"Our eight-hour courses do two things," she says. "They point out the problems which are common among older drivers, and they teach them how to compensate. Our first year for this program was 1979. We had 123 graduates. Last year, the AARP passed over 40,000 graduates. We can't help but feel that this has a positive effect.

"There's no doubt that a good many of them come to capitalize on the lower insurance rates," Labernik says. "But the feedback we get on the program itself is enormous. Many of them are tremendously surprised when we actually demonstrate vision deficiencies they may have—and they're very grateful when we show them ways to compensate for them. They come here to save money, but they leave as safe drivers."

Maybe. I hope I don't sound uncharitable when I say I've yet to see significant evidence of that. My heart and my hopes go out to Labernik and her peers; however, as the population ages, we'll need more like her if we're to avoid a bloodbath on our highways—a bloodbath I could well contribute to in upcoming years.

As my own elderly mother is fond of pointing out to me, I ain't no spring chicken myself. In a few decades, I'll be the codger behind the wheel, and those young bucks on their motorcycles had better keep their eyes peeled. Because there's no way I'm going to give up *my* license.

## REFLECTING ON THE READING

Talk to a person over the age of 70 about the idea of special testing for older drivers. Find out what they think of special testing or required courses for older drivers. Identify at least one argument for and against special testing not mentioned in the article.

◆

# MERCEDES-BENZ
## (JANIS JOPLIN, 1969)

AL YOUNG

◆

*Have you ever wanted a car just for the impression it
would make on other people? What kind of car fits your
image of yourself? What is your image of Mercedes-
Benz owners?*

Janis, your song and my Sadies arrived the same year!

For $600 you couldn't beat it: a sparkling 220 Mercedes-Benz sedan in
the darkest of midnight blue shades that the light would hit and make gleam
just like one of those old British detective cars I used to admire in old J.
Arthur Rank films of 1950s vintage; the kind of no-nonsense motor car Rita
Tushingham seemed perfectly comfortable hopping in and out of between
serio-comic episodes of a romantic story with a bittersweet twist.

I knew when I plunked my money down that I could've been buying a
lemon. But when Adam and Lois Miller told me about that car one Saturday
night at a sweltering dance party, I coolly made up my mind that very moment that they were right when they'd said: "This car's for you; it's you
through and through. It's just the machine for a writer with a flare for simple elegance!"—for words to that special effect.

A few days later I boogie'd right up to the Oakland Hills and offered to
buy the automobile from the owner who had it parked in front of his house
with one of those regulation red and white FOR SALE signs displayed in one
of the rear passenger windows. He was an uptight, prejudiced foothills resident who, I could tell right off, wasn't exactly ecstatic about the idea of selling his treasured, almost-classic vehicle to a mere Negro. Refusing to take
my personal check, he insisted that I either bring cash or a certified bank
draft to his place of business for the precise amount the following day. It just
so happened he was an auto mechanic. Adam Miller, who had gone with me
to check the car over, knew the score. I knew the score. Even though we
were both black and professionally literate, we were still Americans. I
wanted to call the whole thing off. Adam, who'd owned a Mercedes for
years, said: "Just go and get the money and bring it to the bastard, then
you'll have yourself a good car, OK?" I took his advice.

And what a car it was! It still had its original paint job from 1956, shiny
chrome trimmings, white-wall tires (or ought I say *tyres?*), wood panel work

along the dashboard and doors, attractively worn and partially cracked leather seats in a soft, dove gray upholstery; fog lights, scientific-looking meters and gauges, bucket seats, and thick floor carpeting. In short, it had all the right stuff to make you feel every bit as virtuous and glamorous as people treated you once you got behind the wheel, mashed down on the accelerator and started tooling around town. I went right out too and invested in fancy car waxes to while away many a Saturday and Sunday afternoon working like a coolie to make my foreign car shine.

Snappy. That was the word. It was easily the snappiest-looking car I've ever owned. Remember, you're getting this from someone who didn't start driving until he was well into his twenties; someone who had previously owned a $50 Ford and a $200 American Motors Rambler Wagon. In that respect, I was anything but American; if anything, I was a thorough discredit to a nation of auto users and abusers.

Suddenly, though, I was something to be reckoned with. By dint of installing myself behind the wheel of what most people considered to be a luxury car, I was initiated at once into the grand scheme of things automotive according to which people do not ask "Is this your car?" but, rather, "Is this you?"

Is this you? That was the key. No, it wasn't me; it could never be me. It was only an almost antique auto I oughtn't have been fooling with in the first place, but the impression I gave off was that of a well-heeled, successful oddball who just happened to be driving one of Germany's finest industrial products in a country that measured human worth on the basis of an individual's material accumulations.

Was that Mercedes me? For awhile I thought it was; I wanted so for it to be me. How keenly I recall parking it in front of a San Francisco bookstore I've frequented for years and having one of the hip clerks rush out and shout: "Why Al Young, you slick sonofabitch! So you finally sold out!" Or the afternoon I happened to be chatting on the street with another Mercedes owner who also happened to be my color. There we stood at curbside, leaning against our cars, when a derelict white man stumbled from across the street. He stood for a minute, staring at us, then cupped his hands to his mouth and screamed at the top of his ugly voice: "Hey! Hey! You niggers think you're takin over the world, don't you? You think you got everything sewed up! Well, you know what? Fuck you, you black assholes! Fuck everyone of you black nigger bastards!"

Then there were the black people themselves who put me through changes. There was the hefty highway patrolman who pulled me over one summer evening, stomped around the sedan, checking every part of the car out, finally leaning over the hood and fingering the windshield wipers.

"I'm giving you a citation," he said at last.

"A citation for what?"

"Faulty windshield wipers!"

"May I ask what's wrong with the windshield wipers?"

"Sure, you can ask."

"Then, tell me, how are they faulty?"

"They're just faulty, that's all! You got that? Your windshield wipers are faulty! Now, you wanna get belligerent? I been pretty nice to you up till now."

And there were the dents and nicks and the stealing of the Mercedes chrome insignia that customarily graces the front of the hood. Sometimes you felt as if people went out of their way to do bodily harm to your car simply because it was supposed to be a luxury car. It wasn't unusual, for instance, to climb back inside of it at some parking garage to find that the car had been broken into and burglarized.

Mercedes-Benz repairmen—those immaculately garbed gentlemen in greaseless smocks—would take one look at me and sense intuitively that I had no business trying to maintain such a car. In fact, when the oil pump finally blew on the freeway one day and I had to have the car towed by Triple A to the nearest German auto garage, I was informed, forthright and bluntly, that the cost for repairing the frozen pistons was probably going to run higher than the value of the car. "And if you cannot afford to pay our fee," said the head mechanic, "then we want the thing towed from our premises within 48 hours. Do you understand?" I understood. Moreover, I was required to sign a prepared, written statement to that effect.

Oh, Janis, it was all too much! The next time you put in a request in your prayerful song for a Mercedes-Benz, be sure and ask the Lord to throw in some upkeep money to boot. And, while you're at it, you just might want to picture me leaving that alien garage on foot, walking two blocks to the closest bus stop, stepping aboard, plopping down in a window seat and sighing while I thought to myself: "Ahhh, good riddance! That's one more possession that won't be possessing me no more!"

I got myself a brand new Datsun 510 Wagon and drove back into the future.

## REFLECTING ON THE READING

Al Young uses a very wide vocabulary, from very formal to hip to vulgar. List three words that fit each of those categories. Write a sentence describing the effect of this range of language on you as a reader.

◆

# What Harm Can Come from a Few Glasses of Wine?

Anonymous*

◆

*Have you ever driven after drinking? Have you ever
ridden with a driver who had been drinking? Do you
know of anyone harmed by a drunken driver? Keep
your answers in mind as you read a surgeon's account
of driving after drinking.*

*To many of us, four glasses of wine over four hours doesn't seem like
enough to do damage. But this first-person account from a USAA member, a respected surgeon, may make you think twice. He volunteered to
share this story, thinking others might learn from it. We have withheld his
name to protect his privacy.*

We were driving in the slow lane of the freeway, following traffic that Friday
evening when the big red light appeared in the rear-view mirror. I wondered
what would possibly prompt the police to stop us—perhaps a taillight was out.

"You have inadequate rear vision," said the police officer, shining the
flashlight through my rolled-down window and pointing to the pile of presents, suitcases and baby equipment that filled the back of our Jeep. He
looked at me, my wife, our daughter, my son-in-law and our baby.

I started to explain, but he interrupted. "Have you had anything to
drink tonight?"

"I had about four glasses of wine at the rehearsal dinner for my son's
wedding."

"Please get out of the car," he said. He led me to the side of the freeway
where he and his partner administered a field sobriety test, which I passed.

"Now I want you to blow into this Breathalyzer, sir," he said. "You don't
have to, but if you don't, we will assume you're under the influence."

I complied, confident that I had not been impaired by a few glasses of
wine over four hours. But as the cars rushed by and I saw my family wor-
riedly watching me, suddenly I was scared.

"Sir, you are just at the line—0.08 percent blood alcohol. I am going to arrest you for driving under the influence," said the officer.* The cold handcuffs snapped on my wrists, and one officer led me to the patrol car. When he told my family they could find me at the city jail, I saw more fear in my wife's eyes than I had seen during a Vietnam tour when she was a nurse and I was a combat surgeon.

The officers stopped at a hospital to get a more accurate breath test, and again, I registered 0.08 percent. As I walked handcuffed through the hospital's emergency room, I was eternally grateful I was not in my hometown where as a leading surgeon, everyone would have known me. I asked the troopers why they had stopped me, and they said it was for inadequate rear vision; my car was missing an outside mirror. "But, on Friday nights we routinely ask about drinking," one added. "And if you say 'yes,' we test you."

### Six Hours in Jail

At the city jail, the police passed me over to the sheriff's deputy. I was booked, fingerprinted, photographed and relieved of my shoes, watch, wallet, belt, wedding ring and coins. The deputy walked me to a room with a steel door in which there was a 12-inch window. "This is where you'll spend the next six hours. After that, you are free to leave," he said.

The room smelled of urine, vomit, sweat and disinfectant. There were three other men in the 12- by 16-foot windowless concrete space: two college-age kids sitting on the gray floor and an older man stretched out on the single stadium-style wall bench. In the corner was a stainless steel commode with a drinking fountain built into the lid. A black pay telephone sat above it on the wall. I tried to call my wife, but the phone was broken.

"What'd they get you for?" the older man called out. I described the circumstances and he chuckled. "I was riding my bike on the sidewalk downtown," he said, closing his eyes and holding his arms out as if he were riding no-handed.

After 2 a.m. the bars closed, and the steel jail door opened and slammed shut with greater frequency. Over 25 men of all ages, socio-economic groups and ethnicities crowded into the cell. Some were pacing, some sick, some shouting, others sleeping on the sticky floor. Most had stories to tell about how they got there. I listened to them all.

Very few were "bad guys," and nearly to a man, they already regretted what they had done and what lay ahead. At 5 a.m. my name was called on the intercom. I stood up, disheveled and dirty, and was led to the dismissal area.

"You report back here for court at 8 a.m. in two weeks," said a deputy. I walked out into the crisp early morning air, passing through deserted streets

---

*In most states, a driver with a blood alcohol concentration (BAC) of either 0.08 or 0.10 per-cent is legally guilty of driving while intoxicated. The Surgeon General has recommended that level be reduced to 0.04 by the year 2000 for drivers over 21 years of age and 0.00 for drivers under 21.

back to our motel. When I got there, my family looked worse than I did. I felt awful about what I had put them through.

Six hours later, I drank diet cola at the wedding and watched many other guests have too many margaritas in the afternoon sunshine. I wondered who was driving them home.

### Standing Before the Judge

Two weeks later I stood before the judge in a court of flags, secretaries, sheriffs and some of the same men who had been in my cell. The case preceding mine concerned a repeat offender, and the judge sentenced him to a multi-thousand dollar fine, one year loss-of-license, six days in jail and an alcohol treatment program.

I simply told my story; the sheriff corroborated it. The secretary stated I had never had a similar violation or a major accident in 40 years of driving. The judge was surprised I didn't have a lawyer, but I had served on juries in which the testing method and equipment were challenged, and it didn't seem very sensible. I just wanted to get it over with.

Thankfully, I was given a misdemeanor, "reckless driving," and in addition to a fine and a four-month driver's license suspension, I was assigned to "work-fare" for three days.

My work-fare consisted of working as a city janitor. I cleaned bathrooms, mopped floors and carried out trash in the city buildings for those three days.

"Are you the new custodian?" a woman looked up and asked as I quietly replaced the wastebasket beneath her desk.

Bill, the head janitor, who was in the doorway, answered, "No, he's just temporary."

"Oh," she said, "he's good, Billy. You should see that he stays." It made my day. I enjoyed work-fare and gained some insight into the cramped and difficult conditions under which county social workers perform their duties. It also gave me time to reflect. As a surgeon who routinely cares for highway accident victims in the Emergency Room, I had seen the carnage of a drunk driver.

I recalled college days when I am sure I drove while impaired, but I honestly thought I had not done it since. However, after being stopped, I studied the blood alcohol tables, and I realized that tired from work and the new baby, and having had very little to eat at the rehearsal dinner, it was a cinch to be 0.08 percent, and thus legally impaired—which is the level where a driver's reflexes are slow and judgement is imperfect.

### Driver's License Suspended

The work-fare is over now. And as I write this, I am halfway through the four-month driver's license suspension. My wife drives me everywhere. That means taking the baby too. I haven't advertised what is going on; indeed, it is something that in a small town can destroy a professional. I know when my suspension is over, it will cost me $100 to re-take my driver's test, and my auto insurance will triple in cost and remain at that level for three years.

I know if I am stopped again within the next seven years with even a trace of alcohol on board, I will be dealt with as a repeat offender.

I have learned a valuable lesson *the hard way*. But perhaps I saved my family's life and that of someone else. Maybe people reading this will stop and think. The ads all say, "Friends don't let friends drive drunk." I agree; but even friends and family don't realize how easily 0.08 percent comes and how normal you look at that level. While the blood alcohol tables, weight scales, food intake and age can determine how impaired you are, that's too complicated. It's much easier to simply say, "If you drink, don't drive."

Take it from me—the shame, the cost, the inconvenience and the potential to hurt loved ones is too great. A drink, even one, isn't worth it. Stop and think about this the next time you start your car. If you had anything to drink, you should not drive. Trust me. You won't like it when the red light appears in your rearview mirror.

## REFLECTING ON THE READING

Find out what the laws regarding legal intoxication are in your state. Find out the punishment if convicted for driving under the influence of alcohol. Discuss with your classmates whether you think the punishment is appropriate.

◆

# LIMO TO HELL

MERRILL MARKOE

◆

*Going to a social event in a limousine seems to be the ultimate luxury. See how your image compares to Merrill Markoe's experiences.*

My recent invitation to the Emmy Awards got me thinking that the whole premise of the Emmy telecast is a little confusing: that each year there is so much incredible stuff on TV that it is not possible to contain the orgy of awards and self-congratulations, speeches and production numbers in a less-than-four-hour show.

I know this probably sounds jaded. I guess even I had some hopes of an evening of grandeur and glitz the very first time I attended. I fretted for weeks with all the women I knew on the topic of proper attire. I even purchased several outfits so unlike the kind of thing I ordinarily wear that I began to question everything that I knew to be true about the order of the universe.

When all of this dawned on me—the night before the event—I returned the beaded-and-sequined funeral wear and bought myself a woman's tuxedo. I think it was that same evening that my escort and I made the momentous decision to eschew the traditional complimentary limousine and drive ourselves to the big event in his car.

Now, I know that probably sounds goofy if you are one of those people who have always longed to ride in a limousine. But riding in a limousine makes me feel like a geek. First of all, there is the preposterous size of the car, and then there's the *Upstairs, Downstairs* effect concerning the amount of room *you* get versus the amount the driver gets. It's so unlike anything I was taught to be comfortable with that it triggers in me a compulsively compensatory behavior, and I end up encouraging each driver to pour his heart out to me in ways I would generally discourage, even among beloved family members.

And so, on previous limousine rides I have heard (at my own request) the sad tales of the overwork, poor pay and stress that sometimes constitute a limo driver's life. I have listened to stories of abuse suffered at the hands of callous celebrities (one driver told me Warren Beatty made him sit outside a restaurant for sixteen hours and, when he finally came out, didn't even tip him). And then there was the time I listened in polite horror to an excruciating description of the congenital defects of a driver's grandson. Also hard to forget is the time that I looked into the rearview mirror only to notice that my elderly, bloodshot-eyed driver was taking the limo to sleepyland. I was able to rouse him with a brisk slap on the cheek and talk him into making a pit stop at the nearest Denny's, where I watched him drink cup after cup of black coffee before I would agree to get back into the limousine.

### Glamorous Emmy Story Number One

So, driving ourselves seemed like a fine idea to me, right up until the time we joined the unmoving crunch of gridlocked limousines that had converged on the Pasadena Civic Auditorium like salmon headed upstream to ... well, I guess to attend some kind of big salmon media event. The increasing frustration of moving only a vehicle's length per green light was starting to make my sometimes fiery-tempered escort kind of fiery-tempered. Which is why, as soon as he had an opportunity to make any turn that led out of this morass, he did so, even though that meant we were traveling *away* from our destination.

This eventually led us to abandon our valet parking pass and park the car in a department store lot some six or eight blocks away. Next came a brisk walk through two very expansive department stores, followed by a very unpleasant high-speed footrace down many long blocks of city streets in over-a-hundred—degree heat. My escort maintained a constant fifteen-foot distance in front of me, glancing back only occasionally and gesturing significantly at his watch. I hobbled gloomily behind in a pair of high heels, growing increasingly damp in my wood-blend tuxedo and nylons. The good times continued after we were seated. From that moment straight through the last song-and-dance extravaganza involving extras dressed up as cartoon characters, my escort subjected me to a continuous harangue as he grew more and more panicky about the safety of his car in a department-store lot. "You're sure you don't think they're going to lock up the place before we get out of here?" he kept asking. "You think it's okay, right?" About the thousandth time he asked, I turned and looked across the aisle. And there was Bruce (*Scarecrow and Mrs. King*) Boxleitner, knowing he looked cool as he ran his hand through his tousled sable hair.

### Glamorous Emmy Story Number Two

Last year I decided to chuck the tuxedo effect and I went out and bought myself a swell new dress. No one was more amazed than I that I was able to find one I liked, could afford and in which I actually seemed to cut a dashing figure. To protect my new acquisition from the assorted ink and marinara and condiment strains that I manifest like an uncontrollable form of stigmata, I never even took my dress out of the garment bag in which it had been hermetically sealed at purchase.

Emmy day started smoothly. This year my escort was once again planning to drive himself, but *I* was sharing a limousine with a group of friends. Yep, I felt pretty good, right up until the first breath I exhaled as the limousine pulled out of my driveway. It was then that I learned that the belt to my dress, the centerpiece of the design, had been constructed by the Morton Thiokol company. It somehow lacked an adequately engineered system of fastenings—it merely had a thin and useless loop—and in fact slid right off my body every time I breathed out. Maybe this was my fault. Maybe there was an elaborate system of hoists and pulleys that I should have asked to be hooked up to at the store. But now there seemed to be nothing I could do. I experimented during the drive with doubling the belt back on itself as well as with a form of breathing so shallow it probably could not be sustained in cryogenic suspension. As I walked up the auditorium steps I was so preoccupied by the issue of how to carry my purse and my program *and* keep my belt on my body that it took me a couple of minutes to realize that I was walking directly behind Little Miss I'm-Not-Having-Any-Trouble-Keeping-All-My-Clothing-Looking-Perfect herself, Cybill Shepherd. A gigantic wad of photographers clustered around her like iron filings. "Cybill, hey Cybill! Over here!" they were shouting, and at any angle she knew exactly how to make that I'm-a-gorgeous-former-model-and-I'm-not-having-any-belt-problems-at-all face right to the camera.

My worst fear was naturally fated to come true: I actually won something and had to make a long, graceless, belt-clutching walk down the aisle to the stage, all the while being scrutinized by a mobile hand-held camera. Of course, it wasn't only me ... I was enveloped by a group of eleven men with whom I shared the honor. I think I do have the distinction, however, of being the only winner with just one hand free with which to receive the award.

But the glamour didn't stop there. After the show a group of us decided to get together for a celebratory dinner. My escort, as mentioned earlier, had his car there and insisted on driving part of the group. Which is why I found myself sharing the crawl space behind the seats in a two-seat sports car with another good-natured but secretly irritated woman also dressed in formal wear and also being strangled by her various matching accessories. When at one point along the way the car screeched to a halt to obey a traffic light, I almost became the first person in history to meet her death by being impaled on an Emmy. Which brings us to this year.

### Glamorous Emmy Story Number Three

This year my escort and I *both* took the limousine, which, of course, came with the usual drawbacks. Before we left the driveway I learned that our driver had been a cool-guy senior at the high school where my escort had been a dorky freshman. This poignant example of life's cruel ironies depressed me all the way to the gridlock. But we live and we learn. This year when my escort tried to talk me into another formal-attire footrace in the scorching heat, I was able to respond with a jaunty, heartfelt obscenity. And this year, although I chose for my outfit precisely the same thing as last year, my sturdy, unmatching belt stayed exactly where I put it. But even these impressive accomplishments were faint consolation for what turned out to be a night of pure, uninterrupted tedium. You must remember that when you attend a live television show, you do not have your usual remote control changer option.

My escort was called backstage early on, and I was left to spend the duration of the evening with a "seat filler." These are people hired by the networks to show up in their formal wear and occupy any seats abandoned by audience members who are losing their will to live. In this case, a *very* large, round, pale gentleman with a new growth of beard became my new companion for the evening. Which is only one of the reasons that hour three found me pacing with others in the lobby. By the timed I rejoined my escort during hour four, we were both so shell-shocked by boredom that we elected to stand in the back of the auditorium. This afforded us a vantage point from which little could be seen, which in this case didn't turn out to be a drawback.

The following day I spoke to a friend who had attended with a guy who had never been there before. On the ride over, in the limousine they shared, this friend opened a bottle of champagne and proposed a toast: "To the most boring evening of your life." The first-time guy became enraged and lectured my friend about how jaded and cynical he had become. He made my friend feel kind of ashamed, until an hour into the show when they ran into each other in the lobby. "Let's get out of here," Mr. I'm-Not-Jaded said to my friend. "You were right." And they promptly took the limo home.

In the final analysis, it's very nice for anyone who works hard to receive an award for his or her efforts. But in the case of the Emmys, maybe it would be a good idea to try delivering the honors through the U.S. mail.

## REFLECTING ON THE READING

Imagine you were the driver of one of the limo rides described by Markoe. In one paragraph, describe the driver's view of the experience.

# PUTTING IT IN WRITING

## RESPONSES

1. As quickly as possible, write down the first five adjectives that come to mind when you think about the word "car." Pick two of the adjectives and explain why you associate them with a car.
2. Recall your most unusual experience in an automobile. Write for five minutes, describing it in concrete detail so that a reader would know why it was unusual.
3. Study an ad for an automobile that you like. How much of the ad emphasizes safety, how much emphasizes costs, and how much emphasizes status and image? Write a one sentence conclusion based on your analysis of the ad.

## READING FOR MEANING

1. Several of the articles use statistics to support their points. Use the statistics from one of those articles to make a table or chart that makes it easy to understand the significance of the statistics.
2. Some of the articles in this chapter deal with strongly emotional subjects. Pick one paragraph that evoked strong feelings from you. Explain what produced those feelings (e.g., the situation described, the language used, an experience it reminded you of).

3. Pick the last sentence of one of the readings in this chapter and write a paragraph explaining why it is an effective ending to the article.

## ORGANIZING YOUR IDEAS

1. Get a brochure from a car dealer describing the features of a car you would like to own. Now, go the reference section of your community library and find a magazine that also assesses the quality of the same car. Itemize the differences between the dealer's brochure and the assessments in the magazine.
2. Use "speed," "alcohol," and "age" as key word descriptors with "automobile." Do a search in the reference area of your college library to find material that would help you understand the relationship of each category to driving safety.
3. Imagine you are a writer for the David Letterman show (as Merrill Markoe used to be). Write a "Top Ten" list under the heading "Top Ten Reasons Americans Will Never Give Up Their Automobiles." Compare your list with two classmates. Discuss with one another whether a different order would be more effective for each of your lists.

## WRITING A PAPER

1. Compare a car you have owned (or your family has owned) with the car you would own if cost were not a factor. Write a paper that makes clear all of your reasons for making the choice you would make. Draw on the research you did for #1 in "Organizing Your Ideas."
2. Think up three or four criteria that you would consider in purchasing a car. Write a paper which explains the importance of each criteria and cite one or two examples of cars that would fit each criteria.
3. Fatal accidents seem most often related to the driver's age, use of alcohol, and speed of the vehicle. Using the research from #2 in "Organizing Your Ideas," explain which factor is the major cause in automobile fatalities.

Tom Toles' humor is based on irony.
What is the irony in this situation?

# WORK

Just when "work" begins in our lives is not clear. At the age of just three or four, children can "help" mommy or daddy in some task in the house or yard. Most likely, that was your introduction to work. After a few years in school, a child is given homework to supplement the work done in class. In most homes, children must clean their rooms, make beds, wash or dry dishes, cut the lawn, shovel snow, and perform various other forms of housework and yard work. But, ordinarily, none of this work results in a paycheck. "Work" is usually considered those tasks and jobs for which people get paid.

Young people are urged to stay in school so they can "get a good job." Some people believe school exists to prepare us for work. Others, like Michel Montaigne, believe that study exists to learn how to live well and die well. Work is just a part of living. Most college students choose to continue their education to learn skills and develop abilities which they can put to work (i.e., get paid).

Sometimes, work is called a vocation (literally, "a calling"). This idea suggests that some particular work suits you, that fate or God or your heritage determines the work you should do. Other people are interested in work that pays the most money for the least time and effort. Still other people are satisfied with work that can be counted on, that provides a steady income, adequate to pay for food, shelter, and transportation. A wise person once wrote, "Find a job you love and you'll never work another day in your life."

Work also involves the choice of working for someone else, whether in a small business or a large corporation, or working for yourself. When you work for another, you encounter "bosses," or supervisors—people who tell you what to do, schedule and structure your work, or evaluate your performance as a worker. Those relationships often produce conflict and sometimes abuse. A boss who can fire you holds unusual power over your life and may have quite unpleasant effects on how you feel about work. At the same time, when you work for yourself, you must take responsibility both for success and for failure.

Since the beginning of the Industrial Revolution, work outside the home has become the norm. Some work is very unpleasant and even dangerous (e.g., mining, high-rise construction, long-distance truck driving); some work is extremely repetitive and boring (e.g., assembly line or word processing); some work is very active and exhilarating (e.g. professional sports or search and rescue).

To provide some control over the conditions of their work, workers in many industries have formed unions. Both the federal and state governments have passed laws to provide for job safety and against job discrimination. In the past few decades, women have entered the workforce in dramatically increased numbers, raising issues such as pay equity, child care, and sexual harassment.

Before you read the articles in this chapter, reflect on your own work experiences. Think of the work you most enjoyed and the work you least enjoyed. Make lists of the features of each job that contributed to your enjoyment or your lack of it. If you have never held a job for pay, then do this exercise in relation to work you have done for which you were not remunerated.

◆

---

# LETTER TO A KID

ANONYMOUS

---

◆

*Being interviewed for a job makes most people nervous. Can you remember how you prepared for your first job interview? Recall how well you did in your interview as you read "Letter to a Kid."*

Dear Kid,

Today you asked me for a job. From the look of your shoulders as you walked out, I suspect you've been turned down before, and maybe you believe by now that kids out of high school can't find work.

But, I hired a teenager today. You saw him. He was the one with polished shoes and a necktie. What was so special about him? Not experience, neither of you had any. It was his attitude that put him on the payroll instead of you. Attitude, son. A-T-T-I-T-U-D-E. He wanted a job badly enough to shuck the leather jacket, get a haircut, and look in the phone book to find out what this company makes. He did his best to impress me. That's where he edged you out.

You see, Kid, many of the people who hire other people aren't "with" a lot of things. We know more about foxtrots than about discotheques, and we have some Stone-Age ideas about who owes whom a living. Maybe that makes us prehistoric, but there's nothing wrong with the checks we sign, and if you want one you'd better tune us in.

Ever hear of "empathy?" It's the trick of seeing the other fellow's side of things. I couldn't have cared less that you needed "bread for your pad." How you pay your rent is your problem, and your landlord's. What I needed was someone who'd go out in the plant, keep his eyes open, and work for me like he'd work for himself. If you have even the vaguest idea of what I'm trying to say, let it show the next time you ask for a job. You'll be head and shoulders over the rest.

Look kid: The only time jobs grew on trees was while most of our country's manpower was wearing G.I.'s and pulling K.P. For all the rest of history you've had to get a job like you get a girl: "Case" the situation, wear a clean shirt, and try to appear reasonably willing.

Maybe jobs aren't as plentiful right now, but a lot of us can remember when master craftsmen walked the streets. By comparison you don't know the meaning of "scarce."

You may not believe it, but all around you employers are looking for young men smart enough to go after a job in the old-fashioned way. When they find a fellow like that, they can't wait to unload some of their worries on him.

For both our sakes, *get eager*, will you?

## Reflecting on the Reading

The author of "Letter to a Kid" emphasizes the importance of "attitude" in a job interview. However, the author also appears to have an attitude. Describe the author's attitude in two or three sentences.

◆

# Tyrannical Bosses Spawn Naturally in Workplace

Susan Harte

◆

*"Boss" often conveys negative connotations. As you
read the following article, think of how your last boss
fits the picture developed by Susan Harte.*

By now, you know them by sight. Hardly anyone who has ever worked
for pay has not had to suffer at least one.

They hover until you want to scream. They scream until you want to dis-
appear. They harp and carp, demand and demoralize, patronize and insult.
Sometimes, they even tell lies to make themselves look good.

They come in many shades of red, but they're still the bosses from Hades.

These people sap your motivation because nothing you do suits them.
They are doggedly and unfailingly right.

They dampen any joy or creativity you might bring to your job because
you're afraid—of their capricious ways, of doing something wrong.

Bad bosses rob you of your optimum productivity because they pulver-
ize your morale. Worst of all, they feed off weak, malleable people and then
proudly insist that the pablum tastes great.

We all know who bad bosses are, how they behave and how we feel
about them. But where do they come from?

### Whining Children

Some experts say bad bosses may start out as children who whine or
malinger to get their way. They won't share toys. While one will be willful
and self-centered, another will be frightened and domineering.

"These people grow up to be selfish, stubborn and manipulative," says
Judith Segal, a Los Angeles-based management consultant. "They're people
users. The reason subordinates detest them as bosses is that they make you
feel taken advantage of, set up, powerless and off balance."

Bad bosses also can spawn other bad bosses. In this case, the idea is: "I
suffered for 10 years under Joe. Now I've the power to make everyone else
similarly miserable."

And poorly managed companies consistently pick managers for all the wrong reasons, Dr. Segal says. Afterward, those executives, just like bad parents, relinquish their responsibility and rarely monitor lower managers—except about money and product concerns.

### Bad Managers

"Managing people well is usually the last reason someone is made a supervisor," Dr. Segal says.

Consultant Michael Mescon agrees that many companies promote for the wrong reasons. Susceptible to eager, charming people who present themselves well in meetings, corporations tend to glance only superficially at character and managerial aptitude.

"To a great extent, bad bosses are symptomatic of an organization's perverse systems that reward these behaviors," says Dr. Mescon, president of the Mescon consulting group and former dean of Georgia State University's business school.

"Say you have a bad boss, a real (unpleasant person) anyway you look at him or her. Now, how does an individual like this not only survive in organizations, but also be rewarded with both raises and promotions?"

It's because the corporate culture tacitly supports treating people like chattel, as long as the profits look good, Dr. Mescon says.

However absurdly destructive that sounds, Dr. Mescon says, if it's part of the "organizational folkway," and if top management hasn't the will to look into the heart of the operation, then there will always be bosses from hell.

But some American companies are being forced to change their ways.

### Intrinsic Satisfaction

"Why?" Dr. Mescon asks rhetorically. "Because people view work differently now, and they should. Work should be as natural as eating and breathing. We ought to develop an intrinsic satisfaction from it."

In the future, he predicts, fewer workers will allow themselves to be pummeled emotionally. And confident, secure supervisors won't feel the need to assert their power in destructive ways.

"I think the 'age of terrorism' is going."

## REFLECTING ON THE READING

List the qualities of a bad boss as Harte describes them. Think of two other "bad boss" qualities and add them to the list.

◆

# BERYL SIMPSON

STUDS TERKEL

◆

*Working for an airline sounds adventurous. See if you
can find any adventure in Beryl Simpson's description
of her job with an airline.*

My job as a reservationist was very routine, computerized. I hated it
with a passion. Getting sick in the morning, going to work feeling,
Oh, my God! I've got to go to work.

I was on the astrojet desk. It has an unlisted number for people who travel
all the time. This is a special desk for people who spend umpteen millions of
dollars traveling with the airlines. They may spend ten thousand dollars a
month, a hundred thousand a month, depending on the company. I was dealing with the same people every day. This is so-and-so from such-and-such a
company and I want a reservation to New York and return, first class. That
was the end of the conversation. They brought in a computer called Sabre. It's
like an electric typewriter. It has a memory drum and you can retrieve that information forever. Sabre was so expensive, everything was geared to it.
Sabre's down, Sabre's up, Sabre's this and that. Everything was Sabre.

With Sabre being so valuable, you were allowed no more than three
minutes on the telephone. You had twenty seconds, busy-out time it was
called, to put the information into Sabre. Then you had to be available for
another phone call. It was almost like a production line. We adjusted to the
machine. The casualness, the informality that had been there previously was
no longer there. The last three or four years on the job were horrible. The
computer had arrived.

They monitored you and listened to your conversations. If you were a
minute late for work, it went into your file. I had a horrible attendance
record—ten letters in my file for lateness, a total of ten minutes. You took
thirty minutes for your lunch, not thirty-one. If you got a break, you took ten
minutes, not eleven.

When I was with the airlines, I was taking eight tranquilizers a day. I
came into this business, which is supposed to be one of the most hectic, and
I'm down to three a day. Even my doctor remarked, "Your ulcer is healed,

it's going away." With the airline I had no free will. I was just part of that stupid computer.

I remember when I went to work for the airlines, they said, "You will eat, sleep, and drink airlines. There's no time in your life for ballet, theater, music, anything." My first supervisor told me that. Another agent and I were talking about going to the ballet or something. He overheard us and said we should be talking about work. When you get airline people together, they'll talk about planes. That is all they talk about. That and Johnny Carson. They are TV-oriented people.

I had much more status when I was working for the airlines than I have now. I was always introduced as Beryl Simpson, who works for the airlines. Now I'm reduced to plain old Beryl Simpson. I found this with boyfriends. I knew one who never dates a girl with a name. He never dates Judy, he never dates Joan. He dates a stewardess or a model. He picks girls for the glamor of their jobs. He never tells you their names. When I was with the airlines, I was introduced by my company's name. Now I'm just plain old everyday me, thank God.

I have no status in this man's eyes, even though I probably make twice as much as the ones he's proud of. If I'd start to talk about some of the stocks I hold, he'd be impressed. This is true of every guy I ever dated when I was working on the airlines. I knew I had a dumb, stupid, ridiculous, boring job, and these people were glamorizing it. "Oh, she works for the airlines." Big deal. When I used to go back home, the local paper would run my picture and say that I work for the airlines and that I had recently returned from some exotic trip or something. Romance.

A lot of times we get airline stewardesses into our office who are so disillusioned. We'd like to frame their applications when we get a bright-eyed, starry-eyed kid of eighteen who wants a career in the airlines. Big as life disillusionment. We want to say, "It's not what it's cracked up to be, girlie." If a girl's a stewardess, she might as well forget it after twenty-six. They no longer have compulsory retirement, but the girls get into a rut at that age. A lot of them start showing the rough life they've lived.

## Reflecting on the Reading

Underline the key word or phrase in each paragraph of Terkel's interview with Beryl Simpson. Now, thinking about the words you have underlined, write a sentence that describes the dominant attitude expressed by those words.

◆

# A Pipefitter's Dream

Mary Gaddis

◆

*Gaddis teaches a course on women in skilled trades at
Laney College in Oakland, CA.*
*A woman working in a mostly male environment
faces many issues she would not face in a mostly female environment. Consider what those might be and
see if Mary Gaddis experienced the same issues.*

I knew becoming a pipefitter's apprentice was going to be a challenge
when I went in for my oral interview and was asked, "Do you know it gets
muddy when it rains?" When the second question was, "Do you know that
men are kind of ... they can be sort of ... they just might ... and how would
you deal with that?", I was sure this had moved from a challenge to a problem. My response was, "Do you mean they might say _ _ _ _? If so, I would
just ignore them. If they continued, I would say _ _ _ _ you, and if they
grabbed me, I'd kick them between the legs."

At this point my three male interviewers crossed their legs and said the
interview was over.

I thought my new career was over before it started as well. But luckily I was
wrong, and one month later I got called for a job and was told to come in the
next day to be dispatched. For the next three days, though, I kept being told not
to come in—just to wait. Much later I found out that when the union business
agent called the company and told them that the first-year apprentice they'd be
getting was Mary Gaddis, the company said, "We don't want any girls."

As the story goes, my business agent, one of the 10 or so decent men in
the union, told them, "If you don't want any girls, then we won't dispatch
anyone to you—no plumbers, no steamfitters, no nobody." It was the support of the men like him in the union that really helped me survive being a
woman in the trades.

The year was 1979, and I was the first woman in the 1,800-man pipefitter's union. Ten years later there are all of 15 women in the union—less than
1 percent of the membership. In my years as an apprentice and now as a
journeywoman I have had to put up with the most outrageous behavior, not
only because I was a woman, but because I was the only woman. Like the
time when I was working on a ladder and some guy came up and put his
hand between my legs. When I asked what he thought he was doing, he told

me that it looked like I was going to fall so he came up to help me balance. Or when a guy at a construction site told me that women brought bad luck and that if I ever came near him he would bash my head in, and with that comment placed a 40-pound pipe wrench on my shoulder to make his point. Or the guy who would grab my breast or rear end in order to get my attention.

I stand 5'10" and weigh 200 pounds, which gave me an advantage at being able to challenge the men at their own game. I didn't like having to play it like a man, but often it was a matter of survival. And along the way, there were the guys in the union who were truly supportive and would go out of their way to stand with me. There certainly wasn't any help from a governmental agency or system—I was on my own. As other women came in, we would make sure we saw each other twice a month to check in and get support from each other. It helped a lot.

And then I thought I had it made. I had gotten through the apprenticeship program and was a journeywoman; I even made foreman on a site. Boy, was I wrong! When I was made foreman the guys painted graffiti in the outhouse about me. There was a picture of me from behind, with no clothes, looking over a table of blueprints with the comment, "Now that's my kind of foreman and don't forget to kiss your foreman goodnight." When I complained, nothing happened, so I finally quit the job.

I still work summers as a steamfitter, but I've found further purpose in my life by helping other women get into the trades. I helped found Women Empowering Women, which encourages and introduces women into the trades, and I tell my story to women whenever I get the chance.

The problems are real, I tell them, but you can make it. There are some supportive men and a lot of supportive women. And our job is not to give up and let men keep women out of good-paying jobs in the trades, but to advocate and make sure that more and more women have the opportunities.

## REFLECTING ON THE READING

Would you describe Mary Gaddis as optimistic or pessimistic about her work situation? Find three sentences in the article that support your opinion.

◆

# DRUDGE QUEENS OF OFFICE OPINION

DEBRA J. SAUNDERS

◆

*When you hear the word "secretary," what are the first
three words that come to mind? Now read what Debra
J. Saunders, Los Angeles Daily News editorial writer,
says about her work as a secretary.*

This past holiday season I was counting my blessings. Right up there is
the utter joy of writing for a newspaper. But frankly, on another level,
I'm just plain glad not to be working as a secretary anymore.

It's not that I think the job is a bad one. It's just amazingly underrated.
When people want to compliment a secretary, for example, they often say
that she—that's right, she—is "more than just a secretary." There's an implication that the job is so menial that one who does it well must be extraordinary.

Truth be told, secretarial work can be challenging and rewarding. The
rotten part about it stems from other people's attitude about the job. In the
unbending world of public opinion, secretary is synonymous to drudge
queen. Imagewise, they're the ashtrays of the world.

Watching the movie "Working Girl" on cable Christmas Eve was like
confronting my own ghost of Christmas past. The movie stars Melanie Griffith as a Wall Street secretary who wants to work her way up a career ladder
peopled by those who wouldn't take her seriously.

I felt that old choke in the throat, the hard swallow of the knowledge
that people didn't want to hear what I had to say. I wanted to do great
things, but to the wood-paneled world, I was just another twentysomething
curly-hair who could type.

The problem isn't so much that a bad boss doesn't want you to think.
It's just that secretarial work is supposed to seem thoughtless and effortless.
Just get the coffee. Make the reservations. Put together the presentation.

But the employer who acknowledges the effort that goes into being a
secretary, then has to give credit for a job well done. That might give some
women ideas and set them to thinking about a promotion. And then you
might lose a good secretary.

My friend Meg Catzen, a hot-shot lobbyist, was watching "Working Girl"
too. "That's what life was for every working woman who didn't have a grad-

uate degree," she muttered. She graduated from Johns Hopkins University to the copy machine.

The worst part is, that once you've taken a clerical position, the suits start thinking less of you. It's like the pivotal scene in "Working Girl": Griffith's bitchy female boss charges into the board room warning execs not to listen to Griffith because—hold on to your briefcases—she's a secretary.

That's right, an impostor, passing herself off as someone who knows something. That's no hotshot, that's my secretary.

Meanwhile, men our age graduated from school to entry-level jobs that promised glorious futures. Jobs that didn't require typing. Bigger paychecks. An easier row to hoe.

And the biggest benefit of all was that the men got hired under the assumption that they would go on to do greater things. It was understood that these young men with their ties had something to say.

They say that today's young female graduates don't face those problems. That young women today don't have to burn at the indignity of being dismissed as "the girl." I hear that young women today enter the workforce with that same sense of entitlement and self-assurance that jacketed young men have had.

I don't believe it. Maybe that's true for the MBAs and the doctorates, but I'm afraid there's still a good chance that a young woman with a liberal arts degree who can type is destined to start out with a job full of heartache. For that woman is entering a world in which many others have a stake in their not succeeding.

I toughed it out. I went from secretary to administrative assistant. (How gratified that title made me feel because it made it sound as if I were more than just a secretary.) From assistant to account executive.

I got my own office and business cards. And I learned that those higher-up jobs weren't quite as glamorous as they had seemed. I learned that meetings are boring and reading memos can be as tedious as typing them. I found out that you can get paid more, have a fancy title and your boss still may not want to hear what you have to say.

And now it's Christmas every day because, ho ho ho, I actually get paid to mouth off.

Life is good. And I'm no longer afraid that some puffed-up pooh-bah is going to ask me to fetch his coffee.

## REFLECTING ON THE READING

Interview a secretary where you work, where you go to school, or some place you do business. Prepare three questions based on Saunders' views, trying to confirm her generalizations.

♦

# THE MYTH OF MALE POWER

## AN EXCERPT

### WARREN FARRELL

♦

*Women have traditionally held low status jobs. Men have traditionally held high danger jobs. Look for information new to you as you read this excerpt from Warren Farrell's book,* The Myth of Male Power.

I am often asked why men don't get as worked up as they might about women—particularly poor women—having to use their bodies as prostitutes.

Because most men unconsciously experience themselves as prostitutes every day.

The miner, the firefighter, the construction worker, the logger, the soldier, the meatpacker. These men are prostitutes in the direct sense: They sacrifice their bodies for money and for their families.

Thus, 94 percent of workplace deaths happen to men.

The middle-class man is a prostitute of a different sort. He recalls that when his children were born, he gave up his dreams of becoming a novelist and began the nightmare of writing ad copy for a product he didn't believe in—something he would have to do every workday for the rest of his life.

The poorer the man, the more he feels this. To men, prostitution is not a female-only occupation.

We frequently hear that women are segregated into low-paying, dead-end jobs in poor work environments such as factories.

But when the Jobs Related Almanac ranked 250 jobs from best to worst based on a combination of salary, stress, work environment, outlook, security and physical demands, they found that 24 of the 25 worst jobs were almost-all-male jobs.

Some examples: truck driver, sheet-metal worker, roofer, boilermaker, lumberjack, carpenter, construction worker or foreman, construction machinery operator, football player, welder, millwright, ironworker.

All of these "worst jobs" have one thing in common: 95 to 100 percent men.

One reason the jobs men hold pay more, then, is because they are more hazardous. The additional pay might be called the "Death Profession Bonus."

Just as the "glass ceiling" describes the invisible barrier that keeps women out of jobs with the most pay, the "glass cellar" describes the invisible barrier that keeps men in jobs with the most hazards.

What about the male executive jobs—the glamour professions such as law?

Many lawyers enter law with the fantasy of becoming a Perry Mason. Instead they become paper masons. They expect to work with people. They become isolated from people. They desire to be legal pioneers. They become legal prostitutes.

In their search for pay and respect, many lawyers find instead chest pains, hypertension, arthritis and insomnia—in their 30s.

Both male and female lawyers are much more likely to feel like prostitutes when they work for corporations.

It has been my men friends who have been most likely to succumb to the bribe of big salaries and least likely to quit when they hated what they were doing.

Why? In part because they are more likely to be supporting wives financially.

Eighty-seven percent of wives of top executives—vice president and above—work inside, not outside the home.

Conversely, almost all the husbands of female executives work full time outside the home. So the monied male executive has a wife who is a financial burden.

A married female executive has a husband who is a financial buffer.

The married male executive usually has more home support from his wife, but he pays for that by treating his profession more as an obligation. She has less home support, but she can treat her profession more as an opportunity.

In my workshops I have met thousands of men willing to parent, cook, manage the home and arrange the social life in exchange for the income of executive women they love. I meet few executive women volunteering to financially support these men.

When feminist publications discuss construction work, mining and other death professions, they are portrayed as examples of the male power system, as "male-only clubs."

However, when Ms. magazine profiled female miners, the emphasis was on how the woman was "forced" to take a job in the mines because it paid the best, and how taking such a job was the only way she could support her family.

Ms. could never acknowledge that the male-only clubs of hazardous occupations paid best because of their hazards and had been male-only exactly because men risked their lives for the extra pay to support families.

This double standard—of the death professions being a privilege when men did them and an oppression when women did them—has made two generations of men feel unappreciated.

## Reflecting on the Reading

Farrell uses a series of comparisons, often opposites, to make his point. List four contrasts that Farrell uses in this article.

◆

# The Immigrants Have Something to Teach Us

Richard Rodriguez

◆

*While the United States has always been a "nation of immigrants," every so often popular concern is expressed about the effects of immigration on American culture or the American economy. Recall when and how your ancestors came to the United States. Then read the following article, written by Richard Rodriguez, whose parents immigrated from Mexico.*

Californians are afraid of the future and cannot imagine themselves in the great world. To prove it, Gov. Pete Wilson last week published an open letter to President Bill Clinton, urging a constitutional amendment to deny citizenship to the children of illegal immigrants as well as the repeal of federal mandates requiring health and education services for illegal immigrants.

On the same day that the governor published his letter ("on behalf of the people of California"), I was at a chic Los Angeles hotel. All day, I saw Mexicans busily working to maintain California's legendary "quality of life." The common complaint of Californians is that the immigrants, whether legally or illegally here, are destroying our quality of life. But there the Mexicans were—hosing down the tiles by the hotel swimming pool, gardening, everywhere gardening. The woman who could barely speak English was making beds; at the Yuppie restaurant, Mexican men impersonated Italian chefs.

Who could accuse Wilson of xenophobia? The governor was, after all, only concerned with those immigrants illegally here. His presumption was that the illegal immigrants are here only for the umbrella of welfare services. Remove those benefits and they will go back to Mexico, the governor reasoned. Here was a presumption in Wilson's letter that betrayed naiveté about the desperation of the Third World poor and their wild ambition for work.

"God, do they work," a friend confides over martinis in Bel-Air. "I've never seen people work like those Mexicans."

What troubles us about Mexican immigrants is that they work too hard. The myth California has advertised to the world is that here is a place of leisure—the myth of blond beaches and palm trees.

It is embarrassing to watch the Mexican work, like watching a peasant eat. The Mexican, perhaps most especially the illegal immigrant, reminds us how hard life is, he reminds us that in much of this world, one must work or die.

Work becomes life. The feel of work, the assurance of a handle to hold, a hope. The peach is torn from the branch, the knife slits open the fish; the stake is plunged into the earth faster and faster. Work or die. The Mexican works.

Not only Mexicans are working, of course. There are also Vietnamese, Koreans, Guatemalans, Salvadorans, Chinese. Wilson's letter to the president was only concerned with Mexicans and with Mexico, but many Californians probably are made more uneasy with the Asian migration. If, as the governor believes, Mexicans are a burden because they are poor, Asians are a threat because they are poised to take over the city. In San Francisco, people say it all the time: The Chinese are taking over the city.

During the Gold Rush, in the mid–19th century, Chinese miners were chased off the fields by other prospectors. Mexicans (many of whom arrived from northern Mexico, bringing with them mining skills) were also chased away. But many generations later, now, the parent in Walnut Creek, a father of three, tells me that Asians are unfair. (His daughter has not been admitted to Berkeley.) "Asians are unfair because they work so hard."

Californians should be thinking of ways to join with Mexico if we are as modern, as advanced, as we like to tell our fellow Americans we are. We would be imagining a global state. Instead, environmentalists are using the North American Free Trade Agreement as a way of keeping Mexico at bay, under our control. And Gov. Wilson urges the president to tie NAFTA to Mexico's policing of its northern border. Clean yourself, we tell Mexico, clean yourself and then we will embrace you.

Sen. Dianne Feinstein wonders if we shouldn't charge a toll for entering California from Mexico. And her fellow liberal in the Senate, Barbara Boxer, wants to enlist the National Guard to protect our border. But, of course, millions of middle-class Californians assume that they can use Mexico whenever and however they want. They go to Mexico for a tan. They go to Mexico to adopt a baby. They retire to Mexico—get a condo in Cabo. They reach into Mexico for an inexpensive gardener or nanny.

Despite ourselves and because of the immigrants, California is becoming a world society—an extraordinary meeting place of Asia and Latin America with white and black America.

Poor New York, thousands of miles away, senses that something is going on in California but hasn't a clue. All summer, New York has been taken by the notion that the California dream is tarnished. *The New Yorker* dispatched Joan Didion from her upper East Side apartment. Regis Philbin confided to his viewers: "It's so sad—all those poor people going to L.A."

CBS News sent several correspondents to Los Angeles a few weeks ago to view the apocalypse. Except for an eccentric Latino who predicted a Latino takeover of the Southland, the entire hour of "48 Hours" was given to white and black opinions. Lots of blond people said they were fed up with California—"it's not what we had in mind."

No correspondent bothered to ask the Guatemalan teen-ager or the Chinese short-order cook why they had come to California.

Dear Regis Philbin: California does not have an immigrant problem. California has a native-born problem.

Gov. Wilson, I think, would have done better addressing a letter to his fellow Californians—rich, middle-class, poor. The governor might well have asked if, as Californians, we assume too much about our right to leisure, and the government's obligation to our well-being.

Ross Perot may have it half right. Americans are going to have to be harder on ourselves. The government is running out of money for savings-and-loan fat cats, Social Security grandmas and welfare mothers. But Perot is wrong in thinking that we can close ourselves from the world.

Neighbors should not live oblivious of one another. Any coyote in Tijuana can tell you that illegal immigration is inevitable as long as distinctions between rich countries and poor, developed countries and the Third World, are not ameliorated. If we want fewer illegal Mexican immigrants, we must work with Mexico, as Mexico must work with Guatemala.

In time, though, California will turn the Mexican and Chinese teen-agers into rock stars and surfers. But I think the immigrants also will change California—their gift to us—reminding us of what our German and Italian ancestors knew when they came, hopeful, to the brick tenement blocks of the East Coast.

Life is work.

## REFLECTING ON THE READING

Look up the word "paradox." Find three examples of a "paradox" in Rodriguez's article.

◆

---

# LOOKING FOR WORK

GARY SOTO

---

◆

*Most of us earned our first money by running an errand for a neighbor, pulling weeds, babysitting, or similar work. Recall the first work you did for money, and compare your experience to Gary Soto's.*

One July, while killing ants on the kitchen sink with a rolled newspaper, I had a nine-year-old's vision of wealth that would save us from ourselves. For weeks I had drunk Kool-Aid and watched morning reruns of

*Father Knows Best,* whose family was so uncomplicated in its routine that I very much wanted to imitate it. The first step was to get my brother and sister to wear shoes at dinner.

"Come on, Rick—come on, Deb," I whined. But Rick mimicked me and the same day that I asked him to wear shoes he came to the dinner table in only his swim trunks. My mother didn't notice, nor did my sister, as we sat to eat our beans and tortillas in the stifling heat of our kitchen. We all gleamed like cellophane, wiping the sweat from our brows with the backs of our hands as we talked about the day: Frankie our neighbor was beat up by Faustino; the swimming pool at the playground would be closed for a day because the pump was broken.

Such was our life. So that morning, while doing-in the train of ants which arrived each day, I decided to become wealthy, and right away! After downing a bowl of cereal, I took a rake from the garage and started up the block to look for work.

We lived on an ordinary block of mostly working class people: ware-housemen, egg candlers, welders, mechanics, and a union plumber. And there were many retired people who kept their lawns green and the gutters uncluttered of the chewing gum wrappers we dropped as we rode by on our bikes. They bent down to gather our litter, muttering at our evilness.

At the corner house I rapped the screen door and a very large woman in a muu-muu answered. She sized me up and then asked what I could do.

"Rake leaves," I answered, smiling.

"It's summer, and there ain't no leaves," she countered. Her face was pinched with lines; fat jiggled under her chin. She pointed to the lawn, then the flower bed, and said: "You see any leaves there—or there?" I followed her pointing arm, stupidly. But she had a job for me and that was to get her a Coke at the liquor store. She gave me twenty cents, and after ditching my rake in a bush, off I ran. I returned with an unbagged Pepsi, for which she thanked me and gave me a nickel from her apron.

I skipped off her porch, fetched my rake, and crossed the street to the next block where Mrs. Moore, mother of Earl the retarded man, let me weed a flower bed. She handed me a trowel and for a good part of the morning my fingers dipped into the moist dirt, ripping up runners of Bermuda grass. Worms surfaced in my search for deep roots, and I cut them in halves, tossing them to Mrs. Moore's cat who pawed them playfully as they dried in the sun. I made out Earl whose face was pressed to the back window of the house, and although he was calling to me I couldn't understand what he was trying to say. Embarrassed, I worked without looking up, but I imagined his contorted mouth and the ring of keys attached to his belt—keys that jingled with each palsied step. He scared me and I worked quickly to finish the flower bed. When I did finish Mrs. Moore gave me a quarter and two peaches from her tree, which I washed there but ate in the alley behind my house.

I was sucking on the second one, a bit of juice staining the front of my T-shirt, when Little John, my best friend, came walking down the alley with a baseball bat over his shoulder, knocking over trash cans as he made his way toward me.

Little John and I went to St. John's Catholic School, where we sat among the "stupids." Miss Marino, our teacher, alternated the rows of good students with the bad, hoping that by sitting side-by-side with the bright students the stupids might become more intelligent, as though intelligence were contagious. But we didn't progress as she had hoped. She grew frustrated when one day, while dismissing class for recess, Little John couldn't get up because his arms were stuck in the slats of the chair's backrest. She scolded us with a shaking finger when we knocked over the globe, denting the already troubled Africa. She muttered curses when Leroy White, a real stupid but a great softball player with the gift to hit to all fields, openly chewed his host when he made his First Communion; his hands swung at his sides as he returned to the pew looking around with a big smile.

Little John asked what I was doing, and I told him that I was taking a break from work, as I sat comfortably among high weeds. He wanted to join me, but I reminded him that the last time he'd gone door-to-door asking for work his mother had whipped him. I was with him when his mother, a New Jersey Italian who could rise up in anger one moment and love the next, told me in a polite but matter-of-fact voice that I had to leave because she was going to beat her son. She gave me a homemade popsicle, ushered me to the door, and said that I could see Little John the next day. But it was sooner than that. I went around to his bedroom window to suck my popsicle and watch Little John dodge his mother's blows, a few hitting their mark but many whirring air.

It was midday when Little John and I converged in the alley, the sun blazing in the high nineties, and he suggested that we go to Roosevelt High School to swim. He needed five cents to make fifteen, the cost of admission, and I lent him a nickel. We ran home for my bike and when my sister found out that we were going swimming, she started to cry because she didn't have the fifteen cents but only an empty coke bottle. I waved for her to come and three of us mounted the bike—Debra on the cross bar, Little John on the handle bars and holding the Coke bottle which we would cash for a nickel and make up the difference that would allow all of us to get in, and me pumping up the crooked streets, dodging cars and pot holes. We spent the day swimming under the afternoon sun, so that when we got home our mom asked us what was darker, the floor or us? She feigned a stern posture, her hands on her hips and her mouth puckered. We played along. Looking down, Debbie and I said in unison, "Us."

That evening at dinner we all sat down in our bathing suits to eat our beans, laughing and chewing loudly. Our mom was in a good mood, so I took a risk and asked her if sometime we could have turtle soup. A few days before I had watched a television program in which a Polynesian tribe killed a large turtle, gutted it, and then stewed it over an open fire. The turtle, basted in a sugary sauce, looked delicious as I ate an afternoon bowl of cereal, but my sister, who was watching the program with a glass of Kool-Aid between her knees, said, "Caca."

My mother looked at me in bewilderment. "Boy, are you a crazy Mexican. Where did you get the idea that people eat turtles?"

"On television," I said, explaining the program. Then I took it a step further. "Mom, do you think we could get dressed up for dinner one of these days? David King does."

"*Ay, Dios,*" my mother laughed. She started collecting the dinner plates, but my brother wouldn't let go of his. He was still drawing a picture in the bean sauce. Giggling, he said it was me, but I didn't want to listen because I wanted an answer from Mom. This was the summer when I spent the mornings in front of the television that showed the comfortable lives of white kids. There were no beatings, no rifts in the family. They wore bright clothes; toys tumbled from their closets. They hopped into bed with kisses and woke to glasses of fresh orange juice, and to a father sitting before his morning coffee while the mother buttered his toast. They hurried through the day making friends and gobs of money, returning home to a warmly lit living room, and then dinner. *Leave It To Beaver* was the program I replayed in my mind:

"May I have the mashed potatoes?" asks Beaver with a smile.

"Sure, Beav," replies Wally as he taps the corners of his mouth with a starched napkin.

The father looks on in his suit. The mother, decked out in earrings and a pearl necklace, cuts into her steak and blushes. Their conversation is politely clipped.

"Swell," says Beaver, his cheeks puffed with food.

Our own talk at dinner was loud with belly laughs and marked by our pointing forks at one another. The subjects were commonplace.

"Gary, let's go to the ditch tomorrow," my brother suggests. He explains that he has made a life preserver out of four empty detergent bottles strung together with twine and that he will make me one if I can find more bottles. "No way are we going to drown."

"Yeah, then we could have a dirt clod fight," I reply, so happy to be alive.

Whereas the Beaver's family enjoyed dessert in dishes at the table, our mom sent us outside, and more often than not I went into the alley to peek over the neighbor's fences and spy out fruit, apricot or peaches.

I had asked my mom and again she laughed that I was a crazy *chavalo* as she stood in front of the sink, her arms rising and falling with suds, face glistening from the heat. She sent me outside where my brother and sister were sitting in the shade that the fence threw out like a blanket. They were talking about me when I plopped down next to them. They looked at one another and then Debbie, my eight-year-old sister, started in.

"What's this crap about getting dressed up?"

She had entered her profanity stage. A year later she would give up such words and slip into her Catholic uniform, and into squealing on my brother and me when we "cussed this" and "cussed that."

I tried to convince them that if we improved the way we looked we might get along better in life. White people would like us more. They might invite us to places, like their homes or front yards. They might not hate us so much.

My sister called me a "craphead," and got up to leave with a stalk of grass dangling from her mouth. "They'll never like us."

My brother's mood lightened as he talked about the ditch—the white water, the broken pieces of glass, and the rusted car fenders that awaited our knees. There would be toads, and rocks to smash them.

David King, the only person we knew who resembled the middle class, called from over the fence. David was Catholic, of Armenian and French descent, and his closet was filled with toys. A bear-shaped cookie jar, like the ones on television, sat on the kitchen counter. His mother was remarkably kind while she put up with the racket we made on the street. Evenings, she often watered the front yard and it must have upset her to see us—my brother and I and others—jump from trees laughing, the unkillable kids of the very poor, who got up unshaken, brushed off, and climbed into another one to try again.

David called again. Rick got up and slapped grass from his pants. When I asked if I could come along he said no. David said no. They were two years older so their affairs were different from mine. They greeted one another with foul names and took off down the alley to look for trouble.

I went inside the house, turned on the television, and was about to sit down with a glass of Kool-Aid when Mom shooed me outside.

"It's still light," she said. "Later you'll bug me to let you stay out longer. So go on."

I downed my Kool-Aid and went outside to the front yard. No one was around. The day had cooled and a breeze rustled the trees. Mr. Jackson, the plumber, was watering his lawn and when he saw me he turned away to wash off his front steps. There was more than an hour of light left, so I took advantage of it and decided to look for work. I felt suddenly alive as I skipped down the block in search of an overgrown flower bed and the dime that would end the day right.

## Reflecting on the Reading

Write an anecdote describing an instance that you earned some money as a child. Tell the story so that it makes some point about work or money. See Chapter 2, p. 58 for models of effective anecdotes.

# Putting It In Writing

## Response

1. Recall your first paycheck or your first payday (or, your last one). Write for five minutes describing what you did with the money.
2. Write a paragraph describing the job you have enjoyed most. Use very specific details and vivid words to convey your sense of pleasure in

that work. If you haven't had a job you enjoyed, describe one that made you miserable.

3. Imagine "The Interview from Hell." Write for five minutes explaining what it would be like.

## Reading for Meaning

1. Most of the readings see work as more negative than positive. List three negative features of work described by female writers and three negative features of work described by male writers. Decide whether men and women seem to complain about the same things regarding work. State your conclusion in a single sentence.

2. Pick the article you had the most difficulty reading and outline it. See Chapter 2 for ideas about outlining. Write two or three sentences describing how making the outline helped your understanding of the article.

3. Using an article designated by your instructor, use the mapping technique described in Chapter 2 as a way of understanding the key elements of that article.

## Organizing Your Ideas

1. One way of categorizing work would be *training, applying, interviewing, performing on the job.* List examples from the readings in this chapter that apply to each category.

2. Some people refer to jobs as blue collar, white collar, and pink collar. List five jobs that you think fit into each category. Compare your list with the list of a classmate of the opposite sex. Write a sentence that describes what you learned from the comparison.

3. Reread the interview of Beryl Simpson by Studs Terkel. Construct four questions you think he asked to get her answers. Using those questions, interview a classmate about his or her work.

## Writing a Paper

1. Using the first two readings in this chapter as a source of ideas, write a "Letter to a Boss." Include advice that you think would help any boss be more effective with the people he or she supervises.

2. Using the material you developed in #1 or #2 in "Organizing Your Ideas," write a paper explaining the best way to go about getting a job. Make your advice as practical as possible. Explain any differences in the process depending on the type of job (blue collar, white collar, pink collar).

3. Pick a job that you think you would like. Interview a person who is currently doing that work. (Use the interview techniques you practiced in #3 in "Organizing Your Ideas".) Write a paper that demonstrates whether what you learned in your interview increased or decreased your interest in that job.

Sometimes it seems men and women will never understand one another. What does the Feiffer cartoon suggest about relationships and commitment between men and women?

# Men and Women

"Is it a girl or a boy?" Friends and relatives anxiously ask this when they learn of a new birth. For some reason the sex of a child elicits great interest. In this century, issues related to sex, or in more academic terms, gender and sexuality, create some of the liveliest and most controversial discussions among people of all backgrounds. Consider this list of words and phrases and notice which one's evoke positive, negative, or relatively neutral feelings: women's lib, male chauvinist pig, feminism, femi-nazis, radical feminists, men's movement, battle of the sexes, gender equity, abortion rights, sexual harassment, preferential hiring, dumb blonde, macho, mom, dad, brothers, sisters, bachelor, old maid, bitch, bastard, broad, guy, sexy. To make an exercise out of this list, form a group with several classmates. Make a group of equal numbers of males and females. Individually, each person should mark each word or phrase +, −, or 0 signifying positive, negative, or neutral. Then, compare your lists to see if males and females react differently to the same word or phrase.)

*Vive le difference* say the French. The phrase seems to affirm that differences between men and women are not only inevitable, but also desirable. The issue of difference lies at the heart of the debates over gender and the controversies related to sexuality. The physiological differences between men and women are obvious and undisputed. But the social and cultural meanings that become associated with those differences create lively, often heated, conversations. Physically, women have pendulous breasts, men have pendulous sex organs. Few would dispute those facts. But when a commentator speaks of women having "penis envy" or men having a "breast fixation," we quickly enter the area of cultural meanings, interpretations of attitudes or behaviors that some expert or analyst associates with physical differences.

The differences between male and female and modern democratic ideals of equity and equality create tensions that most of us now experience on a daily basis. In families, are boys favored over girls? In school, do boys get more attention from teachers than girls? At work, are men paid more than women for the same work? Should they be paid the same for comparable work? In romance, who should initiate relationships? Who should dominate the relationship? In any of these areas, what kind of touching is acceptable between males and females, between females and females, or between males and males? When one person physically touches another, what rules make some touches acceptable and others not? How are such rules developed in a culture?

The questions that develop from the apparently simple categories "men" and "women" are anything but simple. Traditionally, women have borne the babies and been the nurturers of the young, while men have been the hunters and warriors, providing food and protection. But these traditions are oversimplifications. In modern, industrial societies, women serve in the military, even in combat, and men care for babies and raise children. With modern medicine and technology, birth control is cheap and widely available to both men and women. Some people feel this has changed the nature of both sexual relationships and marriage. Many people think these changes are bad, corrupting modern societies. Many other people think these changes are good and will be the basis for creating fairer, more humane societies. So it's easy to see why discussions of the roles, functions, and relationships of males and females in American society—or any society—lead so easily to controversy and difference of opinion.

Before you read the material in this section, try the following exercise with a group of your classmates (or your entire class). On a small piece of paper, write three statements that are true of men. On the back side, write three statements that are true of women. On the top of the paper, write an "M" or an "F" to indicate your own sex. Collect up all the papers, grouping them according to the sex of the writer. By comparing what men say about men with what women say about men, you may discover some of the issues and controversies in your own group or class. You can do the same exercise by comparing what women say about women with what men say about women. You should have some good material to activate your thinking as you read the articles in this section.

◆

# WHAT WE HAVE HERE IS A FAILURE TO COMMUNICATE

DAVE BARRY

◆

*Notice the effect Dave Barry creates in his opening sentence by contrasting "guys" with "women." How would the effect have differed if he had substituted the words "men" and "gals" in his opening sentence?*

Today's topic for guys is: Communicating With Women.

If there's one thing that women find unsatisfactory about guys—and I base this conclusion on an extensive scientific study of the pile of *Cosmopolitan* magazines where I get my hair cut—it is that guys do not communicate enough.

This problem has arisen in my own personal relationship with my wife, Beth. I'll be reading the newspaper, and the phone will ring; I'll answer it, listen for 10 minutes, hang up, and resume reading. Finally Beth will say: "Who was that?"

And I'll say: "Phil Wonkerman's mom."

Phil is an old friend we haven't heard from in 17 years.

And Beth will say, "Well?"

And I'll say, "Well what?"

And Beth will say, "What did she *say*?"

And I'll say, "She said Phil is fine," making it clear by my tone of voice that, although I do not wish to be rude, I *am* trying to read the newspaper here, and I happen to be right in the middle of an important panel of "Calvin and Hobbes."

But Beth, ignoring this, will say, "That's *all* she said?"

And she will not let up. She will continue to ask district-attorney-style questions, forcing me to recount the conversation until she's satisfied that she has the entire story, which is that Phil just got out of prison after serving a sentence for a murder he committed when he became a drug addict because of the guilt he felt when his wife died in a freak submarine accident while Phil was having an affair with a nun, but now he's all straightened out and has a good job as a trapeze artist and is almost through with the surgical part of his sex change and just became happily engaged to marry a prominent member of the New Kids on the Block, so in other words he is fine, which is *exactly* what I told Beth in the first place, but is that enough? No. She wants to hear *every single detail*.

We have some good friends, Buzz and Libby, whom we see about twice a year. When we get together, Beth and Libby always wind up in a conversa-

tion, lasting several days, during which they discuss virtually every significant event that has occurred in their lives and the lives of those they care
about, sharing their innermost feelings, analyzing and probing, inevitably
coming to a deeper understanding of each other, and a strengthening of a
cherished friendship. Whereas Buzz and I watch the playoffs.

This is not to say Buzz and I don't share our feelings. Sometimes we get
quite emotional.

"That's not a *foul?*" one of us will say.

Or: "You're telling me *that's not a foul?*"

I don't mean to suggest that all we talk about is sports. We also discuss,
openly and without shame, what kind of pizza we need to order. We have a
fine time together, but we don't have heavy conversations, and sometimes,
after the visit is over, I'm surprised to learn—from Beth, who learned it from
Libby—that there has recently been some new wrinkle in Buzz's life, such as
that he now has an artificial leg.

(For the record, Buzz does *not* have an artificial leg. At least he didn't
mention anything about it to me.)

I have another good friend, Gene, who's going through major developments in his life. Our families recently spent a weekend together, during
which Gene and I talked a lot and enjoyed each other's company im-
mensely. In that entire time, the most intimate personal statement he made
to me is that he has reached Level 24 of a video game called "Arkanoid." He
has even seen the Evil Presence, although he refused to tell me what it looks
like. We're very close, but there is a limit.

I know what some of you are saying. You're saying my friends and I are Nean-
derthals, and a lot of guys are different. This is true. A lot of guys don't use words at
*all*. They communicate entirely by non-verbal methods, such as sharing bait.

But my point, guys, is that you must communicate on a deeper level
with a woman, particularly if you are married to her. Open up. Don't assume
that she knows what you're thinking. This will be difficult for guys at first,
so it would help if you women would try to "read between the lines" in determining what the guy is trying to communicate:

Guy statement: "Do we have any peanut butter?"

Inner guy meaning: "I hate my job."

Guy statement: "Is this all we have? Crunchy?"

Inner guy meaning: "I'm not sure I want to stay married."

If both genders work together, you can have a happier, healthier relationship, but the responsibility rests with you guys, who must sincerely . . . hey,
guys, I'm *talking* to you here. Put down the sports section, OK? *Hey! Guys!*

## Reflecting on the Reading

Recall a recent conversation with a person of the opposite sex whom you
know very well. Write out the dialogue for at least four exchanges. How
does your dialogue compare to the one Dave Barry presents?

◆

# IN A MULTI-COIFFEURIAL SOCIETY, THIS IS AN OUTRAGE

FROMA HARROP

◆

*The word "multi-coiffeurial" echoes the more common term "multicultural." How does this title set you up for what Harrop says?*

It is disquieting to learn that a school in Jacksonville, Fla., has banned the book "Snow White" for younger students.

School Superintendent Larry Zenke may be squeamish. The story has a gory scene where a hunter cuts out a boar's lungs and liver, and the Wicked Queen eats them, believing they are the vitals of Snow White.

Whatever his reason, I don't like it.

In suppressing "Snow White," Zenke is depriving dark-haired girls of a rare role model.

In the past, I had never cared much for the notion of a "Rainbow Curriculum." That refers to a proposal requiring New York City grade schools to include positive references in class to the multitude of races, cultures and sexual orientations that make up the American mosaic. After all, I and fellow dark-haired women of Italian, Semitic or other Mediterranean origin made it, although our textbooks blatantly tilted in favor of children with blond, red and auburn locks.

But I had completely forgotten the significance of raven-haired Snow White until Zenke and his ilk came along and tried to take her away from us. Disenfranchised brunettes must join the struggle for recognition of our contributions to American culture. It is time to recognize that this is a multi-coiffeurial society.

During the '50s and '60s, Snow White was the only black-haired heroine to be found in children's stories. The rest are blond, as fans of Walt Disney's feature cartoons can attest to. Alice of Wonderland is blonde. Tinker Bell, Sleeping Beauty, blond. Cinderella, ditto. Pinocchio may have been a little Italian puppet/boy with a shock of black hair, but his benefactress, the Blue Fairy, is as platinum as Jean Harlow.

Of course, the Gentlemen-Prefer-Blonds ethic was in full force long before this century. Consider two Romantic heroes—Lord Byron's Corsair and Sir Walter Scott's Ivanhoe. Both dallied with interesting brunettes before leaving them for home-gal blonds. No wonder so many Mediterranean women go flaxen while their men remain dark and handsome. This has led cynics to remark that the males and females in many southern European cities seem to have dipped into different gene pools.

The whole issue has to be handled sensitively. Snow White is not an exemplary brunette. She is, in fact, one of Disney's more passive heroines. She is chased off by the hunter, led to the cottage by the animals, given a poisoned apple by the witch, and brought back to life by the smooch of a prince. Indeed, she sings the loser's theme song, "Some Day My Prince Will Come." She even cleans up after the dwarfs.

But all of that notwithstanding, Mr. Zenke down in Jacksonville ought to let the little ones have Snow White. The violence is no worse than what they see on television. Otherwise, beware. Brunettes will have their revenge. Soon you might be dealing with books titled "Claudia's Mommy Isn't Really Blond."

We, too, are part of the Rainbow, and we're not all Goldilocks.

## Reflecting on the Reading

Stereotyping women on the basis of hair color has been quite common. Does the same stereotyping occur for men? Design a survey question for your class that would develop an answer to that question.

◆

# Fishing for Love

Joyce Maynard

◆

*You have probably read personals ads seeking a relationship. Have you ever written one or answered one? How did those ads work out for Joyce Maynard?*

*Joyce Maynard became a teen-age media sensation in 1972 with her New York Times Magazine cover story, "An 18-Year-Old Looks Back on Life." Maynard is a former syndicated columnist and the author of the new novel, "To Die For." She lives in New Hampshire.*

Two-and-a-half years ago I left my marriage of twelve years for no better reason than an insufficiency of love. But while I grieved over the end of my marriage and the pain it caused me and everyone else in our family, I came to believe that the wise course, and the only acceptable one, was to do everything I could to make a happy life. Why bring about so much upheaval and grief only to experience more of the same afterward?

And so for me, an important part of the healing process required that I take an active role in seeking out what I had missed for so long in my marriage: namely, someone who would love and treasure me as I was. It didn't seem too much to ask that a woman who had spent a good part of the past dozen years looking out for her family's needs might spend some time and energy on meeting her own, for a change.

When I said as much in the newspaper column I wrote at the time, you might have thought I was advocating running away to join the circus, the outcry was so loud. "Somewhere along the line you seem to have forgotten you're a mother," wrote one man. Then came the capper: "It wouldn't surprise me if the next thing I knew, you were answering ads in the personals." Well, yes, as a matter of fact, I was.

**Write On**

I've learned that the man's letter was a not-uncommon expression of horror (substitute shock, derision, disgust, pity) over the notion that a reasonably intelligent, fit and attractive woman and mother of three would be so brazen, desperate, aggressive and "loose" as to write a letter to a total stranger (and maybe even meet him for dinner) on the basis of an ad in the paper. Even well meaning friends frequently expressed surprise when they asked me how I met this person or that one and I answered, "in the personals."

"Gee," one woman volunteered, "I never would have pictured you as the type."

I try to imagine what the type is. But since evidently I am the type, I will simply tell you that I am a 38-year-old woman with a strong sense of responsibility as a parent, an established career, a home of her own, friends, interests and no shortage of things to do or people to do them with, who nevertheless found herself wishing for a romance.

At first the ads to me were only partly about finding a man I might love who might love me back. In the throes of divorce, I recognized that it wouldn't be such a hot idea to plunge directly into a serious relationship. But because I also knew (at some level, anyway) that the person for me might be one in a million, I figured I'd better get to work eliminating the other 999,999.

I started by answering ads in the local weekly in the medium-size New Hampshire town where I make my home. The first half-dozen men who called me heard my life story, including too much about my marriage. After a few such conversations you learn to peel back the layers like those of an onion, one at a time. (With one's life story or one's onion, there's less crying that way.)

### Talk, Talk, Talk

But even so, those conversations filled a need that wouldn't have been met by any talks I might have had with old friends. The men and I didn't know each other's last name, and in most cases we never would. But as we spun our tales, I began to focus on what I liked and didn't like about a person. I cared less about impressive academic or professional credentials, income and job status, and more about emotional accessibility.

Soon I expanded my horizons to the nearest big city and the new 900-number voice-mail personals.

I ran up a couple of hundred dollars' worth of phone bills just listening to the taped messages of people running the ads. I listened to men talking about themselves, of course. But I also listened to women, and to gay men and gay women. I wanted to know if the kind of love I'd yearned for in my own marriage—unconditional acceptance of another person, without the desire to change him or her—could even exist.

One day an ad caught my eye in the Boston paper. The man said something about not being afraid of smart women—and not much more because he kept the ad under 10 words (which meant that it was free). I dialed the now-familiar 900 number.

The man's voice had a definite Texas/Oklahoma accent, and I liked what little I heard, so I left my number. A day or so later, Bill got in touch. "I just wanted to call because you sounded like a nice woman," he said, "but I'd never get involved with anyone with a New Hampshire area code. I'm a three-hour drive from you. With my luck, we'd fall in love and that would break both our hearts, because I'm never moving and it doesn't sound like you are either." He hadn't even heard about my kids yet.

Bill was already signing off, wishing me luck and a nice life, when I told him he was making a big mistake. "You might find someone to have dinner with a lot closer by," I told him, "but you won't find anyone like me."

Reluctantly he said he'd meet me if I came to Boston. I went. Over dinner he said he'd never get involved with anyone who had children. I said it didn't look as though all his years of going out with childless women had got him far on the relationship front. He said he'd never live someplace where he couldn't get to Fenway Park on public transportation: I said, "All right, I'll drive to your house, then." And for close to a year that's what I did.

I fell in love that year, and more important, maybe, I got back a kind of love I'd never known. But Bill wanted no part of my family life. And one thing I'd learned from my marriage was the futility of trying to change a person to sustain the love between the two of you.

Even though my relationship with Bill was doomed to end, and it nearly broke my heart when it did, it also gave me something I can never lose. That year taught me that unconditional love is not too much to ask for—that a person deserves no less, and that holding out for it isn't selfish or crazy. It's a sign of self-esteem, wisdom and strength.

After Bill and I parted, the prospect of starting all over again telling my story to total strangers seemed exhausting. "It's like going back out on the road," said Bill, who had spent years in a band. Like him, I was weary of the highway. I wanted to go home.

When I began answering the ads again, I found myself comparing every stranger with the man I'd loved. I would hear a person on the other end of the line, and if he didn't have an Oklahoma accent, I barely listened.

### Matchmaker, Matchmaker

In among the personals in a magazine, I read an article about a matchmaking service in Boston. I called Zelda, the proprietor.

In her elegant high-rise apartment, Zelda poured me a cup of tea, sat me down on her couch and asked me to tell my story. She took a few notes as I talked. When I finished she looked at me soberly and said she didn't know for sure if she could help me find what I was looking for, but she would be pleased to try.

Zelda and her assistant, Annette, wrote an ad for me. The ad didn't mention my children, or that I lived a two hours' drive from Boston. It called me "gorgeous"—a word I'd never use to describe myself. "Men pursue me eagerly," it said. "But I await my romantic ideal."

### Past and Present

A month or two later the ad appeared, and Annette told me it elicited a big response from all sorts of eligible-seeming bachelors. I read their letters. Annette and Zelda called in the most promising people to screen them for me.

The man who finally passed Zelda's test was a 38-year-old Boston lawyer who'd answered my ad, he told her, at least partly because it mentioned I was a writer and that was what he'd always wanted to be himself. He wrote that he was quiet and a little shy: "I seldom speak, let alone kiss, on the first date."

His letter carried no airy bravado. Nor did he present a dazzling list of achievements, although from what Annette and Zelda learned in their interviews with him, he had accomplished plenty. Only after he'd passed another round of interviews and Annette had consulted me did she provide him with my name and number.

I wish I could have been there in the room to see Ron's face the day he came back from lunch to find the message from Annette instructing him to call me. Because when he read the name on his message pad, it was more than dimly familiar to him. Nearly 20 years before, when he and I were just 19, he'd read my first book and, smitten with my photograph on its cover, sent a letter to me at the college where I had briefly been enrolled as a student. The letter came back to him with the news that I had since withdrawn from school.

Not surprisingly, Ron had met and been involved with numbers of other women in the two decades since writing that letter. But he had never married, and he wasn't sure he'd ever been truly in love.

One night last October he drove the two hours from Boston to my door. Since then I have stopped looking at the personals. I call this a committed relationship, which to me means not that it's without difficulties, but that we have sufficient stake in what we have that we're willing to work very hard at untangling problems when they arise.

### Personals Best

When my children asked where I met Ron, I told them. (Just as I did with Bill.) I'm encouraged to speak openly about the personals just because some people are apparently shocked by the concept. What does it say about our society that so many of us feel reluctant to admit we want love?

Answering the personals is nothing to be ashamed of. All of us possess the ability (but not all of us make use of it) to shape our destiny rather than passively let life have its way with us. I want my children to grow up knowing that if you aren't satisfied with the way things are, you have the power to change your life. You need to figure out what you're looking for, to begin with. Then you have to articulate it. If you're looking for a used car or an apartment, it makes sense to read the ads, or run one. No reason I know why the same rules shouldn't apply to love.

## REFLECTING ON THE READING

Pair up with a classmate of the opposite sex. Interview one another about what you seek in a relationship and then write a personals ad of no more than 50 words on behalf of your classmate. If your instructor and classmates agree, you could publish the ads in your class and try to guess the author of each.

◆

---

# THE MYTHS OF FEMALE WEAKNESS

CARYL RIVERS*

---

◆

*Rivers develops her argument by accumulating one example after another. Is she successful in disproving the myths of female weakness?*

The images from the sands of Saudi Arabia offer a stark contrast: American servicewomen work in fatigues, while Saudi women are glimpsed briefly, shrouded head to toe in the veil. While the Americans were driving heavy equipment, a group of some 40 Saudi women staged a protest—dismissing their drivers and piloting their luxury cars through the streets of downtown Riyadh. Their demand? The right to drive, forbidden to women in their country. From all appearances, it's the modern, liberated society vs. the Middle Ages, as far as women are concerned.

But before we Americans start congratulating ourselves on how liberated we are, we might check recent headlines. Nobody's asking American women to dress from head to toe in black, but the mythology about women as "the other," in her strange and wondrous forms, has hardly vanished from the landscape. Peculiar notions about women—as flawed, weakling, sexual predator, neglectful mommy or breed mare—float about like toxic smoke as the subtext of recent controversies.

First, there was the incident in which a female sportswriter was surrounded in the locker room of the New England Patriots by naked players, who made obscene comments and suggestions.

Many of the cries of outrage were directed at the victim. Patriots' fans screamed obscenities at sportswriter Lisa Olson as she walked into the stadium. A Cincinnati coach declared people were tired of bitches; some players said their wives didn't like the idea of women in the locker rooms.

The implication of sexual threat—or misbehavior—by women lurked behind all of these comments. Does a woman "ask for it" if she goes about her job wearing something less body-obscuring than the veil? The notion that any woman who strays from proper female territory into male turf is a

---

*Caryl Rivers, a professor of journalism at Boston University, is the author of "Indecent Behavior" (Dutton/NAL). She wrote this article for the *Los Angeles Times*.

sexual aggressor and deserves any punishment she might encounter may be ancient history—but it's not as dead as we thought.

Involving other women to validate the alleged threat should also be ancient history. Do players' wives really worry about sportswriters—when motel lobbies are filled with nubile groupies whose self-esteem is so low that they need to prove they are somebody by sleeping with celebrities? Do wives really believe that a sportswriter is rushing into the locker room each night worried not about a good quote to lead the next day's story, but breathless for a peek at sweaty, half-naked men—of which she has doubtless seen more than enough already?

Not many women get jobs as sportswriters, so another story—also about doors that could be closing to working women—is more ominous. Johnson Controls, one of the nation's largest car-battery manufacturers, barred all women employees of child-bearing age—not just those who were pregnant—from jobs that would expose them to high levels of lead potentially damaging to a fetus. This is the Woman-as-Vessel theory. Women have no value, no lives, no purpose, except as breed mares. So, they should be barred from any activity with even a remote chance of impairing this.

More than half the jobs in the company were suddenly off-limits to women employees. Eight women sued, and the U.S. Supreme Court recently heard arguments. If the court backs the company, about 20 million American jobs—most of them well-paid—could be off limits to women. Other companies that use toxic substances in manufacture have already put "fetal protection" policies into effect.

If women can be barred from working with any toxic substance, can they also be kept away from jobs in scientific research? Could they be prohibited from newspaper copy desks because rays from word processors might affect fertility? Construction workers handle solvents and chemicals. Should women be banned from that field? Women will be protected out of well-paying jobs—but no one is going to "protect" women from low-paying jobs slinging hash, scrubbing toilets or emptying bedpans.

The genes in male sperm can be damaged by toxins. But no one ever talks about taking jobs away from men, even though what's toxic for the goose may also be toxic for the gander.

In the 19th century, it was accepted medical belief that women should not be educated because the brain could not develop at the same time as the ovaries. Today, women are still suspect because they don't have the right "math genes" or think with the wrong side of the brain or will turn into premenstrual-syndrome-crazed witches once a month.

Women in politics are especially up against this myth of female weakness. A woman has to prove she is competent to win; a man often has to prove he is spectacularly incompetent to lose. Dianne Feinstein added a pro-death penalty stance to her liberal persona to prove she was tough, and many of her ads showed her on the job, busily managing. See, a woman can run things. But she still lost.

In Texas, sexism wasn't subtle at all. Republican gubernatorial nominee Clayton Williams suggested that rape was something women ought to enjoy, and there was talk of "honey hunts" on his ranch during which cowboys chased prostitutes. He treated Democrat Ann Richards as if she were a helpless twit, wondering aloud when she was going to start drinking again. Only after his behavior showed him to be a colossal fool did he begin to slip in the polls. A woman who displayed such behavior would have been laughed out of the race early on.

In Massachusetts, Democrat John Silber created a stir when he suggested that the "overweening materialism" of some working mothers could lead to child abuse and neglect. It cost him votes among younger women, but many other voters privately agreed. Despite years of research consistently showing that children of working mothers do not lag behind children of at-home mothers in any area of child development, the "neglectful working mom" image is still readily accepted.

For 50 years, researchers have been trying to find the horrible effects of maternal employment that have never emerged. And the baby-boomers—reared almost exclusively by at-home mothers—have more divorces, drug problems and unstable career patterns than other generations. But mom at (gasp!) work still pushes all the buttons.

Why? Before the industrial revolution, everybody was at home—and everybody worked. It was only after industrialization that the grim reality of factory life created the notion of home as a respite from work's cruelties and women as the ministering angels of the hearth. Motherhood was turned from a natural human function into some strange variety of sainthood. Saints aren't supposed to park their halos and go to work.

For women, the message is clear. Just because you can wear green-and-beige desert camouflage instead of chador black, it doesn't mean things on the home front are just fine. In the parlance of the locker room, never drop your left; you could get sucker-punched. Where sex discrimination is concerned, there is no such thing as yesterday's news. It keeps turning up in tomorrow's headlines.

## REFLECTING ON THE READING

Think of your own example about women in the workplace that either supports or counters Rivers' opinion and develop it in a short paragraph. Now read Warren Farrell's "Myth of Male Power" in Chapter 10. Show how he agrees or disagrees with your opinion by writing another short paragraph.

◆

---

# BROTHERS, PLEASE, STOP, JUST STOP

DONNA BRITT

---

◆

*The first two articles in this chapter make their points
by using humor. Donna Britt, a Washington Post
columnist, uses a different kind of appeal. How would
you describe her attitude in this article?*

I like men, period. But brothers? Oh, man.

The slide-y walk, the mighty talk. The power and glory, their survival
story. I'm so far gone that I love the smell of a brother, even after he's spent
hours taking it to the hoop—or the tennis court or the jogging track. Or the
library, if attacking a book gets him in the flow.

I love each and every one of you so much that I'm going to do what
everybody who has ever utterly loved someone has had to do:

I'm saying "No."

*No.* Stop. This second. Cease and ~~desist~~ from:

Being so angry—righteously or otherwise—all of the time.

Hitting, dissing, lying to, seducing and abandoning your sisters.

Killing each other.

My reasons for saying this are purely selfish.

I need you. Not just the black men who, by birth or fate, belong to me. I
mean all of you. I don't want to lose another one of you.

Not to drugs. Not to the police. Not to immobilization or despair, to the
courts or to blind fury or certainly, for God's sake, to another bullet.

I'm asking a lot. But if you weren't bigger and stronger and more marvelous
than any man has a right to be, you'd never have survived. But here you are.

Let's say right off that most brothers are not hitters, thieves, abusers or
shooters. Anyone who doesn't know that, who doesn't realize that most
want, very much, to Do The Right Thing, is a fool.

So you millions of African-American men who are none of those things:
I applaud and congratulate and offer you my deepest, amazed gratitude. For
you are miraculous.

The rest of you: Just stop.

I am not letting white men off the hook. They are just as liable to hurt
women, white and black. To knowingly and unknowingly stick it to brothers on jobs, in courtrooms, on the streets of every city in this nation. The
reasons are historic, ongoing and must be confronted.

But right now, white men are not my concern.

They aren't dying like you. They haven't learned to hate themselves enough to devalue everyone who looks like them. It's you that I want around tomorrow. And next year.

It's hard, being a black man in America. It's tough, too, being a black woman. Dealing with so much toughness makes us hard. But it is only by uncovering our softness, our love, that we will survive.

So stop it. Despite all you don't have, you still have the keys to the kingdom. Use them to save us all.

Show me your genius. If you're smart enough to run a drug operation, you can run a corporation—and employ your people without killing them. If your anger can terrify a nation, your love can turn the world around.

You've made it this far for a reason. What if it's to create a new blueprint for black maleness? To disarm racism? To learn to love, really love, your sweet black self?

Maybe it's to raise each baby you make, beautifully. To make me, your lady, your mama, your great-granddaddy proud.

Whatever it is, start today. Please, baby, please, please, please, baby, please. I ain't too proud to beg.

You're worth it.

## REFLECTING ON THE READING

Britt's language is very emotional, intended to arouse feelings in her readers. In two or three sentences, explain Britt's meaning in non-emotional language. Discuss with two classmates the different effects of the two ways of expressing a point.

◆

---

# WHY WOMEN REQUIRE SPECIAL TREATMENT

EDWARD ENFIELD

---

◆

*Enfield expresses the bewildered feelings of many older men about the changes in gender relations in this article for the London Observer. See if you feel sympathy for him.*

By profession, until I retired, I used to be a Gray Suit, as my father was before me. We are that sort of family.

In the house where my father was raised, the prevailing attitude to women meant he did not taste chicken breast until he went to Oxford. This was because he was the younger of two sons in a family of five children and, therefore, came last for everything, including chicken.

At dinner time, it was his duty to open the dining room door and stand while the rest of the family filed past. Occasionally, my father would shove his elder brother aside and leave him to shut the door, but he never questioned his sisters having precedence over them both.

My early years were a modernized version of my father's upbringing.

As soon as I could stand, I had to give up my seat in tube trains and buses to any woman of any age. As soon as I could walk, I learned to walk on the outside of any woman I was with so that I and not she should be splashed by passing carriages, although there were none.

At the age of 4, I toddled off down the lane to play with some village children and learned enough foul language to last the rest of my life. On returning I used what is now called the "f-word" to my mother in all innocence and was at once banished to bed. I worked out from this that there is one way to behave when women are present and another when they are not.

Some slight modification of my views took place as a result of a conversation with Douglas, the legendary porter of University College, Oxford. One day, I had arranged to take a young lady to dinner, and she was to call for me at college at 7 p.m. At 6:55, I was waiting on the steps, but by 7:30 she had not arrived.

Douglas came out of the lodge and took up the at-ease position beside me. He gazed morosely at the traffic, then said: "No woman is worth it, sir."

For any male suffering on account of a member of the opposite sex, that slogan can be of inestimable value. All the same, I continued, and still continue, to regard women as superior beings, although my efforts to express this do not always turn out well.

I once wrote an article in which I tried to say that the danger of the feminist movement was that while women were naturally much nicer than men, in striving to be equal they might become equally nasty. In the next issue there was a letter I did not understand, so I asked my wife what she thought the writer meant.

"It is perfectly clear," she said. "She thinks you're a pig."

In spite of such occasional rebuffs, I persist in showing respect in such ways as standing up when women come into the room, or walking all the way around the car to open the passenger door. I never use bad language in front of women and cannot abide to hear it from them.

None of my peculiarities was noticeable in local government, which is a conservative undertaking, but when I retired I became, of all things, first a columnist and then an author, and was plunged into the world of publishing. This I was pleased to find almost entirely in the hands of delightful young women.

My son has a theory that the advantage of being a man is that you can go on flirting longer than if you are a woman. It seemed worth trying, as the young women all treated me as if I were as youthful as themselves, all called me Edward even if we had never met and sometimes sent me official letters with kisses at the bottom.

I cannot claim any success.

They wonder what I am up to when I dodge round behind them to get to the outside of the pavement if we cross the road. They see some sinister motive in my walking round the car to open the passenger door. They cannot understand my pained expression if unladylike words fall from their lips.

In the end, I think they conclude I am just an ambulatory anachronism or walking fossil, although they are too polite to say so.

## REFLECTING ON THE READING

List the ways in which Enfield behaves to show respect for women. Now make a parallel list of the ways you think women behave to show respect for men. Share your lists with a group of classmates, trying to identify areas of agreement or disagreement about how respect is shown.

◆

# HOMOSEXUALITY: HETEROSEXUAL MALES' BOGYMAN

JAMES RICCI

◆

*Not very long ago, the subject of homosexuality was taboo and would not be discussed publicly. Ricci describes how his views of gay men have changed since he was 15. Look for his explanation of what caused the change.*

It was after one in the morning, and I was hitchhiking home from my girlfriend's house when the Volkswagen with Pennsylvania plates stopped for me.

The driver was a small, thin man with a pocked face and a quiet voice. He looked to be in his late 20s.

I was 15 and did a lot of hitchhiking around my hometown. I was accustomed to riding with strangers, making small talk, learning about their lives. This driver, however, made me uneasy from the instant I got into the car.

He seemed very tense. He gripped the steering wheel so tightly his knuckles gleamed in the headlights of oncoming cars. Several times he tried to initiate conversation but stammered to a stop.

After we'd driven about a mile, he put his hand on my thigh.

For an instant, I froze, my head filling with a silent shriek of panic. I shoved his hand away and demanded to be let out. He apologized profusely. With a strange politeness, he insisted on driving me to my destination.

I pressed against the passenger's door to be as far from him as possible. Time would not budge.

When we finally got to my stop, I sprang from the car. The man sat looking straight ahead, his profile rigid. "No hard feelings," he said.

I walked down the long hill to my home, heart pounding, keeping an eye on every set of headlights that appeared in the distance (he might be circling back for me).

I couldn't sleep that night. It was several days before I could bring myself to tell my parents.

This was probably not all that uncommon an experience for an adolescent boy of that time. As sexual accostings go, it was a minor thing. For a long time, however, it confirmed me in an attitude of fear and hatred toward homosexuals.

I thought of this recently when I read of two cases of heterosexual violence against homosexuals.

In one, a Wayne County, Mich., prosecutor indicated his intention to show that robbery victim Roosevelt (Coop) Williams was murdered and mutilated by his assailants because he was known to be gay. In the other, two men sitting together on a park bench in New York City were savagely beaten by a group of youths yelling anti-homosexual slurs.

Homosexuals are probably the single hardest minority for heterosexual males to tolerate. Because their difference lies at the very core of what most men instinctively regard as the definition of gender, they are easier than any race or creed to think of as not exactly human.

The most astonishing proclamations of bigotry I have ever heard from educated men have been voiced in regard to gays.

I think I've come a long way in understanding since that night when I was 15. Professional and social contact with gay men has helped me know they are no more likely than heterosexual men to attempt to force themselves on others. I have come to see that whom a man is capable of sexually loving ought to neither limit his right to live free from harm nor define his worth.

In short, I don't think I have feelings of hatred anymore.

But the Volkswagen with Pennsylvania plates still motors along the back roads of memory's landscape.

I wonder what became of the forlorn little man behind the wheel. I wonder if he found someone to love and made his peace. Or if one dark night he stopped for the wrong hitchhiker and found violent fate instead.

## REFLECTING ON THE READING

Ricci mentions two of the most controversial issues in American society today: uninvited sexual advances from a person of the same sex and gay-bashing, attacks on men who are presumed to be homosexual. In a short paragraph, explain which issue you believe is the greater problem. Be sure to state the reasons for your opinion.

◆

---

# WRITE LIKE A MAN

## MERRILL MARKOE

---

◆

*Markoe uses satire to make her point about certain pop-
ular male images. Look for language that indicates she
is being satiric.*

One thing I have plenty of is crackpot theories about the differences between men and women. (In fact, I was one of the first to point out that
our sexual organs are almost *nothing* alike.) And I stumbled onto another
one this week when I bought a couple of trashy celebrity autobiographies at
my supermarket checkout counter.

The two I picked—*The Boz: Confessions of a Modern Anti Hero,* by
Brian Bosworth with Rick Reilly, and *McMAHON!: The Bare Truth About
Chicago's Brashest Bear,* by Jim McMahon with Bob Verdi—belong to the
cute-guys-in-sunglasses genre. For readers who know even less about the
world of sports than I do (and I doubt that's possible), I will say that both
these people are good-looking white male football players in their twenties.
Both have cool-guy haircuts and very hip-looking matching shades. And on
that particular day in the supermarket, the depth of my uninterest in the
game of football, multiplied by the height of my enthusiasm for cute guys in
sunglasses, gave me the impetus to shell out the necessary dollars to make
these purchases. Which is how it came to pass that I actually sat down and
*read* the books and then came up with my new theory.

### My New Theory

The parading of infantile character flaws as though they were badges of
honor and distinction is a male trait.

Consider the following examples: In a chapter of *The Boz* entitled
"The World According to Me," we are introduced to "two people—Brian
and the Boz." One of those two tells us that "to people under thirty, or people who still had an open mind, the Boz became a symbol of a new kind of
hero: somebody who wasn't afraid to give the finger to The Way Things
Are Supposed to Be and, at the same time, could still accomplish great
things." Presumably it is the Boz who made the decision to begin his autobiography with the following passage: "Miami. The Orange Bowl. New
Year's Night, 1986. And I'm standing on the field between plays, peeling a

huge chunk of skin out of my hand and grinning. I'm not talking about a little skin. I'm talking about *layers* of skin, a big gouge of skin the size of a
big broken rubber band. And it feels good.. . . In fact, it feels great.. . . The
more skin the better. Pain and blood let you know you're playing serious
football."

A short while later, someone—I guess it is Brian—laments, "Somewhere
people got this barbarian image of me.. . . I've learned not to let it bother
me, but it used to." But as we read on, we come to realize that both Brian
and the Boz have a lot more on their collective mind than football. "To me,
girls are just a pain in the ass," says I'm-not-sure-which-one. "They call at all
hours of the night.. . . They leave notes with dirty messages on them." He
goes on to describe a very overt pass made by a female fan one night in a
bar. "It made me sick," perhaps-it-is-Brian bemoans, "partly because she was
ugly. No, she wasn't even ugly. She was past ugly onto *ooooogley*." A little
later in the paragraph he treats us to a sort of Joycean stream of consciousness on various women. "Kathleen Turner is a fox," he tells us. "Cybill Shepherd is not beautiful.. . . Madonna I like because she does her own thing.
She's nice looking and she's got a hard body.. . . But she's probably got the
intellect of a coffee table." And it's clear by now that we should take him at
his word, since he may be one of the few writers today who has had sufficient one-on-one conversations with coffee tables to make this comparison
accurately.

Moving on to *McMAHON!* we immediately hear a similar tone of voice.
"I do carry myself like a bit of a hot dog sometimes," Jim says. "I'm not afraid
of giving lip to some guy twice my size.. . . I was born to be a hellion." He
then launches into reminiscences of his golden childhood. "I particularly enjoyed throwing things at moving objects, especially if these objects were the
heads of classmates I didn't care for.. . . I was also very hyperactive . . .
bored.. . . That still holds today. In kindergarten I'd take tacks and stick them
in the fat rear end of this Hawaiian kid, who never did make it through the
Pledge of Allegiance without screaming.. . . Then, they'd call my mom and
she'd come in. Then they'd call the Hawaiian kid's fat Hawaiian mother and
they'd all ask for an apology.. . . I still haven't said I'm sorry.. . . That kind of
thing helped me get through the day."

The Boz also recalls the days of his adolescence fondly. For instance,
"that summer I worked at this fast-food hamburger place—you'd know the
name. And I used to do some horrendous things to people's hamburgers,
just to break up the boredom. If I didn't like the person much, I'd rub his
hamburger patty along the floor with my shoe before I'd cook it.. . . I'm not
sure what makes me love pissing people off so much but I always have."

I believe that this kind of swaggering talk could only be published under
the names of attractive successful white men. The combination of arrogance
without shame and insensitivity without humility or hindsight is the sole do-
main of attractive successful white men. To test my thesis, I went searching
for an example of a woman who was analogous in any way. I bought and read

the autobiographies of the most willfully self-promoting and egomaniacal female media figures. And, after working my way through the writings of Joan Collins, Suzanne Somers, Shelley Winters, Tina Turner and Pamela des Barres, I couldn't help noticing that most of them were confessions about failed romances, family tragedies or personal foibles. Most were written in a sort of self-mocking tone. Pamela des Barres was even loving in her descriptions of crude sexual liaisons with narcissistic drug addicts. Not one of these women seemed to revel in their inadequacies the way the cute guys in sunglasses do.

So, kicking off what could be a trend for the Nineties, I would like to inaugurate the era of swaggering female autobiographies with chapter 1 of my brand-new work in progress.

### The Merr:

*Confessions of a Great Big Loudmouthed Rude Girl,*
*as Told to Helen Rogan*

"December 20, 1979. 8:00 P.M. I am at the bar in a hip Los Angeles eatery, dressed in one of my smart little sport coat and slacks ensembles. I have just agreed to join a very attractive young television producer at his table for a drink, and as I head across the room carrying a brandy Alexander I feel the soles of my shoes hit a wet spot on the floor and then I feel my feet fly out from underneath me as I go into a seamless skid that sends me sailing like a cartoon animal clear across the room in one long, smooth movement that ends when I land underneath the table of my date. I peer out from beneath the tablecloth at a room full of horrified people, and then I rise to my feet, claiming to have engineered the whole thing. Maybe they bought it. Maybe they didn't. I just don't care. Because I know that the more hideously inappropriate my behavior, the more personal embarrassment I cause myself, the better. That's when I know I am playing serious comedy.

"Perhaps it all goes back to that day in the sixth grade when I was experimenting with a tube of cream depilatory and accidentally removed most of my right eyebrow. As a result, I was forced to retreat behind a Band-Aid accompanied by a lie that had to do with somehow being attacked by a bird. Maybe, that's when THE MERR was born—and since that time I make no excuses. If people don't like how I do things I might yell sarcastic remarks at them and then lock myself in my room and pout for hours. Because I'm THE MERR and I guess I'm just the sort of a free spirit who does what she wants when she wants.

"And if that means living with a constant barrage of people coming up to me and saying, 'Did you cut your hair yourself?' or, 'Do you know there's a price tag hanging from your collar?' well, so be it! I do things my own way.

"Sometimes I'll just walk into a restaurant and sit down at a table and when they bring me my food, if it isn't *just the way I like it,* I'll probably eat it anyway and not say a word because I figure it's still a lot better than anything I would have cooked for myself. And at times like these I might toss back my wild mane of raven hair and break into a gale of gleeful laughter. And in so doing maybe get a great big marinara stain all over an item of clothing that I paid a lot of money for. And in most cases it will turn out to be the kind of stain that can never be removed. But I might go on trying to wear the item of clothing anyway—hoping to hide the stain behind a pin or a scarf. Why? Because I'm THE MERR and that's the way I do things. And if you have a problem with that, well—that's your problem. Don't eat with me.

"I have no use for the old buzzards who try to tie me down with their rules and regulations. When I hear the call of the open road, sometimes I'll just get into my car, the radio blasting, the empty cans rattling around on the floor—my dog sitting beside me getting his light brown hair all over every single item of clothing I'm wearing—and I'll just barrel right on through a yellow light even though I know it's actually borderline legal. And I'll drive on into the sunset, hoping that this won't be one of the days when my dog will suddenly have to throw up. After all, he only does it about half of the time—not a high enough percentage for me to stop inviting him to come along altogether. Because I'm THE MERR. And these are the kinds of risks I am willing to take. It's just part of the way I live life on my own terms.

"Like the way I'll sometimes stay up until three or four in the morning, just worrying and fretting about bad scary things over which I have absolutely no control. And then when I do finally fall asleep it will be about five minutes before I have to get up so I'll be a wreck the rest of the day. Because I'm THE MERR. And that's just the way I do things."

Somehow it doesn't sound the same coming from a girl.

Afterword: How was I to know the impact my theory would have on the world at large? Just months after I wrote this piece, Madonna went on to break the sexist stereotype by being the first public woman to be as proud of her adolescent behavior as any football player, striking another important blow for parity of the sexes.

## REFLECTING ON THE READING

Write a paragraph about yourself in which you "write like a man." That is, write about yourself in the way that Markoe calls "swaggering talk."

◆

---

# THE EDUCATION OF INGRID CANRIGHT

INGRID CANRIGHT

---

◆

*It's been over ten years since Canright published her
views of American youth, especially the reluctance of
young men and women to make commitments in personal relationships. Has this situation changed? If so, in
what way?*

> "Love is an exploding cigar that you willingly smoke."
> —Lynda Barry, cartoonist

Of late the noncommittal self-interest of American youth has captured
the nation's attention. Analysts are examining, deploring, and, in come
cases, celebrating the emotional and political detachment of people under
twenty-five. Why—and whence—this generation of self-absorbed and
largely cynical young people?

In the wake of the recent elections, it is hardly necessary to describe the
political viewpoint of American youth—if indeed such a thing can truly be
said to exist. The Republicans were delighted with the youth vote's support
of the self-interest campaign. The political conservatism of young people has
long ceased to surprise anyone. My generation is apathetic. I include myself
despite the advice of an older friend who told me not to worry—"they're
not your generation." My loyalties are divided: I understand the hidden frustration of modern, trodden youth.

But my interest here is the emotional selves of my peers. Our political apathy is only one expression of a fundamental disengagement from reality. Young
people today, particularly the most detached, describe themselves as "realists,"
ostensibly justifying the intensely self-motivated quality of their every move.
But such self-absorption demands that one's attention be constantly directed
inward, while "realism" implies that one is an observer of reality.

Needless to say, these qualities have profound effects upon personal relationships, particularly romantic ones. It is impossible to fall in love while
maintaining perfect emotional detachment. Young Americans struggle with
the dilemma of their emotional needs versus their precious disengagement.
Getting involved is intrinsically threatening to us. That's the qualitative difference between young politics and young relationships: we can vote for
the self-interest candidate and if he loses, well, we shrug and keep looking

out for number one. There was never any emotional commitment. No risk. No pain. Democrats cry when their candidate loses; Republicans strategize.

The eschewing of emotional attachment is taken to lengths that range from the ridiculous to the pathetic; and nowhere are the young more militantly aloof than on college campuses. American undergraduates are the purest expression of youthful detachment—and the trend is as visible on ostensibly "liberal" campuses as on the most conservative ones. The forming of any meaningful romantic attachments is regarded as inherently dangerous, misguided. Why? One reason, as Christopher Lasch points out, is that sexual freedom (the term "free love" brings a smirk to youthful lips) has released sex from the conventional structures of love, marriage, and children; sexual relationships have become easier to get but also infinitely easier to lose. Sexual or emotional involvement no longer comes with any illusion of permanence, and herein lies the danger. Infidelity is taken for granted, jealousy forbidden, monogamy something to be considered a decade hence—if then. Falling in love is to be avoided at all costs; those whose control slips are the objects of ridicule. Mobility is the modern, mature approach to "cool sex," the typical pattern a series of detached, if "caring," relationships in which there are few, if any, expectations.

If the ways of the world haven't taught us effectively enough, it is now possible to take courses in detachment. "We are afraid to become involved in relationships that don't appear to show any promise of lasting a long time," reads a university evening extension course listing for a class called "Brief Encounters." "Yet the reality for most of us is that fewer of our relationships are lasting for a long time. We are a mobile population changing jobs, locations, ideas, lovers, and spouses. The purpose of this course is to come to terms with change, make the most of relationships that may not last forever or even for a very long time, and develop a different goal for relationships." What's love got to do with it, indeed.

It is not surprising that the separation of sex from attachment doesn't always work. Those who do not succeed, as I have said, are subject to ridicule by youth society and usually to rejection by the object of their attachment ("You're pressuring me"). Possessiveness is a dirty word. "It doesn't take much to be in love; it takes guts to admit it," moans new wavers' "Pop Art." Modern music is in fact fraught with expressions of emotional isolation, both contented and petulant—and of antagonism toward the opposite sex. "Love is a battlefield" in youth culture, nothing sweet or welcome about it— an emotion seen rather as a response to be suppressed or denied as long as one can hold out.

It is perhaps ironic that promiscuity has resulted, finally, in increased distance between lovers, in an almost warlike separation of the sexes into male and female camps. The women's movement has also contributed to sexual divisions, through no fault of its own: according to Lasch, men are still threatened by the idea of feminine equality and women's increasing independence. Men's attempts to dominate, now totally robbed of the veil of patriarchal gentility, have had to become more overt and are apparent in the resurgence of male sexism everywhere. Though infinitely less ready to admit it, young men probably feel as embattled as women do. I have heard college men critiquing shared sexual partners with camaraderie and bravado—flaunting their sexism; this mirrors the attitudes of the increasingly militant female cliques, with which I am more familiar, where "men" are discussed with equal disdain and hostility. In the women's camp, as feminist Linda Singer points out, heterosexuality is viewed by liberated women (not lesbians) with "ambivalence and a recognition of contradiction . . . there is no way for a woman, at this stage in history, to love a man but fully separate herself from his oppressive power." Singer made this comment in late 1984, not 1965. The sexual power struggle exacerbates the antagonistic nature of male-female relations, reinforcing the conviction, on both sides, that to remain aloof is a matter of psychic survival.

The phobia against attachment is essentially a condition of the educated young, largely because of their greater exposure to the conflicts that have resulted from the women's movement and greater awareness of global crises. The decline of political consciousness in the young and their increasingly narrow, self-oriented view are responses to a world seen as out of control: a world of emotional stress, increasing professional competition, and bizarre political events. We are too aware of this world, and as the next generation, about to "inherit" it, are withdrawing. We'd like to pass—but, that denied us we'll pull in the drawbridge and post every guard. And yes, when absolutely required, we'll lob policy statements, disclaimers, and ballots over the wall, rather like missiles.

Less "educated" young people, those less aware of specific conflicts but undoubtedly affected by the modern mood, hurriedly succumb to media trances and beatific manipulators like Reagan and Falwell. This part of my generation is predisposed to traditional romantic patterns: marry early in response to some hormonal primal scream; repent, perhaps, at leisure. But sociologists tell us that despite the strict male-female roles of this group, its members express much less sexual friction than do those of us who think of ourselves as liberated.

I am not saying that such a lifestyle will solve my generation's emotional problems—rather, I'm pointing out that the detachment is most pronounced in those who have tried the hardest to face reality. It's too much for us.

Why is it too much? The world's been in bad shape before. Americans born since 1955 have had it easy, on the whole. People my age are this century's first American generation not to have experienced a war. Older generations complain that today's youth haven't paid their dues, have laid down the banner and picked up the bong. It's true. We have.

I think we're shell-shocked. We grew up watching from the sidelines as the young adults of the sixties gave their lives to changing this country. It really looked like they made a difference—but something happened. About the time of Watergate, resistance grew quiet. Politically, the country drifted back toward conservatism. It's been drifting for over a decade now, and it's gotten pretty dark out there. We wonder if the sixties made a difference at all, except to women. And we face a world in which a threat greater than any war hangs over us every day, a threat so terrifying that it inspires political positions as irrational as they are divergent. We are not united on the nuclear issue. Worse, most of us are paralyzed by it.

You can look at nuclear war as one hell of a reason to become politically active, or you can look at it as one hell of an excuse for apathy, or for electing a trigger-happy old man to the most crucial office on earth: there's a certain security in knowing the whole world handles him with kid gloves. We, American youth, look at it all three ways—when we can bear to look. Excuse us for our squeamishness.

But what's nuclear war got to do with romance? This essay is about disengagement, one of the more striking qualities of my generation. We don't like to admit we're attached to anything (a person, an idea, life on earth) because choices we have made and choices made for us have rendered the objects of our cathexis impermanent, tenuous. We scream "Sour grapes!" even before the fruit is snatched away.

What happens next? We are left with very little to invest in except ourselves, the one object that is truly ours. Self-preoccupation in modern youth arises not so much from complacency as from desperation: it has become the faith of those without a faith. We turn ever inward.

And relationships? Narcissists lack the capacity for empathy. They respond in completely inappropriate ways to others—even those they are "close" to. On campus, a friend laments, "The first time I said I loved him, his response was to ask if I wanted a drink of water."

"I was going through a rough period and told her I needed to talk," fumes another. "She didn't contact me for five days." The fear of attachment confounds communication and leads to despair and anger: "He/she really doesn't care!" Our self-defeating solution is to renounce all romantic notions. Slam goes the drawbridge; we are peacefully, if desolately, alone again.

That's the wrong solution. It amounts to isolation that defends against isolation, and it parallels our political apathy in response to a politically untenable situation. What is required of us is courage.

M. Scott Peck says that the price of emotional attachment is pain; he will get no quarrel with that from my generation. The only real security in life, he goes on, lies in relishing life's insecurity. Here American youth will throw up their hands in disgust and abandon Peck as an imbecile. (Slam goes the drawbridge.) But what he says is true. Love, like other commitments, takes a great deal of courage, work, and acceptance of a certain amount of risk. The premise is that it's worth it. I hope ultimately we decide it is.

We're lazy, too. Maybe we don't think the activism of the sixties did any lasting good and couldn't possibly do any good now. Much as that conclusion may appear to have some basis in fact, it's a cop-out. Activism, a dedication to some cause outside of ourselves, would be excellent generational therapy—and we need it.

I will be accused of blithely bidding my besieged peers to buck up and get to work on saving the world. Please, accuse me of anything but the bootstraps philosophy. I know that overcoming our fear of commitment means changing our entire emotional frame of reference. I'm scared too.

Political and social occurrences have given my generation a well-founded fear of any commitment, an almost instinctive apathy. Whether or not we can overcome our fear is important not only to us individually, but also to the future of society. Yes, I hear their cynical laughter. But what kind of a nation will we be if we cannot even commit ourselves to other people, much less to a set of abstract values? What kind of families can we have if we no longer tolerate interdependence? What kind of a people will we be if we equate attachment with failure, autonomy—at any price—with strength? What kind of politicians will we elect if self-interest is our highest value, humanity an "inoperative" commodity?

Or have we already answered these questions?

## REFLECTING ON THE READING

Canright claims young Americans suffer from an unwillingness to make commitments and from laziness. Decide which of these issues is the most serious and then give three reasons for agreeing or disagreeing with Canright's opinion.

# PUTTING IT IN WRITING

## RESPONSES

1. Think of a stereotype about members of your own sex and write for five minutes explaining what irritates you about that stereotype. Pair up with a classmate of the opposite sex and share your writings.
2. Make a list of topics you prefer not to talk about with members of the opposite sex. Pick one of those topics and explain your reasons for not wanting to talk about it with the other gender.
3. Find the article in this chapter you most disagree with. Write for five minutes, listing all your points of disagreement with the article.

## READING FOR MEANING

1. Sometimes our own feelings and attitudes affect how we understand what we read. Choose an article from this section that appears to address one sex more than the other. Pretending to be a member of the opposite sex, try rereading the article from the point of view of a man

(if you're a woman) or from the point of view of a woman (if you're a man). When you finish, discuss your experience with a classmate. Tell each other what was hardest about doing this exercise.

2. In Edward Enfield's "Why Women Require Special Treatment," he expresses old-fashioned views. Find words and phrases he uses that create sympathy for his views.

3. Donna Britt uses a number of unusual writing techniques to make her point, including slang, rhyme, sentence fragments, and repetition. Copy out examples of each of those four techniques.

## Organizing Your Ideas

1. Write a nutshell of either Caryl Rivers' "The Myths of Female Weakness" or James Ricci's "Homosexuality: Heterosexual Males' Bogyman." (The process of writing in a nutshell is discussed in Chapter 2.) Then, write a single sentence agreeing or disagreeing with the author's main point.

2. Pick any two articles from the chapter that have conflicting opinions. List the points of conflict between the two authors. Then, for each point of conflict, write a statement that balances the two points of view.

3. Choose an article that uses dialogue and quotation for a major part of support in the article and an article that uses very little dialogue and quotation for support. What effect does the use of dialogue and quotation have on persuading you to the writer's viewpoint? What form of evidence does the other article rely on?

## Writing a Paper

1. Recall the last argument you had with a member of the opposite sex. List all the reasons for your position in the argument. Then, pretend to be the other person and construct the best reasons against your position. Write an essay explaining what you learned from the process of trying to argue against yourself. (Use your work in #1 in "Reading for Meaning" and #2 in "Organizing Your Ideas" to help you develop ideas for this paper.)

2. Using the work you did for #1 in "Organizing Your Ideas," develop a paper that argues for the opinion you stated in reaction to one of the articles.

3. Select two writers from this section and pretend they went out on a dinner date. Write a paper in which you describe what happens on the date, what they talk about during dinner, and show how well they get along.

# CREDITS

Colman Andrews, "Everything on the Table" by Colman Andrews from EATING AMERICA: WHAT IS A TACO ANYWAY? AND FEAR OF FOOD. Copyright © 1992 by Colman Andrews. Reprinted by permission of Bantam Books.

James Baldwin, "A Sentence from Notes of a Native Son" by James Baldwin from NOTES OF A NATIVE SON. Copyright © 1995, renewed 1983 by James Baldwin. Reprinted by permission of Beacon Press.

Dave Barry, "What We Have Here Is a Failure to Communicate" by Dave Barry. *San Jose Mercury News*, June 7, 1992. Copyright © 1992 by Dave Barry. Reprinted by permission.

Lynda Barry, "The Telephone Call" by Lynda Barry. Reprinted by permission of the author.

John Berger, From WAYS OF SEEING by John Berger. Copyright © 1972 by Penguin Books Ltd. Used by permission of Viking Penguin, a division of Penguin Books USA Inc.

James E. Bouman, "Snip, Snip: Trading Haircuts is Cherished Father-Son Tradition" by James E. Bouman. Reprinted by permission of the author.

Donna Britt, "Brothers, Please, Stop, Just Stop" by Donna Britt. *San Jose Mercury News*, June 12, 1994. Copyright © 1992 by Donna Britt. Reprinted by permission.

Gwendolyn Brooks, "Mothers and Daughters" by Gwendolyn Brooks. Reprinted by permission of the author.

Ingrid Canright. "The Education of Ingrid Canright" by Ingrid Canright. Reprinted by permission of the author.

Ami Chen, "Getting at the Heart of What's Wrong with this Country " by Ami Chen. Copyright © 1992 by Ami Chen. Reprinted by permission.

Robert Coles, Excerpt form THE CALL OF STORIES by Robert Coles. Copyright © 1989 by Robert Coles. Reprinted by permission of Houghton Mifflin Company. All rights reserved.

Bernard Cooper, "Picking Plums" by Bernard Cooper. Copyright © 1992 by *Harper's Magazine*. All rights reserved. Reproduced from the August issue by special permission.

Julia Cunningham, From DORP DEAD by Julia Cunningham. Copyright © 1965 and renewed 1993 by Julia Cunningham. Reprinted by permission of Pantheon Books, a division of Random House, Inc.

Peter Davis, "Deliverence from Hometown" by Peter Davis. Copyright © 1982 by Peter Davis. Reprinted by permission of Simon & Schuster, Inc.

Joan Didion, "On the Mall" by Joan Didion from THE WHITE ALBUM. Copyright © 1993 by Joan Didion. Reprinted by permission.

Edward Enfield, "Why Women Require Special Treatment" by Edward Enfield. *San Francisco Examiner*, July 13, 1994. Copyright © 1994 by Edward Enfield. Reprinted by permission.

Warren Farrell, "Men Sell Themselves into Lives of Desperation" by Warren Farrell from THE MYTH OF MALE POWER. Copyright © 1993 by Warren Farrell. Reprinted by permission of Simon and Schuster, Inc.

Jules Feiffer, "Feiffer" cartoon by Jules Feiffer. Reprinted by permission of Universal Press Syndicate. All rights reserved.

M.F.K. Fisher, "Soup and Bread" by M.F.K. Fisher. Copyright © 1991 by M.F.K. Fisher. Reprinted by permission.

Mary Gaddis, "A Pipefitter's Dream" by Mary Gaddis. *San Francisco Examiner*, February 7, 1991. Copyright © 1991 by Mary Gaddis. Reprinted by permission.

Freda Garmaise, "Shoppers of the World Unite!" by Freda Garmaise. Copyright ©1991 by Freda Garmaise. Reprinted by permission of Little Brown & Company.

Todd Gitlin, "Is It Really Television's Job to Fan Flames of Unrest" by Todd Gitlin. Reprinted by permission of the author.

Ellen Goodman, "Are We Losing Our Way In $150 Sneakers?" by Ellen Goodman, *Boston Globe*, November 8, 1991. Copyright © 1991 by *The Boston Globe*. Reprinted by permission of *The Boston Globe*.

Cathy Guisewite, "Cathy" cartoon by Cathy Guisewite. Reprinted by permission of Universal Press Syndicate. All rights reserved.

Alex Haley and Betty Shabazz, From THE AUTOBIOGRAPHY OF MALCOLM X by Malcolm X, with the assistance of Alex Haley. Copyright © 1964 by Alex Haley and Malcolm X. Copyright © 1965 by Alex Haley and Betty Shabazz. Reprinted by permission of Random House, Inc.

Lawrence E. Harrison, "Moving into Middle Class" from WHO PROSPERS? by Lawrence E. Harrison. Copyright © 1992 by Lawrence E. Harrison. Reprinted by permission of BasicBooks, a division of HarperCollins Publishers, Inc.

Froma Harrop, "In a Multi-Coiffeurial Society, This Is an Outrage" by Froma Harrop. *San Jose Mercury News*, May 17, 1993. Copyright © 1993 by Froma Harrop. Reprinted by permission.

Susan Harte, "Tyrannical Bosses Spawn Naturally in Workplace" by Susan Harte. *San Jose Mercury News*, June 28, 1992. Copyright © 1992 by Susan Harte. Reprinted by permission.

James A. Herrick, "Kill Your Television" by James A. Herrick. Copyright © 1994 by James A. Herrick. Reprinted by permission.

Shere Hite, "The Case Against Family Values" by Shere Hite. *The Washington Post*, Sunday, July 10, 1994. Reprinted by permission of *The Washington Post*.

Wendy Ho Iwata, "Boy Crazy" by Wendy Ho Iwata. Copyright © 1990 by Wendy Ho Iwata. Reprinted by permission.

Derrick Z. Jackson, "Ice Cube: Buckwheat with a Gutter Rap" by Derrick Z. Jackson. Reprinted courtesy of *The Boston Globe*.

Matt James, "Blest Be the TVs that Bind" by Matt James. Copyright © 1993 by Matt James. Reprinted by permission.

Evan Jones, "Dr. Kellogg and the US Diet" by Evan Jones from AMERICAN FOOD: THE GASTRONOMIC STORY. Copyright © 1974, 1975, 1981, 1990 by Evan Jones and Judith B. Jones. Published by The Overlook Press, Woodstock, NY 12498.

Janis Joplin, "Mercedes-Benz" by Janis Joplin. Copyright © 1993 by Janis Joplin. Reprinted by permission of Henry Holt & Company.

Barbara Karoff, "Food Owes Him the World" by Barbara Karoff, *San Francisco Examiner*, July 15, 1992. Copyright © 1992 by Barbara Karoff. Reprinted by permission.

Maxine Hong Kingston, From THE WOMAN WARRIOR by Maxine Hong Kingston. Copyright © 1975, 1976 by Maxine Hong Kingston. Reprinted by permission of Alfred A. Knopf, Inc.

Koren, Drawing "We motored over to say hi!" by Koren. Copyright © 1993 *The New Yorker* magazine, Inc. Reprinted by permission of the *The New Yorker*.

Ann Landers, "Teen's Mom Horrified by First Rock Concert" by Ann Landers, Creators Syndicate, February 7, 1988. Reprinted by permission of Creators Syndicate.

Frances Moore Lappé, "Diet for a Small Planet" by Frances Moore Lappé from DEMOCRACY AT STAKE. Reprinted by permission of the author.

Mark Leyner, "Pass the Chips" by Mark Leyner. Copyright © 1993 by Mark Leyner. *The New Yorker*, August 16, 1993. Reprinted by permission.

Alan Light, "Sinéad Speaks" by Alan Light. Copyright © 1992 by Alan Light. Reprinted by permission of Straight Arrow Publishers.

Yaacov Luria, "Memories of Father" by Yaacov Luria. *San Francisco Examiner*, June 15, 1991. Copyright © 1991 by Yaacov Luria. Reprinted by permission.

Katharine MacDonald, "Imelda in all of Us" by Katharine MacDonald. *The Washington Post*, April 7, 1986. Copyright © 1986 by Katharine MacDonald. Reprinted by permission of *The Washington Post*.

Susan MacLeod, "Impatient Motorists and Their Middle-Fingered Salute" by Susan MacLeod. *San Francisco Examiner*, July 30, 1993. Copyright © 1993 by Susan MacLeod. Reprinted by permission.

Jeff MacNeely, "Shoe" cartoon. Reprinted by permission of Tribune Media Services.

Merrill Markoe, "Write Like a Man" and "Limo To Hell" by Merrill Markoe from WHAT THE DOGS HAVE TAUGHT ME AND OTHER AMAZING THINGS I'VE LEARNED. Copyright © 1992 by Merrill Markoe. Reprinted by permission of Viking Penguin.

Glen Martin, "Get Off the Road" by Glen Martin. *San Jose Mercury News*, June 18, 1989. Copyright © 1989 by Glen Martin. Reprinted by permission.

Joyce Maynard, "Fishing for Love" by Joyce Maynard. *San Jose Mercury News*, August 16, 1993. Copyright © 1993 by Joyce Maynard. Reprinted by permission.

Joyce Millman, "The Ties That Bind 'Wiseguy'" by Joyce Millman. *San Francisco Examiner*, January 25, 1988. Copyright © 1988 by Joyce Millman. Reprinted by permission.

Newton N. Minow, "Television: How Far It Has Come in 30 Years" by Newton N. Minow. Copyright © 1991 by Newton N. Minow. Reprinted by permission.

Jeffrey Moser, "Sgt. Pepper's Lonely Hearts Club Band" by Jeffrey Moser. Copyright © 1992 by Jeffrey Moser. Reprinted by permission.

T.T. Nhu, "Beware the Boy Who Asks May I Borrow the Car Keys?" by T.T. Nhu. *San Jose Mercury News*, August 11, 1989. Copyright © 1989 by T.T. Nhu. Reprinted by permission.

Elena Oumano, "The Making of a Great American Band" by Elena Oumano. *San Jose Mercury News*, October 25, 1992. Copyright © 1992 by Elena Oumano. Reprinted by permission.

Javier B. Pacheco, "Mozart, the IQ and Music Sales" by Javier B. Pacheco. Copyright © 1993 by Javier B. Pacheco. Reprinted by permission.

Kathleen Parker, "Harried With Children: TV's Bad Scenes for Kids" by Kathleen Parker, June 18, 1990. Reprinted by permission of the *Orlando Sentinel*.

Dan Perkins, "Tom Tomorrow" cartoon by Dan Perkins. Reprinted by permission of the artist.

Barbara McGarry Peters, "Tricks of the Memory Game" by Barbara McGarry Peters. Reprinted by permission of the author.

Norman Podhoretz, "Real Dads Do Not Play Mom" by Norman Podhoretz, *San Jose Mercury News*, June 18, 1986. Reprinted by permission.

Ezra Pound, "ABC of Reading" by Ezra Pound. Copyright 1934 by Ezra Pound. Reprinted by permission of New Directions Publishing Corporation.

Anna Quindlen, "The Legal Drug" by Anna Quindlen. *The New York Times*, June 11, 1994. Copyright © 1994 by *The New York Times* Company. Reprinted by permission.

James Ricci, "Homosexuality: Heterosexual Males' Bogyman" by James Ricci. *Detroit Free Press*, August 17, 1989. Copyright © 1989 by James Ricci. Reprinted by permission.

Caryl Rivers, "The Myths of Female Weakness" by Caryl Rivers. Reprinted by permission of the author.

Richard Rodriguez, "The Immigrants Have Something to Teach Us" and "In a Shopping Mall, A Vision of the Future" by Richard Rodriguez. Copyright © 1990 by Richard Rodriguez. Reprinted by permission.

David Rosenthal, "Do Fathers Still Know Best?" by David Rosenthal. *San Jose Mercury News*, June 19, 1989. Reprinted by permission.

Stephanie Salter, "The Glorification of Anorexic Emaciation" by Stephanie Salter. Copyright © 1993 by *San Francisco Examiner*. Reprinted with permission from the *San Francisco Examiner*.

David Sarasohn, "In Minnesota, the Biggest Megamall Under the Moon" by David Sarasohn. *San Francisco Examiner*, July 25, 1989. Copyright © 1989 by David Sarasohn. Reprinted by permission.

Debra J. Saunders, "Drudge Queens of Office Opinion" by Debra J. Saunders. Copyright © 1993 by Debra J. Saunders. Reprinted by permission.

Lisa Taylor Sims, "A Bias Against Whites" by Lisa Taylor Sims. Copyright © 1992 by Lisa Taylor Sims. Reprinted by permission.

Gary Soto, "Looking for Work" by Gary Soto from LIVING UP THE STREET. Copyright © 1985 by Gary Soto. Reprinted by permission of Strawberry Hill Publishers.

Studs Terkel, "Beryl Simpson" by Studs Terkel. Reprinted by permission.

Ladie Terry, "'Orphans' Speak Out" by Ladie Terry, *San Jose Mercury News*, December 13, 1994. Used by permission.

Bob Thaves, "Frank & Ernest" by Bob Thaves. Reprinted by permission of NEA, Inc.

Tom Toles, "Tom Toles Cartoon" by Tom Toles. Copyright © 1992 by the *Buffalo News*. Reprinted with permission of Universal Press Syndicate. All rights reserved.

Tr. George Fyler Townsend, "The Fox and the Grapes" from AESOP'S FABLES by Tr. George Fyler Townsend. Reprinted by permission of GuldAmerican Books, an imprint of Doubleday Book and Music Club, Inc.

Garry Trudeau, "Doonesbury" cartoon by Garry Trudeau. Reprinted by permission of Universal Press Syndicate. All rights reserved.

Marta Vogel, "Sorry, Friend, My Home Is a No-Selling Zone" by Marta Vogel. *The Washington Post*, September 8, 1992. Copyright © 1992 by Marta Vogel. Reprinted by permission of *The Washington Post*.

Barry Walters, "Still Hot, Still Sexy, Still Dead" by Barry Walters. *San Jose Mercury News*, February 24, 1991. Copyright © 1991 by Barry Walters. Reprinted by permission.

Dan Wasserman, "Dan Wasserman Cartoon" by Dan Wasserman. Copyright © 1988 by Dan Wasserman. Reprinted by permission of the *LA Times*.

Gary Wills, "If We Cannot Save Our Children, We Are Also Doomed" by Gary Wills, *San Jose Mercury News*, May 21, 1992. Reprinted by permission.

Virginia Woolf, Excerpts from THE COMMON READER by Virginia Woolf, copyright 1925 by Harcourt Brace & Company and renewed 1953 by Leonard Woolf, reprinted by permission of the publisher.

# Author Index